THEY TRIED TO CUT IT ALL

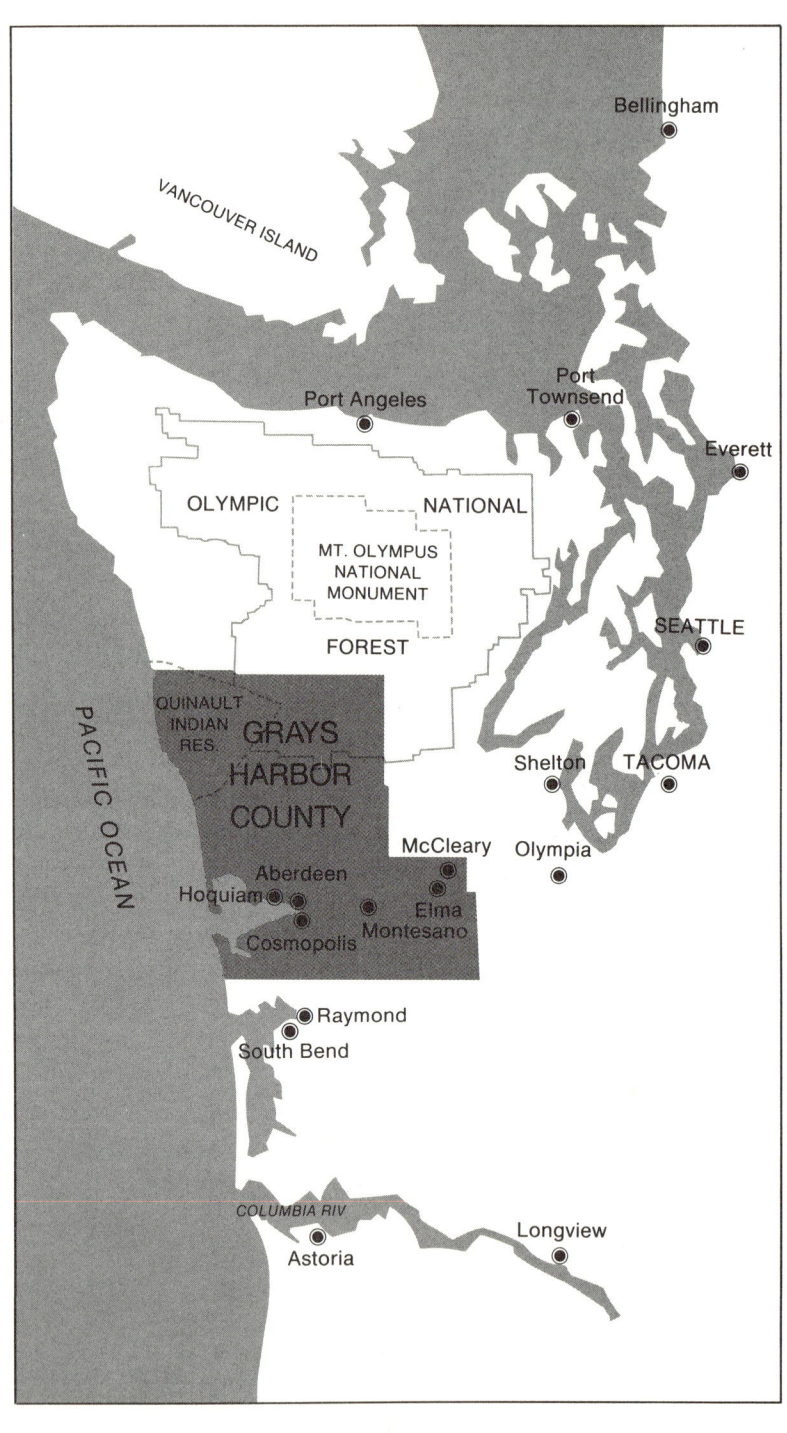

THEY TRIED TO CUT IT ALL

By

Edwin Van Syckle

*Grays Harbor — turbulent years
of greed and greatness*

Pacific Search Press

Pacific Search Press, 222 Dexter Avenue North,
  Seattle, Washington 98109
© 1980 by Edwin Van Syckle. All rights reserved
Printed in the United States of America

First printing 1980 by Friends of the Aberdeen Public Library;
  Henry N. Anderson, grantor
Second printing 1981 by Pacific Search Press
Third printing 1983 by Pacific Search Press

Library of Congress Cataloging in Publication Data

Van Syckle, Edwin.
  They tried to cut it all.

  Bibliography: p.
  Includes index.
  1. Lumbering—Washington (State)—Grays Harbor—
History. 2. Wood-using industries—Washington
(State)—Grays Harbor—History. 3. Grays Harbor
(Wash.)—History. I. Title.
TS806.W2V36 1981   338.1'74982'09797   81-4526
ISBN 0-914718-60-6   AACR2

*To my
Grandchildren*

Acknowledgment

This compilation of the feats and foibles of Grays Harbor's fabulous forest industry comes from many sources, no little of it from my own experiences as a logger and mill hand and my 50 years as a newspaper reporter and editor in Aberdeen and Hoquiam. Much of the material derives from personal interviews and association with men and women who made history, or who had personal contact with the history makers. Among many pioneer residents I interviewed was Mrs. James Gleeson of the Satsop Valley, who had housed and fed Grays Harbor's first white settler, William O'Leary, in the final years of his life. And the incomparable Cyrus "Cy" Blackwell, one of the very first, as a bull team logger, to sink an axe into a Grays Harbor tree. There were scores of others, all connected in some way with the woods, mills and waterways. Others were the descendants of these pioneers.

I am particularly grateful to Dave James of the pioneer Grand Mound and James Rock family, and himself a splice in the timber industry, for laying out the skidroad, or direction, for this work. He was the consultant, the advisor and in many respects the director toward publication. It couldn't have happened without him.

Another invaluable aide was Charles H. Clemons, son of Charlie Clemons, one of the great names in the Grays Harbor timber realm. Charles H. Clemons, a lifelong Harbor resident, was, through the inspiration of his father, a woods historian and researcher. Much of the material he collected was generously placed at my disposal, for which my gratitude.

My sincere thanks also to Rosalie N. Spellman and members of her Aberdeen Public Library staff for encouragement and assistance; to Henry N. "Heine" Anderson for his generosity and dedication to Grays Harbor history, and to my patient wife, Lillian, called Peter, for her suggestions and her tolerance of my taking up so much house space to prepare this volume.

In the bibliography I have listed many others who contributed, or from whom I borrowed facts, tales and figures. I fear I may have omitted many who in one way or another lent knowledge and plausibility. For that I am sorry. This mass of historic information was gleaned and compiled over more than a half century. At this late date there could be many gaps in memory and remisses in inscribing phases of Grays Harbor's illimitable story.

Ed Van Syckle

Contents

Chapter 1.	Beforehand	1
2.	The Early Mills	8
3.	Life in the Camps	54
4.	Bulls and Steam Whistles	81
5.	Polsons, Schafers and The Big Six	98
6.	Cruisers and Scalers	125
7.	Screeching Began the Day	135
8.	Splashers and Boomers	150
9.	Billy with the Big Fists	164
10.	They Got Organized	179
11.	When Nature Turned Mean	192
12.	Plywood, Pulp and Paper	196
13.	The Shipbuilding Years	213
14.	That No Good Billy Gohl	241
15.	Master of the Vigilant	248
16.	The Hills Are Green Again	255

Appendix A: Sawmills 263
Appendix B: Logging Railroads 268
Appendix C: Logging Firms 271
Appendix D: Lumber Vessels 275
Appendix E: Postscripts 277
Appendix F: Ficker's Album 281

Notes 285
Bibliography 297
Index 299

Frontispiece: Map of the Olympic Peninsula

Illustrations .... *Following pages 68, 148 and 228*

THEY TRIED
TO CUT IT ALL

Chapter 1

BEFOREHAND

If the hellions are logging the hogbacks beyond Valhalla, and surely they must, it would be in a stand of Douglas fir. They wouldn't touch anything less, or find anything better. The straight, tall and great-girthed timber, sweet as the waftings of Heaven itself, would be growing on endless hills, section upon section as far as the eye could see. The old bullwhackers would be hammering the canyons with Titanic oaths, and down the skidroads would stomp the hairy-eared giant-killers with chips in their gizzards and pancakes in their craws. Their boots would be spiked, their pants stagged, and their wool underwear would rasp an ordinary mortal raw. They would be the roaringest, cussedest, ring-tailed hell-benders ever to pass from one paradise into another.

It would be like Grays Harbor when it was young and the sap was running strong; when the hills rang with steel and mighty voices, and raw thirsts hit the bars and bordellos like a butt-cut through the underbrush, and ripe for brawling. It would be like Grays Harbor when the benches were going to stumps, snags, and slashings, and the bottoms to oats, spuds, and rutabagas; when cattle bawled belly-deep in tideland grasses, and the be-whiskered pioneer smoked elk hams in a hollow tree. It would be like Grays Harbor when waste was wanton, and the belles of Hume Street also, when itinerant and unwavering men of God scorched the clearings with hellfire, and pious women, prairie-pantsed and sunbonneted, ruled the dooryard with Bible, frying pan, hoe, and rifle; when the Indian, aghast at the white man's excesses, guzzled to insensibility and died of the white man's ills.

This would be the heedless age of sawdust immortals, of guts and the gutless, of tin pants and snoose, of bullchains and headrigs, of ships and seamen from the thirsty deserts of the sea.

Here was the best of the timber country, where Pacific storms brained themselves against Grays Harbor hills, and the summer sun warmed the mudflats to a welcome stench. Here was Utopia! Here the seismic man howled and shook the earth. Here even the meek and the puny could hitch up their britches and reach for the logger's "pie in the sky."

Here was the range of the rampants! And, by God, the wilderness would bend!

AND IT DID!

Not only did the wilderness bend, it shattered.

Within a lifetime the despoilers came and went away, the lumber barons with them. They devastated and raised hell, but their era deserted them. For all their prodigious labor and sweat, their mighty engines roaring on the benches, baring the hills and gutting the canyons, they could not outlast the timber. Though they screeched the tidewater reaches with two dozen sawmills and made the land all around raw with scars, time would take them, and the miracle of abundance would hide their going. But, before the epoch ended, the rampants would make Grays Harbor the greatest lumber port on earth, and turn this region into a new way of life.

So they came, the rampallians, to this unbelievable place to do monumental deeds of curse and blessing. They beat trails from Nova Scotia, Maine, Michigan, churned the seas from Scandinavia, the bogs of Erin and the moors of the Scots, to roam 1,224,000 acres of incredible riches. Here they would find breathtaking expanses of fir, spruce, cedar, and hemlock, seemingly to the end of the earth.

This was the juiciest country loggers and lumbermen would ever find, and they fairly itched to sink an axe into it. They went after the hills hammer and tongs, with bulls and snorting monsters, with greed and carelessness. But, what the hell, there was always more timber over the ridge. Yet when they were done, where they left a wasteland, the vigor of the valleys and the shot-clay on the hills covered the wounds and lesions. If the roisterers of yesterday were to thump down the old skidroads again they would not believe their eyes; their desolation is gone, buried in second-growth, and so is their way of life.

And to some of these, Charlie Jump, who as a waxed-mustached barkeep in Cosmopolis and later a dam-tender on the Wishkah, would say, "Now wouldn't that physic a woodpecker!"

When the rampant set foot upon the landing he found no glory on the skidroads, no fame on the cold deck, hardly any recognition at all save his own bunk in the bunkhouse and a growl from the bull-of-the-woods. He would be at the mercy of the operator for pay and living conditions, with about as much independence as a man in henskin shoes on a peeled hemlock. His "monthly insult" would be a pittance, though better than a mill hand's. Yet despite this when it all added up, by God, he was a logger and otherwise his own man, a fact no one disputed without peril. He tramped with the legions, howled with the wolves, hated pimps and cardsharps as an abomination, and bowed mannerly to anything that hinted of respectability.

The woods drew every hue and breed, all to succumb to a peculiar pride in the nature of their toil. They grew gaunt and giant in the mud and heat, and, if they could survive the whip of a frazzled cable or the bight of a mainline, they began to feel a stubborn vainglory that marked them as men apart.

Some went to the woods well-educated and well-read, perhaps carrying a Bible or a copy of Shakespeare, for not all were the spirited rampageous, although this is not to belittle them. Some were family men earning a living for a wife and covey of children, who often waited anxiously.

However, for the first half-century or more ninety percent of the men in the timber likely would have been young bucks, single and full of pith and vinegar. There would have been a leavening of older hands to keep operations on an even keel, whack the bulls, and give the cook his come-uppance. But mostly the timber was for thin-bellied, fast-footed men, the nimble-witted, quick-trigger "all cat and half wild," many of whom joined the thrashings ere their sixteenth birthday, and became veterans before they could thumb their noses at the "No Minors Allowed" sign and lean a bar in ring-tailed camaraderie.

Some lived to be old, scarred men; others didn't make it. If a man had a sixth sense of danger and was constantly on the alert he could, possibly, survive and the donkey puncher would not have to sound that dreaded signal (seven long whistles and two short) for him. And if he lived the day, he could scratch it off the calendar on the wall beside his bunk . . . so much more on the paycheck. If they carried him away, his bunkhouse mates would doff their hats, wag their heads, and deal another hand of pinochle; not necessarily callous, but after the way of life.

FOR ALL THIS there had to be a beginning. Was it a century ago, two centuries, or a hundred centuries ago? Was it when the last ice of the last Ice Age trickled away, or was it when David Douglas made his painful way through the Grays Harbor country and left his name upon every fir within sixty thousand square miles?

It could have been in many times, but only in this place. It could have been 10,000 years ago when the geology of this region presumably was fairly well fixed, and the terrain, subject to erosion and other natural phenomena, became clothed with one of the greatest forests on earth. True, the trees aged and died and new trees replaced them, but the forest as such remained, to be virgin and mature, and spread over a land rich in hills and valleys and vast stretches of benchlands. It was such a forest the Scottish botanist found, seemingly a whole world of timber, filled with the potential of riches, and pain, tears, hope and death.

It was a place and a forest to be challenged for generations, plundered and ravaged, but never quite conquered. When David Douglas arrived in 1825 he was but a generation away from the invasion, the ring of the axe and the to-hell-with-tomorrow assault upon the hills.

He was less enthused of the timber once he dragged a swollen leg through Grays Harbor's bellicose climate. At the time he did not know the fabulous fir would someday bear his name. He was more concerned with the pain and the inconveniences of the journey than with the majesty of the great fir and the boggling extent of it.

Yet he did report it, and chronicle it, and carry its seeds back to Britain. But he was not the first to "discover" the tree, which he already knew as Pinus taxifolia. In 1795 Archibald Menzies, a surgeon-naturalist, had reported it and carried two specimens back to England. Its present botanical designation, Pseudosuga Menzieii, bears his name. However, Douglas was the first scientist who would have his name perpetuated in the common term for this magnificent tree, the Douglas fir.

Born in Old Scone near Perth, Scotland, Douglas ended his formal education at ten, but went on to become a self-educated botanist of renown. After several years in the famous gardens of Britain, rubbing elbows with men who had traveled the world collecting plants, Douglas determined to become a collector, too. Eventually he was engaged by the Horticultural Society of London, chief promoter of collecting expeditions.

After one trip to the East Coast of America, Douglas was assigned to Northwest America. He left London July 25, 1824 aboard the Hudson's Bay ship *William and Ann*, arriving at the mouth of the Columbia River April 7, 1825, after a journey of eight months and fourteen days.

Once ashore he plunged immediately into the rich botany of the Northwest, finding many species unknown in Great Britain. The first plant to catch his eye as he landed at Baker Bay was the Gaultheria shallon, our common salal. So attracted was Douglas he "could scarcely see anything else." He also found Rubus spectabilis, our common salmonberry, abundant. In fact the vegetation was so lush Douglas was quite beside himself with expectation "of ranging through the long-wished-for spot" and "resuming wonted pursuits and enjoyments."

But all was not to be enjoyments for Douglas. He was to spend 25 days on a distressful journey through the Grays Harbor region about which he wrote: "I experienced more fatigue and misery, and gleaned less than in any trip I have had in this country."

Douglas' troubles began in October, 1825, when, as he was bundling his botanic specimens for shipment to London aboard the *William and Ann*, he fell upon a rusty nail which quickly caused a large abscess on his knee and gave him a badly inflamed leg. This laid him up for three weeks in Fort Vancouver and prevented him from going to Fort George, Astoria, in time to see his precious boxes of plants and seeds put aboard ship.

Contrary winds delayed the *William and Ann* at the mouth of the Columbia. Learning of this, Douglas decided to go to Fort George in hope of seeing to the stowage of his collection, but found the ship had sailed an hour before.

Once at Fort George Douglas set about preparing for a planned journey to "Whitbey Harbor" as he called Grays Harbor. He stayed overnight with Concomly, the great chief of the Chinooks, where he met the chief's brother, Tha-a-muxi (characterized by Douglas as a "fine old man"), who arranged to accompany Douglas northward.

Concomly's big war canoe manned by twelve men almost swamped in the heavy weather crossing the Columbia. Repeatedly seas boarded the craft, washing away most of the food.

Wet and miserable, the party landed on Cape Disappointment and undertook the portage four miles to Willapa Bay, dragging canoes through woods, over rocks, stumps, logs and gullies, only to meet thick fog and rain on the shores of the bay. Douglas' knee had become stiff and painful.

The party paddled up the bay to Cape Shoalwater where they were stormbound for two days by high winds, sleet, hail and rain. There was scarcely any fire and no food except a small amount of chocolate, a few kinnikinick berries, and some roots of sagittaria (arrowroot, a marsh plant) and Lupinus littoralis (somuchtan in Chinook), a wild licorice Douglas found "nutritious and wholesome."

Facing a portage of 16 miles to Grays Harbor, Douglas decided to send the canoe back to the Columbia, two of the Indians being more than glad to take it when they found all the provisions were gone.

The weather now became so violent Douglas' party twice had to shift camp back from the beach because of the rising sea. And then, suffering from his worsening leg, and afoot from four o'clock in the morning until six in the evening, Douglas dragged himself over the portage to Grays Harbor. With no food for two days and his leg tormenting him, Douglas wrote: "I hardly can give an idea of my afflicted state."

That day was followed by an even more miserable night. The

party shivered in a wet, blustery storm over a poor fire in an improvised shelter of pine branches, grass and a few old cedar bark mats. Douglas wrote: "The following day found me so broken down with fatigue and starvation, and my knee so much worse, that I could not stir out."

However, the weather moderated toward dusk and Douglas managed to crawl out with his gun and, as he puts it:

> "Providentially I killed five ducks with one shot, which as might be expected, were soon cooked. I was certainly very hungry, but as soon as I seen the birds fall my appetite fled; it had brought such a change over me that I hardly persuaded myself that I had been in want. I made a basin of tea, in which, with a little duck, I made a good supper. Very little sufficed me."

The campfire drew the attention of Tha-a-muxi's people across the bay. They sent a canoe and took the party to the chief's village on the Chehalis where Douglas rested and recuperated for several days, the first white man to receive such kindness from the Chehalis Indians. After the harsh and trying experiences of the past week, Douglas "was in no mood to find fault with the dirt, filth and stench" in which his hosts lived. On the other hand, Douglas wrote, he had all and every kindness and all the hospitality Indian courtesy could suggest.

Douglas botanized in the vicinity of what is now Aberdeen and Hoquiam and obtained some seeds, including "the interesting bear grass and wild licorice." He then started up the Chehalis, "a large stream, nearly as large as the Thames, very rapid with numerous cascades."

Douglas had intended to follow the Chehalis to its source, but after 60 miles he decided to cross over to the Cowlitz River and then to the Columbia and Fort Vancouver. The Chehalis, he found, was too high and too difficult to navigate.

Tha-a-muxi had accompanied Douglas upriver, but took the canoe and returned to his village when the botanist decided to cross over to the Cowlitz. On the Cowlitz Douglas obtained a boat from Chief Schachanaway and arrived at Fort Vancouver November 15, 1825, gaunt from hunger, with a painful knee, very little botanic accomplishment, and grievous memories of the bay Robert Gray had discovered only 33 years before.

Chapter
2

THE EARLY MILLS

David Douglas was 27 years gone from the Harbor before someone came along to tap the Scot's painful wilderness. He was Benjamin C. Armstrong, age 27, who, accompanied by a Mr. Strahill and a Mr. Cox appeared on the Grays Harbor scene in 1852 cutting a trail from Scatter Creek, near Grand Mound, to Cedar Creek, which empties into the Chehalis a short distance northwest of Oakville. Over this the three men freighted irons for a muley sawmill, which they built at the falls of Cedar Creek, proposing to cut 3 x 12 planks, raft them to tidewater on Grays Harbor and ship them to San Francisco. Whether they did this is not recorded, but the mill proved a success by cutting lumber for virtually every pioneer structure in the Chehalis Valley, including the scows that coursed the river.

Somewhere in those early years history lost sight of Mr. Strahill and Mr. Cox, for they go unmentioned while the mill was referred to always as "Armstrong's mill," the supposition being Armstrong owned the mill with Strahill and Cox his hired hands. Evidence of Armstrong's labors still exists today in the rocks at the falls where he drilled holes for driftbolts to anchor his structure.

Much of the plant's success rested with the praiseworthy quality of the lumber produced. James G. Swan in his book "Northwest Coast," published in 1857, had this to say of Armstrong's product:

"Some ten or fifteen miles above our camp are excellent sawmills of Mr. Armstrong, where timber of all kinds is sawed in the best manner. The cedar and ash plank, and boat-stuff I have seen from Armstrong's, was equal to any I ever met with, while the fir and spruce lumber can not be surpassed by any mills in the Union. Some of our Eastern mill men would be doubtful about attempting to cut a log of spruce measuring six feet through the center, but Mr. Armstrong informed me that he has saws capable of performing such work, although he confessed he would prefer operating on three or four foot logs, as he can handle them easier."

It is pretty well established Armstrong did a satisfactory job of supplying the needs of his neighbor settlers. There exist several accounts of pioneer purchases from the Cedar Creek mill, including one in the autumn of 1853, when John Rogers James and his brothers, Samuel and William, "made a trip to Armstrong's mill down at Cedar Creek and brought home to Grand Mound the first load of lumber for the new house their father, Samuel James Sr., was building."

Five years later Patterson F. Luark would record in his diary:

"First raft of lumber ever run to Grays Harbor was cut at Armstrong mill, hauled to the river (Chehalis) and rafted — consisting of 40,000 feet belonging to P. F. Luark, Charles Byles, David Byles, and W. B. D. Newman to be used in building on Johns River. After many mishaps and one smashup and rerafting reached Johns River — but no homes built — Byles and Newman never built, but left the Harbor."

Luark eventually located on Point Chehalis and most of the lumber was lost the following winter while attempting to move it to the Point.

Luark made another entry in 1857: "Attended sale of property of B. C. Armstrong (deceased) and bought coat etc. and one thousand feet lumber for a house at $15 per M."

In 1855 there had been recorded another of the few substantiated facts of Armstrong's life. In the courthouse at Montesano, in Marriage Record Book A, is this item for May 9, 1855: "Benjamin C. Armstrong to Mary Nechard ... Sidney S. Ford, JP." Mary Nechard was an Indian woman, a daughter of Chief Satsop and well-known among the early settlers. Following Armstrong's death in 1857, she became the wife of John Riddell who had a sawmill on Shoalwater Bay.

It would be 13 years from the time Ben Armstrong cut his first slab on Cedar Creek until the Chehalis Valley got its second waterpowered sawmill, this one on Sylvia Creek northwest of present Montesano. Michael F. Luark found the site and conceived the mill, but it remained for the arrival of John Fry and his distaste for cutting shakes to prompt the building.

John Fry had come to Grays Harbor from Oregon in the bitter winter of 1869-70 upon the urging of his brother Jason Fry, who was then at Taholah teaching reservationed Indians such white skills as farming, carpentering, blacksmithing, or whatever the whites thought the Indians should know. John Fry, in company with his son-in-law, J. N. Markham, intended to prospect the Grays Harbor region, but the weather was so severe the two returned to Oregon. While on the Harbor, however, Fry met M. F. Luark who took him to his prospective mill site at the Sylvia Creek "falls." Fry thought the site excellent.

Despite his experience with the weather of the previous winter, John Fry returned to the Harbor in June, 1870, preparing to settle on Redman Creek, later the site of Ocosta. With the help of his two sons, John Fry began splitting shakes for a house, but after two hours of sweating with a froe and maul he decided it was an "uphill business." What the Harbor needed, he told his sons, was a sawmill and lumber for building. He dropped his froe and headed for Montesano and M. F. Luark.

When Fry had first met Luark and visited the Sylvia Creek site, he told Luark a man in Portland, who was indebted to him, owned a set of mill irons for a sash saw and a circular saw. He suggested Luark attempt to strike a bargain for the equipment. This Luark had done, so that when John Fry returned to Grays Harbor with his family in June, 1870, Luark not only had the irons but also a waterwheel to run the plant, and an empty purse. The equipment had taken his last cent.

Discouraged by shake-cutting, John Fry approached Luark with a proposition to build the mill, taking his pay in lumber. Jason Fry, who had moved back to the Harbor from Taholah, and the Markham brothers agreed to help with the project, to which Luark acquiesced, though advising them he had no means of paying them.

John Fry finally agreed to take cattle to stock his place on Redman Creek, whereupon Luark consented to give him three hundred dollars worth of cows. Fry started to work with the others and, by spring, had the mill ready to cut lumber. John Fry took some of the first lumber to build a store structure for John Eastman of Montesano.

In February, 1883, it was reported that M. F. Luark had gone to Portland for a circular saw and a planer for his mill. By May the machinery was in place and the mill was producing six to ten thousand board feet of lumber per day. Three years later the Montesano Vidette carried a story of Sylvia millmen "rushing a flume from the mill toward Montesano at a lively rate and expect to deliver lumber in June." The flume ended on the Chehalis for delivering lumber to water transportation. D. W. Fleet did surveying for the flume.

In March, 1888, the Sylvia mill was reported running full-time with J. N. Baker as foreman and C. N. "Bud" Wilson "making splendid records as sawyer." The plant was then averaging 15 thousand feet a day.

By April, 1890, the plant had been sold to the Port Blakely Mill Company, which planned to abandon waterpower and install a steam engine. In September of that year the steam plant was in operation, cutting 20 thousand board feet per day.

Sol Simpson and A. H. Anderson, founders of the Simpson Logging Company, purchased the sawmill machinery in September, 1898, moving it to Bucks Prairie, ten miles from Elma, thus ending a quarter century of operations of the mill at Sylvia Creek "falls."[1]

Pioneer events sometimes seemed to have roundabout ways of happening. The North Western, Grays Harbor's second tidewater sawmill, may not have been located in Hoquiam had it not been for Mrs. Campbell's blackberry pie.

It began with Mrs. Campbell's husband, Ed, receiving a permit in December, 1867, to operate a post office out of their home on the Hoquiam River. He was appointed postmaster.

With the permit came the responsibility for Ed Campbell to select a name for his station. This seemed simple enough; he would name it after the nearby river. But first there had to be determination on the spelling, and Anglicizing of the Indian guttural. For help Campbell paddled across the river to consult with the two James boys, William and John. Campbell suggested "Hoquiam." The Jameses, knowing Campbell had been a printer's devil, yielded to what they considered Campbell's superior knowledge of spelling. The three decided upon "Hoquiam," and so it is.

Once he assumed the postmaster job, Ed Campbell and his family had to adjust to the constant coming and going of neighbors and strangers. The Campbells' became a convenient and favorite stopping place for travelers up and down the lower Chehalis and bay. Travelers particularly expected to be fed and housed; thus the Campbells soon found themselves in the boardinghouse business. Their fame spread almost beyond their capacity to perform. They sometimes housed as many as 60 guests, some of necessity being forced to sleep in the barn at 50 cents a head.

Mrs. Campbell, perhaps more than her husband, was responsible for the popularity of the Campbell place. She was recognized far and wide for the meals she prepared and placed upon the board. Wayfarers would travel miles off course just to sit down at her table.

In the summer of 1880 the mailboat brought a stranger to the Campbell landing. He was tall, distinguished, with something of an aristocratic air about him. He was hungry and tired. He had come up from the Columbia River on what was then an uncommon errand. He was looking for a mill site. His name was George H. Emerson, agent for Asa M. Simpson of San Francisco, with an assignment to explore sawmill possibilities on Grays Harbor.

When Emerson spooned up the last bit of blackberry pie and cream, patted his stomach and pushed himself away from the table, he was a contented man. He was captive. He was even more so when Mrs. Campbell provided him with a feather bed, atop the customary straw-filled mattress, filled with the Grays Harbor duck and goose down. The next morning, after a breakfast of homemade ham, eggs and toast, with jam from Grays Harbor blackberries, Emerson vowed he would go no farther. Hoquiam was the place; besides, there was no timber supply on earth quite like what he had found here, unbelievable miles and infinities of timber, and no place else where he could find such blackberry pie.

Emerson first attempted to acquire a mill site in Cosmopolis, but considered he was being "held up" by Ruel Nims on the price of a site. He continued on to Hoquiam to talk to Ed Campbell and James Karr.

Whether it was blackberry pie or land costs in Cosmopolis, Emerson settled on Hoquiam. From Johnny James, he who had helped determine the spelling of "Hoquiam," Emerson bought 300 acres of land, including a riverside site for a sawmill. He then made arrangements in South Bend, on the Willapa River, for a piledriver, and hurried away to San Francisco.

Asa M. Simpson had made a deal for an operating sawmill in Albion, California, and was awaiting Emerson's acquisition of a site on Grays Harbor. After a conference with Simpson, Emerson went to Albion to superintend removal of the machinery and its loading aboard the brig *Orient*, Captain Williams, at Crescent City.

Once the machinery was on board, Emerson returned overland to Hoquiam to await the *Orient*. The last leg of his return journey was by rowboat down the Chehalis. Emerson had hired an oarsman and a boat in Montesano, proposing to stop at the Stevens mill in Cosmopolis to make arrangements for cedar foundation timbers for his mill. As he approached Cosmopolis, the little sawmill toot-tooted his arrival under the searching eyes of J. B. Kesterson, who was to say that Emerson was "a fine looking man" sitting bolt-upright in the sternsheets.

Emerson closely studied the Stevens plant, ordered his timbers, then took off again in the rowboat, his oarsman digging into the murky Chehalis with oar-bending determination. Emerson was in a hurry, but he need not have been. The brig *Orient* was to take several weeks on her voyage and would not arrive until mid-April, 1882.

In Emerson's absence an attempt was made to tow the piledriver from Shoalwater Bay, but the rig capsized and was lost. However, the heavy iron hammer had been put aboard the towing steamer and was saved, to await Emerson when he arrived in Hoquiam. Using logs for a float, piling cut at Higgins slough, just east of Central Park, hewed timbers, and more timbers and lumber cut in the Cosmopolis mill, Emerson built a crude but satisfactory piledriver to construct a wharf upon which to land the machinery and foundations for a warehouse and the sawmill itself. Each day he would climb the steep hill behind the

Campbell house to scan the lower bay for sight of the *Orient*. She already had been several weeks beating up the coast, and was to spend three weeks more standing off and on the Grays Harbor mouth, waiting for weather and bar conditions to permit entry. And then one day, after Emerson had almost despaired, she appeared with everything set before a spanking westerly, rounded Cow Point and swept into the Hoquiam.

Upon the newly-built wharf the *Orient* discharged not only machinery and tools, but a crew of sea-weary millwrights and laborers, who were thoroughly intimidated, not only by weeks at sea but also by the prospects of life in a willow and crabapple thicket. But the mill was built and by September, 1882, smoke was pouring from the single stack, and the circular saws began to whine, creating Hoquiam's first industrial commotion with a capacity of 50 thousand board feet of lumber per day.

The *Orient* returned in October to load the first lumber cargo from the mill to San Francisco. The schooner *James A. Garfield* loaded the second cargo cut by the mill.

Some of the first lumber emerging from the plant was used to construct a messhouse and bunkhouses for the crew, and later, homes for men with families. In time the mill was to supply Emerson with lumber for a home, for he was to become a permanent resident of Hoquiam and the town's outstanding citizen.[2]

Simpson saw the North Western Lumber Company incorporated February 28, 1884, and the sawmill burn down to the piling June 15, 1896. It was immediately rebuilt with more up-to-date machinery. Through all these first years, and on until his death August 2, 1914, George Emerson managed the North Western operations and much of the other business enterprise in Hoquiam.[3]

His name did not appear among those incorporating the North Western Company, the directors being A. M. Simpson, T. B. Morris, M. P. Callender, A. W. Simpson and Samuel Perkins. The firm was capitalized at one million dollars.

CAPTAIN JIM WHITCOMB hunched out the pilothouse window in elbow-leaning absorption. He let the June sun warm his neck while he abstractedly studied the spruce-alder-crabapple-willow shore, with deep shadows underneath and whiskers of moss draped rather elegantly, he thought. And he noted the salmonberries turning color, yellow and red, and showing thickly in the underbrush.

His ears caught the steamer's bow wash, the thrash of her sternpaddles as she beat a steady course up the south channel of the harbor. There was no other sound anywhere, save the fireman slamming the firebox door, a window squeaking.

Ripples hurried away, tumbling the sunlight. A shag stretched its chalk-line course inshore, looking neither to right or left, its wings flailing away in that strange half beat of diving birds.

"It's a shag, Mr. West, what we calls a Montesano goose." Captain Whitcomb answered the inquiring gesture of the man on the deck just outside his window. A stilt-legged great blue heron dipped and waited, fishing the shallow water. "And that over there is what we call a shitepoke."

Captain Whitcomb shifted his weight from one leg to another and rubbed the long hair on the back of his neck. It was peaceful here, and quiet, and soul-filling. The captain's thoughts meshed with the steady thrum of the *Governor Newell*'s sternpaddles. Idly, his eye skipped over his passengers clustered on deck. They seemed to be drinking in the feel of their new home. Michigan people all, they were, following in the wake of the man West, chasing the promise of uncut stands of timber. A good day to look your dream in the face, Whitcomb decided, this sunny Sunday morning, the eighth of June, 1884.

A. J. West stood there on the deck in a reverie of plans, thinking of sawdust and the sweet smell of fir. He was a lumberman with a sharp eye for timber, and here was forest such as he had never before seen, hill after hill, valley after valley even to the blue distance of the snowy Olympics. It brought a smile to his lips and an acknowledging grip on his arm by his wife of almost twenty years. She stood close beside him, enfolding in her arms their youngest, seven-week-old Watson West, who blinked in the sunlight.

Mrs. John G. Lewis clutched the hand of her two-year-old son, George, wondering in what part of this wild land was her husband, who had preceded her.

John Young and his wife, Ellen, travel-wearied, gazed ahead with questioning eyes.

Given to his own ways and keeping his own counsel was "Uncle Tommy" Corlett, who in his day had been a sailor, again a slave driver down south, and now was following in the West train as a general handyman.

Ed McManemy was below and much at home with the comforting throb of machinery, the hiss of steam and the smell of hot oil, and the fraternal gossip of W. H. Clough, the *Governor Newell*'s engineer. He no doubt wondered how things were going to be out here, this notch on the edge of nowhere.

The same thought may have occurred to three young men leaning against the railing. They talked and joked; they were light-hearted enough, although just a little awed by this tremendous landscape. They were used to people and the trappings of human comfort, yet they searched here for one sign of habitation, for there was none save the ship trembling under their feet. There was not a break in all the shore, not a clearing, not a house, not a wharf or structure of any kind, not even a wisp of smoke against that line of snoozing hills.

The three were Arnold "Arne" West, 19-year-old son of the lumberman; E. B. "Brad" Warner; and the tall but stocky young Joseph "Joe" Graham. All were part of the A. J. West party from Edmore up in the Michigan timber country. All had been inspired by West on this venture into Washington Territory. They were following a man in a hurry.

Joe Graham thought of his last 12 days of hectic travel, by freight train roaring across the wind-swept plains and down the Columbia gorge, the hop-skip-and-jump portage via Ilwaco, North Cove, and Peterson's Point. He squinted into the sun, as if he expected to see the hills explode with the promise that had propelled A. J. West back to Grays Harbor, his party in tow.

West had been to Washington Territory the year before and had picked a mill and timber site on the Skagit River; but, while mulling over the problems of setting up operations, he happened upon a copy of the Montesano Vidette in which Samuel Benn had advertised "the embryo Chicago of the West," meaning Aberdeen. The advertisement was persuasive, for it sent West hurrying to Grays Harbor, and changed the whole course of his

THE EARLY MILLS

life and that of scores of other persons. The new town was not as fully developed as he expected or Benn's advertisement indicated, but he was not disappointed. In fact, he readily shared Benn's enthusiasm. He found the country a lumberman's paradise.

So taken was West by the Harbor country he immediately picked a site, left instructions for clearing it and for building two small rowboats, then hurried back to Michigan for machinery. Back in Edmore where he had been cutting shingles, West speeded up work on his final job. As the last bolt disappeared, his men stood ready. While the machines slowed down and even before the wheels stopped they had the belts off and were pulling out the anchoring bolts. Before the main bearings had cooled the machinery was on a flatcar on its way to Portland, half way across the continent. West had fairly itched to get into the big timber country where trees grew thick as hair on a dog's back and as big as a house . . . great giants without limb for 100 to 200 feet.

Now as Graham leaned on the railing staring into the distance, he shared West's urge to be up and doing in this sleeping land. Looking toward the pilot house, he caught the captain's eye and called out a question. Captain Whitcomb, jettisoning his wistful dreaming, focused on young Graham to answer, "Hoquiam's comin' up pretty soon. Be time to get out and stretch your legs if you've a mind to." He gave his attention to his ship.

The *Governor Newell* swung around the upper end of an island that would someday be called Rennie.[4] In the North Channel her pace slowed perceptibly as she bucked the incoming tide along a solid wall of forest.

As the *Governor Newell* turned into the Hoquiam, Captain Newcomb caught Graham's eye again and wagged a finger toward a huddle of whitewashed houses in a clearing. In the foreground was a small sawmill, its single stack dwarfed by some stubborn tideland spruces towering beyond it. Must be the new Simpson mill, and moored there almost scuppers deep with newly-sawed deckload was a three-mast schooner, the *Portland*. Curious and in Sunday idleness, her crew watched the steamer pound by.

Not more than three or four cable lengths upstream another

spindly wharf sprouted from the Hoquiam River mud. As yet barely worn, its deck carried half of Hoquiam's population, about equally divided, whites and pigtailed Chinese. They crowded forward eagerly. For years to come this would be a familiar picture . . . similar wharves thronged at steamer time by people awaiting parcels, mail, freight and friends. But today was special. It wasn't every day that 12 new faces appeared on Grays Harbor.

The *Governor Newell* fumed and splashed, and backed, fetching up with a thump against the piling, teetering the onlookers. On board two deckhands, the young Marden twins, passed the lines to idlers ashore, while their brother, mate Bob Marden, pawed through the luggage for freight to be unloaded at Hoquiam, scarce that day. Another Marden, Harry the purser, scanned the wharf for a likely passenger up the bay, but found none.

While the crew restocked the steamer's wood supply, piling it on either side of the engine room door and chuting more into the hold, Joe Graham took his turn ashore. As he stood on the wharf, he could take in all of Hoquiam in one glance; the Campbell home across the river, lonely under a frowning bluff . . . the scattered houses standing on cedar blocks and hoisting their skirts above winter tides seeping across the flats . . . a few boardwalks, a cow grazing along the river bank. A store building stood near the wharf where someday Levee and Ninth Streets would intersect, standing out from the other buildings and overshadowed only by the A. M. Simpson mill, George H. Emerson, superintendent. The mill had been operating only a few months and was almost as new as the lumber it cut.

As Graham walked closer, his experienced eye could tell at a glance it was "picaroon plant," that is, there were no live rolls and all lumber had to be handled by hand. He noticed the main cutting rig was a double circular, one circular saw above the other.

Joe Graham stood reflectively. In 12 days he had left settled, civilized Edmore to come to this. Hoquiam: 17 white men, 13 Chinese and a patch of swamp grass. The Chinese, grinning, jabbering, nudging one another . . . standing with their hands in their sleeves . . . their long black queues dangling down their backs. The white men fingering their long mustaches ... gallused and sleeve-holdered in their Sunday best, some with coats over their arms, stiff hats on their heads. And dwarfing them all, the background of timber, the never-ending timber.

Joe raced back to the wharf as the *Governor Newell* was casting off and leaped aboard. Soon she edged around Cow Point (so named because of a peculiar snag on the beach resembling a cow) and squared away almost due northeast. The bay narrowed into the Chehalis, the hills loomed higher and closer. The passengers edged forward. Excitement quickened, but still no break appeared on the shore.

Not until Captain Whitcomb swung into the Wishkah River did the newcomers realize how primitive was their new home. Although somewhat prepared by Hoquiam, they had expected more than this. But here was Aberdeen — they had the captain's word for it — six lonesome buildings cringing on the bank of a strangely-named stream that snaked through a tree-choked vastness. A raw clearing, helped somewhat by patches of tidal prairie, had been hacked out of the woods.

Graham stood on the bow, peering intently at the buildings as they came into view. Clinging to the riverbank at the foot of what was to be known as Hume Street was the barn-like Hume cannery. He stole a quick glance to the east across the mouth of the Wishkah River where some clearing had been done on the A. J. West mill site, selected by West on his first trip to Grays Harbor the year before. The larger trees still lay where they had fallen. Some of the brush had been slashed, and piling had been driven for a wharf but they were still uncut and uncapped.

Aberdeen House, the only hotel, loomed nakedly and alone where the Wishkah River ended Heron Street. Skittishly it crept out over the river, one corner supported by piling. An eight-foot plank sidewalk ran in front of it and onto a small wharf. Graham spotted a man bustling out of the building.

J. C. Fairfield, owner of Aberdeen House, heard the engines of the approaching *Governor Newell*. Telling his bartender, Billy Pedler, to get ready for some customers, he hurried out the door onto the wharf to greet his guests.

North from Aberdeen House a two-plank sidewalk lifted on stilts about four feet off the ground, a mere catwalk, and trailed off down F Street to four buildings on Wishkah Street. It vibrated to the heavy footfalls of a broad, skookum-looking man. Sam Benn, the city's founder, had walked in from his family's temporary home, a shack east of what was to be Arnold Street. He passed a vacant spot on F and Wishkah where his first house had been. Looking to the left at what had been his orchard, he noticed the J. M. Stout house, under construction, was coming right along.

Half a block away Adolphus Payette waved to Benn from the doorway of his new store, north of Wishkah between F and G streets. Big Adolphus had just moved into the building with its frontier-West false front and was still putting stock on the shelves. He was a handsome French-Canadian, dark, curly-haired, with a winning quietude about him. Peering around his legs was his son, three-year-old Ed, who had left off pawing through the new merchandise to see what the commotion was.

Next door, separated from Payette by a single lot, was the new saloon. Through the window two more curious faces, those of Ed Clark and Leon Emont, proprietors, checked out doings.

Benn hurried on south down F Street, past the building on the river which Judge John C. Pearson had moved into only a few days before. Pearson was inside, still straightening up. In the fore part of the structure were his offices with a few law books on shelves and an old desk; in the rear were his living quarters.

Keeping to the raised plank walkway Benn covered the last half-block to the Aberdeen House wharf. The town had been platted that year, and he could see stakes here and there in the brush, hesitantly marking the non-existing streets. None of the streets was cleared, but sled trails, deeply cross-rutted, threaded between stumps where teams of oxen had pulled their loads. Benn stepped onto the wharf just as the *Governor Newell* was coming in. It was early afternoon and half tide on the flood.

An hour later Joe Graham sat on his pile of baggage right inside the hotel door, waiting. His friend, Warner, slumped beside him. Idly watching the town to pass the time, he had caught sight of barely a dozen men and fewer women. Joe tried to sort out the names of those who had met them at the wharf. Sam Benn was the man who gave them a grinning welcome. There was George Weatherwax, the brother of J. M. Weatherwax.

THE EARLY MILLS

There was Austin I. Fox, the carpenter who said he'd come to town to do some building and never got around to leaving. And there was Fairfield, of course, who had eyed them critically and allowed as how he had rooms ready for West and his family and maybe he could put up some of the other folks. Then, suitcase in either hand, he had disappeared up the stairway.

Finally Fairfield returned, hurrying up to them bustling and breathless. "Well, boys, I got you fixed up." They tramped behind him up the steep stairway. Half way up they flattened against the wall as two paperhangers pounded down with their paste pails, brushes and rolls of paper. One of them was E. L. Koehler.

Fairfield with a flourish of his arm ushered them into a frugal room on the west side of the building, so newly papered they could smell the paste and see damp smears not yet dried. A cheap bed filled one corner. There was a single chair and a rough spruce commode.

Warner, none too pleased and a little superstitious, halted abruptly on his way in. The room was number 13, the numerals obviously cut from a calendar. Graham gave him a push. "What the hell, Brad, it's just another number."

Once inside and the door closed, they stood there, both a little uncertain. Warner broke the silence. "So this is Aberdeen. It cost me ninety dollars to get here and I've got seventy-five dollars left. If I had another fifteen, I'd take the boat right out again."

Neither Graham nor Warner had much chance for second thoughts. They were too busy. West lost no time in getting his mill construction under way. The next day, West and several of his men took one of the rowboats, built over the winter by W. T. Jackson in the Hume cannery, and headed at the turn of the tide for Cosmopolis. There facing the river on Front Street was the William Nims and Stockton store,[5] perhaps the best all-around trading center on the Harbor in its day. West bought a crosscut saw, axes, shovels, grubhoes and other tools. Then he went on to the Cosmopolis mill, steam operated by this time, to arrange for some foundation timbers for his own plant in Aberdeen. McManemy went with West to pay a professional and social call on Charley Lyons, the plant engineer. The others sought another Cosmopolis attraction, a far-famed spring of crystal-clear water bubbling from under the roots of an old, gnarled spruce near present C and Second streets.

Returning to the West mill site at the mouth of the Wishkah, the men put the tools ashore. As they finished unloading, Joe Graham satisfied a need to make his own personal bit of history. His mother had told him how his grandfather had broken ground for the Rideau Canal connecting the St. Lawrence and Ottawa rivers. Not to be outdone by his forebear, Graham grabbed a grubhoe, fitted on a handle and dug a small crabapple growing between the roots of a large stump.

"You're in a bit of a hurry, aren't you, Joe?" West asked.

"Well, I got a reason," Graham replied. "I'll tell you some day." He had turned the first earth for Aberdeen's first sawmill.

Actual construction of the mill got underway the next day, June 10, 1884. There was a deadline to meet since the mill machinery so hastily shipped from Michigan to Portland was on its way. Piling was already in place, having been driven the previous winter by a crew from Hoquiam.[6] Now Joe Graham and Tom Manley worked to cut, cap and deck the piling. A crew put down three rows of mud sill, and across these laid cedar ties. Twelve by twelve cedar timbers, cut in the Cosmopolis mill and dragged from the river by a yoke of oxen, went atop the ties. The decking was in place just in time for the little steamer *Gypsy* to make delivery of the mill machinery.

Late in July the West mill cut its first board. Though it was merely machinery on a foundation not yet covered, it was a going mill. Lumber was then cut to side and roof it, and more lumber for a boarding house and bunkhouse, which West built north of his plant.

And then, on the hottest day of summer, West's crew raised the mill stack, hoisting it into the sky with block and tackle and guying it to handy stumps. Fairfield, the hotel owner, stood appraising the job.

He turned to West. "It won't draw in this here climate. Needs to be higher."

"Well," said West, "that's all the stack we have. If we need more, we'll get it." However, there never was another inch added.

It was during this summer that D. W. Fleet and the Waite girl of Montesano were married and given a "honeymoon ride" on the West mill carriage.

On another day, West was setting up a Perkins shingle machine, a hand rig, as the always dogmatic Fairfield watched.

"What's that?"

"It's a shingle machine."

"Ain't gonna cut shingles, are you?"

"Sure," West explained. "We had room on the railway car so I just put it aboard. Might be a chance to cut a few shingles here."

"Oh," Fairfield nodded knowingly. "I didn't think you were going into the shingle business. Why man, there ain't enough cedar tributary to Grays Harbor to last that machine six months." He spat for emphasis. "No, sir, there ain't."

Despite Fairfield, cedar turned out to be one of Grays Harbor's more abundant raw materials, feeding almost a century of shingle, shake and cedar lumber cutting.

West found no problem finding logs of all varieties. The first came from the mill site itself, then small quantities came from settlers clearing land. Small rafts of cedar began arriving from the Voorhies place on Johns River. Other logs came from Henry Beaver, who was logging with his brother on Preacher Slough. The bluff at the present Aberdeen city entrance was being logged by Ike Woods, Jerry and Flora McGillicuddy, and Alex Polson. These logs, put into the slough that ran up Wilson gulch, were also bought by West.

Meanwhile the infant Aberdeen dragged on through the wet and stormy winter of 1884-85. When the pussywillows came out and the salmonberries budded, a crew began clearing Sam Benn's meadow on East Market Street. A new mill was being planned by Peter Emory, Gilbert F. Mack and A. D. Wood.

As West had obtained foundation timbers from the Cosmopolis mill, so now his mill provided the foundation timbers for this new mill. It fell to Joe Graham and John G. Lewis to deliver them. For the job they used a small scow which they drifted up-river to the mill site. With the timbers delivered it was only a matter of weeks before Aberdeen's second sawmill was in operation. The new plant, however, had its troubles. A bandsaw had been installed in place of the customary circular saws. The bandsaw could not, even after weeks of experimenting, cut a straight course. It was replaced by circular saws.

Once in operation the plant cut lumber for a needed store building, which Emory, Mack and Wood raised at Market and D streets. Irwin Emory came out from Michigan to operate the store.[7] The building was a two-story affair with a large hall on the second floor which served Aberdeen's social functions for years.

The year 1886 saw the first cargo of lumber shipped from Aberdeen, a full load aboard the schooner *Charles Hanson*, and cut by West's circular saws.

The West mill clearly was gaining its own share of the infant but growing Grays Harbor lumber business. In the first eleven months of 1889, West shipped coast-wide 9,204,000 board feet of lumber, a good part of the total 28,779,000 feet shipped by all four Aberdeen mills. By 1890, the West plant was cutting 13 million board feet per year. In time West had installed in his mill Aberdeen's first electric light plant.

A generation later, in 1905, West was to sell his original sawmill and build the Michigan mill at Junction City, placing it under the management of his sons, Watson West and E. R. West. By then A. J. West had left his mark on the community in ways other than sawmilling. He had been a member of the state constitutional convention. He built the first general traffic bridge across the Chehalis, the A. J. West bridge, which served until the state spanned the Chehalis with a new highway bridge.

The West mill has long since disappeared. The Slade interests, which bought the mill from West, had it dismantled just before World War I. West himself died in 1921. Yet his name is still used in ways other than identifying one of Aberdeen's elementary schools. One of the prime thoroughfares in South Aberdeen is West Boulevard, while seemingly in his memory the shore piers of his bridge still stand.[8]

RAIN WAS PELTING remorselessly as a second "Michigan party" disembarked from the little steamer *Garfield* at the foot of Heron Street April 7, 1885. Across the gangplank gingered Captain J. M. Weatherwax, who was to build Aberdeen's third sawmill. Following him was his brother George, who was to die in China years later, Bion Weatherwax, a nephew, and Addis Weatherwax, daughter of George. Others in the string of passengers putting ashore were James B. Haynes, who was to make a future in logging, his wife and their flock of six children: Ora, Irene, Tom, Harry, Jessie and Ted. William Miner also disembarked to found an ironworking plant, later to be acquired by the Douglas brothers, Bert Morse, Casper "Cap" Phelps, and three men who had joined the party in Astoria. One of the three was Cyrus "Cy" Blackwell, who had been on Grays Harbor in the 1870s and was returning to become one of the first and perhaps the best known of Harbor loggers.

For Mrs. Haynes the last bitter mile was over as she climbed the narrow stairs in the Riverside Hotel, her year-old child whimpering. To the din of April rain she wept.

Mrs. Haynes was to remember that day as the most discouraging of her life. Under all Heaven she knew of no more grievous wilderness than this, or a time when tears were more a solace. And Cy Blackwell was to provide the crowning disillusionment of her journey.

Mrs. Haynes and Blackwell were standing together on the *Garfield's* deck as the steamer churned past the mouth of the Hoquiam. She remarked to Blackwell: "Hoquiam is such a small place; is Aberdeen larger?"

"Nope, smaller," Blackwell replied.

Aberdeen was, indeed, smaller. There were hardly forty buildings in sight, including chicken coops. There were no streets, no sidewalks; a town wallowing in mud, reeking of mud, and probably with its whole future of the sticky blue-black stuff that clung so tenaciously to the boot soles.

April was only a few days older by the time Captain Weatherwax had a crew hacking and grubbing a mill site in the muck at the foot of I Street. As alders, willows, crabapple, tideland spruce and salmonberry disappeared, Abe Boyer, Weatherwax's master mechanic, Ross Pinckney and A. I. Fox, with planks from the West mill, built a small scow on the bank of the Wishkah to transport timbers from West's wharf to the Weatherwax site. Anthony Damitio, a master builder, superintended construction of the mill and, after completion, started a business of his own, a woodworking plant which fashioned everything from cabinets to steering wheels for ships. Meanwhile J. M. Weatherwax was staying with Mr. and Mrs. William "Uncle Billy" Keyes, who had a home at I and Wishkah Streets.

Weatherwax had his plant ready for operation in October 1886. Its completion signaled a rapid increase in Aberdeen's population, for 30 to 40 men trooped into the mill the first day. There was no ceremony or fanfare. The mill's throaty whistle bellowed, and in time it was to become an Aberdeen fixture. Weatherwax had said facetiously he had purchased the Colby mill in Michigan "just to get the whistle." He shipped the machinery around the Horn in the *Lottie Carson* which, in delivering the cargo, made her one and only trip to Grays Harbor.[9]

Tom Tew was the Weatherwax plant's first superintendent and his son, Fred Tew, the first engineer. Henry "Hank" Ruffe was the original sawyer, while John G. Lewis quit the West plant to take the job of setter with Weatherwax. Charles Fish was dogger on the head rig, behind which Joe Graham was offbearer, operating the live rolls, the first on Grays Harbor. Harry Van Metter was the plant's first edgerman, while Ben Johnson operated what was called the "bull saw," a large circular cut-off saw used to cut slabs and edgings into four-foot lengths for Aberdeen's first fills, and to feed the boilers of the sternwheelers plowing up and down the Chehalis. Lyman Babcock, who had worked for Weatherwax back in Michigan, helped build the mill and later was to become sawyer, filer and then foreman.

The busy saws and conveyors in the Weatherwax plant started one of Aberdeen's most far-famed institutions — sawdust streets. Weatherwax bought two teams of horses for general hauling around the plant, lumber from the "drop" to the wharf, and delivery to local building sites. Billy Pearson drove one team, Billy Dodridge the other. They also did the sawdust hauling for the first fill.

Then one day came Martin Spellissy down the Chehalis on a scow with a span of sorrel mules. After he had gotten his animals, his pots and pans, a tent and a stack of hay ashore, he pitched camp just downstream from the mouth of the Wishkah and started scouting for work. Before he could land his first job, one of the mules died. It was a blow to Spellissy and was to change all his plans. Instead of independence and a career of heavy hauling, he was sentenced to years of labor on a sawdust dump cart, while his remaining mule was to grow old between the shafts of the same lumbering vehicle. Together they were to trudge back and forth between the Weatherwax mill and the ever lengthening fill of Aberdeen's streets. Together they were to create something that brought oaths to men's lips for years to come, for when Aberdeen put in permanent streets, every last bit of sawdust had to be removed. Not only that, but while the sawdust fills served, they caught fire in summer and were a constant menace to sidewalks and wooden buildings, and floated with the tides of winter.

Spellissy's mule at first had a fairly easy haul, dumping sawdust almost within the shadow of the mill. Slowly, day by day, month by month, the springy, sweet-smelling, almost everlasting fill worked up I Street, turned right at Hume, and crawled eastward to G Street, where it swung left and slowly inched northward to Heron. No one really knew whether it was a Spellissy whim or town planning that turned the filling eastward to terminate on the bank of the Wishkah. Halted there, Spellissy then took the other "fork" and worked west from G Street along Heron. In time the lumbering cart pulled by the aging mule was to fill F Street to Wishkah Street and carry the fill across the big slough there. Down the middle of the slough two walls were built two feet apart at the top, planked over, and the whole covered with sawdust and some of Ben Johnson's four-foot cuts of slabs.

Another laborer in that neighborhood was the Rev. Charles McDermoth, who had come down from Cosmopolis to build the first Methodist Church in Aberdeen, at First and I streets. Often he could be seen puffing behind a two-wheel truck, trundling lumber from the bank of the Wishkah at Heron Street to the site of his church.

Spellissy had little trouble at first keeping up with the mill's output of sawdust. The plant was cutting 65 thousand board feet of lumber in a 10-hour shift. But by 1889 he had his work cut out for him. The mill's capacity was boosted to 22.128 million feet for a 12-month period ending November 30, 1889. The increase was brought about by installation of a new 18-inch engine. Like all mills cutting fir at that time, the plant had a double circular saw rig with upper and lower saws 60 inches in diameter, turning at a speed of 700 to 750 revolutions. The pony rig was also double-sawed with a steam feed, which was faster. A gang edger with a 6½-foot opening, three trimmers, three planers, a molding machine, resaw, band saw and pig saw, completed the machinery.

J. M. Weatherwax incorporated his holdings in 1889 as the J. M. Weatherwax Lumber Company, with capitalization of $250,000. Others were C. B. Weatherwax, secretary; J. G. Weatherwax, Eugene France and Carl S. Weatherwax. The company by then maintained two logging camps, two barkentines and a schooner, with another schooner building adjacent to the mill (to be named the *J. M. Weatherwax*), a tug, the *Herald*, and only recently had disposed of the steamer *Aberdeen*, which carried passengers and freight between Montesano and the lower Harbor. The company was planning a shingle mill alongside the lumber mill with the shingle machinery already on the ground. The big boiler and another engine were at the time on their way around Cape Horn.

Aberdeen had a fourth sawmill in 1899, the Wilson plant upstream from the mouth of the Wishkah at Wilson Creek.

Into these a-building years of sawdust empires came the Wilson Brothers, who turned know-how into one of the outstanding sawmill and ship operations on the Coast.

Charles R. Wilson was born in Goteborg (Gothenburg), Sweden, July 24, 1846. He was 22 years old when he came to the United States with his brother, Fred Wilson. The two young men spent a few months on the East Coast learning the country and the language; then they headed for what they had heard was a paradise of timber in the Pacific Northwest. In 1870 they landed on the Columbia to find work on a small river steamer plying the Columbia and Willamette rivers. They liked the situation so well they sent for a third brother, Henry, who joined them a few months later. Together they bought a river boat of their own. As their profits increased, Fred Wilson took his share to purchase a larger boat. The three brothers operated the vessels on the Columbia for the next ten years. In 1881 they had amassed enough funds to buy a small sawmill in the river town of Rainier,

Oregon, which they operated until 1887, when, running out of timber, they looked around for new fields. They had heard about and now determined to investigate Grays Harbor. Because Aberdeen had the best choice of hotel, Charles Wilson put up at the Pratsch Hotel, where he met Sam Benn.

Sam Benn listened to Charles Wilson and enlisted A. J. West to persuade the Wilsons to settle in Aberdeen. This they did after West helped pick a site for a sawmill a quarter mile east of his own mill. The site had a creek and a riverside location for a wharf. The creek was to become known as Wilson Creek, eventually smothered by culverts and community development, but the site was to produce one of the largest of Grays Harbor's lumber enterprises.

Wilson Brothers, known as concerned and careful operators, kept their sawmill operating through the 1893 Cleveland "panic." Charles Wilson found time to serve on the Aberdeen city council, while the family home on Front Street became a center of social activity. Here the three sons of Charles Wilson grew to manhood, and when their father died in 1908, took over control of the Wilson affairs for the next 20 years.

Soon after Charles Wilson and his brothers became established, Grays Harbor was "discovered again," and to his liking by a man from England, he, too, by way of Michigan. He was Edward Hulbert, born January 15, 1855, in England and at 18 an emigrant to the United States. He was drawn to Michigan's lumber and shingle industry, in which he worked until he got his first whiff of western red cedar in 1890.[10]

Once on Grays Harbor, Edward Hulbert took to shingle weaving as naturally as a ruffed grouse to a crabapple tree, come autumn. He soon discovered, however, there were better things to do than run double-block and nine-block shingle machines. Besides, opportunity was knocking all around, so with some associates Ed Hulbert established the Union Shingle mill on the south side of the Chehalis, opposite and a little distance upstream of the mouth of the Wishkah. The mill was not long in running until it burned. Undaunted, Ed Hulbert joined another group of Harborites, W. McClymont, Jim Hackett, A. H. Farnum, B. B. Averill and Robert Coats, in developing the Aberdeen Lumber & Shingle Company plant in South Aberdeen. Farnam was president, Averill vice-president, while Hulbert shouldered the load of secretary and treasurer and for 11 years was the mill operator, until the plant was sold to a firm of which C. M. Weatherwax was president.

Ed Hulbert was not to be denied his fascination with logs and lumber. He immediately became interested in the Michigan mill in South Aberdeen, roughly on the Harbor end of Macfarlane Street. The Michigan mill burned, turning Hulbert to another venture, this time, in company with E. A. Christenson of San Francisco, the purchase of the American mill on the Wishkah at Market and B streets.

In January, 1913, Ed Hulbert purchased the Federal mill at the foot of Heron Street and renamed it the Hulbert mill.

Hulbert managed both plants until his final illness. Upon his death October 17, 1918, his son A. E. Hulbert became manager of both the American and Hulbert mills.[11]

While the Wilson Brothers were weathering the depression of "Cleveland's panic" of 1893 and Edward Hulbert was still shingle weaving, Captain J. M. Weatherwax's empire began to crumble. Caught in the nation's financial mudslide, when 600 banks across the continent failed and 15 thousand firms went to the wall, Weatherwax's enterprises also collapsed. But he was not alone in Chehalis County. There were several others, notably D. W. "Daddy" Fleet, who saw his million-dollar collection of properties and bank accounts go down the drain.

As the depression deepened, the Weatherwax mill went into receivership, with Eugene France the receiver. He paid off $40,000 of the defunct firm's $54,500 liabilities and placed the lumber mill upon the block for sale. Captain Weatherwax, however, remained in the timber business with a stand he owned on Sylvia creek near Montesano. He started logging the timber in 1903, later selling his holdings to the Chehalis County Lumber & Timber Company when C. F. White was manager.

At the time the Weatherwax mill came up for auction, a farseeing lumberman from the white pine of Michigan, Henry Neff Anderson the 1st, and his son-in-law Albert W. "Bert" Middleton, who had married Anderson's daughter Martha and was to be partner and finance man, were on hand for the bidding. They bid successfully, the deal being closed in February 1898, launching the saga of lumbering to last through four generations, and making two families irremovable fixtures in the life of Grays Harbor.

The Andersons and Middletons zeroed in on Grays Harbor like a "V" of geese to the South Bay flats, with Henry N. "Pap" Anderson the lead gander. He was the man of vision, the organizer, the opportunist who led the flock out of the Michigan woods to the denser stands of Grays Harbor fir. He took root readily, as did his sons Samuel Miles Anderson, Henry Neff Anderson Jr., and George Edgar Anderson, but he was not to see his dreams fully fruitful.

"Pap" Anderson was born in Altoona, Pennsylvania, in 1839, of parentage that stemmed from Aberdeen, Scotland. He went into the lumber business in Altoona but, in 1878, with the Pennsylvania forests dwindling, shifted to the white pine and the town of Greenville, Michigan. He had already worked the pine for 20 years when he heard, from other "Michiganders" who had gone to the Northwest, that the Weatherwax mill was for sale. He lost little time hightailing it to Grays Harbor's "tall and uncut," with his son-in-law to look after the office and handle finances while he got the wheels turning. Not long after the bullchain began to groan, Samuel "Sam" Anderson came from Greenville, then Henry Neff Anderson Jr., known as "Hal." George Edgar Anderson, known as "Ed," who operated a retail lumber yard in Greenville, was to follow three years later when it was decided he could be used for better results in the manufacturing end. Upon the urging of his father, Ed Anderson sold the lumber yard and followed the summons to Aberdeen, where he soon found himself being educated in the mysteries of the log-scaling stick and log appraisal. He was also induced into lumber tallying for the coastwise trade to California, eventually taking over company sales and the general managership of the entire Anderson & Middleton operation.

These moves left Charlie Middleton, brother to Bert Middleton, still in Greenville where he operated the family flour-milling business. However, he became financially interested in the Grays Harbor enterprise, sharing equally with his brother in financing the purchase of the lumber mill.

The Ed Anderson family would never forget the day they

departed Greenville for the far-away Northwest. They stood on the depot platform awaiting the train, uneasy and anxious. And then, at the first train whistle, the stationmaster rushed out waving a telegram. He put it into Ed Anderson's hand. It was from "Pap." It said: "Don't come. Aberdeen has just burned down."

Their house had been sold, and all their worldly goods were in a boxcar already on its way to Aberdeen. All the goodbyes had been said, and all the ties with Greenville presumably had been severed.

"What," asked the worried and pleading wife, "are we to do?"

Ed Anderson had already made up his mind. "We'll go anyway!"

And so it was that another family in the Greenville "V" arrived on Grays Harbor five days after Aberdeen's disastrous fire, while portions of the sawdust fill still smoldered.

Young Henry Neff Anderson the 3rd, then but six, would vividly remember that time, that journey, and being set down in a devastation of fire, and a wooden town straggling away into the slashings and underbrush.

Pap Anderson was on hand, as was Samuel and Henry Neff Anderson Jr., when the train pulled into Aberdeen. The Anderson & Middleton mill was roaring and thumping, while Aberdeen merchants were busily scurrying around retrieving goods hauled hastily away from the path of the fire. Housewives whose homes had been spared were rearranging their lives temporarily to accommodate the homeless. The travel-weary Andersons, however, had a place to rest. They went to Pap's big house, later to be converted into a hospital by Dr. A. S. Austin, who had married Pap's daughter Carrie. Dr. Austin also was to bring his brother, Dr. O. R. Austin, recently graduated from the University of Michigan Medical School, to Aberdeen to become one of the town's far-known citizens.[12]

With Sam Anderson looking after the lumber manufacturing and Hal Anderson looking after procurement of logs, an opportunity opened to log a section of timber by rail west of Oakville on Cedar Creek. Hal would supervise the show and Andrews, the cook, would become famous for his pea soup. This was signal enough for Pap Anderson to start looking for other fields.

He soon fastened upon a sawmilling promotion that had gone bankrupt in the California redwoods. He was soon there to learn the promoters had all but finished a rail line up the Eel River to a magnificent stand of timber 12 miles from the coast near Garberville, with the little settlement of Piercy available as the post office for possible Anderson operations.

Pap, dreaming of a new realm of lumber, began beating the brush for capital. He soon recruited the Grays Harbor Andersons and Middletons, McPherson of Grand Ledge, Michigan, and the Pollard Steamship Company of San Francisco. This was enough for Pap to complete the rail line, build a sawmill, dam Indian Creek (a tributary to the Eel) for a log pond, fill the pond with redwood logs, lay out cottages, gardens and orchards for his crewmen, build tram-loading facilities on Bear Harbor to put lumber aboard three steam schooners supplied by the Pollard company, the *Newburg, Chehalis* and *Coronado*, all Grays Harbor built.

When the locomotives arrived they were offloaded to the new wharf, placed on their carriages, stoked with firewood, then huffed and puffed up the long grade to the mill site and its roundhouse. Flatcars to carry logs, freight and lumber were assembled, and for a time were busy hauling machinery for the new sawmill. Crewman were assembled, some from Grays Harbor, some from Michigan, some locally. The mill boiler was fired up, the machinery tested. Pap Anderson was ready to saw lumber.

The day was the 1st of October, 1905. The mill and the village were draped in flags and bunting. A crowd assembled. The crew was posted. Pap blew the mill whistle vigorously, then took his place behind the sawyer to be able to see how the carriage, the bandsaw and the live rolls operated. A perfect specimen of redwood was rolled onto the carriage. The sawyer gave his signal for the first cut. The carriage moved, the saw sent a shower of red-brown sawdust, the slab dropped to the rolls. And then, as though Fate had somehow planned it, a brace that had been merely "tacked" in place jarred loose. The brace fell upon Pap Anderson, striking him upon the head. He was carried away as all the machinery was silenced and the crew stood benumbed.

Pap lived a hopeless week, and with his death his dream of

redwoods died with him. From that day the mill remained silent. All the works went into decay and rust. The self-same log, with but one slab removed, rested on the carriage, a monument to Pap's tragedy. The crew drifted away; new redwoods grew between the railway ties and even through the sheds and the mill itself.[13]

The place was to remain so for 40 years after Pap's death, abandoned save for a watchman who kept a lonely vigil over Pap's dream. No Anderson approached the place save one, Henry Neff Anderson the 3rd, known as "Heine," who was married August 31, 1921, to Marjorie Abel, daughter of W. H. and Ella Rosmond Abel. On their honeymoon, 16 years after the tragedy, Heine Anderson and his bride visited the old mill site to find the same log on the same carriage, the mill pond, by then mostly drained, choked with moss-covered logs, and the same old watchman prowling.

Not until after World War II did the redwood enterprise lure the Andersons, this time Sam Anderson Jr. and his brothers Reginald and Harold, along with their father Sam Anderson Sr., who had paid the combination ownership of the redwood $2,000 and underwritten all the unpaid taxes of many years. The four went to Piercy ostensibly to recondition the operation and cut the redwood timber. But the long-unused plant was found too far gone to be rehabilitated. The plan was dropped and the timber sold to several Northern California gyppo mill operators who, on the basis of paying for the timber as they cut it, all in all made themselves fortunes.

When George Edgar Anderson became incapacitated at the age of 55, Henry Neff "Heine" Anderson shouldered much of the family's responsibilities, and in time built these and his own fortunes into one of the most far-reaching lumber conglomerates in the nation and around the rim of the Pacific.[14]

When Heine married Marjory Abel he inadvertently opened a completely new and vibrant span in his life. His bride and life-long wife was the daughter of perhaps the most brilliant legal mind ever to haunt Grays Harbor, W. H. Abel. Heine profited from W. H. Abel's wide experiences, legal expertise and business acumen. Abel not only was almost unbeatable in a lawsuit or courtroom battle, but was farsighted in acquiring properties and advising the rising Heine Anderson. And more, he invested in Anderson's far-reaching enterprises.[15]

In 1921, upon return from his honeymoon, Heine Anderson began casting about for a life career. It was virtually foreordained that a grandson of Pap Anderson would find a career in lumber, and it could have been equally prophesied such a chip from the old block would become a widely-known lumberman on the coast. To launch Heine Anderson into his future of sawdust and scantlings, Heine's father, George Anderson, and his uncles Sam Sr. and Henry Neff Anderson Jr., each tossed $1,000 into the poke and told Heine to go start a lumber wholesale business. This he did, parlaying the original $3,000 into a lumber-selling dominion that encompassed most of the United States, largely because Heine Anderson was an organizer like his grandfather, and also because of the excellence of Grays Harbor fir.

In the late 1920s there was a considerable amount of Washington lumber required in the Midwestern states due to the fact that the southern pine, which had been supplying most of the lumber there, was about exhausted and because it took rail transportation to supply the market. The railroads themselves needed huge amounts of lumber for car stringers, decking, sheathing and roofing. There were three wholesalers supplying a large part of the requirements, George T. Mickel of Portland, Oregon, Fred Carlin of Tacoma, and Twin Harbors Lumber Company, which at this time had offices in Chicago, New York and San Francisco, all specializing in that type of business.

In addition, the export business was beginning to increase in volume with demands from Japan, China, Australia, New Zealand, the United Kingdom and the West Coast of South America. The Douglas Fir Exportation & Export Company was recognized as the largest supplier of these markets. However, there were twelve mills on Grays Harbor not members of this organization. It seemed reasonable another export outfit could be in the field, so Heine Anderson, along with Harry Dollar of Vance Lumber Company, Bob Fox of the Schafer Company, Cliff Shaw of the Polson Lumber & Shingle Company, Henry and Clarence Blagen of the Grays Harbor Lumber Company, and Sam Anderson of the Bay City Lumber Company, organized the Grays Harbor Exportation Company which, due to the quality of

Grays Harbor spruce and Douglas fir, became well-known throughout the industry and increased its business to rival that of the Douglas Fir Company.

Heine Anderson already had been doing some intercoastal trading, being one of the first to ship Northwest lumber through the Panama Canal and, like his offshore shipping, found he needed an organization to handle a promising lumber movement to the East Coast. This prompted building lumber yards in Boston, Philadelphia and Baltimore, and an additional distributing yard in Wilmington, Delaware, to be operated jointly by the Anderson & Middleton Company, the Grays Harbor Lumber Company and the Bay City Lumber Company, all to handle lumber supplied through Anderson's intercoastal organization. The Wilmington yard was placed under management of William "Billy" Mack, already a well-known lumberman on Grays Harbor, who had managed the S. E. Slade Lumber Company before it went out of business, not long after establishment of the Wilmington yard.

Then came the worst depression the lumber business had ever seen. Only a few mills operated during the first months of the Great Depression, and along came General Hugh "Iron Pants" Johnson and the NRA, which virtually dictated, but also aided, the industry. In 1933 the NRA called a nation-wide meeting in Chicago of lumber company and association leaders. In view of the export volume they handled, Heine Anderson, representing the Grays Harbor Exportation Company, and Lee Forest, general manager of the Douglas Fir Exportation Company, were asked to participate. The NRA meetings set lumber price controls, and laid out a schedule of mill operations permitting mills to cut only on certain days depending upon the amount of lumber business available. It was during this Chicago meeting that the noted Shelton lumberman, Mark E. Reed, contracted an illness which caused his death.

The "emergence" from the lumber depression began sometime in the mid-'30s, permitting Anderson and associates to start a portable sawmill on the Weber branch of the Satsop cutting alder. The plant was to be moved to a location near the newly built chair factory on the Port of Grays Harbor complex, to cut alder lumber for furniture manufacture by Grays Harbor Chair. The plant operated as Olympic Hardwood Company.

His operation was significant in that it began volume use of Grays Harbor's vast stand of red alder, long considered a nuisance or trash tree. Alder grew rapidly and could be of lumber size in 20 years. It was soft, prone to stain and early decay, but when dried properly it became a hardwood well suited for furniture. In fact it worked up like many better known hardwoods, and was much cheaper and in greater abundance.

The Olympic Hardwood mill proved such a success Anderson had Ed Davidson build another one in Raymond, calling it Olympic Hardwood No. 2.

However, alder lumber was not all that sweet an operation. Anderson, after much delay of lumber on his wharf because of a seamen's strike and longshore strike, had a whole steam schooner load of alder sent to Califonia. The same sort of delay put the lumber on the wharf there weeks later. When the buyer saw the lot and condition it was in, he turned thumbs down on the whole shipload. The lumber was stained, some had already begun to rot, and where bark fragments still showed on the edges sprouts had begun to appear. Some of the lumber actually had started to grow in transit.

Anderson had to take his losses. This ended his venture into alder-cutting.

In 1938-39 Anderson, who always seemed to know what and where the bear did it in the buckwheat, noticed a steady increase in house-building and also an increase in California and East Coast demand for western lumber: this with the knowledge that 16-foot 2 x 4s brought from $3.00 to $5.00 more per thousand than any other length because they could be cut in two for studs (eight-foot 2 x 4s). Why cut 16-foot lumber into eight-foot studs? Anderson mulled the question, finally concluding it was worth a try to get retail yards to stock studs.

Working upon his conviction, Heine Anderson converted his eight-foot hardwood mill in Raymond with but a few changes into a fast stud mill, the first of its kind. Olympic Mill No. 2 soon had many copiers throughout the Northwest and British Columbia, but remained the largest single producer.

The intercoastal trade was booming by the time the United States entered World War II, but Heine Anderson was forced to slight the trade to join the Navy. His was no routine enlistment, but a "draft" by the War Department of a lumber procurement officer. The Navy would not permit Anderson to serve as a "Dollar a Year" man but required he join the ranks. This he did as a lieutenant commander, to become a full commander later on.

His first job was procuring all lumber for Navy needs. Then he was established in the Central Procurement Agency to procure lumber for all military branches. This he did for three years with headquarters in Portland, Oregon. As part of the procurement, Twin Harbors Lumber Company was the largest supplier of tent poles for the government and later received a Navy "E" flag. The tent-pole orders added up eventually to 13 million, with the hardest kind of specifications. They were to be 20 vertical grain to the inch, clear and flawless. Grays Harbor fir answered the requirements, as it did for lumber for submarine chasers, because wood is not magnetic. Wooden hulls fooled the mine fields laid by the enemy.

Back in civilian life with W. H. Abel, Anderson became heavily interested in five mills in Oregon and California, as well as two plywood plants in California. By now he had spent 30 years with the West Coast Lumbermen's Association and 21 years with the Pacific Lumber Inspection Bureau. Pointing up the importance of Grays Harbor in the lumber trade, Anderson was selected to represent the industry on the War Production Board and during the NRA days. For much the same reason and because of Heine Anderson's prominence in the industry, President Dwight Eisenhower, on January 1, 1958, appointed him chairman and member of the board for the Seattle branch of the Federal Reserve Bank of California, a position he held until December 31, 1963.

By 1979 and in his 80's, Anderson decided to call it quits with the lumber business, liquidating the Twin Harbors Company and ending more than 60 years in the trade. He had started in the sawdust and shavings in the Anderson & Middleton mill, which was being dismantled in 1978-79, falling only a year short of

Anderson's "dismantling" of his own career, the last of the giants to leave the Grays Harbor scene.

Coincident with the Anderson story was that of Benjamin Johnson, also a co-arrival from Michigan (Iron River). He was 25 when he bought a ticket on the newly-completed Northern Pacific for Tacoma. A stage ride put him in Montesano, which served briefly as home base for his scouting expeditions. Finally he filed on a claim of 160 acres on the Hoquiam near a place that would be known as New London. He had already married in West Branch, Michigan, a Scottish lassie, Grace Clark, 17, from Hamilton, Ontario. He could not honestly paint a very pleasant picture for her of a wilderness clearing, but he could enthuse of the timber and the possibilities of lumbering. She came west to share what would be his considerable fortunes.

Benjamin Johnson was born Johnston, without a middle name. This he supplied himself when he first noticed the shortcoming. It seemed logical that the name should be "Franklin," and Franklin it was and remained. He never gave a reason for dropping the "t" in his name, but it is supposed out here with so many Scandinavians around "Johnston" was always causing problems in spelling. The customary "Johnson" in these parts saved a lot of explanations.

However, in the family James, Leo and Vera all retained the "t." Mary Johnson did not.

Once established in Aberdeen, Johnson helped build the J. M. Weatherwax mill, Aberdeen's third, and became the plant's first sawyer.

Next, Al Coats put together the original American Mill Company with some money of his own, some from Eastern promoters and the Hanify interests in San Francisco. B. J. Johnson was invited in, and was also retained to operate the plant located on the Wishkah River at the foot of B Street. Al Coats next formed the A. F. Coats Logging Company, with Johnson taking a fourth interest. Johnson then operated both the American mill and the Coats Logging Company. Not long thereafter Congressman Joe Fordney of Michigan bought into the Coats company, the firm then becoming the Coats-Fordney Logging Company, which operated on the Wishkah-Wynooche divide for years. Joe Fordney sent his son-in-law, J. J. Stout, west to look after the Fordney interests. Some time later Johnson suspected there were some financial shenanigans in the Fordney woodshed and went back to Michigan to talk the matter over with Fordney. Fordney immediately bristled, refused to discuss the matter, and told Johnson to leave the house. Fordney soon offered Johnson $50,000 and two half-sections of timber on North River for the Johnson interest in the Coats-Fordney company. This Johnson accepted without hesitation.

Then trouble developed in the American Mill Company. Coats was convinced the San Francisco interests were "ripping him off" in the handling of lumber buying, shipping and sales. Anderson was asked to go to San Francisco to confer with Hanify. While there, and through Hanify, he sold his interest in the mill to Ed Hulbert.

Not exactly at loose ends but momentarily out of a job, B. J. logged for a short time on Hood Canal, then with Fred Hart, A. D. Wood and Will and Eugene France formed the Hart-Wood company in Raymond and built a mill there. Johnson, already a stockholder in Hart-Wood, formed the Nemah River Logging Company and, in 1919, hired Victor Morrison, who was to become his son-in-law a year later. Hart-Wood meanwhile had built the Olympic mill in South Bend. Johnson sold all his Willapa Harbor interests to form the B. F. Johnson & Sons Logging Company, Johnson himself putting up $50,000 worth of his North River timber. Vic Morrison had a 10 percent interest and Ray Johnston the same amount. By 1927 the timber tract had been logged, and with Ray Johnston wishing to quit logging, the firm was disbanded, with B. F. then forming the B. F. Johnson Lumber Company. As such he bought a mill at Linnton, Oregon, near Portland, but lived to see it operate only four years. He died at the age of 69, March 16, 1931, in Aberdeen.

The timber tradition so well preserved by B. J. Johnson was carried on by his son-in-law, Vic Morrison, and eventually his grandson, B. F. "Bim" Morrison. Vic Morrison switched to the Ul-Mid-Mor Company (Ultican, Middleton, Morrison) to log Ultican timber and some Weyerhaeuser timber, until a damaging woods fire broke up the company. Morrison then (1923) joined William Rosenkrantz in the Western Machinery Exchange, a leader in buying and selling of mill and logging machinery in Western Washington since 1905. He stayed with Rosenkrantz until 1943, when he purchased the Grays Harbor Public Log Dump at the eastern entrance to Aberdeen from R. J. Ultican, W. H. Tucker and Rosenkrantz.

When the log dump finally was phased out, Vic Morrison and his son Bim logged for the Rayonier company at the top of what was called the "Cosy Hill." Then in 1947 he and his son formed the Morrison Logging Company to log a billion feet of timber for Rayonier in the next ten years. The company was liquidated in 1971.

Bim Morrison then formed the Clearwater Timber Company with an outstanding logging operator, Jim Gotsis, to continue logging in the Queets-Clearwater country. It was perhaps of no consequence in the logging world, but Bim Morrison was the only offspring of B. J. Johnson to be named Benjamin Franklin, and the only one to be left-handed like his grandfather.

BEFORE ALL THIS, events had shaped at Cosmopolis to give Grays Harbor its first tidewater sawmill and eventually the largest lumber operation in the world. It would seem remote, but the first step was the arrival of George W. Byles, his cousin David Byles, and a partner George Lee. They were Tumwater tanners, moving their enterprise to Grays Harbor in hopes of more business tanning elk and cattle hides.

At the mouth of what was to be named Mill Slough, the partners put up a building of hand-hewn timbers and constructed huge tanning vats. Their efforts lasted hardly more than two years, and succeeded mostly in giving Cosmopolis the name "Stinkopolis" because of the odors from the tanning process.

Tanning, as an industry, failed on Grays Harbor because of the lack of sufficient hides and because the tannery was too far from markets over hard routes of transport. The huge vats and hand-hewn building were still in evidence when Ruel Nims bought the Byles and Young interests in the townsite. Nims converted the building into a warehouse (he was a merchant), but saw the structures burned when an exceptionally high tide wet a large quantity of stored lime.

After failure of the tannery and burning of the warehouse, the scene seemed to await the coming of the next man to try the location. He was Charles Stevens, said to have been a successful and money-making miller "down South." He arrived on the Humptulips supposedly with a considerable quantity of gold and silver to claim a homestead. He located on a mile-wide, two-miles-long prairie, to be called Stevens Prairie and the site eventually for Humptulips City.

However, homesteading was not to Stevens' liking, so, hearing of the industrial troubles in Cosmopolis, he determined to acquire the site and establish a grist mill. This he did in 1877, the year when a future partner, J. B. Kesterson, on March 13 was sitting beside Alexander Hamilton, whipping a rig through the Black Hills toward Elma.

With the help of N. W. Fletcher, Stevens built his two-story structure and more than a half-mile of flume from Beaver Creek, later known as Mill Creek, with lumber cut in the Estes muley mill on the Cloquallum, about two miles from Elma.

At the Stevens mill the flume was 15 feet off the ground, giving the waterwheel a good "head." In summer the flume was something of a construction epoch-maker, but in winter it was a spectacle. It leaked badly and in freezing weather was draped, festooned and swathed in ice for all to see and wonder.

Yet, for all the effort the grist mill proved to be another failure. Stevens desperately tried to convert damp wheat into passable flour, but found he had barely passable shorts and bran. By 1879 he had enough of milling and decided to quit.

The mill structure itself had impressed Jason Fry with possibilities for a sawmill. He persuaded Stevens, who by now was ready for most any suggestion, to convert the ground floor to lumber-cutting, using power from the existing flume and water turbine. Stevens readily fell in with Jason Fry's idea, started the conversion, but soon ran out of money.

At this juncture J. B. Kesterson appeared upon Charles Stevens' scene of trouble. Kesterson had arrived on Grays Harbor but the year before, as a youth of 17 years. He bumped and jolted on a cold and blustery day into, and was not much taken with, his new-found region. However, at the urging of "Uncle Jimmy" Gleeson on the Satsop, Kesterson agreed to stay a month, work on the Gleeson farm, and see if he would change his mind about the Chehalis Valley. He stayed and grew to like the valley, so much in fact he would take up a homestead and spend the rest of his life working the hills and bottoms of the Grays Harbor country.

After the month of trial, Kesterson wrote his stepfather in California, Nelson Waite, the father of someday-to-be Mrs. D. W. "Daddy" Fleet, requesting him to sell the California farm and come to Washington Territory. Waite carried out the instructions, bringing $1,000 as Kesterson's share of the farm sale, while with his own share he became one of the first merchants on Montesano's Main Street, with J. D. Mace as a partner.

Nelson Waite, after he had established his store, became interested financially with Michael "Mike" Luark in the Sylvia Creek mill Luark had built in 1873. This in turn led to young Kesterson becoming a logger, handling logs for Luark and Waite.

Thus engaged, Kesterson learned of Charles Stevens' troubles in Cosmopolis and began to investigate particularly the Portland market as an outlet for "good, clear cedar lumber." His findings proved favorable and Kesterson agreed to put his still-retained $1,000 into Stevens' enterprise. Doing this, Kesterson set out for California to buy sawmill irons, muley saws and other necessary equipment.

Jason Fry, with Stevens and Kesterson, began to convert the mill, but soon proposed Stevens write to John Fry at Oysterville to come to Cosmopolis and put the mill into working order, saying he would pay John Fry upon sale of the first lumber.

The proposal did not appeal to John Fry, who failed to answer Stevens' letter. This was another trouble piled upon Stevens' many but not the last. Characterized by Kesterson as "a cranky old man with ideas of his own," Stevens and his youthful partner parted after a quarrel. He promised Kesterson to repay the full amount put into the enterprise. This in time he did.

A year later Jason Fry, who had taken up a tract of cedar on Johns River and had made a deal with Stevens to saw on shares, appealed again to John Fry to investigate the condition of the mill and if possible put it in running order.

This time John Fry acceded to the appeal and moved to Cosmopolis in 1880. By that time Stevens had his mill heavily mortgaged to Esmond & Anderson of Montesano. Acting upon a John Fry suggestion they agreed to supply materials, whereupon John Fry proceeded with the work, aided by his son-in-law Fred Carter, and Fletcher who did the iron work.

Before Jason Fry and his Johns River crew could get out cedar timber, John Fry and his son Charles, who had come over from Oregon, and Fred Carter went up the Mill Slough to bring out some spruce, hemlock and small fir for the mill's first run.

In the spring of 1881 the waterpowered mill produced the first lumber cargo ever to leave Grays Harbor, a load of cedar in the little two-masted schooner *Kate & Ann*, Captain Lutchins, for delivery in Portland. Captain Lutchins was still making calls on Grays Harbor in his *Kate & Ann* in 1885 when, as was his want, he stopped in Lovelace's saloon for a game of cards. Someone came around selling raffle tickets for a piano. The captain, flushed by success at cards and by a drink or two, bought several chances and immediately called over a carpenter from the bar, instructing him to crate the piano forthwith. Nor was his confidence misplaced. He won the piano and a few jingling gold pieces that night. The piano was awaiting him the next time the *Kate & Ann* called.

Some of the mill's initial output in 1881 was used to build the first houses in Cosmopolis, homes for John Fry, Charles Fry and Fred Carter (not counting the one built by Pilkington much earlier).

Stevens had shown no business ability, so Jason Fry encouraged Esmond and William Anderson to buy Stevens out. They could have foreclosed on him, but instead they paid him $700 cash and took the property. John Fry was placed in full charge of the operation. An edger was installed and for three years water powered the wheels profitably. In fact the final year of the three-year waterpower operation the plant cleared $3,000 for its owners besides cutting timber for the boiler room and other additions to a proposed steam mill.

John Fry left the plant in 1884, the year it was converted to steam, and took up a homestead on Mox Chuck (where the Grays Harbor Country Club is now located).

When Stevens and Kesterson parted company, soon after the

sawmill machinery was installed. Kesterson, then 20 years of age, went into the logging business on his own. He soon had the money from Stevens he had invested in the Cosmopolis mill but hardly enough to set up a sizable bull-team operation. Teams of five yokes cost anywhere from $1,200 to $1,500, while a whole outfit from falling tools to boom sticks cost from $2,500 to $3,000. And, in many years, logging was restricted by weather or the log market to but three months of logging, hardly enough for the operator to break even.

Kesterson did manage with a "jawbone loan" to set himself up as a logger, but not a very successful one. He later recalled Robert and Alex Polson were hand-logging on the Hoquiam within the Hoquiam city limits when he, Kesterson, was becoming discouraged. When Alex Polson decided to buy his first bull team, he went to look at Kesterson's cattle. Kesterson by then had decided to go out of the logging business because he had a wife and four children and couldn't "make ends meet" with logs selling for $3.50 a thousand, sometimes for $5.00, but not often. Only two mills were buying logs in 1886-87. Kesterson's bull team didn't please Polson. The animals were too light, he said. He went elsewhere, purchased heavier animals quit hand logging and began bull-team shows in 1887.

That year, 1887, was something momentous in the lumber history of Grays Harbor. W. H. Perry of the Perry Lumber & Mill Company of Los Angeles, purchased the Cosmopolis mill, an event eventually leading to the Grays Harbor Commercial Company, which had to be but one of its kind. There was nothing else like it anywhere in the Northwest lumber industry, and no outfit was more bedamned and belabored.

Perry bought both the mill and its site, and immediately set about to improve the plant and boost its capacity.

In 1887 logs were selling on Grays Harbor for from $4.50 to $5.00 per thousand feet, while on Puget Sound the going price was $4.50 to $7.00 per thousand feet. The price difference allowed Grays Harbor mills to offer rough lumber for the price Puget Sound operators were paying for logs, a situation that nettled W. H. Talbot of the Pacific Pine Lumber Company and other operators on the Sound, to a point where they decided to have a Grays Harbor mill of their own. Consequently, Talbot started scouting for a mill to purchase but found only one, the one in Cosmopolis.

Convincing mill owners who belonged to the Pacific Pine Lumber Company, Talbot sent Captain G. S. Hindsdale, then general manager of Pacific Pine of Los Angeles, to offer Perry $125,000 for his Grays Harbor property. Perry refused to sell. Captain Hinsdale was then instructed to purchase for the account of Pacific Pine a site on Grays Harbor and start construction of a mill. Hinsdale purchased a quarter section of land just west of the Town of Cosmopolis on what was to be called "Big Slough, or as some called it, "Shingle Mill Slough." The tract, however, had no frontage on the Chehalis River.

By April, 1888, machinery had been ordered, and George Stetson of the Stetson & Post Mill Company in Seattle was sent to Cosmopolis to start construction of a plant. He had already built a warehouse and staked out a mill site when, in May, Perry reconsidered and offered to sell. Talbot, Stetson, Cyrus Walker and Will Walker all were displeased with the site of the proposed mill and were well content to drop plans for its construction. They then negotiated a $135,000 price for Perry's Cosmopolis Mill & Trading Company.

Under new ownership the Cosmopolis mill was operated under the name Grays Harbor Mill Company which, in 1895, was changed to Grays Harbor Commercial Company, with a sales outlet through the Pope & Talbot yard in San Francisco. As a matter of fact the Cosmopolis mill was, through ownerships, a Pope & Talbot operation from the day Perry sold, though there were other stockholders like William Walker, E. B. Ames, C. F. White, A. W. Jackson and Neil Cooney.

In 1890 E. M. Herrick of San Francisco was president of the Grays Harbor Commercial Company, succeeded in the mid-1890s by A. W. Jackson. George Stetson became manager in 1888 and served until 1892, C. F. White succeeding him until 1914. However, White's headquarters were in Seattle, and Neil Cooney, the assistant manager, was the controlling figure. Cooney became manager of the Grays Harbor operation upon White's retirement in 1929 and governed until the company was liquidated and the mill razed, still under a cloud as an exploiter of cheap labor.

Pope & Talbot built a wooden tank factory, a box factory, a planing mill, dry kilns and two large shingle mills, one on the Chehalis near the western city limits of Cosmopolis, the other on the west side of the mouth of what what called "Big Slough" in Cosmopolis. In time the firm built a huge messhouse and operated a large general store, several barracks or bunkhouses, and a logging system called the Chehalis County Logging & Timber Company. It also installed a much-berated policy of cheap labor, a tight company town, payment with script and an ingrained contempt for organized labor. The policy seemed to work, for the plant operated through good times and bad, its only concession being a switch from the 10-hour to the 8-hour day with the rest of the industry.

The Chehalis County Logging & Timber Company already had a six-year history before it was acquired by the Grays Harbor Commercial Company. The firm was organized in 1901 by Cliff M. Weatherwax, son of J. M. Weatherwax, who was named the president and remained so until its sale to the Commercial company in 1907. Cliff Weatherwax was born in Stanton, Michigan, in 1878 and was 12 years old when he arrived in Aberdeen. He was graduated from the Aberdeen high school, attended the University of Washington, Leland Stanford University, graduating from Harvard University with the class of 1901. In 1902 he formed a partnership with John Soule, E. S. Hartwell of Chicago, and C. F. White of Seattle, to continue the business of the Chehalis County Logging & Timber Company until its sale.

In 1908 Weatherwax bought out the Aberdeen Lumber & Shingle Company which had been incorporated in 1899 by Edward Hulbert, J. M. Hackett, A. H. Farnum and Sam McClymont. Actually Weatherwax purchased the interests of Hulbert, Hackett and Farnum, and became treasurer and manager of the company, with Sam McClymont as president and E. T. Taylor, secretary.

And then the Grays Harbor Commercial company hired Neil Cooney, who was to become a most capable manager, a man of energy and foresight, also a man reviled and maligned throughout the timber country. Neil Cooney came to Cosmopolis from Port Madison as a shipbuilder in 1890. He was engaged in construction of the steamer *Montesano;* later he built the tug *Chehalis.* George W. Stetson (later of Stetson & Post in Seattle), first manager for Pope & Talbot in Cosmopolis, hired Cooney as a foreman upon Cooney's completion of the *Chehalis.* He was afterwards made general foreman and, still later, superintendent and assistant manager. Within a few years Cooney succeeded C. F. White as manager.

By then the mill was cutting 600 thousand feet of lumber per day, using 1,200 men who, under the company's labor policy, were largely down-and-outer bums, wanderers, the broke and hungry recruited in Seattle where there was a standing order for so many men a week for Cosmopolis. Any man, regardless of his age, color, race or nationality, could get a job, a meal and a bunk. About the only requirement was a suitcase or a bundle that could be "held" in the company's time shack until the man had worked out his fare to Cosmopolis. This gave rise to the common practice of buying or somehow acquiring (perhaps from someone who had been over the route before) a cheap cardboard "telescope" suitcase, filling it with a few bricks, gunnysacks and wadded newspapers, and climbing aboard a train for Cosmopolis. A man could always count on a job, a place in the messhall with 600 other men, and a place to sleep, but he would earn very little.

The arrangement seemed to satisfy not only the company, which had a crew coming, a crew on the job and a crew going, but also many of the men themselves. An unexpected number stayed on to build homes and raise families in Cosmopolis. Others proved strangely loyal even in trying times, especially during labor unrest on Grays Harbor when strikers from other plants besieged the gates of the Commercial company plant in a vain effort to get the men to walk out. They never did. Even during the height of the I.W.W.'s (Wobblies) aggressive activity the Cosmopolis men clung to their jobs.

The cheap labor policy, including that of opening the gates to any man who wanted a job, drew thousands of men, many who came merely to eat and "serve their time" for fare out again. This was the reason the Commercial company plant often was called the "Western Penitentiary." However, the food was plentiful and fairly good, served on long tables in the cavernous messhouse under the direction of a hatless and baldheaded man called "Steward." The cooks were mostly Chinese and good at their monumental job of feeding 600 men at one sitting, three times a day. The messhouse had its own slaughter house, bakery, gigantic stoves and dishwashing sinks. The floor was covered with an inch of sawdust through which an army of flunkies scuffed. There was also a row of wire cages in which ferrets were kept to prey upon the rats.

Another remarkable edifice maintained by the Commercial company was the shipping shed, which could load a whole train with lumber at a time. Deepwater ships loaded at the wharf. The planing mill was one of the largest in the industry, tanks were sold all over the world, and the box factory was the prime source of containers for packers and producers on the West Coast, and inland fruit growers as well.

And nowhere could a man go, with the possible exceptions of the Poles, the Sahara and the Gobi, but what he would find another man who had "worked for Cooney," or "worked at Cosmopolis." Men from all walks of life, and from most everywhere, trudged through the gates, having been awakened by three whistles at 6 o'clock, warned by two whistles at 6:30 and set to work by one whistle at 7 o'clock. The same one-whistle blast would shut down the machinery at 6 p.m. The men got, with suitable whistles, an hour's mealtime at noon. Some men working in the box factory were paid 75 cents for a 10-hour day.

What the militant Wobblies failed to do, economics succeeded in doing. By 1931 the Grays Harbor Commercial company had cut out its own timber and had to purchase in the open market. Too, the huge mill and its satellite plants were badly worn and patched from long years of hard driving. So the gates were closed.

Neil Cooney, by then a rich man, bought the mill site and other company properties, disclosing a firm faith in the future of Cosmopolis. Cooney stayed on until his death in 1943 at the age of 82, and in his will left the 500-acre site and $100,000 to anyone or firm agreeing to build a sulphite pulp plant of not less than 150 tons daily capacity and have it in operation seven months after his death. The offer found no takers, and the executors of Cooney's estate sought to sell the site to the city of Cosmopolis for $4,500, but the city was unable to finance the offer. Cooney also willed enough funds to build a new St. Joseph hospital in Aberdeen.

The Cosmopolis mill site did, however, change hands during World War II, when R. J. "Dick" Ultican of Aberdeen purchased it and upon it built a yard for the construction of wooden barges for the United States Army Engineers.

With the war and the barge business ended, Ultican, who also operated the Ultican Tugboat Company, built a sawmill upon the site. The mill burned in 1951.

Cosmopolis eventually got its pulp mill when the Weyerhaeuser Company acquired the long-unused mill site from R. J. Ultican. Weyerhaeuser built a sulphite mill, one of the largest in the industry, converting Cosmopolis, which had long since ceased to be a "company" town, into one of the richest municipalities (per capita-tax base) in the state.

However, back in 1887 when the Cosmopolis mill was buying logs from the first loggers and Alex Polson was trying to convert to bull-team logging, Kesterson, tired of muscling logs into tidewater, had much to say about pioneer struggles in getting logs to the mills. In his estimation, shared no doubt by many others, hand logging with jacks was brutal, a spirit-breaking, man-killing job that did much to speed the appearance of the bull team, and later of steam to supplant the animals.

Hand logging was done with three types of jacks — screw jacks, crank jacks and pump jacks (operated as the name implies with the up-and-down motion of a long handle). The mechanisms were back-breakingly heavy, and dangerous. The pump jack particularly had to be handled with caution. It often had a tendency for the pawl to slip a cog, causing the handle to fly up with rib-crushing power. The jack had two engaging elements, that is, two points that would engage a log. One was the foot, the others were on a swivel head, two so-called ears that would bite into a log. It took almost as much labor to move this 60-pound steel monster as to lift a log.

The pump jack, in later years called the Gilcrist jack, was

made in South Bend by the Willapa Iron Works, and the screw jack survived the hand-logging era by many years. The pump jack was used for any number of heavy lifts, particularly on construction jobs.

Men like Kesterson led the trend toward training animals to move the massive logs, which wore out the arms and shoulders of loggers working by hand. Later came steam and gasoline.

Greenville, Michigan, produced another luminary for the Grays Harbor lumber industry, and another member of Pap Anderson's entourage. He was E. C. Miller, who began his career first as a real estate operator in Detroit, and then, when Pap Anderson waved him on, shifted to Skagit County, Washington. There he built the Washington Portland Cement plant and named his surrounding community Concrete.

There was no school in Concrete, and Miller's two children had to cross an unbridged river each day to a distant school. This, he decided, was no way to bring up a family. Miller had married Pap Anderson's daughter Sarah Manola, and was now ready to listen to the summons of the Anderson clan, though Pap himself had been dead seven years.

As was the custom of the times, E. C. Miller founded the Grays Harbor Shingle Company in 1912, later adding a cooperage plant, and in 1923 a sawmill, cutting cedar. The outfit was then incorporated as the E. C. Miller Cedar Lumber Company, and took in Robert Ingram, who had married Miller's daughter, Catherine. Another induction was Miller's son, Harold Miller.

Ingram had already claimed some distinction in Grays Harbor County. He arrived from Quinault by way of being graduated from the Hoquiam high school and the University of Washington, where he distinguished himself academically, and as captain of the football team and the rowing crew. He served in the USS South Dakota in the first World War, later in submarine chasers. He returned to the lumber business after the war's end, but was called again for World War II in which he spent four years in command of an attack transport in the South Pacific. After the war he again returned to cedar lumber, becoming president of the Red Cedar Shingle and Hand-Split Shake Bureau, a director of the West Coast Lumberman's Association, a director of the National Forest Products Association, a director of Harbor

Plywood Corporation, the Aberdeen school board for 17 years, and a Grays Harbor port commissioner.

Upon his death the E. C. Miller operation, now with two mills, the first in South Aberdeen and the other in South Montesano, passed to three sons, Robert Ingram, Jr., president and general manager, James "Jim" Ingram, vice-president and sales manager, and Ernest Ingram, secretary.

There is no tougher way to start a logging career than in a depression-time pulp woodlot. For sheer back-breaking labor nothing excelled it but Grays Harbor's earliest jack logging. But that was the beginning for the Mayr brothers, Werner and Marzell, who were to parlay a horse named "Bess" into a multi-million family enterprise in a matter of a half century.

It would never have happened had not Bavaria-born Marzellinus Mayr been inquisitive about a crudely-fashioned sign on the San Francisco waterfront. This forerunner of modern graffiti said: "Don't Go To Cosmopolis."

There was a steam schooner at the pier loading freight for Grays Harbor. Marzellinus Mayr took passage. That was in 1912, on Mayr's second visit to the United States. He was to go back to Bavaria to return with his wife, working his way across the country as he had done before. This time a son, Werner, was born in 1913 in Columbus, Ohio. Two years later in the Wishkah Valley a second son, Marzell, joined the family.

Eighteen years later came the depression years and any job, however hard, was better than no job. So the Mayr brothers took to the woods south of the cemetery in Cosmopolis, with old "Bess" their mainstay in yarding pulpwood to a truck landing. "Bess" had a history of her own in that she was once owned by Russ Ellison, who sold her to John D. Huffman, who in turn gave her to the Mayrs, all because she had a non-healing sore on one leg. Not ones to look at a gift horse too closely, the Mayrs, by some magic, healed her and put her to work. From there a long hard road led to eminence in the world of timber, two sawmills, several logging "shows," a fleet of 60 logging trucks and a wealth in logging equipment.

Sometime along the way the brothers became Mayr Brothers, a company, on the long climb out of the woodlot. By 1936 they were getting out short alder logs on the Newskah for Heine

THE EARLY MILLS

Anderson's Olympic Hardwood mill. In 1938 they mortgaged their team of horses and put an old car down on a tractor, bought some hemlock stumpage from Barney Stout and started getting out pulp timber for Rayonier. Then logging out a parcel of timber purchased from Earl Karshner on the Wishkah, the brothers switched to the Carlson claim on the north shore of Lake Quinault. In 1942 they made their first purchase of Forest Service timber, hauling to the Polson rail line in the Quinault country. The following year they bought a block of Polson timber on the Queets, bridged the Queets River in May of 1943, and logged with two big 100-horsepower tractors, selling the "peelers" to the Grays Harbor Veneer Company.

Within three years the Mayrs acquired a Washington and a Skagit donkey engine, moved to Washington state timber on the Queets watershed and started trucking logs to the Harbor.

While still logging on Matheny Creek the brothers acquired a chipping plant once operated by the Grays Harbor Lumber Company (Blagens), and started a log-sorting yard to handle export logs. In 1974-75 they built, on the bank of the Hoquiam River, what was considered the most modern of sawmills, a "grade" mill to cut high-grade lumber and convert the waste to chips for pulp and paper. More recently they acquired a mill and a huge holding in timber in the Willapa region, with logging operations as far south as the Columbia River.

Meanwhile, in keeping with their concern for the timberlands, ecology and wildlife, the brothers built a fish-rearing pond and other facilities on the upper Wishkah in conjunction with the Washington fish and game departments. It is primarily a steelhead enhancement program, hailed as a model in fish rearing.

Mayr Brothers remains a family ownership with Werner Mayr, president; Marzell Mayr, vice-president; Jennie Mayr (Mrs. Werner Mayr), secretary; Tom Mayr, treasurer and forester; Mary Nelson, assistant secretary. Many family members fit into the enterprise: son-in-law Oliver Mackey is supervisor of the chip mill; Mike Mayr, supervisor of the Raymond log yard with Dan Mayr assistant supervisor; daughter Cathy Mackey works in the office; Steve Nelson, another son-in-law, is a logging foreman, while young David Mayr, just out of high school, is a mechanic.

Chapter
3

LIFE IN THE CAMPS

The logger would live, in early shows, under a roof of shakes through which the stars would shine (but not a drop of rain). He would sleep in a bunk on straw, called "California Feathers," and warm himself by a big iron stove in the middle of the bunkhouse. He would hang his wet underwear and socks on lines around and above the stove where they would steam and reek of sweaty wool. The tin pants, stiff when wet and with their permanent knee bend, would be stood in the corner near the bunk, like a half-man ready to jump.

Not all loggers, however, turned in early or slept the honest sleep of a hard labor and exhaustion. In one end of the bunkhouse, likely as not, in a draw poker game cards were slapped and ruffled until almost crow-cawing time. On a Saturday night the players would knock off for Sunday breakfast, especially if a player or two came over from another camp. Stakes were gold coins, of which there seemed to be plenty, and all of which one or two men in camp would collect before the Fourth of July.

The logger would be roused out in the morning before daylight by a flunky banging on the triangle, or "gut hammer." He would dash cold water in his face from a wash basin on a bench outside the bunkhouse door, and traipse sleepily to the messhouse for breakfast, downed forthrightly in silence. Some privileged old hand might comment on the weather — "it'll be colder (or hotter) than Billy-be-damned." Other than that the crew most likely was mute, for the business of eating was eating. The same for the noon meal and supper. And the food was the best to be had, for no camp could exist without a good cook, expert with a pot of beans, beef and potatoes. His rating went up with the excellence of his cakes and pies. The same for the women cooks of whom there were many in the early days of logging. Many a crew quit camps where the biscuits were rock hard, the beef burned, or the potatoes soggy.

Loggers have been known to indicate their displeasure with the food by heaving it out of the window without bothering to raise the sash. And there have been irritable ones who, when having asked with just the right amount of deference and with what a logger would consider a polite tone, "pass the goddam beans," and getting no response, have mounted the table and tramped its length to fetch the pot of beans themselves.

The supper table was the likely place for the cook to be judged. It was the time of abundance, the better dishes, and the most flurry of hurrying flunkies with replenishments. The logger himself was apt to be a little mellow, after he scrubbed his neck and combed his hair, having taken a pull on a bottle of whisky on the bunkhouse table. It was a custom, whenever a man from camp went to town, to let a generous saloon keeper know he was about to hit for the woods. The saloon keeper invariably handed him a bottle or two "for the boys." If two men went to town, patronizing different saloons of course, and especially if they returned on Saturday broke and to be on hand for the Sunday meals, the camp would have a "shindig" which was something to see.

The men who took the part of women tied a sock or handkerchief around their arms. The boys chose their partners. In most all camps there was a violin player and a harmonica player who struck up the music and the dance was on, while the bunkhouse rocked and coyotes howled. There were always a few good callers, and some of the boys were high and fancy steppers. They bowed and honored their partners as though they were the real thing.

Free firewater had another way of getting into camp, but only once a year. About a month before Christmas a tailor from Aberdeen, usually Anderson of Anderson & Nettelblad, and possibly one from Hoquiam, would visit the camp taking orders for made-to-measure suits. Invariably he brought two sample cases, one full of cloth and the other with three or four bottles of high-grade whisky. He placed the bottles on the bunkhouse table before the "boys" went to supper. After supper, with his prospects suitably genial, he would measure them for suits.

A logger in town could buy hand-me-downs for $20 to $30. Many ordered tailor-made suits which ran from $45 to $70. The logger would pick up his suit when he hit town for Christmas time. When he was ready to return to the woods he would return the suit to the tailor, who would hang it in his shop until the Fourth of July, the logger's second annual trip to town.

Loggers were surprisingly finicky about their clothes, all of which, work clothes and town clothes, had to be the best obtainable. In the early days they asked for Belgian serge, made in Bohemia, 20-ounce stuff that would turn water. Most loggers preferred mohair lining, strong stuff that wouldn't wear out. Ed Bailey, for instance, had such a suit for 24 years and then had it made into a new suit. Where they demanded stout cloth, loggers also demanded stout seams and often would pick their own stitches, either a pull stitch or a cross stitch. Early shingleweavers, a clan unto themselves, were in some respect like the loggers. They liked to dress "fancy" when "on the town." They wore box suits and peg-top pants and could be spotted a mile away as shingleweavers.

In his bedroll wrapped in a tarp the early-day logger would have a change of underwear, two blankets, a box of soap (often a sweet-smelling variety), a shaving outfit and always a toothbrush, but he never carried a hot water bottle to heat his cold feet.[12] Some loggers carried a "powder puff" — a snuff box — but most relied on the long-familiar round box of Copenhagen. Virtually every pair of tin pants in the woods had the telltale round mark on the hip pocket where the logger kept his "snoose."

While most loggers stayed in the woods for their six-months-at-a-time stint, others were "camp inspectors," staying only a few days until moving on to another camp. Such a man was "Three-Day Red" who was well known throughout the woods for taking a job on Saturday afternoon, washing up on Sunday and clearing out on Monday — five meals without a lick of work. Sunday was wash day and clothes-patching day in the camps.

Although "Walkin' Dudley" was not a camp inspector, he did have a peculiarity that made him known to all. He walked everywhere, perhaps all his life. Cy Blackwell had met him in Maine, again in Minnesota and California, and finally Grays Harbor, always walking. In fact he was such a well-known character that a particular type of logging donkey was named for him, the "Walkin' Dudley."

And then of course there was "Poots" Woodland, renowned throughout the timber country as the greatest cusser of them all. He was so capable in his profanity he could berate the object of his ire for a full minute without using the same word twice. And he had other claims to fame as well. He was a first-rate line splicer, a skill in great demand where steel cable streaked, slashed and strummed on every hillside. And what raised more eyebrows and fetched more grins was Poots' recitations from the poets. With the slightest provocation, and often without it, Poots would mount a three-springboard stump and recite Burns and Byron with zest and fervor and a dramatic flailing of arms. It filled his soul, frightened the chipmunks and awed the windfall buckers.

While loggers observed many of the niceties, in their own ways of course, their language was not for polite society. It perhaps was the most colorful in the West (not as profane as the sailors', but colorful), inspired in many respects by various aspects of the human body. You could find this predilection even in the description of a forked-trunk tree with a crotch, which would be a "schoolmarm." A ring woven of a haulback strand was a "Molly Hogan." A certain kind of line splice, where the ends were bypassed and then tucked, had a name which would cause a circuit rider to ripple with redness. A woman working in the messhouse was a "slide-valve" flunky, whereas a man would be a "ball-bearing" flunky.

"Burning a stump" was a "siwash" or "Oregon lead"; "cherry picker," a car-mounted crane for picking up logs along a railroad; "crummy," the caboose; "farmer's hitch," an amateur splice; "haywire side," the rig-up crew; "hardtack outfit," poor feeders; "tong shaker," man who releases tongs from logs; "nose bag," cold lunch; "Port Blakely snipe," a crude sniping job; "rattler," a railroad logging truck; "sister hooks," similar hooks on opposite side of pin; "choke-bore pants," pants worn by city guys in the woods.

The masculine-oriented term was more apt to be slanted toward strength than sex. There was the "bull of the woods," the boss or superintendent; the "bull bucker" or "bull buck" who supervised the cutting crews; the "bullcook," the handyman around camp; the "bullwhacker," and so on to anything strong, massive, overly influential, either actually or facetiously. The origin of the term "snatch block" was never included in the patent numbers.

Even in the peculiar parlance of the woods, a block is hard to describe. The dictionary says it is a pulley in a frame, and a pulley is a grooved wheel in a block. That sounds like using something to describe itself. And describing a "snatch block" is almost as singular. "Snatch" in the dictionary means "to grab or seize suddenly." The logger accepted the various interpretations or applications of the word, but in the woods it was strictly usage. The snatch block did snatch; that is, it could be said to snatch when a logger put the bight of a line upon the sheave and closed the block. Whether the "grab" or "seize" was or was not sudden depended entirely upon the disposition of the logger and how much slack he had in the line. If he had just returned from town, a certain laxity in his agility could be expected.

Once the block had "grabbed" or "snatched" the line it could change a lead (direction), get extra pull, lift, or give a rigging slinger fits. It was often used as a "tail" block. (It should be recognized the logger used the word "tail" in many ways, whether it be nomenclature, used in town, or as a bit of spice in bunkhouse gab.) In any event, the "tail" block, as it may be assumed, was away down there (yarders usually were on higher ground), the last bit of far-out mechanism in the setting. From the tail block everything went back to the donkey puncher, who could give you all you wanted, or take away everything but your lunch pail . . . and sometimes that, especially if the pig jumped the pole road.

The snatch block was one of the handiest tools in the timber, largely because of its facility and adaptability. It could be opened to admit a line, and closed and pinned to keep it there. It could be hung almost anywhere with its attached swiveled hook, and easily lost in the slashings and rubble around a small donkey called halfbreed. This peculiarity became so common and aggravating some logging shows painted the blocks bright colors so as to be easily found. It could be used to string haulback around a setting, lift rigging for a highclimber, drag a log for the wood buck, build a skidroad, move a cook shack, and belabor the blacksmith.

But a snatch block was not always on the plus side. It had an aggravating habit of occasionally spewing its locking pin, in which case the block would pop open and the line would start running on the casing, sometimes cutting off a section of the casing along with the locking mechanism. And blocks had to be carefully attended, which meant mostly the grease cups had to be filled and tightened often. If not, the bearings would overheat and start smoking, squealing and calling upon the hooktender to give with the best of his vocabulary. And the situation could be dangerous, for many woods fires were started by blocks running red hot.

Among prized possessions of early Grays Harbor logging works were snatch blocks hand-forged by Nels Nelson and his son, Carl, who operated a machine shop in Aberdeen under the name of Nelson & Son. They forged the casings of steel, forged their own hooks and swivels, but used cast sheaves. Some logging outfits would have half a dozen Nelson productions, while the multitude of camps kept the Nelson anvils ringing sometimes night and day.

Even in his not-so-ribald moments a logger was apt to be vivid and picturesque in speech, and compellingly scornful of lesser men. A "sheepherder" for instance was a logger who wore bib overalls; or he might be called, not necessarily to his face, a dash-board logger, or a "hay-shaker," automatically identifying him as a farmer come to the woods. A "Coos Bay logger" was one who tucked his pants into his boot tops, an unforgivable practice in the Grays Harbor woods. However, it was woods-wise and ethnically proper for a logger to tie a double turn around his pantlegs at the calk-shoe tops. This kept the deep mud at the landing from filtering, and sometimes gushing, into his boots.

A bucker, according to a faller, was a faller who had been hit on the head by a falling limb or "widow-maker."

For some reason Grays Harbor loggers were disdainful of their Oregon counterparts. Logging terms constantly degraded the Oregon logger . . . like the "Oregon lead," and the "Coos Bay" logger who was sometimes called a "sheepherder" because he wore bib overalls. Oh, well!

And his lingo could be waggish too. "Bunkhouse": the logger's home and the place where logging records were set every night. There was a saying that loggers did their logging in town and their bawdying around the bunkhouse stove. Siwash, a common name for Coast Indians, was borrowed by the logger to indicate when the bight of a line (a curve or loop) was thrown over a stump to change the direction of the lead, also called an "Oregon lead."

A "Quebec choker" was a peavey; "Nova Scotia steam," human muscle; "cat's paw," an amateurish eye splice; "Cosmopolis flush," a four-card flush in a poker game; "gopher," a powder man who shoots a choker hole under a log; "hemlock show," logging in scrubby timber; "meow," a badly kinked or tangled steel cable; "Peter hook," a type of choker, and a later development, the "ukulele choker"; "pung," the logger's pocketbook; "necktie," a steel choker; "pull the pin," quit; "rigging crew," four men if they wore hats, eight if they wore caps; "skybound," main yarder line fouled in the high lead; "scaler," a bushel bucker's enemy; "solo," sung by the rigging crew, music by the whistlepunk; "whistlepunk," usually a young logger jerking a long wire to a whistle on the yarding donkey, signaling the donkey puncher; "soogan," logger's quilt or blanket; "steam choker," donkey puncher; "donkey puncher," donkey engineer; "Swedish fiddle," more often a bucking saw sometimes called a "misery whip;" "turkey," pack sack; "monthly insult," logger's pay; "windfall bucker," according to fallers a bucker accustomed to talking to himself who has slipped further to the stage of answering himself; "windfall bucker," a man bucking long-fallen trees, some perhaps on the ground for a century; "whiskers," jaggers on worn cable; "setup," seating arrangement in the messhall.

"Logger's delight," a complete tour of all the honkytonks in town; "bushel bucker," a bucker working by the thousand board feet; "splash," release of water and logs in a splash dam; "sack the river," to follow the river releasing grounded logs. And then, of course, there was the classic comparison between a logger and a pig; the pig makes his bed with his nose, the logger with his feet.

Some loggers were called chasers because of women, but the work-a-day term "chaser" was the man who unhooked logs at a landing. A "chokerman" was one who set chokers; "sidewinder," a tree knocked sideways by another tree; logging "side," one complete logging unit with machines, gear and rigging crew. A rigging crew in the high-ball, high-lead days consisted of a hook-tender, the boss of the rigging crew, rigging-slinger who picked the turns and directed setting of the chokers, four chokermen, a whistlepunk and a chaser at the spar tree.

As logging methods changed, the "ground lead" — dragging logs on the ground — gave way to the "high-lead," a method whereby the mainline from the yarding engine was led through a bull-block high in a topped and guyed "spar tree." The spar tree was guyed at the top with cable let to handy stumps. Often the tree was "buckle-guyed," guys fastened half way up to keep the tree from buckling under strain. Because of its height, up to 200 feet, the spar tree lifted the front end of a turn, avoiding many of the obstructions which plagued the ground lead. Even with the high-lead, rigging crews spent a lot of time freeing hang-ups.

High-lead logging was made possible by agile men with steel nerves, men who feared neither height nor the drunken motions of a windswept tree top. They were called high climbers, high riggers or tree toppers.

Chopping and sawing the top off a tall Douglas fir selected to hold the enormous pulleys which elevated cables between yarding donkeys and logs on the forest floor was only the first part of the high climber's task. More important and arduous was his fastening the blocks and the guy wires which stabilized the spar tree against tons of strain.

The first high-lead logging in Grays Harbor county was accomplished by George Townsend, logging boss for the Henry McCleary Timber Company, in 1910. His "climber" was a nervy faller named Sylvester Boling, who volunteered to work his way 60 feet up a tree by alternately mounting the springboards, ascending board by board to the point where he would cut off the top of the tree. At 60 feet, Boling looped a rope around the tree and his belt to save him if he fell off his springboard while chopping. Years later, recalling this daring act, Townsend wondered how anyone could have got up to Boling if he had tumbled and hung head down 40 feet or so from the ground.

Townsend improved the mortality prospects of his climbers by a system of ladders built eight feet long and four feet wide with steps two feet apart. These heavily-spiked ladder sections ran 70 to 80 feet up a tree.

It wasn't long before alert loggers decided to try climbing trees with spurs and belts. If telephone linemen could climb poles with spurred feet, why not loggers? With practice and extended spikes, men learned to climb speedily and safely to far greater heights than had been possible with springboards or ladders.

There were dangers in tree topping. If the undercut and back cut weren't put in right, the top might cause the tree to split as it tumbled, crushing the belted climber against the tree. Or, having the safety rope looped too close to the undercut could cause it to jump free and drop the climber to earth, or a descending climber losing control of his safety rope could tumble "inside out" and be left hanging upside down until rescued.

Climbers were a rare breed, self-confident and usually inclined to keep to themselves. Climbing is still done in a few Grays Harbor logging operations, but it lessens each year as mechanical towers replace live standing spar trees. What the public sees of high climbers today is limited to logging exhibitions at county fairs and sports shows. Most of the new "speed climbers" are spunky young fellows who get their kicks out of jogging perpendicularly. They couldn't hang a block or string a tree if their lives depended on it.

After the spar tree and its high lead was considered the ultimate in log-yarding, loggers would say all we need now is a "sky hook" to create a lead out of impossible terrain. It was facetious, of course. There was no such thing as a "sky hook."

But now loggers are not so sure. The mythical "sky hook" could well be the modern helicopter, used sparingly so far, but with a brilliant future. In the Grays Harbor country small helicopters are used to lift shake bolts out of unreachable positions ground yarding cannot reach.

The future for helicopters is perhaps being written more in British Columbia than on Grays Harbor. There huge military-style choppers are taking over coastal logging in difficult country, and most of the coast is difficult. One large American-made military style chopper capable of carrying 35 passengers and converted to forestry use, is said to replace an 80-man to 100-man logging camp. Imagine what an old bullwhacker would think, or say, if he saw such a thing.

A pile of logs collected at a spar tree, or anyplace else for that matter, was called a "cold deck," perhaps because the logs were in temporary storage and inactive. When logs or "round stuff" were pulled away from a cold deck, the donkey engine was "taking 'em hot."

After years of the fixed spar tree, the "skidder" came to the woods. This was a self-contained logging unit, with a steel tower, skyline and other gear, which could be moved from one logging "show" to another.

When a howl was heard in the slashings, likely it was a bucker who had answered a call of nature and used a wad of moss grabbed from the forest floor. The moss of course would be full of sharp fir and hemlock needles.

And when a logger had pulled the pin for the last time, he wanted to go to "Section 37," the logger's heaven, where there was no brush, the ground was level, the rigging small, with a good place to rest and a cook whose specialty was apple pie with lots of cinnamon.

The whistlepunk must have special mention, for now he is gone, vanished, a dodo of the woods. His place has been taken by an electronic gadget permitting a hooktender to flash signals to the donkey puncher directly, and this is no doubt much faster and better. But the whistlepunk was an institution of his day, and the woods will never be the same without this time-honored, mosquito-slapping worker in the tall timber.

When things were going well and the haywire was holding,

the whistlepunk was an important cog in the logging machine. He was the signalman of the woods, the virtuoso of the jerkwire. He converted the whoops, yells and hollers of the chokersetter into whistle toots for the donkey puncher, and woe unto him who made a mistake.

The whistlepunk operated a simple but highly ingenious apparatus. It consisted of a long wire stretched from the donkey engine out to where the rigging slingers worked. The wire was slung from hemlock saplings, high-butted stumps, old snags, and eventually wound up at the springpoles projecting above the donkey roof. A quick jerk or blow on the wire was carried from the springpoles to the whistle by another set of connecting wires. The jerk drew a jet of steam and a whistle to which the donkey puncher was supposed to respond. A good whistlepunk could skin the mainline back to the woods, slack the main or the haulback, go ahead slow or just put a strain on the line. Or, upon signal, he could start a thunderous symphony of snorting engines and crashing timber. It was something to see.

Whistlepunks usually had scabby ears, burned to a crisp by loud and imprecating hooktenders and chokersetters. In a whistlepunk's life there was no room for error or miscue. Wrath fell upon him in great slabs and slices.

But withal, there he stood in fair weather and foul, with the wire over his shoulder and belayed to a hemlock at his back. Mosquitos buzzed and deer flies stung. He stomped his feet in frost and sweated in July. Rainwater ran down his forearms, and at 11 o'clock his stomach growled with hunger. And kind words were seldom.

A whistlepunk often wondered why his job was necessary. Rigging-slingers yelled so loud the donkey puncher should have heard them. But the puncher played his obbligato by ear, the donkey engine made a fearful racket and it was up to the whistlepunk to supply the necessary notes.

And now, with the whistlepunk gone, there are not so many oaths in the canyons, which in a way is regrettable.

But in his day the whistlepunk was an important figure. Upon his alertness depended the health and longevity of the men who snared the logs. He had a carefully prepared and carefully followed array of whistle signals, all of which had to be instantly given and instantly responded to. There could be no delay or mistakes or the hooktender would come storming out of the canyon with fire in his eyes and his tongue spurting flames.

One blast, for instance, meant the donkey puncher should start, while a following one blast meant he should stop his machine.

Two whistles meant go ahead on the haulback or "skin 'er back."

Three whistles: ahead easy on the main line.

Two whistles and two whistles: come back easy on the haulback.

Series of short blasts: slack the mainline.

Two whistles and four more: slack the haulback.

No whistles: the puncher could renew his chaw.

One whistle plus two: tighten the mainline.

Two whistles plus three: ease the tight line.

Then there was the five long blast signal which meant the chokersetter was in trouble and needed help. It meant "call the camp foreman." Another signal sometimes used, mainly when setting up a "show," was three blasts and then one: "go ahead on the guinea line," a quarter-inch line used to pull the haulback.

And then of course the classic of the woods — a series of several angry short blasts, which meant "you son of a bitch, with the compliments of the chokersetter."

The one signal a logger never wanted to hear was the seven-long-two-short whistles which meant someone was injured. The extent of the dread perhaps reached a height in 1925 when there were more than 100 fatal accidents in the Grays Harbor woods. This sent an alarm clanging throughout the industry, prompting severe safety measures which reduced fatalities to 18 by 1952. Safety records are much improved in modern logging.

Most of the jobs in the woods became specialty jobs. Not everyone could be a good donkey puncher, or a timber faller, or a chokersetter, or for that matter a good bullcook, the doer of all chores around a camp, mostly janitor work.

For instance, the "bull bucker" headed all the cutting crew. He was the man who made the decisions where to fall timber, which direction it should be felled and who should do it. The fallers worked in pairs, one at each end of a falling saw. In chopping this made it necessary for one man to chop left-handed, the other right-handed, and fallers often were paired with this capability in mind. Each pair had a "head faller" and a "second faller."

A set of fallers tramped into the timber carrying axes, saws, wedges, a maul, springboards, oil bottles, a lunch pail (if far from the messhouse), a water bag or jug, and often a can of snoose and plug of tobacco. In the early day of logging when most swell-butted trees were high-stumped, fallers carried two springboards apiece, and worked themselves up the tree from one springboard hole to another. The springboard, little used now, was a six-foot length of straight-grained fir or spruce two by seven or eight inches, slightly tapered at one end where an iron "shoe" or "plate" was attached. The off end of the "shoe" had a sharp upturned edge, which would bite into the upper part of a springboard hole cut into a tree. A springboard notch had to be carefully cut, with the bottom straight into the tree. The upper part could slope down, but not too much, for the sharp edge of the "shoe" had to engage the upper part of the cut. Properly fitted the springboard served as a fine and handy working platform for the faller, who could shift the position of the board by hooking the toe of one calked shoe under the back of the board and giving himself a little mid-air hop. A good hole would allow a faller to make as much as a 30- to 45-degree shift as he sawed through the tree. On larger trees two or more springboard holes on the same level on the same side often were needed to make the undercut and allow the faller to shift to the opposite side to make the back cut.

Fallers were required to be expert, not only to get a tree down in a reasonable amount of time but to do it without damage to the tree. Inexpert falling could break a lot of timber, or leave a "barber chair" on the stump, or jackstraw felled trees, leaving an impossible situation for the buckers. And falling skill also meant staying alive, for the work was dangerous and falling trees are not always predictable. A tree in falling could kick back over the stump, or roll off the stump if another tree interfered. Falling limbs were called "widowmakers" because of the fatalities they caused, and so were snags, which had a tendency to break aloft or shower the area with inches-thick bark slabs.

Fallers, when they jumped from their springboards yelling

"timber-r-r" or some other warning, always headed for safety to either side of the stump, never to the rear, for fear of the "kickback." Usually they sought another stump or tree for safety.

Following the fallers through the woods were the buckers, who cut the trees into log lengths, usually 24-, 32- or 40-foot lengths.

Theirs was a solitary job, for they worked alone in the tangle of the tops, limbs and brush, swamping the debris to get a place to work, then dragging a heavy bucking saw for hours on end. Normally the bucker sawed "down" on a log, but by using an adapter he could saw "up" as well, especially if the tree was "bridged" and the cut would bind at the top. Usually he could open the cut with a wedge and could continue his cut with a well-oiled saw.

There was danger for the bucker, too. Never would he buck a log from the downhill side, for that would be inviting the severed log to roll and crush him. Severed trees often acted in strange and unpredictable ways, and only a careful bucker survived to make it to town on the Fourth of July.

In an enterprise that depended so heavily upon a saw, logging called for expert saw filers. Fallers and buckers were finicky about how their saws were filed. The "set" had to be just so, the "rakes" just so long and shaped to the user's satisfaction, and of course the cutting teeth had to be razor sharp, with the proper bevel and length.

Saws were brought in from the woods each day and swapped for sharp ones. There was some danger even in this exchange, for there was a method and knack in carrying a limber saw eight to ten feet long. It was carried on the shoulder with the teeth out to avoid a slashed neck in case of a fall. And the step or stride was synchronized with the bounce of the saw, or broken so there was little or no bounce.

After the buckers came the rigging crews and the chokersetters and their crews, including the choker hole diggers who did just that. They dug holes under a log so the choker "eye" could be passed through. They often used narrow shovels shaped like a clam shovel, but if the digging was hard, dynamite was used. A digger would cut a third or a half stick of Hercules blasting powder with his pocketknife, take a dynamite cap from his pocket, insert a length of fuse, crimp the cap with his teeth, and tuck the charge under the log. Many times a number of charges were placed, and just before lunchtime the fuses were lit to a warning yell: "Fire in the hole." The choker hole diggers would listen to the number of explosions. If one failed, it was a problem, for no one wanted to approach a live charge. There was always the possibility of fire still in the hole. In such cases it was a practice to wait several hours before investigating. Dynamiters, called powder monkeys, sometimes disappeared into space when careless.

Donkey "punchers" or engineers were a breed unto themselves. And yarder engineers were the most unique of the breed. In normal life the engineer was apt to be a silent, self-effacing individual given to reading and singular contemplation. But once he had his hand on the throttle and the friction jammed, he was another man, a tyrant of the woods; an unapproachable, hard-eyed, single-purpose phenomenon who made his monster machine roar like a thousand storms while the whole "side" trembled.

Such a man was John Freeland, weight 130 pounds, who was a deacon in his church and wore bib overalls, in the bib pocket of which he carried a small Bible. This he read between whistles or when some rigging was broken. But when he was whistled again, he opened his big 12 x 14 Willamette and its 225 pounds of steam to full throttle, and to hell with the rigging and the men in the woods.

Freeland's haulback wasn't fast enough to suit him, so he spent a Sunday pulling all the haulback off the drum and then facing the drum with six inches of wood lagging. This increased the diameter of the drum and, consequently, the speed of the haulback. This pleased Johnny to no end, for now when the mainline went back to the woods it fairly whistled, with the choker flailing, wrapping around small trees, and either pulling the tree down or unwinding and sizzling in circles through the woods, cutting a wide swath until stopped by the whistlepunk. The waiting choker setters were either hidden under a log or far away from danger.

Johnny, like most engineers, had his mainline marked for distance to the choker setters and would slow down when the

Early Grays Harbor loggers sometimes had to squirm sideways to penetrate walls of Douglas fir giants in the thickest forest on earth.

—CLEMONS COLLECTION

Fallers taking a breather before felling a buxom spruce. Wedges in the back cut will help topple the tree.

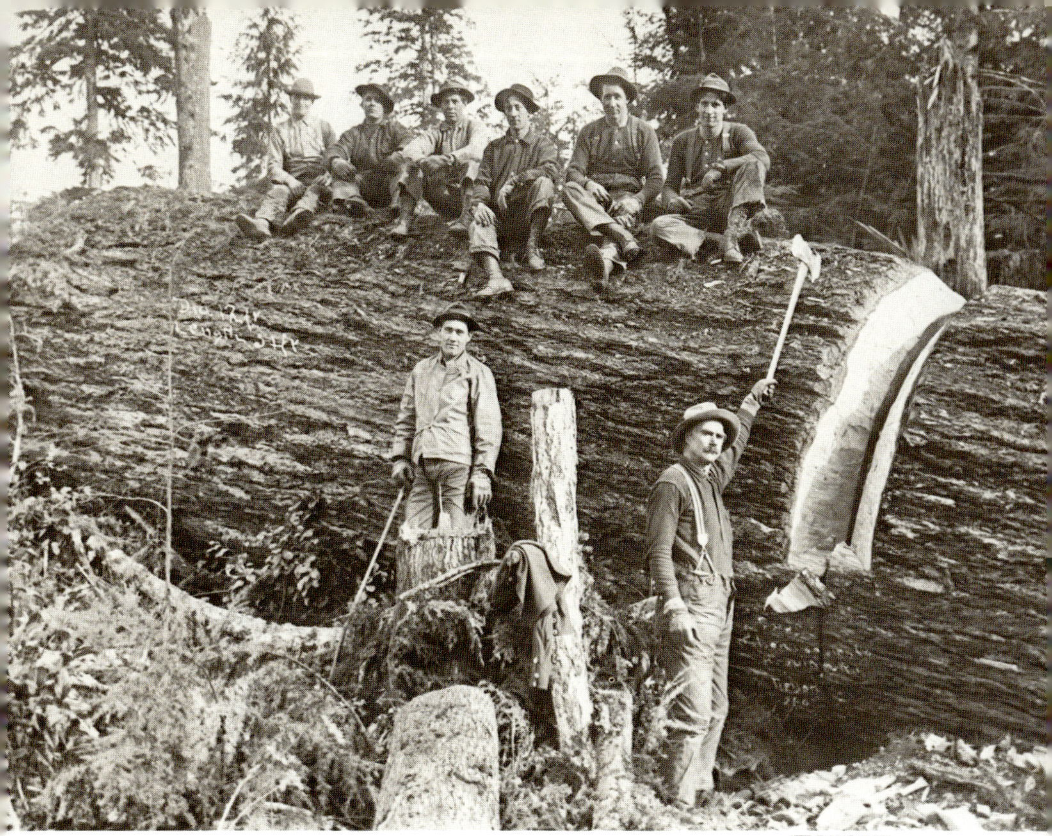

—ITT RAYONIER

Polson loggers pondered how to handle this 12-foot Douglas fir on the Humptulips. The sniper is tapering the logs so they will slide.

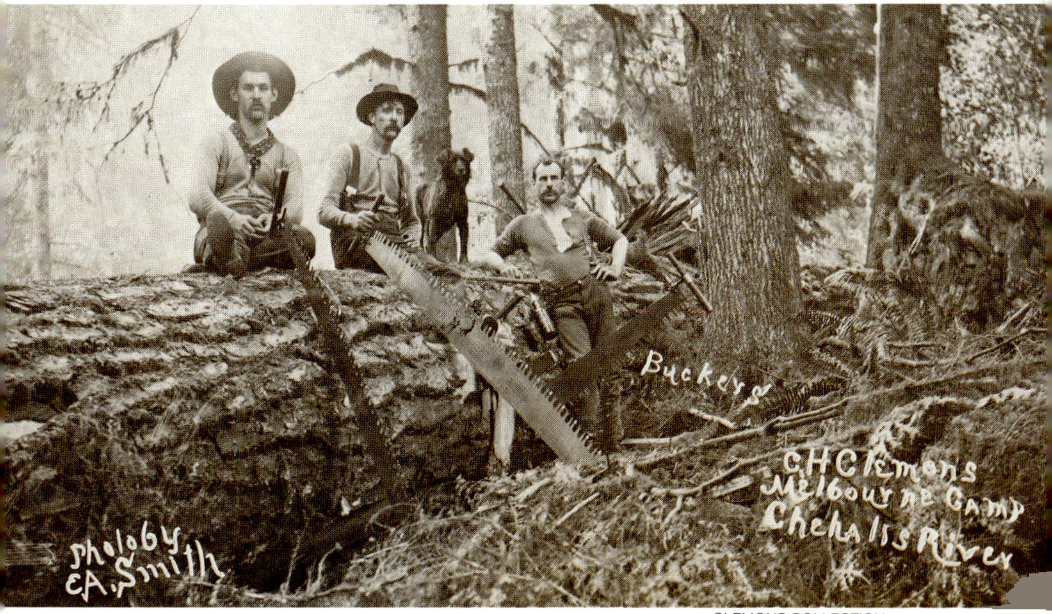

—CLEMONS COLLECTION

Log buckers relax their biceps between sweaty sessions with heavy crosscut saws. Logger at right has wedged his final cut. Dogs no longer work in the woods.

—POLSON MUSEUM

Winds of the 1890s whistled freely through split-cedar shantys in Cy Blackwell's Wishkah logging camp. Cy called it good ventilation.

Cy Blackwell, a master of purple prose, stood in tin pants at age 81. He whacked more bulls, felled more trees and cussed more bosses than anybody.

—ED VAN SYCKLE

—MRS. J. A. McDONALD

Jim Haynes' bull-logging show on the Wishkah in 1890. This is a classic study of the entire bull-powered log-moving process.

—DOROTHY Z. COLLINS

Benjamin Franklin Armstrong, Jr., son of the first Chehalis Valley lumberman, hauling camp supplies, including a butchered sheep, in 1900.

—MRS. J. A. McDONALD

Jim Haynes had this early Dolbeer donkey tugging at enormous logs in the Wishkah valley in 1900. That's Haynes at left near the donkey frame.

That old faithful of early donkey logging, the line horse, served until loggers developed a haulback system. This was C. E. Burrows' camp.

—CLEMONS COLLECTION

Five cuts of a nine-foot spruce waiting to be yarded at Clemons camp near Melbourne, 1904. Charles Leavitt, at left; Henry Thompson with saw.

—CLEMONS COLLECTION

Clemons had one of the earliest drum donkeys, 1900. Haughty youth up front pictures pride of loggers who knew their skills.

This massive 13x14 Washington Flyer could reel in a half mile of slackline two inches in diameter for Willapa Harbor Lumber Company's Camp One.

—EUGENE PATTERSON COLLECTION

Neither rivers nor deep canyons stopped the cross-country migrations of donkey engines when camps moved in the Wishkah country.

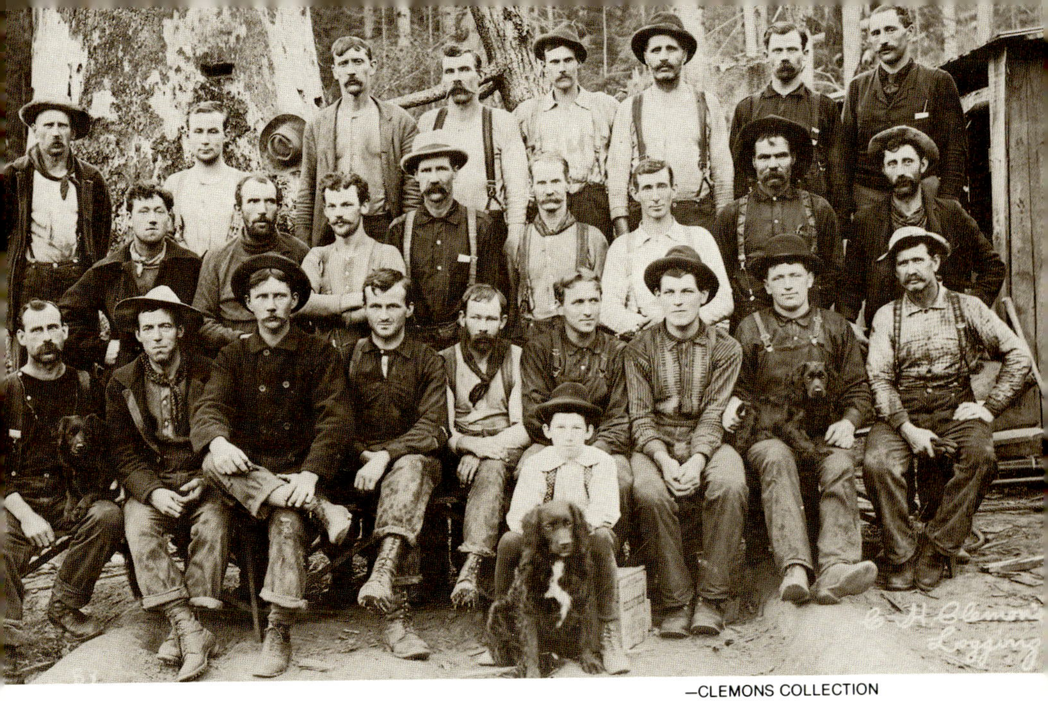

—CLEMONS COLLECTION

Charles Clemons, fourth from left, middle row, with his Higgins Slough crew. Boy up front is his son, George, killed in a 1919 logging train runaway.

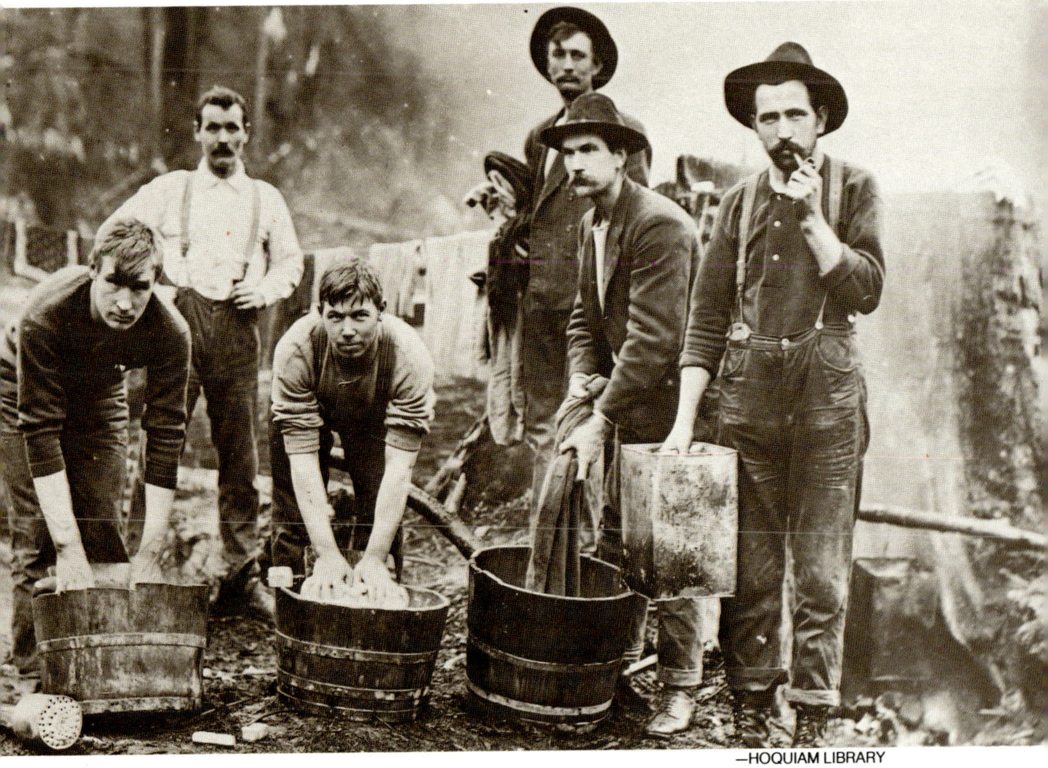

—HOQUIAM LIBRARY

No matter how muddy the week, loggers came clean with Sunday washing. Punctured can (left) worked as a plunger to foment suds.

—JONES COLLECTION

They didn't like the gut-robber's grub, so the whole crew pulled the pin at Polson's Camp Three in 1901. They up and quit.

—ITT RAYONIER

Old Betsy in her heyday of pooping logs out of the Polson works. Now she rests as the Minnetonka in a Chicago railway museum.

When unstoppable loggers came to a canyon, they brought in a piledriver and trestled across to the next bank. No problem.

—JONES COLLECTION

Geared for climbing, Shay locomotives hurtled through the highest hills in the Grays Harbor country to bring logs mill-ward.

—JONES COLLECTION

Men who operated this geared Climax lokie for Coats-Fordney had their meals well tamped down by the jerky up-down drivers.

—JONES COLLECTION

A proud young logger of 1930, his name lost in the shufflings of history, stands with his "jewelry" in Godamighty timber country.

—JONES COLLECTION

It was sawing a "bridged" tree, taut with tension, that gave buckers a dry mouth. To avoid stress, they sawed upwards.

—JONES COLLECTION

In the lives of all working men there comes a day when the saws stick, logs bind and the weary bucker says, "Aw, To Hell With It."

—DAVE JAMES COLLECTION

Rare view of trees laddered for high-climbing at Henry McCleary's Summit Lake camp in 1910. This was before men climbed with spurs.

—JONES COLLECTION

High climber topping a Douglas fir prior to rigging the tree.

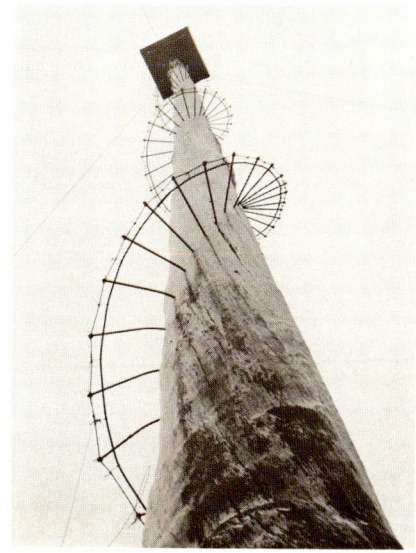

—DEL MULKEY

Daring men walked these corkscrew spikes to the Cook Creek lookout.

H Clemons 1904   Wm. Maloney   Geo. Arland   Joe Bernard   E.K. Bishop   Dan McCloskey (Maloneys bro-law)   Ben Kesterson   Geo. Nine

—JONES COLLECTION

Early logging bosses of Grays Harbor paused to eat lunch and trade wisdom while cruising an old timber burn.

—DAVE JAMES COLLECTION

Each year the countryside gets higher and the hills steeper around Simpson's Camp Grisdale, the industry's last major woods camp.

rigging approached that area. Some engineers were known to pull the mainline through the tailblock when something happened to the whistle.

And Johnny Freeland once did this on purpose. Johnny had a hotshot hooktender from Oregon who was out to set a record. He insisted always that the line be run back to the woods after the noon whistle blew, so the crew could set another choker during their lunch hour. Johnny got tired of this and warned the rigging crew to get out of the bight of the line the next time the hotshot ordered the line returned to the woods at noon time. The signal came and Johnny opened 'er up. The haulback fairly smoked through the blocks. The choker fetched up with the tail block and side blocks in turn. All were carried, screaming with frenzied speed, back to the haulback drum.

Johnny Freeland strode into camp, demanded his check and was ready to "hit the pike." But the camp foreman fired the hooktender instead.

Donkey engineers or "punchers" came into their own during the era of the fore-and-aft skidroad, often truthfully called the "pole road," which was built of three and four logs to form a trough. The "four pole" road was good enough for early loggers who pulled the first log in a turn with succeeding logs tailed on. But when the big road engines began operation with the hitch on the stern log, the leading logs being pushed would jackknife in the skidroad and foul up the whole turn. So the much simpler three-log road, narrower and easier to build, was devised and worked admirably until truck roads and railroads phased out the skidroads.

This then was the realm of the steam donkey puncher, who was monumental in some of his accomplishments. An epochal example was the "move" of the Carlson & Callow works from Chenois Creek to the East Hoquiam, thence to Black Creek in the Wynooche country. While Carlson & Callow logged on Chenois Creek, they eventually crossed the road to Copalis Crossing in Section 12-18-11. When they reached this point they purchased a 14 x 14 Willamette wide-face donkey engine. For a time they had it on the side of the Beach highway with a sign proclaiming it the "largest donkey in the world." It could have been, for it was monstrous. It could pull logs on a pole road for more than a mile.

The giant machine carried 250 pounds of steam, and the firebox measured nine feet wide, twelve feet deep and six feet high. When it was running steadily, one man could not possibly keep up with the machine's demand for firewood. The mainline was 1¼" diameter, and the wide-face drum held 6,300 feet of line. The haulback was ⅝-inch line with the haulback drum holding 13,500 feet of haulback. Ernest Lammey was engineer for this monster.

When Carlson & Callow started to shift from the East Hoquiam to Black Creek, they decided to move their engines directly over the hills and through the timber rather than by railroad. And hereby hangs a tale of donkey "Mass Transit" unmatched in Harbor history. There were ten engines all told, including three wide-faces which were the hardest to move. A yarder without a "lagged" drum could move itself with a straight line on level ground, but a wide-face required at least two blocks and sometimes more.

In this move, which was highly unusual, a small 7 x 9 Tacoma led the procession, with the road machines last. As soon as the route was determined, woodcutters were sent ahead to stockpile fuel. Then line was set for the lead donkey, and as it moved ahead it pulled line out for the second donkey, and so on down the line. As soon as the first two or three had moved, the first ones' lines were put out and the cycle started over again.

Although the procession crossed many creeks and two rivers, water for the boilers was a constant problem. There were times when water didn't show in the boiler water glass, and once when they were too long without water they had to let the boilers cool before water could be injected.

One river was too deep to cross with the ordinary method so, after lines were strung across the stream, fires were pulled after a full head of steam had been attained, and the donkey engines under full throttle pulled themselves across, even through deep water. The road engines got help from the big yarders in making stream crossings. The yarders, first across, merely hooked on to their roaders and horsed them across on a straight line.

This proved to be some sort of a record in camp moving. Carlson & Callow moved four logging camps and all their donkey engines and equipment a distance of 20 miles as the shitepoke flies, not counting the ups and downs of terrain, the detours for better slopes, water and firewood, and shallower water in the rivers. Shortly after all this labor of moving, the entire outfit was sold to the Wynooche Timber Company.

In the era and place of these Herculean doings, especially in poleroad days, there was a certain established routine, not only in the lives of the men but also in the practice of their logging. If the day, for instance, was one in December, it would begin cold and drearily with rain drumming the tarpaper roof of the bunkhouse, while the bullcook rattled the stovelid and thumped wood into the big sheet-iron heater. The fir wood popped and crackled pleasantly. When the sides of the stove began to glow and the stovepipe blushed red almost to the roof, an old bucker roused himself and closed the draft to save the bunkhouse from burning down.

Most of the sixteen men in the bunkhouse would be wide awake, with a few still lost in sonorous snores, but all would be jarred alert as a flunky, beating on the drill-steel triangle, hammered the camp into action.

The cook already had a kerosene lamp lit in his room to the rear of the cookhouse. He fumbled and puffed, for this day he would treat the crew to a clean apron, which he hung around his neck and tied methodically in back. At precisely 4:35 a.m. he ambled into the kitchen and lit the overhead lamp. He then touched a match to the pre-laid fire in the long, wood-burning range. As smoke began to seep around the lids, he opened a cover plate beneath the first oven and inserted a piece of burning, oil-soaked rag to create a draft and encourage the fire.

The range drawing with a satisfying but subdued roar, the cook shuffled to the screened meat room for the big drip pans of sliced bacon, some of which had been served the day before. He also brought out pans of boiled and sliced potatoes and a dishpan of eggs. Now he mixed the sourdough pancake batter using a starter carried over from day to day. He made gigantic swirls with a heavy spoon until, with a knowing eye, he could judge the consistency as logger-ready and rib-sticking. Next he prepared a big pot of oatmeal and pushed the coffeepot to a glowing stovelid. Now was the time to awaken the two flunkies and the dishwasher. In a short time they trooped in sleepy-eyed and, with the donkey punchers, sat down to breakfast. The donkey punchers ate early for they had to fire up their boilers a half-hour before the crew hit the woods, smear gear grease and tend to last-minute chores before daybreak.

The bullcook now built a roaring fire in the sheet-iron stove in the middle of the dining room while one of the flunkies, having finished his breakfast, stepped outside the cookhouse and beat mightily upon the triangle, which could have been heard perhaps clear over on the Wynooche. It was the signal for the crew to turn out.

The men roused reluctantly, stretching and belching, pulling on their wool shirts and tin pants with permanent knee bends. Their socks, dried over the rafters or the hanging rack around the stove, were beaten over the edge of the benches to soften them from dried mud. They pulled on their "stags" (worn-out calk shoes cut down to slipper size). Most all went out to a fir stump behind the bunkhouse to relieve themselves. Some went into the dark to wash their faces in cold water in the tin wash basins; some didn't. Some combed their hair; others left it in a bunk-pillow tangle. They all filed into the messhall when a flunky sounded the signal, another vigorous beating inside of the triangle — as though this would be his delight for the day.

The tables were already set and groaning under the breakfast dishes. It took a lot of pancakes to ready the crew for the day's work. The men ate in verbal silence except for the "pass me this" or "pass me that" necessary to keep the plates supplied. No time was lost in idle conversation.

As each man completed his breakfast, and if the logging area was some distance from camp, he walked over to the lunch table to pick up his lunch bucket filled with meat sandwiches, boiled eggs, pie and cake, or perhaps a doughnut or two. Some of the heavy eaters went to the "extra" section for additional fare, mostly pie, cake or doughnuts. Most all filled the top of their lunch pail, a flat, tank-like container fitted with a cupola on top covered with a cup-shaped tin lid, with coffee or tea, often with generous helpings of canned milk and sugar. Thermos bottles were years away from the woods at that time. The coffee or tea would be cold at lunchtime, but for the donkey crew there was warm-up heat in the boiler. The same privilege often was extended to a few members of the rigging crew.

After breakfast, and with their lunch pails in hand, the loggers filed back into the bunkhouse where they laced on their calked shoes, soles bristling with steel nails for safe footing on slippery logs. Loggers never put their shoes near the fire to dry them. Heat stiffened the leather. The loggers preferred to wear their "corks" damp.

In a few minutes the foreman appeared with a yell "roll out" and, if he felt testy that day, "roll out" or "roll up." And later in the day, if he was cantankerous and displeased, he might tell some lagging logger: "The timekeeper has a letter for you ... we're running a logging camp and not a rest home." The offending logger would "hit the pike" without question, blow his pay in town, and get a job just over the ridge from his last.

Daylight would be some time away as the men trooped out of camp, so about every fifth man carried a coal oil lantern. The fallers and buckers stopped at the filing shack to pick up sharp saws to replace the ones they had dropped off the day before to be sharpened. They then proceeded to the cutting area single file and about twelve feet apart, the long saws over their shoulders, carried teeth out, flopping up and down at each stride.

The rigging-slinger and his chokermen stopped at the blacksmith shop to pick up a new choker. This tool was 30 feet long and made of 1⅜-inch cable, the flat hook, swivel and links at one end weighing about 50 pounds. The rigging-slinger threw the "jewelry" over his shoulder while the chokermen picked up the wire.

There was a well-worn trail to the road donkey, where the rigging men dumped their choker in the skidroad for the chaser to send to the woods. The chaser, pond man, the fireman and the woodbucker were backed up to the boiler warming their backsides. The rest of the crew tramped up the skidroad.

The roader engineer had his engines turning over slowly, steam hissing from the petcocks in the cold, coming dawn, while he applied warmed-up gear dope to the bullwheel by the light of a lantern.

The fireman turned from his backside-warming, shoved the

chaser and pondman aside, and opened the firebox. The flickering glare lit up the whole after-end of the donkey, reflections dancing upon the big water tank, and picking out lights upon the slash to either side. He grabbed a heavy iron poker and shook down the wood and coals to the grates, then carefully filled the firebox tight with wood. He slammed the door with a bang, darkness returning.

About half way up the skidroad the fallers and buckers halted to await daylight. It was too dark to cut out across the fallen timber and slashings carrying saws, lunch pails and what other gear they were taking into the woods. They had left their springboards, sledges, wedges, oil bottles and other gear in the cutting area the day before. They stood in droopy misery, with rain rattling upon their coats and dripping from their felt hats.

At the breed donkey the fireman, the handyman (who was to chase for the breed this day) and the wood buck fell out of the line of loggers and climbed upon the donkey skids. They put their lunch pails upon the shelf above the water tank and backed up to the boiler.

The yarder crew went on, stumbling through the debris alongside the breed road for another thousand feet. At the yarder the whistlepunk picked up a bundle of kindling the fireman had prepared the day before. When he reached his station he lighted a fire around which the rigging crew gathered to warm their chilly bones.

The yarder engineer took a long look into the woods and judged there was enough daylight to see hand signals. He jerked the whistle lanyard: one long, one short. The woods began to move; the logging day had started.

Back at the roader the chaser had started the gas engine, turning the pump which supplied water to the three donkey engines. He returned to the skidroad, hooked the new choker into the butt rigging, then picked up a small can of cup grease for the haulback blocks. He did not ride the pig this trip for there were five or six bearings to be greased on the way out. The road engineer blew two sharp blasts on the whistle and started the line up the road and back to the woods. He would know when to stop the line for he had marked the stopping place with a gob of gear grease. Now the whole show was under way.

The camp foreman, who had stayed in camp to take care of two men quitting, did not need to be in the woods to know how his show was performing. He could tell from the donkey whistles exactly what was going on.

The two quitting men had rolled up their bedding, tied calked shoes to the rolls, and walked over to the office to get their time slips. Not a word was spoken, for it would have been unethical for the two to give reasons for quitting or for the foreman to ask. The two stomped out and headed for town, their time slips tucked into their shirt pockets. The slips would be exchanged for checks at the company office, cashable at any saloon in town.

Meanwhile, the bullcook had brought in two or three wheelbarrow loads of dry fir wood for the kitchen stove, stowing it under the long dish-up table. Then the flunkies started to scrub the cookhouse and messhouse floors. Next, the bullcook loaded the swill barrel upon his wheelbarrow and went plodding off to the squealing pigs, which most camps kept for fresh meat. Next, he replenished the woodboxes in the bunkhouses, office, engineer's shack and filing shack. He swept the floors with some difficulty, for they had been badly chewed by spiked boots. The rest of the day he would spend cutting wood and doing odd jobs around camp. Some bullcooks were not above taking a nip or two from bottles stowed at several places around the bunkhouses.

Upon the cook, perhaps even more than upon the camp superintendent, depended the camp's smooth performance. Satisfied men seemingly did better and more work. So the cook was a busy man seven days a week. Few could stand the pressure for many months without going to town for a "bust," or hitting the lemon extract after the second month.

No sooner was one meal over than the next must be prepared. There was much baking done, meat to cut, then the actual cooking of meals, to say nothing of "snacks," coffee and other incidentals. No small amount of the cook's time was spent herding, admonishing and often cussing his helpers.

And then dusk fell, or more likely the dark day just grew darker almost imperceptibly. The yarder engineer blew the quitting whistle: one long, one short. Within about 15 minutes the string of lanterns began to bob down the trail, heading for the bunkhouses. All except the firemen and engineers would be sopping wet, some with their boots squishing. Once inside, some of the loggers peeled off their clothes and put on dry underwear, but many merely shed their calk shoes, socks, tin pants and shirts, leaving their wet wool underwear to dry on their hides. Most all "cleaned up" for the evening meal.

The men trooped to the messhouse in lines when the signal sounded. To hasten the descent upon the dinner tables, some messhouses had more than one entrance. Even with one entrance, the pecking order and some restraint on the part of the famished made the entry more or less orderly. When the meal ended the men swung their legs over their benches and departed to their own timing. Some ate faster than others, while some prolonged the eating until the messhall was virtually deserted.

After the meal the cookhouse crew cleaned up the tables and put up lunches for the next day. The lights were turned out.

In the bunkhouse a couple of old hands played a game of cribbage, with a few onlookers. Poker games mostly were reserved for Saturday night. Besides, some hooktender probably had won all the money in camp anyhow, and there would not be much poker in camp until after Christmas. At 9:30 p.m. all lights were out and the loggers lapsed into work-drugged sleep, to wake up hours later as surly as a she-bear with a sore paw.

The routine differed on Sunday, for it was said in the woods: "Six days shalt thou labor, and on the seventh wash thy dirty socks." So it was.

After breakfast donkey engineers grabbed up armloads of greasy clothes and hiked for their respective donkeys. The boilers had to be washed out every two weeks, but on other Sundays the donkey punchers found it necessary to file rod brasses, take out shims or just "monkey wrench." All this was not necessary, but it gave the engineers an extra day's pay while at the same time they did their washing. They would fill a tub with hot water, put in some soap powder and lye, then work on their machines. When they finished washing out the boiler and puttering around, they fired up the boiler, finished their washing and headed for camp.

Meanwhile, the camp crew, or at least most of them, filled an oil drum with water and built a fire under it. Then they bailed the hot water into tubs and stamped their clothes with their homemade washing machine apparatus, which consisted of a gallon fruit can with several dozen nail holes punched in the bottom. Through the open end a handle was inserted and nailed firmly through the bottom. The apparatus, churned up and down in the tub of clothing, did a surprisingly efficient job of washing. Some modern washing machines use the same principle.

Many loggers, however, never bothered to wash their clothes, contributing much to the customary bunkhouse odor which consisted of a blend of tobacco juice, snoose squirtings, saw oil, fir pitch, pipe smoke, wet wool, lamp kerosene, over-ripe socks, whale oil, bear grease and stale jokes, to say nothing of unwashed hides and the cook's onions, all heated in the square box of dirt upon which the sheet-iron stove rested.

In the rain the logger would wear a coat made of the same paraffined, canvas-like material as his tin pants. Later he took to wearing a heavy wool coat with double shoulder and double-thickness sleeves which shed or absorbed a tremendous amount of water. It was warm, durable, comfortable, and normally would outlast a riggin' slinger. But whatever, he was ready. With his calk shoes over his shoulder and a farewell shot of whisky in his belly, often a bonus from the bartender, he headed for camp.

At heart he was a rebel, though not often rebellious until logging operations became outsized. The first logging camps were apt to be owner-operated, with the owner working along with his crew. It was a close and friendly relationship, with all sharing the good and the bad, with the chopper, for example, knowing as much about camp affairs as the owner himself. Then, as the logging enterprise grew, there would be several camps with the owner operating from an office in town and the camps themselves under management of superintendents or "bulls of the woods." The close personal relationship was gone and, with working or living conditions no better, the logger began to grouse, then bedamn, and in time, under spur of the union organizer, to rebel.

In fact all the synonyms bubbled to the surface. The logger was defiant, intractable, recalcitrant, insubordinate, pugnacious, refractory and often quarrelsome. He was unattached and footloose, and mostly unencumbered by matrimony. He became a drifter in the sense that he had no fixed home, but moved with the camps as the timberline retreated, or moved from one operation to another according to his whim. As compared to the mill hand, the logger was not tied to one spot by repetitious work, or to a set of rolls, an edger or trimsaw, green chain, deafening planer, or the monotony of piling lumber. His was an outdoors job with nature and peril, in places where misery was rain six or more months of the year, mixed often with squaw-deep snows of winter and the scorchers of summer and early autumn. However, he did not complain of the work itself, for there was savor to it, but he did rebel if the rigging was bad, the food poor, the bunkhouse lousy, the pay low or the bull of the woods overbearing.

Thus was the legend of the "timber beast" enhanced, though a logger was never called such. He called himself a logger, wet with the rain, cold with the cold, hot with the summer sun and the lures of the flesh and waggles of Hume street; never a "lumberjack," or a hireling, nobody's lackey. He was his own man, hard-muscled, hard-working, not too concerned with the niceties, but a gallant at heart, a cougar on the prowl, a wildcat in a fight, and better left alone.

It is almost fundamental in the woods and sawmills that a wheel will not turn or a line move without snoose, or if you wish to be polite, a "pinch of snuff." This time-honored institution, which once boasted jeweled snuff boxes and a whole ritual of social decorum, fell to the hoi polloi as one of the basic necessities of labor. The custom has survived largely as "Copenhagen," of which of course there must be ample supply.

Twice within the memory of modern man there has been a snoose scarcity in the woods and paucity of industry thereby. The first, properly called the "Great Snoose Famine," was in the winter of 1926-27, while the other was in January 1969, this comparison being but a mere interruption of supply.

Both were caused by blizzards on the Great Plains, notably in Montana and the Dakotas. Snow smothered rail lines and no traffic was moving toward the Coast and eventually Grays Harbor. It must be noted too: Grays Harbor on both occasions had deep snows also, which may have compounded the problem. Some

LIFE IN THE CAMPS

would have said snowstorms were the main cause of the industrial shutdowns. However, there was no getting around the fact that the woods or mills could not move without snoose, for when you wanted to step up an operation you would say "give 'er snoose"; or when the steam pressure was low the half-breed "didn't have enough snoose." And for that matter when anything was a little on the weak side, it "needed more snoose." If you didn't have snoose you couldn't operate, you couldn't get the headrigs rolling, the wood hogs roaring or tne haulback spliced.

There was a spell when it looked like not a wheel would be turned, a gear meshed or a slackline tightened. There wasn't any snoose around, certainly not enough to muscle the mills, camps and gillnets. That was the Great Snoose Famine. Somewhere on the white wastes of the Dakotas was a freight train or an express with tons of snoose, and not a single little round box to reach the Coast. Not a single rare for the snoose-starved, no help for the tall and uncut and the deep and unfished. From the Cascades to the Pacific countless thousands of lower lips quivered, and dejected souls pined. Men would walk all the way to Hoquiam just for an outside chance for a can of snoose. And, in Ballard, halibut fishermen refused to leave the wharf until a supply of snoose was assured.

In time both dearths were relieved by snowplows and thaws, and the shelves of Grays Harbor were replenished. Most of the snuff or snoose was Copenhagen, the old reliable that had been bulging lips for decades. But in January, 1969, relief came also in the form of wintergreen and raspberry flavors, a thing that was profane and had old hooktenders tapping their Copenhagen cans indignantly. It was enough to make an old bullwhacker weep into his warmed-over coffee.

To know the industrial importance of snoose you would know it took 500 to 600 rolls a week (eight cans to a roll) to keep the belts tight, the shafts turning, the trees falling and the plywood glued, plus give or take a few cans of evergreen or raspberry.

And the Copenhagen had to be fresh. There was no more finicky consumer anywhere than a setter on a headrig who was about to purchase a can of snoose. Copenhagen was dated at the factory and was closely inspected as it crossed the cigar counter.

An eager lower lip would tolerate a few days of age, but not much more. Anything over two weeks caused misgivings, while if the can was a month old the merchant might as well have dumped it into the ash can. The stuff would have been dry and couldn't pull a short-rake crosscut through a four-year cottonwood.

But, as it was said, the Great Snoose Famine finally ended about the time the water pipe to the wide-face roader thawed, and things began to happen again. Lips bulged with new vigor, the yarder puncher grew testy and irascible, while the yard boss in the shipping shed passed a compliment to the carloading crews. Even the lumber market bettered, and log scalers had a twinge of conscience and put their scaling sticks clear down to the bottom of the log. Paradise was regained.

Chapter 4

BULLS AND STEAM WHISTLES

The first logging in the Chehalis valley was for the first three waterpower mills: Armstrong's, Estes' and Luark's. These were what might have been called "family logging" shows in that when the mill was in need of logs it was shut down and the crew turned loggers. A half-dozen trees would be felled nearby, a bull team borrowed, and the logs snaked to a landing. This would not necessarily be an oft-repeated procedure, for six or eight trees might last the mill a month. The output often was no more than a thousand feet a day, with the muley up-and-down saws shaking the environs for a hundred feet around.

It was a common practice when "logging into tidewater" to fall a tree into the water, then limb it and buck it into lengths and let the logs float away. But there came a time when few trees were available for this type of logging. Then the logger had to cut trees away from easy access to tidewater or deep, freshwater streams. This took much more than bulging biceps. Then came the bull teams and spans of horses, for in no way, come flying-ant time, could human muscle meet the weight of a four-foot butt cut. Even on a cross-skidroad with a six-yoke team and well-greased skids the skidder had to give the first log of a turn a "rock" with a peavey or a length of vine maple to get it started.

And J. B. Kesterson would know; he hand-logged on Elliott Slough in the spring of 1881 with Rollie Van Winkle, a partner he had found the spring before while getting out ties in the Blue Mountains of Oregon for the Northern Pacific railroad. Kesterson persuaded Van Winkle to come to Grays Harbor and to join in a logging venture, not only on Elliott Slough but also on Van Winkle Creek where Rollie Van Winkle settled. The creek empties into and drains from man-made Lake Aberdeen, a link in Aberdeen's industrial water system. The logs were towed to the newly-built North Western mill in Hoquiam.

Prior to logging on these two sites, the partners cut piling at the mouth of Delezene Creek to build the Hoquiam mill. The pilings were floated down the Chehalis to Montesano where they were rafted, but Kesterson and Van Winkle had no luck in attempts to float the raft to Hoquiam, so they hired the little steamer *General Newell* to tow the raft to the millsite.

Also in 1881, while Kesterson and Van Winkle were grunting logs into the water, several other men were muscling timber. William "Uncle Bill" Reid, he the uncle of Jerry and Dan McGillicuddy, was logging the Scammon place at Lower Montesano. In 1883 he was to shut down his camp for a time because of the scarcity of hay for his animals. At the same time J. W. Milroy, logging near Sharon, was "going full blast," getting feed for his animals from Fords Prairie.

Hamilton & Smith, who began hand logging on the Wishkah in 1883, by the end of March had an accumulation of 120,000 board feet of logs for delivery to the North Western mill. Upon delivery they were paid $5.50 per M for the logs at the North Western boom.

W. D. Mack, one of the first loggers on the Hoquiam, did some hand logging, then acquired a bull team and a partner, Pete Autzen, to organize the company of Mack & Autzen. Later Autzen was to become a county commissioner. He and Mack built one of the first logging railroads in the Grays Harbor County, a three-mile line on the Hoquiam.

It soon became evident, once the North Western mill demanded logs, that hand-logging was no way to operate. With this realization, bull team operations sprang up throughout the region. Blackwell began in 1883, followed by a host including two logging crews brought in by the North Western Company, one with Jim Perkins as foreman; the other was Jim Cowan, foreman, a brother-in-law of the elder Jerry McGillicuddy. In later years Jim Perkins became sheriff of Chehalis County.

There were bulls bawling in the logging works of Leavitt & Clemons on Delezene Creek, Tom Madden, Frank Wedekind, A. W. Silby and Ed Chalmers' works in the Wynooche and Satsop valleys. Charles W. Arland ran a bull team show, as did the Schafers in the Satsop Valley, J. B. Haynes on the Wishkah, and short-lived John Brown on the Neushkah and Charley Creek.

Preceding the Schafers on the Satsop a firm composed of William "Bill" Ray and Ed Loveless logged where the Schafers later were to establish their Camp No. 1, and bought timber off the Schafer homestead. The pair, logging through 1889-90, also bought timber on the Dan Gleeson homestead, Gleeson and C. P. Look being employed by them.

For very good reasons Delezene Creek was an early and popular logging area. The stream wiggled into a vast body of prime timber with a large amount reachable from the creek, while the stream itself was just large enough to handle the sluicing of logs to the Chehalis.

These favorable circumstances Leavitt & Clemons found in 1886 when they formed a logging partnership. They spent three years in the valley with their bull teams and a splash dam.

Some time later Mike Woods was to log four miles of the Delezene Creek bottom, building three splash dams and two camps. He did his last logging out of his camp northeast of Dam No. 3 over a pole road with steam donkey engines. While in this operation, Mike Wood sold all his holdings to Morley Brothers and Willis Hopkins, who formed the Saginaw Timber Company.

For a time the Saginaw company continued to use the splash dams, but the stream bed was becoming unfit for sluicing logs, and the company started to build a logging railroad. Saginaw last splashed on Delezene Creek in the winter of 1909 when they had such a bad log jam the stream was abandoned. However, there were some who continued to use the dams, one being Milton "Slim" Duval, who was building a pole road into the hills to log into Dam No. 2 about the time Saginaw decided to switch to a railroad.

In 1910 when Amos Ing was foreman at Saginaw Camp No. 1,

he had two donkeys scraping cuts and making fills for the rail line, then on Sundays any man in camp who wanted to work overtime was given a long-handle shovel and taken down to Saginaw Station to shovel gravel on cars for rail line ballast.

By 1912 Saginaw had a new Camp 2 on a high ridge behind the old camp, with "Cranky Jack" Moore as foreman and seven donkeys lined up on one pole road. It was about this time too, Saginaw put a new Baldwin 2-8-2 locomotive on its rail line, and Willis Hopkins sold his interest in the company to his partner A. J. Morley.

In connection with his operations Morley built a six- to eight-machine shingle mill near Saginaw Station, operated it for a number of years and closed the plant when logging operations ceased. In turn Morley acquired two milling operations built by Ed Lester in the North River country above Vesta.

With the first few sawmills in operation there came an increasing demand for logs, and as a consequence, an influx of loggers. They came from most everywhere, but first perhaps from Maine with its timber tradition dating back to 1631, from Michigan's "mitten country" and Wisconsin's Green Bay region. They were the spawning grounds for much of Grays Harbor's timber muscle, men and money.

Yet it was A. M. Simpson of San Francisco, lumberman and financier, who gave Grays Harbor in 1882 its first fulfilling of the term "sawmilling." His North Western mill in Hoquiam was the initial volume producer, the first real demander of logs, and the first to set the woods bawling and brawling.

Simpson's mill, a circular saw plant, had a cutting capacity of 18 million board feet a year, which meant something more than jacks and "Nova Scotia steam" was needed to supply the mill with logs. This meant in turn logging operations of considerable scale would have to be started. Insofar as bullteam logging was the only kind then known to the industry, Simpson's agent, George Emerson, imported a team of six yoke of logging-trained oxen from Oregon along with a logging crew and an experienced bullwhacker. James A. Perkins and William S. Reid started the operation with James Cowan and James Murphy running the camp. It was soon evident a team with a hauling capacity of hardly 1.5 million feet a year could not meet the demands on the mill.

In 1883 J. A. Perkins was reported putting in logs for Emerson from the William Henry "One Arm" Carter place in South Montesano.

Also in 1883 W. S. Reid, in the Lower Town Montesano, was shut down because of a scarcity of hay for his animals. A year later, February 2, 1884, he was to register the first log brand in Chehalis county. In 1883, too, J. W. Milroy & Co. commenced logging near the Murray place at Sharon.

In 1891, Milroy & Perkins moved their logging outfit from Higgins' Slough to the Campbell place at Alder Grove to log spruce, the location to become known as the Rufus Arland place. A year before they had been logging with horse team behind the location of the present Grays Harbor courthouse in Montesano. At the same time Charley McCormick was rolling logs downhill from the same vicinity, fetching $3.50 to $4 a thousand, mill scale.

Onto this scene a year before, 1883, stalked Cy Blackwell, who was to win a reputation as an outstanding logger and extend his career and reputation well into the twentieth century despite another distinction as a studious astronomer with a penchant for observing the stars through the bottom of an upturned bottle. However, in that he was not alone, for similar observations were frequently made throughout the industry.

Cy Blackwell was born in Franklin County, Maine, and at 15 was driving a two-yoke team of bulls in his father's logging works. At 21 he shifted to Minnesota and Wisconsin where he worked in the woods for three years, then succumbed to the lure of California. In 1873 he was driving logs down the Truckee, and the following year went to Seattle, taking a swing down through the Grays Harbor country. He returned to the Truckee, but could not forget the Washington coast, where a logger could elbow through fir running better than 20 million feet to the quarter section. He returned to Grays Harbor in 1883.

Blackwell's first job was with the North Western Company as a bullwhacker in a small show above Melbourne. Within four months he started out on his own in company with Jim Gillies, working as Gillies & Blackwell under contract to the North Western Company. The camp was on the west branch of the Hoquiam above New London. It was a one-team show using a crew of 17 men.

This operation was significant in that it was here in 1884 Cy Blackwell built the first splash dam on Grays Harbor. There were many skeptics as Blackwell cribbed up his structure, but he had seen this type of dam work in Maine. He was confident. The dam did work, even with the giant logs pulled into the pond. In fact it worked so well that similar, but larger dams were built by the dozen on Grays Harbor streams, notably the Humptulips, Hoquiam and Wishkah.

However it remained for Leavitt & Clemons, who were punching bulls on Delezene Creek, first to substantiate Blackwell. They built a splash dam on the stream, which was but a trickle compared to some other Grays Harbor waterways, but it was capable of sluicing logs to the Chehalis. In fact the sluice dam concept worked so well Dan Gillis, Mike Woods and A. J. Morley built a series of dams on Delezene Creek and for years logged the flanking hills.

After two years on the Hoquiam Gillies & Blackwell moved to the Wishkah. Blackwell soon sold to Gillies and started a show of his own on the Wishkah above tidewater. Later he logged with Archie Murray, and again with Jim Gillies. In 1891 after completing the Grays Harbor City clearing, Blackwell again was on the Wishkah, building a splash dam 500 yards above the falls.

Fred Green had a fairly large stand of timber up Parker Creek, which emptied into Blackwell's pond. Green built a camp and a splash dam on Parker Creek, felled a lot of timber and hauled it into the stream. With his first splash the water and logs gouged so much shale from the stream bed and carried it into Blackwell's dam that Green had to quit. He folded up, pulled out and left his downed timber on the ground.

In 1910 Blackwell and Archie Murray split up, Blackwell and his son, Ira, logging what is now Pioneer Park in Aberdeen, then moving in 1915 to an area between Stafford Creek and Markham on the south shore of the harbor.

It was these and bigger shows to follow that loosed the rampants. They were skilled and expert, each prideful in his craft, from the skidroad greaser to the bullwhacker, including the cook and his helper, the skidroad builder, the rigging man, roustabout, skidroad man, barker, sniper, swamper, bucker, faller, foreman, hand skidder, second faller, greaser, and finally the key man, the bullwhacker.

The bull teams worked within reach of the streams, either fresh water or tidal, for they were capable only of short hauls and could not pull the grades into distant hills. But there was plenty of timber the bulls could handle especially if the skidroad builder knew his trade. The road was by far the most important construction in the woods, and Jim Rogers was considered the best.

A well-built skidroad was something to see, and was one of the determining factors in the success or failure of a logging show. For a bull team the skids, usually eight- to ten-foot hemlock (because it was hard) and 14 to 16 inches in diameter, were laid crosswise or athwart the road, just far enough apart so a log could ride two skids at a time. The spacing also was adjusted to accommodate the animals so they could step over a skid without breaking stride.

The skidroad builder laid out the road, almost always by eye, to give the teams the easiest grade and with no turn-binding sharp curves. It was essential to provide a grade that was not too steep, for the turn might run down the team, and one where the teams had the least or preferably no upgrade.

The first roads were swamped and chunked out to avoid the stumps, but later the stumps were blown with powder. If the skidroad builder had the necessary expertise little grading was needed save some work with a grubhoe and shovel. The skids were seated in trenches and sighted in for level by the head skidder. The skids themselves were handled by "skidding tongs" built like a pair of heavy-duty ice tongs with a long handle on each side like a peavey stock. With two men to a pair of tongs and several pair to a skid, the skid was carried and placed in its trench. At curves the skidders put in slanting slue or slew skids to shunt the turn back into the road. At low spots, or where a log had a tendency to bite into the ground or dig out a cross skid, slanting fore and aft skids were placed to lift the head end of the log.

The skids often were "saddled," that is, the center was given a little hollow to keep the logs in the middle of the road. A finished "saddle" was skillfully done as though with a plane. The axmen were expert, and the same could be said of the sniper who beveled, or "sniped" the rim of the head end of the logs to allow them to engage, or come up on a skid without a hangup. A skilled sniper could turn a snipe as smooth as his axe handle, and woe unto a man who picked up a sniper's axe, which was a razor-sharp, six-pound instrument with the handle trimmed to about 30 inches.

If a skid became badly worn from long, hard use it was "glutted," that is a length of vine maple was mortised into the top, or "ride."

All this was preliminary — including the falling and bucking, sniping and barking (bark was removed from the bottom or "ride" of the log) and the cook's biscuits — all this was but window dressing for the moment when the bullwhacker grasped his goad, rolled his chaw into the other cheek, spat mightily into the underbrush and shook the hills with a roar.

It was magnificent. The bawlings rumbled. The tremendous oaths thundered from canyon to canyon. All the woods creatures stopped tiptoe. The cosmos was jilpoked. If the pull was troublesome the bullwhacker tore the hat from his head, hurled it to the ground, and jumped upon it in a tantrum of spikes, felt, and leather. He summoned the Almighty himself to come down and give a hand. He called upon all the powers of the universe including "Fattie Sadie" on River street. It was masterful. It was beautiful. It was like moving an empire with a straight-away pull.

There he was, the bullwhacker come into his own, even more than the skidroad builder the indispensable man. The timber hushed while he lifted his goad and his voice. Upon his skill, his rages and withering vocabulary rested the fate of the logging show. And the woods rang to one of the great epics of the West, a drama monumental in sheer brute force — a turn of big timber to tidewater.

And the skidroad greaser scooted down the road with his five-gallon can and his swab.

The bullwhacker of course, had already boasted his team could pull anything loose and with two ends, and, given good footing, could pull Hell out by the roots, plumb out. "Have 'nother drink!"

So there he stood at the flank of the near animal in the second yoke. Say it was August and "hotter'n blue hell" in the idiom. Sweat oozed under the bullwhacker's galluses. Dust rose as a restless animal stomped, but most of the six yoke stood, patiently chewing cuds and swishing tails — the big-bellied flies were pesky.

The bullwhacker looked back searchingly over his turn; five logs, all big ones, the five-foot butt log in front. Behind were the other four, all sniped and the rides barked. They were short-coupled with dogs and a running length of chain, barely a foot apart.

The whacker shook his head. The skids were biting into the sapwood; it would be a hard turn to start.

Into the head log had been driven two heavy dogs on a running chain with a ring in the middle. Some outfits used a bridle, a loop of line set into notches on either side of the head log and laid in a channel over the top from notch to notch.

The whacker stooped and hooked his team's butt chain into the ring. Then, almost gently: "Hi-you, Babe, you ready?" Babe was the near ox on the wheel, teamed with Paddy, a sleek, black beast bulging with muscle. Babe nonchalantly cocked an eye at the driver and continued leisurely to chew his cud. He knew from experience the furious moment had not yet arrived. It would come when the whacker had worked himself into a proper rage, cursing the heat, the flies, the corn on his off foot, and just to make them alert, the lead yoke of Jerry and Bright, the smart pair that quickened the team, set the pace and piloted the turn.

Then without a signal, Babe swallowed his cud and shuffled his feet restlessly. The action sense was contagious. All down the line of six yoke, tails stopped swishing, jaws were stilled, heads bowed.

The whacker bit off a new and satisfying chaw of plug tobacco (perhaps Star or Horseshoe), settled it comfortably in his cheek, spat into the dust, raised his goad. The moment had arrived.

"Hi-yo-o-o, Jerry! Bright! Get up! He whacked a laggard or

two. The bulls lunged, stomped, throwing their heavily-muscled shoulders into the bows indiscriminately. The whacker cursed.

"Damn your black hides! Up! Jerry!"

The head log jumped a barely perceptible inch; the butt chain sang, but the turn remained firm.

With an oath of disgust, the whacker rested on his goad, relaxed. The bulls ceased their lunging and relaxed also. They cast a wary eye at the bellowing monster at their flanks, knowing the halt was only momentary. The whacker waited until his team was settled.

Again he straightened, his goad poised. Then, swinging it down with a sudden motion, he roared — and the hills echoed.

"Jerry! Bright! Ge-e-e-t up! Yo-o-o, Jerry! By gad I'm a comin'!"

He whacked a dawdling rump. Louder he roared. Louder he cursed. The bulls lunged and staggered as before, only this time the action was more concerted. The chains strummed under tension. Dust rolled up in choking clouds as the bulls pawed frantically. Still the turn failed to budge.

The animals, breathing heavily, halted as suddenly as they had started; it was an old ritual. They knew as well as the whacker that a turn as heavy as this was never started on the first two pulls. The third was the charm.

Nevertheless the whacker spit in wrath, he cursed, he implored the Heavens. He stomped up and down beside his team in vexation. Then he stopped and waited. The bulls tightened, flanks quivering. The butt chain was still taut.

It was a rite. The whacker swiped his face with a wool-sleeved arm, again took his stand, goad upraised. He swung it down as before. A fearsome bellow exploded from his lips. The canyon rocked.

"Hi-e-e, Jerry! Bri-i-te! Ge-e-et up! You, Jerrie-e-e!" It mounted to a mighty thunder. "Jerrie-e-e, you black son of a bitch! Yeo-w-w, Jerry!"

As one animal the bulls heaved mightily into the yokes. Muscles bulged like iron folds under their sweating hides. The effort was gigantic. Chains quivered with stress. Yokes creaked in protest. The whacker yelled like a maniac, waving, flailing his arms, whacking wildly.

There was a rasping, a piping squeal of wood on wood. The butt log swayed, swung. The motion carried down the turn. The last log moved. The turn was started. The epic had begun.

"Pull you bastards, pull! Pull you beauties, pull!"

As early-day logging assumed epochal proportions, it could have been created by several men, not many; men like Cy Blackwell, Jim Perkins, Jack McClay, Lycia Skeen, Arthur Austin, Dan Monroe, George Keith, Hugh Byles, Mel Jerome or Jack Cooper, all bullwhackers of skill, voice and vocabulary.

Bullwhackers were paid $80 to $150 a month, some as much as $180, according to their skill. Other loggers were paid around $65, with board and bunk, of course. The difference in wages was some indication of the importance of the bullwhacker in the woods.

However, the heyday of the bull team was short-lived. For all the aura of might, color and power that surrounded them, bulls actually were ill-suited for work in the big timber. They were often contrary and hard to manage, they lacked sufficient stamina for the work required and their strength was more legendary than real, despite a bullwhacker's boasting. Two or three span of well-cared horses could out-pull 10 to 12 yoke of oxen and do it with discipline and without goring the driver. And horses were faster than the slogging bull teams, even the well-fed and cared-for ones. Many bull teams were abused badly by goad-wielders, who actually worked the animals to death. It was a common saying in the woods that a man could hang his hat on the hip bones of a poor team.

Although the reign of the bullwhacker was clouded by incoming horses, his actual demise was laid to a mechanical contraption called a Dolbeer donkey engine, which not only ended the bull teams, and horses, but revolutionized logging and the ways of loggers.

It, too, lasted only a few years, but while it was driving the bull out of the woods, it created an episode of colorful miscues and achievements.

The Dolbeer, developed by Dolbeer & Carson for the redwoods of California, was simplicity itself — an upright capstan (not unlike a ship's capstan) geared to a single-cylinder (sometimes two) upright steam engine fed by a small wood-fired upright boiler. The unit was set on an iron frame and, for use in the woods, bolted to a set of skids.

From the very first the Dolbeer created problems. Loggers tried the same rigging they had used with bull teams. But for all its small size, the Dolbeer was powerful. It could match several bull teams, and as a consequence walked through dogs, hooks, line, chain and blocks. Another problem was the use at first of five and six-inch manila line. When the line was wet it would slip and harden and double in size, and under strain would shed a halo of water. It became so stiff and hard the spooltender had difficulty making turns around the spool or capstan, or to get the turns to grip the spool. Still another problem was the tendency of manila line to stretch like a rubber band. When the log finally moved it would jump ahead 10 to 20 feet, making the turn hard to control.

The Dolbeer was operated by an engineer who manned the throttle on the off side, and a spool-tender, on the near side usually, who took the turns of line off the capstan as the engine reeled it in. He had to keep just the right tension on the five or six turns on the capstan, and if the log hung up, quickly release the tension, otherwise the engine would stop on center, to the engineer's disgust and calling heavily upon the spool-tender's ample vocabulary. The engineer then put his foot upon a spoke in the flywheel and gave it a kick off center, starting the logging show again.

Some of the remembered spooltenders in the Grays Harbor woods were Huey McKinley, Dave Murphy, Tom Keeley, Buster Crawford and Rube Crowley.

Manila line proved a hazard and almost a failure in the big stuff, and it wasn't until steel wire was introduced that logging could gain momentum. The first flexible steel wire, ¾-inch cable, was brought to the Grays Harbor woods in 1885 by George Emerson for the North Western Company's works. At first steel cable caused as many, perhaps more, problems than manila line. Loggers started to use the same blocks as they had used with six-inch manila, but the steel soon cut into the soft iron sheaves, scored the capstans, and walked through tongs, dogs, hooks and other gear previously sufficient for manila line.

Damage to the capstans, or spools, on the donkeys was particularly disruptive, for a cast iron capstan would last only a few days and had to be replaced. It weighed hundreds of pounds, and the work and cost of transporting it from the foundry to the logging show was something with which to reckon. The cost often was more than the cost of the spool itself. And the line kinked badly, while the bights invariably caught the spooltender across the shins or the nose — hence his pungent vocabulary, second only to that of a bullwhacker.

The spooltender usually handled about 1,000 feet of ⅞-inch line (steel) with six turns around the spool. He had to coil it down methodically so that the line horse could pull the line to the woods without the coils fouling. Most line horses were the pets, friends and pride of their drivers. They were knowledgeable in the woods like the loggers. They knew which way to pull a line, when it was pulled far enough, and when to get out of the way when the Dolbeer began to puff steam.

Cy Blackwell, through the North Western Lumber Company, brought the first Dolbeer into the Grays Harbor country. It came out of California and was first used in clearing the site for the boom town Grays Harbor City. The job, according to A. S. Coats, then a Dolbeer crew member who was to become one of the foremost loggers on Grays Harbor, was started July 2, 1889. Others in the crew were his brother A. F. Coats, Lee Braden, George Monroe, Simon Monroe, William LaVoice, John Shaw, William Cameron, Cy Blackwell and "Penny," the blacksmith.

The second Dolbeer reputedly was brought here by the Wishkah Boom Company for its operation near its dam on the main Wishkah River. Years later it was sold to Arthur Biggs, 18 miles up the Wishkah above Aberdeen.

It wasn't long before the Dolbeer donkey went the way of the bull team. It was slow and cantankerous, too unhandy and with not enough muscle for the big stuff. The innovating logger soon turned the capstan or spool to the horizontal, and the drum donkey came into its own. The drum lent itself to innumerable arrangements to meet the needs of fast-developing logging methods.

It was Cy Blackwell who one day said: "Why do we have to have a line horse . . . why not run a small line through a tail block and pull the mainline into the woods?" There and then was born the "haulback," one of the great innovations of the logging industry. At first the haulback was reeled in on a "gypsy," a spool on the end of the main shaft from which a spooltender took off and coiled down the turns. Then the haulback line was given a drum of its own and loggers were in business.

Next came the sometimes complicated assembly of drums, which took care of several special operations, one of which was the drum for the guinea line (often called the straw line), a very light line which pulled the haulback into the woods as the crew rigged the side or area of operations. It did away with the backbreaking job of pulling haulback, although the guinea line itself had to be dragged and run through blocks on the perimeter of the setting. Only a three-eighths-inch line, the guinea could easily be carried in coils on men's shoulders, strung around the setting and back to the donkey engine to pick up the haulback line.

Another line similarly used was the "pass line," a seven-sixteenths inch line drawn to the top of a spar tree by a half-inch manila line carried aloft by the highclimber. The pass line in turn carried up all the rigging for the spar tree, save the bullblock which often weighed a ton or more.

The drum donkey quickly developed into a machine of singular purposes, especially when loggers began using the fore-and-aft skidroad, or pole road, some of which sinuated into the hills for miles. The yarder with its narrower and powerfully-geared drums was the farthest-out machine. It pulled logs from where they were felled and bucked to a landing, from where a smaller machine, often called a "half-breed" or swing donkey, took over and snaked the logs to the head of skidroad, or in later years to the railway spur or other loading operation. Then in the skidroad days the roader took over to pull a turn of several logs to the river, the butt log in back hooked to the mainline, the smaller logs in front. A turn often would contain 15,000 feet or more.

The roader, like some of the big yarders, grew into a wood-consuming, spark-showering monster (all carried spark arresters). It was a massive machine with wide drums and was often called a "wide face." One drum carried the mainline, the other the haulback. It was not uncommon for a road engine to carry a mile or more of mainline, and of course twice that of haulback.

On the long skidroad hauls a turn often was passed from one roader to another, the last one being on the bank of a river, shunting the logs into the water. At one time the Humptulips Logging Company had five road engines on one skidroad, hauling four to five miles. The operation was so expensive, however, the company went broke.

On many skidroads a "pig" or hollowed-out section of log like a stubby dugout canoe was tailed onto a turn with which to return the tongs, dogs or whatever gear went in with the turn, along with the loggers' lunch, which would be headed for the "mulligan shack," an eating shelter for use when operations were a long way from camp. Loggers in their peculiar sex-laced phraseology (never used in polite company) had a befitting name for the man who rode the pig.

Among several other special drum arrangements was the sometimes-called rigging donkey, used for "rigging up" a spar tree for highlead logging and the skyline apparatus for a skyline show. It had two drums out in front of its basic two to handle the lines necessary for this heavy yet delicate task.

In the skidroad days the big yarder was the "signal" donkey; that is, it controlled the pace of the logging operation. If it yarded fast, the operation hummed; if it was slow, the half-breed and roader would stand waiting. The yarder, when it halted operations, would "whistle 'em off," telling the road engine to bank its fires because yarding had halted temporarily to change setting or make repairs. It also whistled one long, one short, for the noon meal, and quitting time at 6 o'clock. Work in the woods, and sawmills as well, began at 7 o'clock in the morning. Loggers in winter often went from camp and back by lantern light. There was one operation in the "Promised Land" (Humptulips country, Cameron & Hoover camp) loggers facetiously called "Land of the Midnight Sun," because the men went to work in the dark and quit in the dark.

In later years, when skidroads gave way to railroads and truck roads, the loading donkey, variously rigged, became a specialty machine. It could be multiple drummed, and in most cases carried only a small amount of line, for its purpose was, as its name denotes, as a loading machine onto rail cars or motor trucks.

Where the railroads ended at a rollway on tidewater, there

often was a small donkey to parbuckle logs into the stream. In many cases this task was assumed by the "jilpoke," a swinging boom mounted on a mast so the end could be made to engage the side of a carload of logs, and as the locomotive advanced the boom swung with the load and pushed the logs overboard.

Many rollways were tilted to allow logs to roll off cars, once the retaining stakes on the water side were cut far enough through to break under pressure of the load. Cutting stakes often was a dangerous job for the rollway man, who had to be careful not to cut too deep and allow the logs to roll prematurely.

Some rollways were double-tracked with the train shunting its string of cars along the browskid side, while on a parallel track a machine of varying descriptions would roll along pushing loads into the water.

In all cases donkey engines were rated by the diameter of the cylinder and the stroke of the piston. Each size had a rated horsepower, and the logger knew, or should have known (some didn't), which size machine was needed. Popular machines in the Grays Harbor woods were the "Seattles," built by the Washington Iron Works; the "Tacomas," built by the Puget Sound Iron & Steel Company; and the "Willamettes," built by the Willamette Iron & Steel Company, Portland, Oregon. A few Skagit and some Clyde donkey engines found their way to the Harbor. They were good machines, but most loggers preferred the Seattles, Tacomas and Willamettes as proven mechanisms. Once or twice a Vulcan was brought in from California (it was California-made) but failed to operate efficiently.

Steel wire was probably the most important single item in the woods. Without good line there was no logging, for "haywire rigging and a hemlock show" could break a logger in a hurry.

Line of course was bought for the job, say a ⅝-inch line, or possibly three-eighths-inch line (this for yarders of 170 to 200 horsepower), while the big 13 x 14-teens needed 1⅜-inch mainline and seven-eighths-inch haulback. Loading lines were mostly seven-eighths-inch stuff. The duplexes used the same size.

Much of the cable used in the Grays Harbor woods was made in Seattle. Polsons obtained about one-third their supply from Seattle plants. Yet local suppliers had a big chunk of the business. Yellow Strand Wire Rope was popular in the woods and supplied by the Isaacson Company, while Edwards wire rope was good but more expensive. There were others, of course, including some second-hand dealers who often sold good rope and as often sold frayed and inferior stuff.

And then came the blocks, another vital item. The Young Iron Works, Seattle, the Lamb Company, Hoquiam, and the Rope Master Company, Portland, built some of the most common types found in the woods, while the Skookum block built in Portland was also popular. In the days of highlead logging the bullblock, hung high on the spar tree for the main rigging, was from 30 to 40 inches sheave diameter. The 36-inch sheave, weighing 2,000 pounds, was the most common. Just below the bullblock was hung the haulback block, usually a 16-inch to 18-inch block. Around the perimeter of the setting were the haulback blocks of 10-inch sheave diameter. The tailblock was usually the same, though in some settings it was an eight-inch block. Pass blocks, usually five or six inches in diameter, were used to hoist rigging to a spar tree. There was another type of block, and what was called a "moving strap," a length of heavy line much heavier than similar equipment in a logging show, for moving a donkey engine from one location to another, the donkey engine pulling itself.

Coincident with the skidroad was the splash (or sluice) dam, a method of releasing a large head of water into a stream bed to wash out collections of logs. It was first used by bullteam loggers, and later was highly instrumental in making the fore-and-aft skidroad a success. Logs pulled down from the hills were dumped into the rivers and in many cases splash-dam ponds. When water in the splash dams was released, the logs were carried in a torrent to tidewater — that is, those that did not hang up on gravel bars — and then it was the job of a crew and a small donkey engine, or sometimes other means, to "sack" the river, moving the stranded logs into the water.

Chapter
5

POLSONS, SCHAFERS AND THE BIG SIX

The Polson name had surfaced before in Washington Territory, first when Alex Polson rode horseback into Goldendale, Klickitat County, saddle-sore after a 1,500-mile ride from Tucson, Arizona. It may have seemed a round-about way from his birthplace in Nova Scotia, but Alex Polson had asthma and went to the Southwest seeking a helpful climate. Earlier, as a 23-year-old fortune hunter, he had gone in 1876 to Deadwood in the Dakotas, but stayed only three months. He then made his way to Carson City, Nevada, where he engaged in mining and lumbering for three years, and in 1879 made a trip to Tucson.

In Goldendale at the end of his long ride Alex Polson took a job getting out logs for construction of the Northern Pacific Railway from the Columbia River to Montana.

In the winter of 1880 Alex Polson went to Olympia where he worked for one and a half years in the woods for Amos Brown. A horseback exploring trip to Grays Harbor finally stopped him in Montesano, which he liked so much he lived there long enough to become a charter member of the Montesano Masonic Lodge. He then shifted to Shoalwater Bay on Willapa Harbor where he built the first splash dam in Pacific County.

In 1882 he was in Hoquiam to become a permanent resident and to marry Miss Ella Arnold February 18, 1891, a native of Iowa and a graduate of Iowa College at Des Moines. The couple moved into a "spacious home" built as the second residence in Hoquiam in 1884.[16]

By April 1886 Polson was working as county assessor, and in August of that year he reported property in Chehalis County had an assessed value of $1,033,011. From 1884 until 1886 Alex Polson was the first assessor for Hoquiam.

Alex Polson was dabbling in real estate and logging in 1887, the year J. B. Haynes announced on February 25 he was preparing to log on Elliott Slough for the North Western Company in Hoquiam. The announcement seemed so casual as to be of little importance, but it shook the industry, became a landmark in the Grays Harbor woods and was to become a ruling factor in the liberal labor policy of the Polson logging empire. Haynes announced not only was he to log on Elliott Slough but he would do it with the 10-hour day, the first operator in the region to switch from the 12-hour work day.

Haynes was quoted as saying in this regard: "Ten hours of faithful labor is long enough for either man or beast, and will produce all the logs and lumber that can be sold at a paying price; besides, it will be a safeguard against over-production, which is always followed by low prices." Logs at this time were selling for $4.50 per thousand.

As Alex Polson dabbled in 1887, another outsized Nova Scotian, his 24-year-old brother Robert Polson, arrived on Grays Harbor, presumably upon Alex Polson's advice. He came directly from Nova Scotia and not by a way as circuitous as that taken by Alexander. Robert Polson had learned the blacksmithing trade in his birthplace, and logging on Grays Harbor seemed a good field in which to ply it. But logging proved to be more rewarding than blacksmithing, so Robert Polson took to the Grays Harbor woods for one year, followed by a year of logging in British Columbia. He returned to Hoquiam in 1888 to operate a logging show with his brother for a year. Again, in 1889, Robert started a logging operation on his own. This lasted until 1891 when he and Alex Polson combined their operations as the Polson Brothers Logging Company, a name changed to Polson Logging Company in 1903. Robert Polson was manager of operations under both names.

The first logging as Polson Brothers was done with jacks and bull teams on the flanks of what was to become known as Think-Of-Me hill in Aberdeen, then on the Newskah (then spelled Neushkah), and finally working northward from the head of tidewater on the west fork of the Hoquiam. Here they discarded their bullteam operation and took to the Dolbeer donkey engine and, in turn, the many spool donkey engines that followed.

By 1894 the Polsons were planning a railroad from a landing on the West Hoquiam into timber a little distant for logging into tidewater. Their first move was purchase of a locomotive, the tiny "Minnetonka," to become affectionately known in years of service as "Old Fartin' Betsy," and to end her career in a locomotive "hall of fame."

Betsy, as the Minnetonka, had already become famous long before she was acquired by Polson Brothers. She had been the second locomotive put into service by the Northern Pacific Railroad and the first to chug her way across the Cascades. In 1870 she was sold by the Northern Pacific to Ainsworth & Simpson for use in their Spokane lumber yard. In 1894 she became the property of the Polson Brothers Logging Company, along with six sets of Russell trucks for $800. Almost three-quarters of a century later, still with her original boiler, "Old Fartin' Betsy" was still puffing around Polsons' camps as a switch engine. Eventually she was shunted aside and later returned to the Northern Pacific Railroad in exchange for a big mainline locomotive. She now rests in the Northern Pacific museum.

The year following purchase of the Minnetonka, Alex Polson went to Centralia to arrange for shipment of a quantity of iron rails formerly used in the Centralia trolley system. Once the rails were landed on the bank of the West Hoquiam, Polson Brothers were on their way to becoming the biggest logging firm in the Northwest.

From a landing on what was commonly known as the "Middle Fork" of the Hoquiam, before it branches into the "West Fork," Polsons laid steel in a generally northerly course to what would be the long-used Railroad Camp, then swung generally north-westerly to circuit the Humptulips City area and continued northerly, crossing and re-crossing the Olympic highway toward

Quinault. The rail line bypassed the Quinault or Neilton Burn and eventually reached the Quinault several miles below Lake Quinault. The lower Quinault River was bridged in 1930, with rail line continuing to Crane Creek. The Polson Company had acquired the "Quinault Unit" of timber on the Quinault Indian Reservation in 1924 and continued to log it once the river was spanned.

Several projections were made beyond Quinault for the Polson-owned Ozette Railway Company, but the plans were never implemented. Polsons sold their entire empire lock, stock and rail spike in 1948 to Rayonier, Inc., except for 4,000 acres of "family timber" located mostly in the westerly regions of Grays Harbor County.

Meanwhile Alexander Polson had branched out into another field — sawmilling. He purchased a half interest in the A. J. West sawmill in Aberdeen, which he sold later to S. E. Slade.

And in 1901, November 8 exactly, he tried his hand at fisticuffs. It was on that day that two brawny Scots, Alexander Polson and Edward Campbell, the town's first Postmaster, "squared off" on the streets of Hoquiam. The dispute was over a difference of opinion on the sale of school lands, which was to be resolved in the heat of argument by some hefty punches. However, it was reported in the prints of the day that "bystanders interfered before any blood was shed."

And then on April 18, 1902, Polson Brothers received a large locomotive and 30 log cars. They already had three locomotives, 24 donkey engines and were operating four camps with 250 men. They had two camps on the lower Hoquiam above their log boom and rollway, and were virtually logged out in this area when the "great fire" of September 12, 1902, the damnable "dark day" of Western Washington, killed nearly all of the Merrill & Ring timber north of the Polson works on the West Hoquiam. The fire, one of many in the Northwest that day, started in the Decker settlement not far from Sol Simpson's old Camp No. 5, in the Satsop watershed. A homesteader clearing land let a slash fire get away. The fire, taking off in the dry fir and "crowning" with a high wind, swept swiftly across the Wynooche Valley, all forks of the Wishkah and Hoquiam, and played out in the hemlock of the Shaw & Nelson works on Big Creek in the Humptulips country, and on Chenois and Grass Creek watersheds not far from North Bay, Grays Harbor.

The crown fire killed some of the best fir stands in the county, including half a township owned by Merrill & Ring. Polsons at the time were working four sides on the Hoquiam and they lost two camps and one man, a log bucker, in the fire.

The ashes had barely cooled before Merrill & Ring approached the Polsons to organize a new company and log the killed timber before it decayed. The Polson Logging Company, with the Polsons retaining control, immediately moved into the dead timber with six sides to get it out before the worms got it.

The Polsons spent something like five years logging Merrill & Ring fire-damaged timber, for by 1907 the rail line had reached what was to be called the Railroad Camp on the far side of the damaged timber area.

After Merrill & Ring timber had been logged, the Polson Logging Company took off into timber the firm had purchased, back in June, 1903, some 2,000 acres of valuable timber from Congressman J. W. Fordney. The company also had purchased 15 quarter sections from D. A. Blodgett of Saginaw, Michigan, and about as much from R. F. Lytle. It was rumored at the time the Polson Company was negotiating with the Weyerhaeuser Company for 100 million feet in the same vicinity, all located in what was called the "worm belt," fire-killed timber already attacked by worms.

Both Alex and Robert Polson became interested in sawmilling and shingle-cutting. In 1903 Robert Polson with Alexander McLean Matheson organized the Polson Shingle Company, the mill site donated by the Grays Harbor Land Company. The plant began operations in June, 1904, with a capacity of 300 thousand shingles a day.

Matheson, who also came from Nova Scotia, became president and manager of the company, with Robert Polson vice-president. The mill operated until 1913, when the company decided to build a sawmill as a new company with Matheson as president. Following completion of the mill in 1914, the operation was reorganized with Robert Polson as president, Alexander

Polson vice-president, and A. M. Matheson manager. The operation became the Eureka Lumber & Shingle Company. Some time later Robert Polson was named president of the Hoquiam Timber Company.

In 1934 the Polson Logging Company purchased the North Western lumber mill, rebuilt it and operated it as the Polson Mill Company, with a daily cutting capacity of 225 thousand board feet. The firm also acquired an interest in the Bay City Lumber Company with Alex Polson vice-president. Alex Polson, who was also vice-president of the Eureka mill and the Hoquiam Timber Company, became active in public life. He served on the city council of Hoquiam and one term in the Washington state senate.

At the peak of their operations the Polson Company owned and operated two tidewater sawmills, a shingle mill, twelve logging and construction camps, 100 miles of logging railroad, a huge quantity of logging equipment, and boasted an annual output of 300 million feet of logs.

Even before Alex Polson and Ed Campbell tried to out-bluff each other on the streets of Hoquiam, Charles H. "Charlie" Clemons had put in four years on logging camp beans and mashed potatoes near Olympia. He felled timber for Amos Brown, Sam Willey and Ben Turner as an apprenticeship to a lifetime in the woods, then came in 1881 to the Chehalis Valley and its just-beginning logging industry. It took Charlie Clemons five years to accumulate enough money and a hankering to go into the logging business on his own. This he did in company with Charles Leavitt, a State-of-Mainer who had come to the Northwest in 1877, the same year Charlie Clemons had brought the Clemons name to the territory by a rather devious way, not all of his own making. Charlie Clemons had nothing to do, for instance, with Isaac Clemons deserting a British man-of-war in Massachusetts colony in 1700, or the fact that the Clemons name did not surface again until June, 1833, when George E. Clemons was born in Hiram, Maine.

Actually the name, or at least the Grays Harbor branch, began its journey to the colonies from the ancestral home on the Channel island of Guernsey, where 16-year-old Isaac Clemons and his brother were shanghaied (pressed is the more polite term) by a British navy press gang and forced to serve on a voyage to America.

Once their ship had anchored, the two young Clemons lost no time going over the side and into the hinterland. More than a century later the woods of Maine had claimed the family as lumbermen. George Clemons, however, was to spend most of his life in Vermont and New Hampshire in the lumber business and to leave that region but twice, first to Washington Territory with his son Charlie Clemons in 1877 to stay only six months, again to Montesano in 1900, to die in 1901 and be buried in the Wynooche cemetery.[17]

The Delezene Creek logging operation apparently did not take all of Charlie Clemons' time, for in that three-year period he filed on a homestead three miles west of Montesano on Higgins Slough, and married Margaret A. Murray, daughter of Patrick and Anna Keenan Murray, homesteaders at Saginaw Station near Elma. The marriage was April 22, 1888.

Before Leavitt & Clemons dissolved their partnership, they had one last involvement with their log buyer, Captain J. M. Weatherwax, and his mill in Aberdeen. Leavitt & Clemons had a splash dam full of logs and not enough water to sluice them to the Chehalis. If they couldn't deliver the logs they could not get their pay, and they could not pay the crew or other camp expenses. So they went to Captain Weatherwax for a loan to tide them over to the first rain.

Weatherwax seemed exuberant, for no reason the two loggers could determine, but nevertheless when they made their proposition Weatherwax exclaimed: "Glad you came in at this time ... I'm just leaving for the East to get financing." He gave Clemons and Leavitt a check with no delay or argument. The loggers were a little taken aback by the alacrity of the check-writer. Later they looked at the check. It was dated 60 days ahead.

They finally cashed the check, but not until after the rains came and the logs had gone to tidewater.

Events were not to continue amusing for Charlie Clemons. The winter of 1887-1888 was the most severe the Chehalis Valley had experienced in years. In December flooding of the valley broke many booms, washing away 2 million feet of logs, "mostly the property of Mack, Ray, and Leavitt & Clemons." It was also noted that Charlie Clemons "had recently suffered an eye injury when struck by a piece of steel from a wedge he was driving. He had the eye removed in Portland." And in the first week of January the Chehalis froze over making it possible to cross on the ice, but not to move logs.

After Clemons and Leavitt quit as partners and a year after his marriage Clemons, in 1889, moved to a new house he had built on Higgins Slough homestead (now the eastern environs of Central Park). There Clemons, operating as the C. H. Clemons Company, began bull-team logging into Higgins slough. Ten years later, just after the turn of the century when steam was ousting the bull teams, Clemons bought steam machines himself, using them on Higgins Slough until 1903 when he moved to a new logging show at Melbourne.

At Melbourne, which was to be his logging headquarters for 16 years, Clemons first logged by skidroad (pole road) into the tidal Chehalis. When his cutting reached beyond skidroad capabilities, he began building a railroad which eventually was to extend 14 miles through the hills until Clemons and Weyerhaeuser, who owned most of the timber south of the Chehalis, formed the Clemons Logging Company, with Clemons retaining one-third interest in the new corporation.

Clemons was persuaded into partnership with Weyerhaeuser primarily because his operation was getting too big for one man to handle and finance. And, possibly, because of a near-fatal speeder accident on his rail line in October, 1918, and the death of his son, George, on a runaway logging train in April, 1919. And Weyerhaeuser at that time had timber to spare for such joint ventures.

Clemons remained as manager of the consolidation until 1922 when he sold his one-third interest to Weyerhaeuser. Logging was completed on this "show" in 1946.

When Clemons joined with the Weyerhaeuser company, he had no idea the move would perpetuate the Clemons name in the timber industry. But it did in the dedication of the now-famed Clemons Tree Farm.

The Clemons Logging Company was incorporated by Clemons, Minot Davis and Hugh Stewart, the latter two well-known representatives for Weyerhaeuser. Minot Davis was named president of the new firm.[18]

The corporation launched Weyerhaeuser into active logging operations in Grays Harbor, first using Clemons' rail line, then extensions into other sections of Weyerhaeuser timber.

Before the logging operation ended, Weyerhaeuser dissolved the Clemons Logging Company, and in 1941 looked back upon 130 thousand acres of cutover lands, some of it already with a fuzz of second growth, and some actually of cutting size.

Across the Chehalis in Montesano, Chapin Collins, a native of Seattle and graduate of the University of Washington, had purchased the Montesano Vidette in 1927, after having put in a newspapering stint with several Washington dailies. He was in his office one eventful day about the time Weyerhaeuser was pulling its logging equipment out of the Clemons works. Collins had called in several interested men to discuss a possible future for Grays Harbor's cutover timberlands. In the course of the discussion Chapin Collins, inspired by a suggestion made years earlier by J. E. Calder, one of the founders of the Vidette, proposed the cutover lands be consolidated into "tree farms," areas set aside and dedicated to the growing of new trees. He suggested that whoever dedicated lands to "tree farms" would pledge certain procedures of good forestry, fire protection, land management and culture.

Thus the "tree farm" idea was sown, but it took Weyerhaeuser, the county commissioners and Roderic Olzendam, a New Englander who had never seen a tree larger than a telephone pole, to put the idea in motion.

Weyerhaeuser had 130 thousand acres of its own between the Chehalis and North River. The State of Washington had 15 thousand acres, Grays Harbor County 16 thousand acres, with the rest in scattered ownerships. In order to make a compact "farm" or tree-growing region, Weyerhaeuser approached Grays Harbor County for its 16 thousand acres through the appearance of W. H. Price and Paul Meyer before the commissioners April 24, 1941. The commission opened a sale of logged-off lands wanted by Weyerhaeuser. On July 21, 1941, the county posted for sale certain descriptions to be auctioned September 13, 1941. When the day arrived, Weyerhaeuser purchased 15 thousand acres at approximately 75 cents an acre to increase its "tree farm" acreage to 145 thousand acres. The land purchased was to be assessed under state reforestation laws at $1 per acre, with an additional yield tax of 12½ percent whenever any of the land was cropped.

Roderic Olzendam was brought in to promote the "tree farm" concept. He had already successfully promoted the "Keep Washington Green" campaign to the wide-eyed anguish of the backers when he presented an expense account for the "kickoff" celebration in Seattle's Olympic Hotel.

Nevertheless Olzendam was retained to give the "tree farm" a send-off, especially since the Clemons Tree Farm was the first, the largest, the most promising of all tree farms, an idea in years to spread across the continent and pledge millions of acres to the growing of timber.

Olzendam, to publicize the tree farm plan, proposed and organized with his usual flair and elegance a whopping ceremony in Grays Harbor June 12, 1941, inviting writers and cameramen from across the nation. Minot Davis, fearing the founding program was getting out of hand, is said to have attempted to "soften" the celebration. But it was too late; Olzendam had the plan off and running, and it proved to be a whale of a dedication. Then Minot Davis got the bill. He leaped so high his skull nearly stuck in the ceiling.

But the tree farm conception was a goer; it caught on throughout the industry, from the northern woods to southern pine, from the hardwoods to the softwoods of the Pacific Coast. And now, thanks to that determined conversation in Chape Collins' Vidette office, no state is without its tree farms, and countless acres are growing trees, where before they would have been left to haphazard seeding.

Years after he had made his original suggestion for re-growing trees and perpetuating the forests, J. E. Calder made another proposal, that upon his death his ashes be scattered over the Clemons Tree Farm. This was done in silent commemoration of a man who couldn't tell a spruce from a spiraea, but who somehow fitted well into Grays Harbor's timber story.

While Alex Polson was subcontracting in 1884 the right-of-way clearing for the Montesano trestle to Lower Montesano, and toying with the idea of becoming a logger, J. E. "Joe" Calder was thinking of the same thing. But fate made an unlikely choice in Joe Calder, a selection to be proved in financial disaster. The logger-to-be didn't know a pine tree from a pica stick, his knowledge of timber and the logging thereof being limited to publishing timber claim notices in the Montesano Vidette, then called the Chehalis Valley Vidette.

The Vidette was largely the creature of Calder who, as a young printer's apprentice in Iowa and more familiar with hominy than hemlocks, got taken with a bad case of "Western fever" in 1882. At 22 years of age he landed in Seattle and gravitated to the print shops. There he met a printer and itinerant newspaperman named J. W. Walsh, who hankered to start a newspaper of his own. However, there was the matter of money, a location, and immediate income.

Casting about for an opportunity, Calder and Walsh fell for the stories of timber wealth and growth in the Chehalis Valley, and settled upon Montesano where, it was said, there was plenty of government printing concerning land and timber claims. They landed in Montesano the latter part of January, 1883, and by February 1 were setting up an old U.S. Army press and a few fonts of type upstairs in the Marcy store building. Two days later they put out their first edition.

However, J. E. Calder found weekly newspaper publishing a slow way to make money, especially when he watched so many other men supposedly making a stake in the logging business.

The Vidette, 11 months after its first edition, printed a brief notice: "J. E. Calder, formerly with the Vidette, has acquired control of the Milroy & Co. logging camp near Elma and is now operating the camp."[19]

It was noted in print that "J. E. Calder ran a large raft of logs down the Chehalis March 2, 1884," this the first raft to be run down the Chehalis from above Elma. This was followed by another news bit in April 1884, that "Calder has moved his logging camp to the Hoquiam River."

It was here on the Hoquiam Calder met his downfall as a logger. He had undertaken to do contract logging for George H. Emerson, manager for the North Western Lumber Company.

Camp wages at that time were running between $65 and $75 for teamsters; $45 to $55 for choppers and hooktenders; $40 to $50 for skidders; $26 for skid greaser; $30 to $40 for swampers; $40 to $45 for sawyers; $30 to $40 for common hands; $25 to $30 for cooks, in this case "Chiney cook." Calder was hiring around 15 men, including himself. His "Weekly Statement ending June 20, 1885, for Camp of J. E. Calder" for instance contained the names of the following men: H. Richling, Wm. Gibbon, Joe Wood, J. Hood, J. E. Calder, Joe Mathews, Wm. Ritman, China cook, H. Bowers, T. Boyles, R. H. Evans, D. Varmer, T. Moulton, C. Clemons. Clemons, who was to become one of Grays Harbor foremost loggers, was paid $2.11 per day.

Calder's book of "Weekly Statements" ends with a page dated August 15, 1885, with only four employees listed. Whether this marked the end of Calder's logging dreams the statements do not say, but it is known Calder "went broke" on the Hoquiam. He had given George Emerson a note which, with the inevitability of notes, came due. Calder could not meet the payment. Emerson called in the note and claimed all of Calder's logging possessions, hoof, hide and hang-ups; then, in a moment of magnanimity, he called Calder himself into his office.

"Joe, I've got to leave you something," Emerson said. "I'll tell you what I'll do. You go over to the store [a general store operated by F. G. Foster for the North West Company] and pick out a suit of clothes for yourself." He gave Calder a note to Foster.

Calder stomped over to the store, not exactly in the best frame of mind. Foster pointed up the stairs saying all the suits were on the second floor. Joe climbed. He took his time picking out a suit. It had to be, in his estimation, the best on the racks, and it had to fit. Then, just for good measure, Calder found himself the most expensive overcoat in the place; and it fit. This Calder carried to a side window, opened the sash, and calmly tossed the coat to the ground. On his way out, carrying the suit over his arm, Calder waved farewell to Foster, went around the side of the building, retrieved the overcoat, and whistled his way to the Hoquiam wharf where, in due time, he found passage to Montesano and a real estate business he pursued until his death.

At 80 he became mayor of Montesano, wherein with his

flowing white beard he became a county landmark, the beard to be playfully tugged by President Franklin D. Roosevelt during the President's visit to the Olympic Peninsula.

Often, when asked about his beard, Calder would explain that when he first hit Grays Harbor the price of a meal was two bits and the price of a shave and haircut also two bits, but he would rather eat.

THE SCHAFERS in their time were the second largest timber operators in the county. Like the Polsons they became rail-borne after years of bull-team logging and, like the Polsons, stretched steel strands deep into the timberlands toward the Olympics.

Schafer Brothers, loggers and mill owners, were rooted in the little town of Witterslicht near Bonn, Germany. There John D. Schafer was born April 6, 1821, the son of a schoolmaster. After graduation from Bonn University, John D. Schafer married Margaret Schumacher in 1849 and soon after sailed for America, a voyage of two months. They settled at Springfield near Cross Plains and not far from Madison, Wisconsin.

While living in Springfield, John D. Schafer and his wife, Margaret, had two children born, the first a daughter, Margaret, born September 19, 1850, and then Anton Dennis Schafer, born August 29, 1852. Soon after, Mrs. Margaret Schafer died and in 1853, restless and in sorrow over the death of his wife, John D. Schafer left Wisconsin and journeyed overland to Sacramento and the Rogue River gold country. He was unsuccessful in his search for gold and, selling his watch for money to get home, returned to Wisconsin by way of Cape Horn after an absence of eight years.

April 24, 1863, John D. Schafer married Mrs. Anna Bullenbeck Muller, a widow with three children who lived on a nearby farm. Peter Schafer was born to them September 25, 1869. In the fall of 1870, the Schafer family, then consisting of Mr. and Mrs. John D. Schafer, Margaret, Anton Dennis and Peter, and the three children of Mrs. Schafer, Christine, Julia and Chris Muller, and a number of friends, Hubert Kramer, William Cook, Charles Stroeder and Mr. and Mrs. Joe Miller and four children, Arnold, Anton, Kate and Joseph, left for Washington Territory by rail to

San Francisco, by ship to Victoria, B.C., and by steamer to Olympia, where they arrived in the fall of 1870.

The men of the party left the women in Olympia while they went exploring for farmland. They had heard of the Satsop Valley, so they trailed off into the wilderness by way of Little Rock and the Black River, where they built a small scow for passage down the Black to the Chehalis River, a route used by fur traders a century earlier.

All went well until they entered the Chehalis where the scow ran onto a snag and spilled the men and their tools into the water. Charles Stroeder, the only man who could swim, flailed his way to shore with a line and snubbed the scow to a tree. Indians living nearby came in their canoes and helped the party salvage the material spilled overboard.

At the mouth of the Satsop the party engaged other Indians to take them up river to what was later known as Schafer Prairie. The Schafers built their log cabin on the river bank near a small spring. The Millers built about a half-mile upriver, while Charles Stroeder and William Cook built about two miles above Schafers, Cook on the right bank near a stream still known as Cook Creek. The Stroeders located across the Satsop from Cook. Hubert Kramer chose the Cloquallum Valley and later homesteaded there.

With good weather in the spring of 1871 the men had their cabins ready and returned to Olympia for the women and children. Anton Dennis Schafer in that year was 19 years old and ready to strike out for himself. He took a job with government engineers and helped survey Townships 18 and 19 in the Satsop watershed. Later he and his father, John D. Schafer, surveyed and opened the first road to the homestead of David Shelton on an inlet of Puget Sound, now the site of Shelton, one of Washington's most important lumbering communities. In time the Satsop settlers could take a wagonload of eggs, butter and other farm products to Shelton, borrow a boat from David Shelton and deliver the produce to Olympia, where it was exchanged for groceries and drygoods.

Two more children, Hubert, June 19, 1873, and Albert, July 17, 1879, were born to John D. Schafer and his wife Anna, after they moved into the Satsop Valley.

By 1893 the Schafers had three sons — Peter, 24; Hubert, 20; and Albert, 14 — who had an itch to start logging. The family had enough bottom land for farming, a few head of stock and a sizable stand of timber on higher ground. The parents gave consent for the sons to log the timber, but attached as conditions that they hire Ben Kesterson, who had gone broke attempting to log on the Satsop, and that the farm be farmed and not neglected.

With this in mind the three brothers, with a single yoke of bulls, began logging, with Peter the bullwhacker, Hubert, the huskiest, as faller, and young Albert, the hooktender.

Within a short time the brothers hired Tom Osborn, Will Norman, John Comfort, Herman Muller, John Minckler and Ed Kesterson, along with two Indians, Billy Quaick and Hyasman, who could serve in any capacity from bullcook to canoe-building.

At first the Schafers built a cross-skidroad into 40 acres of choice timber on the John Schafer homestead, dragging their logs into the Satsop with a single yoke of animals. Soon they purchased five more yoke and considered themselves in the "big time." The men ate at the Schafer farmhouse, stuffing themselves with a table fare that was to become traditional in later Schafer camps.

The first logs were floated down the Satsop and delivered to the A. J. West mill in Aberdeen, where they brought $2.50 per thousand feet. For pay the Schafers took 90-day paper.

The three Schafer sons worked under a stern dictum from their mother, who ruled the roost as far as they were concerned. They could buy and hire what and whom they chose, but they could "borrow nothing, mortgage nothing, and pay for what you get — now!" It was a formula that worked well, and built the bull-team operation into one of the greatest industrial undertakings in the Northwest.

By 1897 the brothers were delivering to Grays Harbor mills four times their output of but a few years before. And about this time Hubert Schafer joined the gold rush to Alaska. He returned in 1899 with $500 in his pocket, the rewards of deckhanding on an Alaskan steamer, to find that a gadget called a "donkey engine" had invaded the woods, dooming the bull team.

In order to raise money to buy one of these new contraptions, Hubert hurried up to the Washington Iron Works in Seattle, where he hired out. He told the iron works owners he wanted to learn all he could about donkey engines. He also asked them to hold out all but the bare necessities from his pay and apply it to the purchase of one of these machines. They agreed, and it was not long before Hubert and a 9 x 19 roader arrived on the Satsop. The roader by later standards was a mere toy, but it put the bulls to pasture and Schafer Brothers on their way. Hyasman, the all-around Indian, had this to say about steam donkeys: "He eat no hay, and he no mess up the stable. Good!"

It was soon apparent Schafer Brothers would have to do something else besides float logs down the Satsop, so in 1913 the firm purchased a 45-ton Heisler locomotive, six logging cars and two miles of steel. They were railroad logging, but the Heisler was wrecked a few days later when Scotty Meadows, who'd try anything once, piled it up on six percent grade. After $4,000 in repairs to the $10,000 engine, the lokey continued service for many years and became Schafer's famous "One Spot."

In 1914 the Schafer Brothers Logging Company was incorporated with a capitalization of $300,000. Up to this point the Schafers had been primarily loggers. However, during World War I they operated a small plank mill in Brady, and in 1919 purchased the Sunset Shingle Company, Montesano, a plant they operated until 1940.

This touched off a whole series of purchases, including the Fir Products Company at a bankruptcy sale in 1921, which in the same year led to the incorporation of the Schafer Brothers Lumber and Door Company with a capital of $500,000. This capitalization was doubled in 1939 and the name changed to Schafer Brothers Lumber and Shingle Company, with all the stock held by the Schafer family.

Seventeen years before, however, the Schafers had entered into what was their biggest deal to date: purchase of the Chehalis County Logging and Timber Company, timber, railroad and logging equipment for $500,000 from the Grays Harbor Commercial Company of Cosmopolis. In that year, 1922, Schafer Brothers established Schafer Park on the Satsop River as a memorial to their parents John D. and Anna Schafer. They later added another tract to the park, which now gives pleasure to thousands of visitors.

In 1924 Schafer Brothers paid $1,000,000 for timber and land owned by the Wynooche Timber Company. This purchase set tongues to wagging . . . "had the Schafers bitten off more than they could chew?"

However, tongues did wag when on July 18, 1925, Schafers concluded the deal with Wynooche Timber Company, taking all timber, land, railroad and camps, for an over-all figure of $3,500,000.

Schafers purchased the National Lumber Manufacturing Company for $1,000,000 in 1927; the Doty Lumber and Shingle Company for $500,000 in 1928; the Markham & Callow operation in 1928; and the Independence Logging Company in 1929.

In 1929 Schafers paid $500,000 for the Leudinghaus Lumber Company of Dryad, including the townsite, just before the stock market crashed. The company weathered the crash, meeting all their payrolls, although a little behind in paying some of their bills. Yet, within a few years the Schafers were able to purchase a lake-type steel ship at a San Francisco federal sale and named her *Hubert Schafer* in memory of one of the original brothers who had died September 6, 1931. This was the beginning of the Schafer Steamship Company, which later added the *Anna Schafer*, 1932, and *Margaret Schafer*.

Fourteen years later the two remaining Schafer brothers died, Peter in April, 1945, Albert in November, 1945.

And then in May, 1955, Schafer Brothers' descendants concluded the largest business transaction in Grays Harbor history. They sold all their holdings including a billion feet of timber, a railroad, logging camps and equipment, and mills, to the Simpson Logging Company at Shelton, a company founded in 1895 by Sol G. Simpson. The Simpson company at that time was headed by W. G. Reed, Seattle, grandson of Sol Simpson, as chairman, and Thomas F. Gleed, Seattle, president. Within a few months Simpson traded much of the Schafer properties to Weyerhaeuser for timberlands within Simpson's operating base at Shelton and McCleary.

POLSONS, SCHAFERS AND THE BIG SIX

THE BIG SIX, however large they loomed on Grays Harbor, were not native growth. They were transplants from Ontario, Canada, but no less for size, brawn, integrity, fair dealing and faith in the Almighty.

Forerunners of the Caldwells rumbled into Grays Harbor as early as 1884 like an invasion of giants, for every man of them stood better than six-foot-two in his wool socks. George and Jack Caldwell, when unburdened of long-handled peaveys and snatch blocks, each reared up to six-foot-six, a towering height for men a century ago.

They were the offspring of Henry Caldwell, a native of Ottawa, who died in 1880. Their mother, Frances Blaney Caldwell, died in Montesano in 1907 at the age of 76. Henry Caldwell, as might be surmised, was a huge man, while his wife was outsized for a woman. Together they engendered perhaps the best-known family in Grays Harbor logging history, the "Caldwell Brothers," or better "The Big Six," which came naturally enough.

William Caldwell, born August 20, 1861, in Ontario, Canada, was the oldest of the brood, reputedly the most handsome, and by a fraction of an inch saved from being the "midget" of the six; weight, 235 pounds. He and his brother John L. "Jack" Caldwell were the first of the family to come west. They arrived on Grays Harbor in 1884 accompanied by W. Frank Bower, a druggist who was to become their brother-in-law by marrying Lucinda Jane "Lucy" Caldwell.

The two brothers went to the David Wilkie farm of the Wynooche where they spent the summer and fall slashing brush for Wilkie. Late in the fall, with Frank Bower the brothers rented the James Wilson farm, stock and equipment in the Wynooche Valley and made their home with the Wilson family for more than a year. For neighbors they had David Wilkie and his family, the Oliver C. Moaks, the George Wades, the Calvin Birdwells, the Charles Sheasbys, the E. Garrisons, the Charles Garrisons and, upriver, the Henry Wedekind family.

The two brothers, like the four others to follow shortly, took to logging to have some cash to jingle. William Caldwell, who was 24 years old when he arrived on Grays Harbor, took two years off and attended Willamette University in 1888 and 1889. Within a few years he became a minister of the gospel and sandwiched preaching with his logging.

It was but a matter of time until he quit logging entirely to spend more than a half-century with various church denominations. In this respect he became the better known of the Big Six for he had far more public exposure than his brothers.

While living in the Wynooche Valley William Caldwell took up a homestead on Black Creek and became a member of the Methodist Church.

This venture into the biblical field gave way to the Christian Church when Frank Hutton and Harvey Fry started the First Christian Church in the schoolhouse on Black Creek. Caldwell was ordained as a minister in 1896 and from thereon was known as "Preacher Bill." He did his first active preaching on Johns River in 1898, leading the flock there for 20 years and serving congregations in Markham, Ocosta and Westport. He also had a regular preaching assignment at Vesta and Brooklyn on North River for 24 years.

"Bill" Caldwell in his years with the Big Six was the organizer, the business manager and director of the company's operations. The firm's first venture was a logging operation on the East Hoquiam, an eight-horse team show, where the Big Six first used their famed log brand, a numeral 6 inside a circle. The brand was of such repute that the lumber mills seldom bothered to scale a Big Six raft of logs, so well established was the firm's integrity, honesty and fair dealing.

The horse team soon gave way to a logging engine like the one Alex Polson and another Robert Lytle were using on the Hoquiam.

In 1900 the outfit moved to the red cedar stands on Elk River and Andrews Creek in the South Bay region. Later they manufactured shingles in Ocosta, switched to logging on the Satsop, and finally sold their holdings to the E. C. Deming Lumber & Shingle Company of Aberdeen.

"Jack" Caldwell at 205 pounds and six-foot-six-plus was the tallest of the Big Six. He was a quiet, studious man, given to reading the classics. Notably he had a strong aversion to profanity, perhaps because so much of it, along with guts, muscle and snoose, was used to move logs out of the woods.

George A. Caldwell at 240 pounds stood exactly six-foot-six and was the strongest of the brothers. One of his feats of strength was to pick up a 300-pound anvil by the tapered end with one hand. It was easily understood that no one ever rubbed George Caldwell the wrong way or challenged him to arm wrestle. For that matter hardly anyone ever crossed any of the Caldwells save "Little Sister" Lucinda, and whenever she told the Big Six to scratch, they scratched. Lucy was diminutive by comparison with her brothers; until her marriage to W. Frank Bower she assisted her mother keeping house for the "boys." It was no secret in the Caldwell family that Lucinda was the "bull of the woods" when it came to food, clothing, family conduct and general run of the "home camp." She did not meddle in their logging.

Oliver B. Caldwell, 210 pounds, was the shortest of the Big Six, and disliked being called "Shorty" even in fun. So none called him "Shorty." Oliver was the woods manager of the outfit. He hired and fired and ran the show, and particularly liked to "punch" donkey when called upon. He was doing this one day on Andrews Creek, with his young nephew Earl Bower standing nearby, when the boiler exploded with a roar heard at the whaling station five miles away. The concussion hurled Oliver and his nephew into the brush and on either side of a big windfall, while parts of the boiler went whistling into a distant canyon. Young Bower, unhurt, looked up to see his uncle peering over the windfall, grinning from ear to ear and giving him a big wink.

Henry "Hank" Caldwell, 235 pounds, was another of the strong men in the outfit, with road-building as his specialty. Muscling skids and tackle seemed to fit Hank's ability, with no complaints from his brothers. He was also noted as a powerful faller and bucker, chores all the brothers shared at times.

Bryon Caldwell, 220 pounds, was the youngest of the Six and the only bearded member of the family. For years he sported a Van Dyke and was regarded as the best-dressed of the Caldwell "boys," that is, when he sported his "town clothes." Also he was said to have shared honors with his brother Bill for good looks. Of all the jobs with the Big Six Bryon preferred donkey punching, which he did with skill and without stripping the spar trees of their rigging.

The brothers logged until 1911 when they sold their last holdings on Andrews Creek. Bryon and Oliver tried farming in Oregon but grew dissatisfied and returned to Grays Harbor. Again together as the "Big Six," the brothers cleared the right-of-way and graded for the first plank road from Ocosta to Bay City. Then George and Henry started a transportation business between Westport and Tokeland. The company also received the first daily mail contract for the Lake Quinault area. George and Henry organized the Caldwell Bearing and Parts Company in Aberdeen, while William continued to preach and log for many years. Oliver kept on working in the woods as a foreman; Jack finally settled in California. Bryon moved to Westport in 1920 to become a driver for his brother's stage line, later to work as a logger and finally as a maintenance man for the county on South Beach roads.

HAD IT NOT BEEN for the logger's stomach and his ravenous appetite, Ninemire & Morgan might never have prospered on Grays Harbor. Theirs was a touch-and-go meat business until logger appetites called for more and more meat, mostly beef; pork appeared more often as bacon and ham on messhall tables, although many camps had their own pigpens. The beef demand in camps and mill messhalls stretched Ninemire & Morgan from cattle raisers to slaughterhouse operators, then to wholesalers and retailers and a fortune thereby. They delivered to camps throughout the Grays Harbor region by freight boat, wagons, railroads and packhorses, always to an anxiously-waiting market.

The two partners, George W. Ninemire, the leading figure in the firm, and Thomas Grant Morgan, could not have mingled with loggers without thinking of becoming lumbermen themselves. The money-making appeal was there; besides, they were already closely connected with the logger through his stomach. They had learned something about the timber business and found it far more appealing than slaughtering cattle.[20]

The firm of Ninemire & Morgan, beginning as cattlemen, owned large blocks of Grays Harbor land, a thousand acres near Cedarville, including the Blockhouse Smith ranch and nearby lands. The partnership also held a large block of range south of Grays Harbor, including most of Westport and coastal land south to North Cove. Another holding was on Fry Creek between Aberdeen and Hoquiam where the slaughterhouse became a landmark on Myrtle Street. The bulk of the business was supplying meat to Grays Harbor's innumerable logging camps. There was, too, a retail outlet in Aberdeen and a summer store in Westport.

In 1901, while ranging cattle along the south beach, Ninemire & Morgan ran into a freshwater problem following a rather dry winter, but the solution was readily devised. The partnership would form an "oil drilling company" to be known as the Grays Harbor Oil Co., with C. F. White, manager of the Grays Harbor Commercial Company, as president; G. W. Ninemire, vice-president; Thomas Morgan, treasurer; J. A. Sells, secretary-manager. A well was drilled, but when a good flow of artesian water was encountered the drilling was stopped.[21]

In 1912 Ninemire & Morgan formed a corporation with $100,000 capital to build and operate a sawmill at Helsing Junction near Independence, Washington. The mill burned in 1924.

In 1923-24 Ninemire & Morgan, logging from a 100-year-old burn, had a railway running westerly along the divide between Independence Creek and the Chehalis Valley. Their supply of timber was limited because Wilson Brothers Logging Company of Aberdeen had a railroad up Independence Creek and were pushing into the hills ahead of Ninemire & Morgan.

About this time Wilson Brothers sold their logging operations to the Humptulips Logging Company which carried on as the Independence Logging Company until it failed in one of the biggest collapses in Grays Harbor lumbering history. John Markham of Centralia and Bert Callow were appointed receivers in the failure.

After the Independence Logging Company failed, Schafer

Brothers purchased the National holdings, the Independence layout and Leudinghouse Company and built their own railroad from Brady to connect through Doty. The Weyerhaeuser Company had made the Leudinghouse acquisition valuable because it had committed the timber behind the Independence operations to Leudinghouse.

After their mill at Helsing Junction burned, Ninemire & Morgan shifted their sights to Oregon where they purchased the Stevens & Ferris sawmill on Chickahoming Creek, located on the Coos Bay branch of the Southern Pacific Railroad. The mill had no timber of its own, but Ninemire & Morgan were able to purchase timber some distance away. They borrowed from a Eugene, Oregon, bank to build two and one-half miles of railway to reach the timber, creating an under-financed situation which caused the whole enterprise to fold.

At some time in this era the partnership was dissolved, Ninemire taking up farming while Morgan established a so-called "cancer sanatorium" between Chehalis and Centralia. His supposed cure was based on an Indian remedy derived from the sap of some tree. The remedy proved ineffective and Morgan's enterprise vanished. Morgan died in Chehalis.

In 1890, the same year Ninemire & Morgan moved into the Chehalis Valley, another retailer, Robert F. Lytle, set up shop in Hoquiam. However his was a grocery store, continuing what seemed to be a family tradition which followed him from Lincoln, Nebraska, to Fairhaven, Washington Territory, in 1889. In Fairhaven he formed a partnership with his brother Joseph Lytle. The following year the two shifted to Hoquiam, again opening a grocery store with Robert Lytle emerging as the "power" in the partnership.[22]

The Lytle brothers had operated their Hoquiam grocery store for several years when, much against their will, they were forced to accept a small logging outfit in payment of a bill. It was an oxen outfit, to be changed in a few years to steam. The Lytles hired John D. Sparling as foreman for the debt-acquired camp and purchased more timber to keep the camp going. Additional purchases, at the low timber prices prevailing at the time, and a profitable and expanding logging enterprise within a few years made the Lytles a power in the timber business. A considerable portion of their timber purchases had been cedar, which led to building one of the largest shingle operations on the Coast. Later the Lytles organized the Hoquiam Lumber & Shingle Company, built a large plant on the Hoquiam River and capitalized on the lumber boom of 1907.

In 1911 Robert Lytle moved to Portland but continued his business interests on Grays Harbor. In 1915 Robert Lytle organized the Panama-Eastern Lumber Company and built a sawmill on the East Hoquiam across the river from the Hoquiam Lumber & Shingle Company plant. He also was instrumental in organizing and establishing the Woodlawn Mill & Boom Company with a public log dam and boom and an all-electric shingle mill.

It may seem remote to connect Montesano's busy waterfront at the turn of the century with the burgeoning railway systems in the woods, but there is a relationship. Schafer and Clemons' activities stemmed from the Montesano area, while the biggest railroader of them all, Alex Polson, was busy with the Montesano waterfront even before he had visions of a logging empire.

Montesano was thumping fir cants and cedar shingle bolts before the Luark mill on Sylvia Creek was sold and the machinery moved away in 1890. As early as May, 1883, the framework for the M. E. Goodell sawmill in Elma was being constructed by John J. Carney, and later that same month Goodell went to Montesano to pick up his mill machinery, which came in on the steamer *General Miles*. Goodell loaded the machinery on a scow and towed it to Elma. By July of that year, 1883, the mill had cut enough lumber to build 18 new houses in Elma.

A year from the time he started sawing in Elma, Goodell moved his plant to Montesano, locating it "just back of the C. N. Byles residence where plenty of good timber is available."

While Goodell was busy sawing lumber in Elma in 1883, the Wishkah Lumber Company, J. A. McGillicuddy, president, leased a mill site in August from T. J. Carter on the south side of the Chehalis at Montesano. Machinery for the plant arrived the following month on the *General Miles*, and in November began cutting rough lumber. A year later the company was planning to move its plant to Aberdeen, but before the move could be made it was damaged on January 15, 1885, by high water. A quantity of recently-cut lumber was floated away. The same flood in the

Chehalis swept away the Selby & Waite wharf and inundated the entire townsite of Lower Montesano with two to twenty feet of water. Some buildings were also carried away, and it was feared public records and much private property would be damaged.

In the years to follow Montesano was to have nine other mills, all but one along the Chehalis waterfront in Lower Montesano. One of the first was a mill built by the Stetson Lumber Company (George W. Stetson and Neil Cooney) after Stetson had managed the Grays Harbor Commercial Company in Cosmopolis from 1888 to 1894. The mill was located to the east of what was called the "long bridge" from upper Montesano. The mill was taken over within a few years by the Montesano Lumber Company, with George W. Ninemire and C. H. Clemons as majority stockholders, and with Stetson returning to Seattle to operate as the Post-Stetson Lumber Company. The mill was closed down sometime between 1910 and 1912, Ninemire taking the machinery to Helsing Junction near Independence, where it was installed in a mill operated as Ninemire & Morgan, until it burned in 1924.

In April, 1910, the Syverson Lumber & Shingle Company was incorporated with G. A. Onn as president, H. B. Onn as vice-president, and H. Syverson, secretary-treasurer. The firm built a mill on the north waterfront between the Montesano Lumber Company and the Sunset Shingle Company plant, which was near where the present highway bridge crosses the Chehalis. The operation did not last long. By January 24, 1913, it had gone into receivership and was put up for sale on that date. The plant was bid in for $45,000 by Montecoma Investment Company, then sold a month later to the Hoquiam Sash & Door Company and re-opened as the Hartung plant. The sale to the Hoquiam firm was handled by Reuben Fleet of Montesano.

The Hartung mill was operated as such until 1917, when it was acquired by Schafer Brothers, who operated it until it burned in the 1930s. The site remained unoccupied until the early 1940s when it was acquired by Ed Picco, who built a modern sawmill upon the location. Upon Picco's death in 1954 the Grays Harbor Lumber Company was liquidated. The mill then was purchased by the E. C. Miller Cedar Lumber Company.

The Sunset Shingle Company was operated by Thomas Connor, W. H. Bush and Patrick Maloney. They sold to Schafer Brothers early in the 1920s.

E. K. Bishop had two operations on either side of the county road near the waterfront. The E. K. Bishop Cedar Bolt Mill was just north of the county road at the end of the "long bridge." The bolts were brought under the roadway on a slip to the mill. The mill not long after went as many mills did; it burned.

The E. K. Bishop lumber mill, just west of the bolt mill, cut mostly spruce, was discontinued in 1919 and moved to Junction City near Aberdeen.

The Hillview shingle mill, owned and operated by Kinyon & (Mike) Dzamaria, was between the county road and the OWRR&N tracks (Montesano branch), just west of the Chehalis River "wagon bridge" approach. This mill was phased out in the 1920s.

The South Side Mill, just below where the Wynooche merges with the Chehalis and on the south bank of the Chehalis, was built by a group of 22 Croatians in the early 1920s as a semi-co-op, but did not operate as such for there were "too many chiefs and not enough Indians" in the operation. Schafer Brothers acquired the plant within a few years, only to lose it by fire.

The Chehalis County Logging & Timber Company, a subsidiary of the Grays Harbor Commercial Company in Cosmopolis, built a shingle mill on Sylvia Creek.

During this period of lumber-cutting activity, Lower Montesano had a pronounced waterfront air with both lumber and commercial wharves. One early-day picture showed two sailing schooners and a steam schooner loading. Longshore wages in the '90s were $3.00 a day; bricklayers, $4.50; painters, $2.50; carpenters, $3.00; blacksmiths, $4.00; laborers, $2.00; farm laborers, $1.00 and board; mill hands, $35 to $55 per month. Logging company wages per month were: foreman, $75 to $100; teamsters, $75 to $100; choppers, $55 to $65; skidders and swampers, $35 to $50; hooktenders, $45 to $55; sawyers, $45 to $55; cooks, $35 to $50 per month and board.

The waterfront in Lower Montesano was so busy the town decided to build a trestle from lower Main Street to the Chehalis River to carry the ever-increasing traffic. On August 28, 1884, a contract was let to the Pacific Bridge Company of Portland for $6,500 for construction of the trestle, which was to be built on pilings and decked with 16-foot planks. The Portland company subcontracted site clearing to Alex Polson for $122. Polson hired three men to do the right-of-way clearing, the work starting in May, 1884. By August 5, 1885, the trestle had been completed, and Montesano turned out for a parade of horse-drawn vehicles and pedestrians or "marching persons" to celebrate the opening. Mayor Lewis B. Bignold of Montesano introduced Governor Watson Squire as speaker of the day. Ex-Governor Newell was on hand as second speaker.

Chapter
6

CRUISERS AND SCALERS

Before the woods were filled with the high pitch of donkey whistles, and the Shays and Climaxes puffed across the plateaus of timber, there were two other fellowships essential to logging and sawmilling. They were the timber cruisers and log scalers, many of them praised, as many of them bedamned.

The timber cruiser was the pronounced specialist among all woodsmen. His was a peculiar skill, calling for more than ordinary know-how about trees and terrain. W. G. "Watt" Peebles, a top cruiser in his own right, once said, "The best guesser is the best cruiser." Peebles listed the qualifications as knowledge of the terrain, legs like a sprinter, the constitution of a bear, and the ability to count 2,000 paces, the number of paces along a section line.

The cruiser was, and still is, the man who estimated the amount of timber in a stand, whether it be an acre, a section or township. Upon his estimate, or guess as Watt Peebles put it, was based the price to be paid. If the cruiser was good at his job the timber buyer got what was to be expected out of the stand. If the cruiser was slovenly, the "cruise" could be thousands of board feet off one way or another.

Watt Peebles, after leaving Wisconsin in 1884, had forsaken a dream of becoming a Nebraska cattle baron when he arrived on Grays Harbor in 1885. There was too much sand blowing across

Nebraska to suit him, so he sought greener country. He wandered down through New Mexico, made San Francisco in September 1884, then Eureka and eventually Grays Harbor.

Peebles' first job was in 1885 on Delezene Creek where Leavitt & Clemons were logging. He started timber cruising, however, with O. P. Burrows for the North Western Lumber Company on the East Hoquiam, where he prowled the woods for three years before becoming the top-rated cruiser in the Grays Harbor timber.

Watt Peebles and Cleve Jackson, an Indian cruiser and a good one, were working on Widow Creek in the Humptulips country when the great hurricane of 1921 struck the Washington coast. They hit for cover, and as the winds died, found downed timber "piled higher than a house" all around them.

Among the better known cruisers remembered by Watt Peebles was Jerry McGillicuddy, who rates special mention. He was Jeremiah H. McGillicuddy, son of John and Bridget McGillicuddy, who left Kerry County Ireland, in 1847 following the Irish potato famine of the 1840s. Their ship was wrecked on the south coast of New Brunswick, Canada. With several other immigrant families they settled near Harvey Station, New Brunswick, and there Jeremiah Ambrose McGillicuddy was born in 1852. He worked in the woods of Maine, moved to Driftwood, Pennsylvania, then to San Francisco and Eureka, California. When he learned Capt. A. M. Simpson was building a mill at Gardiner, Oregon, McGillicuddy hurried north to logging operations on the Smith River, which led to his coming to Grays Harbor.

Through his brother-in-law, Jim Cowen, a bachelor who filed on a homestead seven miles above Hoquiam on the West Hoquiam River, McGillicuddy heard of the fabulous timber stands in Chehalis County (now Grays Harbor County) Washington. In 1882 McGillicuddy came to Grays Harbor via Olympia, portaged to Black Lake, by canoe down Black River and the Chehalis to Hoquiam. He took up a homestead at the head of tidewater on the Hoquiam. In time he named the place New London.[23]

At New London homesteaders and timber prospectors found a good jumping-off place for the hard, and often grueling trek into the Humptulips Valley forest. In time Jerry McGillicuddy became a "locator" for those seeking homesteads, and at the same time did some timber cruising for those seeking timber claims. Years later he became a full-fledged timber cruiser, perhaps the first in the Grays Harbor region, and had covered virtually every section in the county prior to his death in 1927.

From 1901 to 1913 Jerry McGillicuddy was chief cruiser for Chehalis county. He made the first comprehensive cruise of timber in the county for tax purposes, the first cruise of its kind in the state. The nine-volume record of the McGillicuddy timber cruises is deposited at the College of Forest Resources, University of Washington, in Seattle.

The county cruise was the biggest thing of its kind ever undertaken. Eventually it was determined there were 22.5 billion feet of timber to be inventoried. To make the inventory the county commission (newly-elected C. N. (Bud) Wilson, Willis Hopkins and George L. Davis) in its April 4, 1911 meeting decided to hire McGillicuddy as chief cruiser at a wage of $10 a day, 13 cruisers at $7 a day, 15 compassmen at $4 per day and six packers at $3.50 per day. The cruisers were James L. Shearner, P. J. Moriarity, H. N. Dunbar, P. J. McElfresh, J. C. McElfresh, J. T. Leahy, Alex Laberge, George D. Davidson, E. O. Elliott and James E. Empey, Frank A. O'Brien, J. B. "Uncle Ben" Kesterson and J. L. Nethery.

There was quite a turnover of cruisers before the long undertaking was completed, due primarily to the large number of cruisers who had been hired from east of the Cascades and were unfamiliar with timberlands on the west side of the Cascades. Others could not perform in the dense woods of the Grays Harbor country.

Cruisers and compassmen worked in pairs and by July, 1912 had completed field work on 800 thousand acres of timber in 58 townships. They found in the 22.5 billion board feet of timber 13 billion feet of Douglas fir, 1.75 billion feet of spruce, 3 billion or more of cedar, and 2.75 billion feet of hemlock. They also found 1 billion, 500 million feet of dead fir, pine, cottonwood and "larch," the local name for white fir. And the greatest stand of all was the famous "21-9," (Township 21 North, Range 9 West) 36 sections, 23,040 acres of Douglas fir, standing so big and thick a timber cruiser was hard put even to count the trees. The timber was variously estimated at 180 to 300 feet tall, and to have an average diameter, breast high, of three to eight feet. There were many trees from 11 to 14 feet in diameter.

Twenty-eight of the 36 square mile sections in "21-9" were available for logging when operations began in 1909. Customarily two sections in each Township were set aside as school lands, and six of the most northerly sections were inside the Olympic National Forest and not available to early loggers.

In 1936 timber cruisers and loggers estimated the township had yielded more than two billion feet of timber, with several more billions to be logged. As late as 1950 the township was still producing.[24]

In harvesting such a dense stand of big timber, there were certain drawbacks. The timber had to be felled in one direction; even then there was a lot of breakage. With fallen timber so thick upon the ground, buckers had difficulty cutting trees into log lengths.

And then there was the problem of moving such a vast amount of timber to tidewater. A. P. Stockwell of Aberdeen, manager of the Humptulips Boom and Driving Company, constructed 27 splash dams on the Humptulips and tributaries, to bring the logs out, most of which were rafted in Jesse Slough near the mouth of the Humptulips.

The Wishkah Boom Company, owned by the North Western Company, had a similar operation on the Wishkah. It splashed logs down the west branch of the river, and caught and rafted logs which were splashed down both the west and east branches. The two booming companies acted as common carriers and handled all logs sent down the rivers.

The cruise put Chehalis County on its feet financially, for it paved the way for taxing untold riches in standing timber, providing funds for personnel, roads, buildings and other county works. It did, however, have an adverse effect; private timber owners stampeded to liquidate their holdings to avoid taxes. This liquidation, coupled with a seeming unlimited lumber market, produced the great timber cut and exportation of the 1920s. Twenty to 30 tidewater mills, and others inland, ran three shifts a day, six days a week for years on end to produce an incomprehensible volume of lumber, the greatest ever moved from any port in the world.

Jeremiah McGillicuddy and the host of his cruiser peers left their marks literally in the Grays Harbor County. Each had his own mark or insignia which he left at section corners and on "witness trees." That of Jerry McGillicuddy was four notches on a blaze. Lem Nethery used a diamond-shaped cut on a tree. John Markham, who was phenomenally accurate in his cruises, used a "big mitt," and the famous cruiser Holland had a lizard mark. Jim Empey used a "coonskin" while many cruisers used only a blaze with their name written on it.

Other cruisers prominent in the Grays Harbor woods were John Farquan, D. S. Harris, Jim Hemphill, Willis Hopkins, A. D. Devonshire, Ben Kesterson, Jack Scanlon, Dan Gillis, Tip O'Neal, Dan Dineen, Archie Moore, Patrick Hogan, Frank Dotson, Frank Webster, Charley Phillips, John Rankin, Joseph Egerer, Patrick Doyle, Frank Dineen, Al Wade, Ed Markham, C. Harris, Cliff Gillis, Lafe Heath.

One of Jerry McGillicuddy's sons, Daniel, in turn became one of the better known cruisers in the county, while Jeremiah Ambrose McGillicuddy Jr. who became Chehalis County treasurer, later affiliated with William Boeing in Seattle to organize the Greenwood Logging Company and operate on the upper Wiskah and east branch of the Hoquiam. Cornelius McGillicuddy became a log buyer for Harbor Plywood Corporation on Grays Harbor, while Blaine McGillicuddy became a civil and logging engineer. Dan McGillicuddy, like his father, became chief forester for Chehalis (Grays Harbor) county.

Another fraternity of the timber was that of the log scaler. Where the timber cruiser "estimated," the log scaler was supposed to make precise measurements. He was the man with the scaling stick who not only was supposed to measure a log, but to grade it. Thus he often was a logger's affliction, for upon his "scale" or measurement and grading depended the logger's price for his logs and most of the scalers worked for the mills that bought the logs. There was constant conflict, for a scaler hardly ever was known to favor a logger. It was common practice for scalers to cut a log 10 percent for "hidden defects," and then deduct 100 percent for visible defects. As a consequence a logger often had but little log left.

There were many witticisms connected with early-day scaling, one concerning the tendency of red cedar to be hollow-butted and swell-butted with a sharp taper. The scaler, so the logger claimed, would measure the diameter on the small end, then measure the hollow on the butt end, which often was larger than the log on the small end. Thus the scaler would find the log all hole, or no log at all. In other words the scaler would make the logger's log vanish simply by using his scaling stick.

Better illustrating the scaler's ability, and tendency, to scale down the size of a log was the old woods jape; if a log was too big to go through a sluice gate or into a mill, "why just get a scaler to scale it and it will go through." William "Billy" Mack, scaler for West & Slade, often was the butt of this gag. However, he went on to be a logging operator himself, having a camp a mile or so east of Satsop.

While in early-day logging logs were "graded with a scaling stick," in later years there were grades, and if a scaler complied, a logger was more apt to know where he stood regarding the price of his logs. For many years there was only one log grade, and that was "Number One." Anything inferior was left in the woods. And the mills paid only one price.

It was a common practice for the mills to pay loggers with "90-day paper," which the banks promptly discounted two percent, adding to the logger's woes.

Before the logger ever got his "90-day paper" he may have suffered many perils between the woods and the mill booms. He could have a fortune hung up on gravel bars, his logs could get lost in a mixture of brands in the booming grounds. Log thieves, a busy supplement to the industry, got half price from some mills for the thefts. Many mills would not take logs sluiced down certain streams for often the logs were "broomed"; that is, the ends were frayed and spread by the pounding taken going through the splash dams and beating the stream beds on the way down. Some logs often were heavily embedded with rocks picked up on the stream beds and would be refused by the mills. Rocks played havoc with the mill's saws.

And the vagaries of the weather were not always in the logger's favor. As a matter of fact he often suffered from lack of rain, or too much rain, snow, fire-causing drought, low streams, and even danger to his logs while in the streambeds. Cy Blackwell, wanting to clean up his logging show, dumped his logs into the Wishkah and some piled 80 feet high. The Wishkah Boom Company was in litigation with farmers along the river and could not splash its dams. Blackwell's pile of logs caught fire and burned. He was able to recover damages because it was the boom company's responsibility to move the logs.

In another instance, also on the Wishkah, William Boeing and his Greenwood Logging Company had a roll dam with some logs in the pond. The company also had a large collection of logs felled and bucked in the woods. The logs burned. The company sued the boom company, but collected no damages because it was shown Greenwood had room in the roll dam pond for all the logs which burned.

Log prices usually were at the whim and wants of the mill operators. Where Perkins & Milroyd and Charles McCormack at Montesano were getting $3.50 to $4 per thousand in the early 80s, by the time of the San Francisco quake, 1906, the price rose to $7 per thousand. The Wishkah Logging Company, owned by Roy Sargent and Hiram Hulet, and Carlson Brothers, Adolph and Gus, each bought a stand of state timber which they expected to log at $7.50 a thousand, but the San Francisco disaster boosted the price of lumber while the log market went to $12 per thousand. The companies made fortunes. Larkin Brothers were almost broke because of the dry season and no freshets to move their logs collected in the Wishkah. Cy Blackwell, more modestly, was in the same situation. He had a million feet of logs in the river.

Almost coincident with news of a rise in lumber prices came the rains. Rivers rose rapidly with the downpour and within a short time millions of feet of $12 logs were on their way to tidewater.

This stimulus, besides giving rise to development of the steam schooner to carry the lumber, built one of the greatest collections of sawmills in the Northwest, virtually all on seven miles of Grays Harbor waterfront. These were "tidewater," or so-called "cargo" mills, for they loaded directly into ships for the California and world trade. By 1924 there were 22 such mills working night and day, filling the air with burner smoke and the roar of saws and edgers. Docks were piled high with new lumber, while ships thumped against the wharves filling gaping holds with a thousand million board feet of lumber a year.

Among these tidewater plants were the giant Grays Harbor Commercial Company mill in Cosmopolis, actually a combination of sawmill, planing mill, box factory, tank factory; the A. J. West Lumber Company, Bishop Lumber Company, Bay City Lumber Company, Aberdeen Lumber & Shingle Company, Wilson Brothers Lumber Company, American Mill Company, Donovan Lumber Company, Anderson & Middleton, Donovan Mill No. 2, Hulbert Mill Company, Saginaw Timber Company, Eureka Cedar Lumber & Shingle Company, National Lumber & Manufacturing Company, North Western Lumber Company, E. K. Wood Lumber Company, Hoquiam Lumber & Shingle Company, Grays Harbor Lumber Company, Woodlawn Mill & Boom Company, E. C. Miller Cedar Lumber Company.

There were other mills in the hinterland, some of them sizable, such as the Carlisle Lumber Company, Aloha Lumber Company, White Star Lumber Company, Vance Lumber Company, Henry McCleary Timber Company and a host of small plants largely in the eastern end of the county.

Besides the sawmills there were 27 shingle mills hacking away at Grays Harbor timber. The whine of shingle saws joined the sawmills to assail Grays Harbor eardrums for almost three quarters of a century.

It all began of course with the stiff-blade muley saw, a power-driven saw that worked up and down. Then came the circular saw, then the double circular (one saw above the other). But Grays Harbor's logs were too big for the circular saws, and besides they took a half-inch kerf, or cut, the width of the teeth, with a resulting waste in sawdust. The bandsaw was next, and a logical development, but its use took some doing.

The first bandsaw on Grays Harbor was installed in the Emery & Mack mill in Aberdeen late in December 1885. Other millmen up and down the coast watched with interest, for it was an experiment for all. However, the saw "snaked" badly and had to be controlled, but once under control it revolutionized lumber cutting. First the bandsaws had teeth on but one edge, then came the "double cut," a bandsaw with teeth on both edges, permitting cuts to be made as the carriage advanced and as it returned, while lumber rolled out of mills almost faster than the ships could haul it away.

The first lumber was pulled by hand along on "dead" rolls but in time they were made "live" with shafts and gears, and lumber fairly flew into the edger, the trimmer, and to the "drop" where it was graded and sorted.

For the California trade lumber was shipped green, for that was the California demand, and California was virtually the only early market. Later with the coming of the railroads, lumber began to go by rail, and because of the freight rates, was mostly dried and finished. This necessitated dry kilns, and most all mills installed them.

Opening of the Eastern market by rail and ship put some stability into the Grays Harbor lumber business. Prior to that lumber was sold in California according to the buyer's whims, his economy and upon his own tally and inspection. The lumberman in a way got a taste of his own medicine for he once virtually controlled the logger with his scale, his grading and his price. For years, particularly in 1889 and 1890, San Francisco dealers ruled the lumbermen, dictating prices that in many cases were almost confiscation. Mill owners landed their product on San Francisco wharves often without a solid commitment by a buyer. They faced the prospect of having a portion declared "refuse," or subject to the dealer or buyer's tally, which always was lower than the mill's tally. This was particularly bad for the mills when California had a bad crop year or when lumber sales slumped for some other reason. It was a different story after 1906, and when millmen were able to ship east by rail.

Grays Harbor had a long and profitable lumber trade with the Hawaiian Islands, and one substantial item was what became know as "Honolulu flooring." It was 1 x 6 stock with one side finished, the other rough, so native carpenters could not mistake which side went down. One large shipment was carried in the four-mast barkentine *Aurora* owned by the Charles Nelson Company and skippered by Captain Hans K. "Drawbucket"

Johnson, who put his cargo ashore at Hilo. Another cargo went in the schooner *King Cyrus*, Captain George Rosendal, who once told a strange story concerning his command. The *King Cyrus* was en route from Adelaide to Grays Harbor when hordes of hungry fish attacked a heavy encrustation of barnacles on the ship's bottom. So ravenous was the attack the schooner had to go into drydock for repair to her bottom planking where fish had actually torn out pieces of wood. The shipyard, incidentally, scraped the barnacles from other portions of the hull before the *King Cyrus* put to sea again.

Chapter
7

SCREECHING BEGAN THE DAY

Rumbling the tidewater mills into action called for more than the mere turning of a steam valve or blowing a whistle. It took a whole dissonance of whistles, of shrills and bellows like some mad orchestration. The sawmills boomed in throaty bass, while the shingle mills seemed always to pierce their obbligato, awakening a half-dozen townships to a crispy dawn, and all the stump-ranchers therein arousing with groans, moans and blasphemies, turning toward their windows to see if in truth the day had begun, for the cows had not yet bawled, or the dogs barked.

Adding to the clamor, tugboats whistled for sleepy bridge-tenders to open their spans. They alerted indifferent boommen, and matched vibrations with incoming and outgoing deepwater tramps. Locomotives steam-hissing in the dawn, demanded right-of-way at crossings for long strings of lumber-laden box cars, gondolas, slat-sided cattle cars, flatcars, double-deck sheep cars (an abomination to carloaders) and other rolling stock capable of carrying anything sawn or bundled.

Steam schooners elbowed into the harbor, blowing impatiently for bridge passage, and demanding a man on the wharf to take a heaving line, longshoremen to stand by with cargo hooks in hand, and winch-drivers to storm aboard the minute a line was on the cleat, or before. Sternwheelers on the first of the ebb, pulled at their lines, their wheels turning idly and spouting demanding jets of steam.... "Board! Hurry up! We're pulling in the gangplank!" Deckhands hastily slid the last of the slabwood into the firerooms, or piled it haphazardly on deck beside the fireroom door, this remindful that the shipyards, too, would be adding their pipings to the din.

Grays Harbor is 46-47 degrees north latitude; twilights are long, winter days short. So the reveille of three whistle blasts would come before dawn, if in winter, the millhand in his long underwear awakening grumpily, stumbling to the kitchen to light the coal oil lamp. Curling his toes from the cold floor, he carefully built a fire in the Round Oak range with kindling he had prepared the night before, including, of course, a few pieces of dark fir pitch which virtually leaped afire. He hefted the teakettle to be sure there was enough water for coffee and a pot of rolled oats.

Back in the bedroom he pulled on his pants; then with his galluses dangling, made his way in the damp chill to the privy, which miraculously had stood throughout the first winter storm. The rooster in the chicken yard crowed, which meant somehow another day was about to dawn.

The housewife, who on another day may have been the first out, meanwhile swung to the floor as reluctantly as her husband, pulled a shapeless dress over her chemise and bloomers, swished her pillow-rumpled hair into a knot, and headed for the kitchen. She held her hands over the now-hot stove for a moment of warmth, then began banging pots and pans in a brisk display of housewifey determination. It would be mush, pancakes or eggs, depending upon the day of the week, and whether or not the hens had been productive. The routine was fairly tight with no time or inclination for innovations.

The first whistles had sounded either at 6 o'clock or 7 o'clock for the ten-hour or eight-hour day, depending whether it was before or after the Wobblies came. By the same token the quitting whistle in the evening would be either at 6 o'clock or 5 o'clock, the sound as often as not trailing eerily in the dim light on a howling so'wester.

A half hour after reveille the dissonance was repeated with two blasts, warning the millhand he had better be mopping his breakfast plate, gulping the last of his coffee, grabbing his lunch pail and hightailing it to his day of toil.

By the final whistle an hour after the first, the dogger on the headrig would be on his carriage, the dog handle in hand, awaiting the "nigger"* to jam the first log against the blocks. The peanut whistle in the engine room would have sounded, warning all hands the great main engine would be turning, whipping the line shaft and its many appurtenances into action. All stand clear! Then the fireman, with an eye on the clock, pulled the whistle lanyard, loosing a rumble that out-sounded the squeaking sawdust conveyor and all the other shrieks, groans, thuds, whines and cacophony erupting from the now roaring lumber plant.

It was an unvarying ritual to which thousands of souls responded, a whole terraqueous range tied to the raucous jets of steam, the pace of the headrig saw and snarl of the edger. The only difference day to day would be the seasons and their weather; otherwise the machine operators arrived barely in time to oil the bearings, unless the mill had an oiler, who would know every oil hole and grease cup in the plant. The "hunkies" on the green chain, or they could have been Finns, Scots, Norwegians, Crows, Hindus, Filipinos, Japanese, Chinamen, Swedes, Hawaiians, long-lost Britishers, Indians, a scattering of French-Canadians, an Eskimo or two, a few wanderers from Australia and Chile — name them and Grays Harbor had them — tied on their heavy aprons. The planerman had tightened his knives, and the lumber-pilers out in the yard awaited the first truckloads of the day. At first these would be two-wheeled, horse-drawn trucks, later pulled by "jitneys" made of a Model T chassis with hard rubber tires. Still later lumber would be moved with load-straddling carriers, first electric, then powered with gasoline engines.

The lumber pilers, some working under contract, also tied on their heavy splinter-proof aprons, and drew on split-leather mittens that would become slick and slimy in the rain, wrinkling the hands and turning them death-white by quitting time. Thus

---

*A mechanical term used in sawmills for more than 100 years.

all around the mill men poised, but not a lick of work done before the starting whistle and, for that matter, not a lick after the quitting whistle. It was axiomatic.

The foreman had stopped at the mill office to pick up the day's cutting orders, which the head sawyer tacked at his shoulder to the housing of his big bandsaw. Another set went to the side rig sawyer who, like the headrig sawyer, pulled on his canvas gloves, gave a finger signal to the setter and settled down to the shift routine just as the whistle echoed its last in the cavernous reaches of the mill.

The edgerman with but one leather glove on took his snoose can from the left breast pocket (right over his heart, it might be noted) of his timeworn and timberworn coat, tapped the lid sharply, removed the lid, took a healthy pinch of snoose between thumb and forefinger, deposited the pinch snugly in his lower lip, licking his fingers carefully to intake every last smidgen, then capped the can and returned it to its pocket. He pulled on the other glove. Now he was ready for the day. He had performed the most satisfying rite he knew, or perhaps was to know, and sent the first cant of the day snarling through his machine.

On the other side the riven pieces were shunted on the spiral-grooved live rolls to the trimmerman, who like a virtuoso on his trimsaw console, cut out defects, screeched the rough lumber to lengths and sent it on its way. He too, had cutting orders tacked over his bank of levers, for sometime during the day he must provide so many pieces of a certain size lumber of a certain length. The edgings and slabs were cut for slabwood or for the lath mill. The pieces dropped into the main conveyor which squeaked and groaned through one side of the mill toward the mammoth burner, which smoked and glowed for years on end.

The burners themselves were great tubes of steel, faced inside with fire brick, and capped with a dome of heavy screen. Some early burners were entirely of brick. Later the so-called wigwam burner became popular, so named because of its shape, not unlike a wigwam. Some plants, notably the shingle mills had no burners, but conveyored their refuse to open fire heaps surrounded by ugly walls of sheet metal hung on steel frames. No one knew, or cared, **how much unused wood went up in smoke** in the fires, which seemingly never cooled until the mills ended their cutting and were sold for junk, including the burners.

A man in the lath mill picarooned the lath stock from the conveyor, while another farther up the conveyor picked slabwood out of the trash and sent it down a chute to a pile from where it would be hauled and piled by some slogging oldster and his work-worn horse and cart. Some mills further resawed the slabs into household firewood, which would be delivered around town in a four-wheeled "wood wagon" with sliding body boxes to be upended to dump the loads, and cranked aboard again with mighty huffs and puffs from the driver. The same wagons also carried "planer wood," trimmings from the planing mill, and wood-length dimension, both rough and planed. Planer wood, slippery and in small pieces, was the bane of Grays Harbor youngsters. The stuff had to be wheeled into the woodshed on a wheelbarrow from which it was forever sliding. And it took equally forever to get an armload, for it slid and slithered. This was an acknowledged side factor in the lumber business.

Back in the mill the trimmed lumber, minus the trimmings, slabwood and lath stock, started out on the green chain to the grader with his crayon (black, red or blue, according to his taste or that of the bookkeeper in the office) to be graded with one sweeping glance and marked for delivery down the line. Some pieces went directly to the resaw, which would split them and send them back to the chain again to pass once more before the grader. Beyond the grader a dozen or so men on either side of the green chain pulled the lumber off and onto flanking piles to be moved to any number of destinations around the plant. Much would go to the dry kilns for finished lumber, while some dimension stuff would go to the speedy and loud-roaring bull planer. Other stuff would be trundled to the drying yards to be piled high for air drying. Rough cargo lumber, once the only kind taken by the California trade, would be hauled to the wharf in readiness for the next ship.

Many mills had mechanical "stackers" to load lumber on knock-down or small-wheel bunks, for a trip through the kilns. This could have been any one of several contrivances to stack lumber on edge with sticks between tiers, all using a tilting mechanism. Other mills stacked the lumber flat by hand with sticks between layers to give heat circulation. The kilns themselves were heated by steam from the main mill boilers, the lines carried on bents above yard traffic, swathed in asbestos and jetting the inevitable leaks. The lines made the drykiln man the cold-day envy of every man in the plant; it was warm against the kiln doors, and warmer still when the cars of dried lumber were run out to the "unloader" or as some said, the "unstacker." Once unstacked the lumber was again sorted for its trip to the planers. The planing mill did just that, smoothing the lumber with razor-sharp blades fastened to high-speed drums. Planing machines were of two types. The ordinary "planer" had opposing blades offset, while the "matcher" had blades exactly opposite. The "matcher" was so-called because the opposite blades cut the full length of the piece of lumber precisely so the finished edges could be put side by side and match perfectly. The regular "planer" with one blade ahead of its companion on the other side, was prone to error, however slight depending upon the alignment of the feeding mechanism.

The product may have been S4S (surfaced four sides) or surfaced one, two or three sides, whatever the order. The blades cut the tongue and groove of flooring, ceiling, decking or whatever, shaped drop siding, the lap of shiplap, and the delicate moldings that went through the "sticker." On the off-end of the planers were the offbearers-trimmermen and the tiers, those who sorted the planed lumber and trimmed it to length, and the tiers who tied the lumber into bundles.

The first days of the tiers were apt to be painful, first with a scored and often bloody or blistered offshore edge of the little finger where the twine lodged each time the tie was jerked tight; again a throbbing headache from the incessant thrashing mixed with a high-pitched whine of the planers. The job itself often was the lowest paid in the mill and fell, likely as not, to teenage labor for 50 cents to $1.50 a ten-hour day. Each planer had a feeder, who did his job mechanically, with the only break in the monotony the arrival of a new load of rough lumber. The entire pandemonium was under the watchful eye of a planing mill foreman, who often doubled as a knife-filer, for the filing had to be done precisely with no latitude or tolerance of error, especially the form-cutting blades, the ones cutting the "V's" and beads, the tongues and grooves, or the fancy shapes for molding. Emil Gustafson in the Grays Harbor Commercial plant was perhaps the best-known foreman.

In their cutting the planers threw out a storm of chips and shavings, virtually all of which were caught up by blower pipes, which joined one large pipe flung across the yard on bents to the big "cyclone" (sometimes there were several in a plant) atop the fuel bin. The cyclone itself was a large retort shaped not greatly unlike a nun channel buoy, and within it a hurricane or cyclone of whirling chips and sawdust, hence its name. The chips escaped the turmoil by beating themselves against a rotating fan and dropping into the fuel bin below.

A conveyor running under the bin, carried the chips and sawdust to the boilers where they chuted upon call into the fireboxes, to blaze almost white-hot and sending a stream of hot cinders up the multiple stacks where, cooled to black, they gushed into the heavens to settle eventually upon the housewife's new tablecloth or her line of laundry, and blow helter-skelter in the gutters of the town.

There was thus a close relationship between the mills and the surrounding communities. The mills were ever present to most of the senses, the noise, smells, sight, the touch of lumber, including sawdust in the streets, bars and butcher shops. The relationship may not have gone so far as taste, but if you pulled a splinter of fir, spruce, cedar or hemlock to pick your teeth, you could taste the difference.

At the other end or beginning of the lumber process, the boomman would have emptied another raft of logs and closed his boom "gap" or "gate" with a toggled "stick." He would have tied the set of empty raft "sticks" to the boom "race sticks" for the tug to pick up and return to the rafting grounds.

A "stick" in the parlance of the river, was an 18- to 24-inch log normally 40 feet long with a six-inch hole augered through about eight inches to a foot back from each end. The holes received the toggle chains or "boom chains" (heavy chain possibly six feet long with a ring in one end and a toggle or cross-rod in the other) to link the sticks together. A set of "sticks" would be those enclosing a raft of logs, usually six to eight sections of 40-foot logs, and tied across by "swifters," lengths of cable the width of the raft.

Grays Harbor used the long raft, from 240 to 320 feet, and about 40 feet wide, because of the narrow tidal streams, and to pass through the bridge openings easily. The rafts could be moored without obstructing river traffic, and few logs were lost because of the binding "swifters." Another advantage was that a set of sticks could be run into a rafting boom, filled with logs, "swiftered," closed and towed away with a minimum amount of time or trouble. And then there was the praiseworthy feature extolled by the log scaler. The orderly arrangement of logs in a raft made it easier for a scaler to keep track of his logs, scaled and unscaled. In comparison, the round raft used on the Harbor in the very early days and popular for years on Puget Sound, had logs every which way; they were harder to tow, logs were lost by jumping the "sticks," and the scaler was fit to be tied by the time he had finished scaling a raft. The contour of the long raft was much that of the waterline of a square-stern ship, the stern being the "butt stick" toggled across the after end of the raft, while the bow was the raft peak composed of two sticks brought together and toggled, leaving a handy ring for the tug's towline.

Towing was usually done with the tides, either upstream or down according to the flow and ebb, for bucking a tide with a long raft or two was fuel and time-consuming and was done only in emergencies.

However, there were other forms of log towing on the Harbor, largely of a surreptitious nature — the stealthy towing of stolen logs. It was no trick at all for thieves to run a "dog line" across the rear section of a raft, open the butt stick and drop the section out of the raft, and away they'd go to the expectant mill. Even two or three prime logs were a good night's work for a pair of thieves, who often shared their "take" with the boomman, who either looked the other way or helped the thieves to get the stolen logs into the mill boom. Some referred to these boom bandits as "Moonlight Loggers."

There were several mills on the Harbor suspected of receiving stolen logs — and if they were suspected, it was a safe bet they were engaged. Stolen logs usually were hustled right up the slip with their identity disappearing in the multitude of cuttings and trimmings, and eventually the fire pit. However, it was an open secret as to the more prominent thieves. Millmen and log owners knew who they were, but rarely were they caught and prosecuted, perhaps because the cost of apprehension and prosecution was more than the logs were worth. In any event, thievery was a thriving business, and more than one upstanding citizen-millman could have been shamed by disclosures the thieves may have made. Sometimes it was suspected this was the reason more thieves were not caught.

In any event, regardless of how the logs got into the boom, the boomman at slack water puttered around lining up the logs for the slip man, whose job was to guide the logs to the slip, thence into the mill.

The slip was a massive trough with walkways on either side. It was lined with steel bands or strips fore and aft, and curved gracefully with an artist's eye from the water to the log deck or landing just inside the upper deck of the mill. In the bottom of the trough was a steel-guarded channel through which the bull chain dragged itself slowly when the landing man activated the bullwheel with his friction lever. About every twelve to fourteen feet on the bullchain was a square, four-toothed link that grabbed the log and hauled it bodily out of the water. This square link has been variously called the "bucket," "grab," "dog," even a "chair," but more "bucket" than anything else. Whatever, the function was still the same. The logs disappeared, dripping, into the maw, never to be the same again. They were rolled, slabbed, turned, canted, edgered, trimmed, sorted, kilned, planed, marked, stacked and loaded for where only the tallyman and shipping clerk knew.

Once the log was on the deck, the operator could roll it, mostly according to size and the load on the pony rig, either to the headrig or the pony rig. At this point the sawyer had at his command some ponderous apparatus upon which sawmill machinery and mechanism designers had shown some of their most sagacious and penetrating skills, including making massive and unwieldy machinery operate delicately.

The sawyer could release a log from the stop, let it roll against the carriage blocks, or as in many mills, carry the log against the blocks with chains called the "live lift." After the first slab was sawn the sawyer normally turned the slabbed side down to take off another slab and square the log. To do this he had a long steel shaft with a hook on the end, which came from somewhere down in the bowels of the mill, hooked onto the top of the log and pulled it upon its face. In some mills the log at this juncture was pulled upon two "half rounds" or "half moons" on a shaft, the half rounds automatically shunting the log back against the blocks. The hook in later years was often called a "Simonson hook," after its designer. If the plant were small and handling small logs, peaveys and muscle power were used to turn the logs against the half rounds.

Another ingenious apparatus at the command of the sawyer was the "nigger," a square shaft of steel faced with three teeth on the carriage side. Often it was mounted on two cylinders so the sawyer could manipulate it to push a log against the blocks, or in difficult situations one end at a time. He could also engage the teeth into a log or cant and heave or turn it against the blocks. The "nigger," too, rose from the bowels of the mill and disappeared into the same recesses amid dripping scatterings of bark and other debris, including an occasional rubber intimacy picked up by a raft as it passed a sanitary sewer discharge. The object would have been carefully placed upon a log by the slip man with his pike for the edification of the landing man, and amusement of others including the slabwood man, who would behold it in its passage and sigh that his youth had largely been already spent.

However, before the trinket reached the ultimate man on the conveyor, the head sawyer would have signalled his setter for the first cant off the log. The sawyer would have quickly studied the face of the log to determine what type of lumber the log would best produce. Say he wanted to take off a four-inch cant; he would hold up four fingers. The setter would glance upon his "set works," move the blocks out four and one-quarter inches and brace himself as the carriage moved past the saw. From then on a whole system of hand signals could apply. The little finger and the whole hand pulled sideways meant a six-inch cut. The hand with but the index finger down meant eight inches; two fingers down, nine inches. A fist meant ten inches; thumb down twelve inches, while 'teen figures would take extended fingers with the hand drawn sideways. A pinch of the thumb and forefinger meant a quarter inch.

Different regions of the sawmilling industry used hand signals varying somewhat, but all carrying the same basic information. Grays Harbor and Puget Sound were closely allied, while Southern Oregon and Northern California signals differed from the Washington ones. Another variation prevailed eastward of the Cascades.

With this system of signals coupled with the more obvious pantomime, the whole mill could communicate, overcoming the almost unbearable, but eventually accepted roar. Time of day could easily be told with hand signals, while a dogger, who had been shifting to one leg then the other, eventually would have to signal the sawyer he wanted off the carriage for quick relief. He would do this with a pulling motion about two buttons below his belt. If the sawyer were in a good mood he might comply immediately; if not, then the poor dogger would have to jump up and down a few more times.

Carriages in the early sawmills, the big mills cutting big timber, had log openings, or could take logs of 60"-72"-84"-96"-108" diameter. For instance if the carriage opening was 60 inches, the setter's dial would be calibrated zero to 60 inches with ⅛-inch fractions between the whole numbers — ⅛-¼-⅜-½-⅝-¾-⅞.

On smaller carriages the setter's dial was calibrated in single circle of numbers. One revolution of the dial meant from zero to 60 inches, where by contrast a carriage equipped with an opening to take logs up to 108 inches in diameter would have a double set of numbers on the dial, zero to 54 inches on top of the dial indicators, and 55 to 108 inches on the bottom. It would take two revolutions of the dial to indicate 108 inches of opening.

When the sawyer set up for a run, he had two things of immediate concern; he had to figure the scarf (often called cerf) the width of cut the saw teeth would make, usually ¼ inch — and his "back stand." He would want to come out on a standard "back stand" — that is 6-8-10-12 inches, the amount of the log left in the "knees," that is the angle between the upright blocks and what has been variously called "carriage bed plates," "skids" or "bunks"; in any event the steel tracks upon which the dog-carrying blocks traveled back and forth at the bidding to the sawyer, and execution by the setter. In other words the "back stand" was the last cant on the carriage.

Say the sawyer wanted a "back stand" of eight inches out of a 22-inch set up. Long experience would give him a mental sequence like this: 22"-2"-¼ cerf = 20¾"-4"-¼ cerf = 16½-4"-¼ cerf = 12¼"-4"-¼ cerf = 8". That may seem a little complicated; but nothing about a sawmill, however ponderous, was simple.

Most early mills sawed lumber "full sawn," that is a two-by-four was sawed full 2 x 4 inches; while the modern method is known as "scant sawing" or "standard sawing," the actual rough size of a 2 x 4 being 1¾ by 3¾ inches. Scant sawing gives the mill owner a little more out of his log.

It may seem a little strange, but sawmills were known as "right handed" and "left handed" mills. The distinction was important, especially to the sawyer. If the bandsaw (or bandmill as it was sometimes called) was located to the left of the sawyer, it was a "left-handed mill." If the bandsaw was located to the right of a sawyer, it was a "right-handed" mill.

The importance to the sawyer was how he used his hands — and feet. If it was a left-hand mill the sawyer would feed the carriage — that is, make it run past the saw — with his left hand on the control lever, while with his right hand he would operate the nigger bar, and hook and push-arms levers. With his feet he stepped on pedals to activate the log-stop and loader — this in some mills the cradle in which the logs lay prior to being loaded on the carriage. With the other foot he often used a pedal to operate the "dead skids" — again in some mills a type of skids when activated, raised a few inches above the carriage bed plates so the edge of the log would catch on the end of the skids to help the sawyer roll a log with the hook and replace it on the carriage.

In a "right-hand" mill the whole procedure would be reversed, even to the sawyer giving signals with his left hand. In the left-hand mill he gave signals with his right hand — in other words the sawyer did not remove his hand from the carriage control lever.

Some big mills had both right and left-handed rigs. The headrig may have been a right-hand set-up, while the "side rig" or "pony rig" — they usually were back-to-back — would be left-handed. Sawyers of course, had preferences, but upon call they could be ambidextrous.

Sawyers could get help from their doggers when it came to handling logs too large to see over. The head dogger, the one on the front of the carriage, or the tail dogger — the one on the rear — would relay the hand signals to the setter, and do so until the log was whittled down to size.

Long logs created a problem of a different kind. Some mills like the one at Bordeaux, could handle logs up to 120 feet in length, but they had to do it with a "trailer" tagged to the main carriage, and only for special occasions.

It may have been said by some the head sawyer was the top man in the mill, the key to the whole operation for he was the one to judge the log and determine from his vast experience just what the log would cut out, whether it would be top-grade vertical grain, slash grain, pitch-pocketed planks, two-by-fours or whatever, but that often would be open to argument. Others would say the filer outranked all others in the plant. All lumber depended upon how it was sawn, and all sawing technology depended upon the skill of the saw filer. How the saw performed was definitely his province. The sawyer may have determined what could be gotten from a log, but the filer with his skill told him how he was to get it.

Most big bandsaws in Grays Harbor tidewater mills were eleven gauge with a tooth space of two to three inches. It was the filer's job and that of his assistant, or "fitter," to see to the scarf, although this was largely determined when the saw was purchased, the "benching" or "rolling tension," the swaging, the brazing, stretching, the gumming, grinding and all the other things necessary to put a saw in top shape, not forgetting the gullet-grinding (after all a gullet can carry just so much sawdust).

It was up to the filer, too, to see that the bandsaw ran true, without snaking, cut smoothly and speedily. He was always on hand when the saw was "lined" to cut true, perhaps with just a small adjustment of the guide, and to see the saw speed was compatible with the timber and the disposition of the sawyer. After all, a sawyer should not jam his saw, choke the gullets and give the mill foreman fits, which would bring on the run, chomping his cud of Union Leader and breathing like a horse with the heaves, that miracle man, the millwright.

Through the dark and massive intricacies of the sawmill, a nether region of complaining machinery, all roaring, squealing, squeaking, and thunderous beyond compare, the millwright moved furtively. His ears told him, despite the tumult, which squeal meant trouble and which squeak was the normal dissatisfaction of a conveyor chain crawling up its steel-lined trough. If there was trouble, the millwright had a job to do; and there seemed always to be trouble.

The millwright's responsibility was to keep all this huge pile of noise in running condition, from the peanut whistle in the engine room to the sticker's trimsaw in the far end of the planing mill. He traditionally worked while other men rested, for then the machines were stilled and there was no danger of becoming entangled in a line shaft, but at other times emergency said he must joust with danger while the mill was alive and rumbling. The nature of his toil made the millwright a Sunday worker, for then the pandemonium was arrested and even the demonic thrashing of the woodhog was throttled. About the only sound to be heard was a leaky steamline to the dry kilns, the tide slapping under the wharf, and the millwright's hammer.

The millwright would seem furtive because he normally toiled in the dark recesses, coming only occasionally into the sunlight on his way to the blacksmith shop for another bolt. He was at home in a maze of posts, beams, braces, shafts, belts, gears, pulleys, saws, chains, engines and the saw filer's loft. His uniform was overalls, a jumper and a battered hat, always covered by oily sawdust and grease. He could be seen occasionally carrying a tool or two, sometimes a whole kit, depending upon the magnitude of his task.

Sunday was the time for major repairs, a new link in the bullchain, a new sheetiron apron for the main conveyor, a new gear for the live rolls. There may have been a bearing to pour, a stringer to replace. He had to realign this, readjust that; the job may have entailed anything from a new sheet of corrugated roofing, recapping a piling under the headrig, a new arm on the "nigger," to a new length of chain on the drop.

Necessarily the millwright was on speaking terms with the

—LYONS COLLECTION

Grays Harbor's first tidewater sawmill, 1883, formerly the Stevens grist mill, began water-powered sawing, later converted to steam.

(Right) Michael Luark built a water-powered sawmill at Lake Sylvia, 1873. (Above) First Wilson Bros. sawmill on Wilson Creek, Aberdeen.

—HOQUIAM LIBRARY

North Western Mill, Hoquiam, a year before it burned on June 15, 1896. Barrels on the roof were put there to stop fires. But they didn't.

—BRONCO COLLECTION

S. E. Slade's mill stood on the old A. J. West mill site. Railroad was the Northern Pacific approach to Wishkah River bridge.

This steel-engraving of early Aberdeen appeared in The Northwest Magazine for January, 1890. Weatherwax sawmill is shown at left.

—(INSET) BILLEE HOLBROOK COLLECTION

Hoquiam in 1884. North Western Mill at far left. Inset: Mrs. Ed Campbell, whose blackberry pies lured first lumbermen to Hoquiam.

E. K. Wood sawmill at the bend of the Hoquiam River. Wood sawed much of the lumber used in Hoquiam's shipbuilding industry.

A pause in pandemonium within the North Western sawmill. Headrig in distance, edger at left, "pony rig" at right. Hell itself couldn't have been noisier when this mill was running.

—HOQUIAM LIBRARY

—DEWEY WILSON COLLECTION

Schooners loading lumber in Chehalis River at Wilson mill, 1905. Stump ranches out yonder later became South Aberdeen.

—ANDERSON COLLECTION

Biggest fir log ever whittled into lumber in Anderson & Middleton mill, Aberdeen, sawed out 11,844 board feet. That's "Pap" Anderson by the log.

—DEWEY WILSON COLLECTION

Called the "Western Penitentiary" because of cheap wages, Grays Harbor Commercial Co., mill in Cosmopolis was termed "world's largest" in 1900.

—MARIE GUSTAFSON WAHL

Manager Neil Cooney, known beyond earshot as "The Warden," never shifted his Marmon beyond second gear. He didn't want to strain it.

Martin N. Deggeller

E. W. Daniels

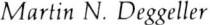
Grays Harbor's booming plywood industry unravelled mile upon mile of thin veneer which went into mountains of panels.

Behind mustaches are Montesano's famed Caldwell Brothers, called The Big Six, with their mother and "Little Sister Lucy" in 1901.

Alex MacLean Polson, center, between brothers Marzell and Werner Mayr.

—MONTESANO VIDETTE
J. E. Calder

Henry Neff "Pap" Anderson

George Edgar Anderson

A. W. "Bert" Middleton

Henry Neff "Heine" Anderson, 3d

William Donovan and friends.

—HORSECLAM STUDIO

Charles R. Wilson

Henry McCleary

E. K. "Ned" Bishop

Robert Polson

Alex Polson

Samuel Benn

Peter, Albert and Hubert Schafer

Nels J. Blagen

J. A. Vance

 E. C. Miller
 R. M. "Bob Ingram
 A. J. Morley
 Frank Lamb
 R. J. "Dick" Ultican
 Joseph Graham
 Al Stockwell
 Ben Johnson
 Ben Averill

Jeremiah A. McGillicuddy

Robert F. Lytle

A. J. West

Capt. J. M. Weatherwax

Jason Fry

John Fry

Edward E. Hulbert

Sol G. Simpson

Asa Mead Simpson

—JONES COLLECTION

Big Fred Hewett's Humboldt Saloon on F Street, Aberdeen, where loggers got their belts as they bellied up to the bar.

Hewett's watering hole featured long bar, wall curios, brass footrail, nine spittoons and two bartender-bouncers. Photo taken just before the rush.

—JONES COLLECTION

Young Dick Ultican, left, felt big lining up with grown men in front of the Batchelor Bar in Cosmopolis. Oh yes he did.

—DEL MULKEY

Vic Lindberg in boyhood delivered papers to many rowdy places in Aberdeen but grew up pure.

—ANDERSON COLLECTION

Heine Anderson's novel stud mill in Raymond revolutionized mass production of eight-foot 2x4's for home builders. Anderson Mill is in foreground.

—ANDERSON COLLECTION

Ill-fated Andersonia, Calif. redwood sawmill never cut a board after "Pap" Anderson was fatally injured the day it was dedicated.

blacksmith and the electrician, with a fleeting word occasionally with the engineer. He knew the sawmill sign language from A to Z. He knew the sound of every machine, and the location of every nut and bolt, every key and pin, every bearing and coupling in the plant. He was a master of improvisation. Tough problems were his meat, tight corners and inaccessible dungeon jobs his daily fare. He was sought out by the engineer, the sawyer, the fireman, edgermen, the cleanup man, the planer mill foreman, the trimmerman, the setter on the pony rig, and just about anyone in the plant who wanted something done.

The millwright knocked off at 11 o'clock for his lunch hour, so he could work during the normal noon hour. He often ate in the engineroom, and on cold days he emerged from an inner door into the fireroom, which was warm with sawdust fires drawing white hot and noisy with draft, and flickering through the peepholes. The rhythmic pulse of the great steam engine lulled the millwright into an after-lunch snooze, to be shattered at noon when the fireman pulled mightily on the whistle lanyard. Then it was back to the recesses, always badly in need of whitewash.

The millwright kept his tools in a painstakingly-locked box, for someone was always wanting to borrow a hammer, a wrench, a chew of snoose, whatever, and forgetting to return any or all. And on Monday, his day off, the millwright built a shelf for his wife, shingle-patched his roof, half-soled his shoes with belt leather scraps from the belt shop, and cleaned his pocket of nails he had inadvertently forgotten to return to their kegs in a corner of the blacksmith shop. He also profited by mislaid pieces of pipefitting and hardware, to say nothing of lengths of prime vertical grain fir, kiln-dried and surfaced four sides, which he shouldered out of the millyard as boldly as he did his empty lunch pail.

The millwright was the one indispensable man . . . they could always hire a new sawyer, but who would know where to find a new spline for the bullwheel?

Chapter 8

SPLASHERS AND BOOMERS

The splash dam was a unique structure, and very few men were skilled enough to build one. Among these were Jack Byard, Nels Ess and Bob Turner. Byard was perhaps the better builder. He constructed some 30 dams in the Grays Harbor country without having a single one "blow out," that is, to have the dam wash out at the bottom or sides because of faulty construction. Turner, who built by his own hand and owned a hotel in Aberdeen, was the more colorful. He was trigger-tempered and known afar for his proficiency with profanity, and was described as "a great cusser." In his fits of temper he would upon occasion pick up a pump jack and hurl it into the canyon, a feat only the strongest of men could perform.

The splash dam was built of cribbed logs with its upper slope faced with small logs or planks and covered with earth. The earth was dragged off adjacent hillsides with a Bagley scraper pulled by a small donkey engine. The Bagley was an ingenious scoop five feet wide, thirty inches high in front and four feet high in back, with a row of heavy teeth along the lip to bite into the ground. The scraper was a tremendous work-saver for the logging industry, not only in building dams but in gouging right-of-way for a skidroad or making a cut or fill for a rail line. It was the forerunner of the bulldozer.

In the high, or deep, portions of the dam were the sluice gates and the waste gates. Some had but a single sluice gate, some two. Large dams had two or three sluice gates and possibly three waste gates. The more efficient dams had what were called "false gates" to trigger the splashing system. This was an inspired arrangement. The main gate, or gates, fitted into channels on either side held back the head of water. When they were hoisted, the head of water in the pond suddenly was released, carrying the accumulation of logs with it. The false gate was the mechanism that "pulled the plug."

The false gate was a structure of planks or timbers a foot or two narrower than the main gate. It was hinged at the bottom just downstream from the bottom of the main gate, and then raised to an angle of about 30 degrees to the main gate. It was held in this position by two cables which passed over sheaves on the superstructure and down to the top of the main gate, or lift gate. The lift gate had two or three "lift boards," sometimes called "splash boards," resting on top, held in place by the channels on either end. When water in the dam reached the top of the splash boards (the excess going over the waste gates) the dam was ready for "splashing," that is, release of the torrent.

To do this the damtender pulled up the splash boards with attached hand ropes, permitting water to pour over the main gate and into the "V" between the main gate and the false gate. The weight of water soon forced the false gate down, the connecting cables raising the main gate. With the release of water all hell seemed to break loose. The sluiceway filled with foaming water, logs caught in the swirl plunged headlong into the deep pool below, then raced in a fury toward tidewater, some riding end up for a quarter of a mile.

At the head of the sluiceway on their floats and racesticks the damtender and his helper worked feverishly with their pikepoles to keep the logs headed. One misstep here meant certain death for no one was ever known to survive a plunge down the sluiceway.

On some streams there were several dams "splashed" in series, that is, the upper dam first, the next downstream just as the influx began to show in the pond; and so on down the string of dams. In this way a whole river system could be cleared of logs, with luck, in one series of "splashes."

Then it was up to the booms at tidewater to catch the logs, sort them according to brands and ownership, and raft them for towing to the mill. It was also the time the irate rancher went out to his riverbank to see how much land he had lost in the splash.

A number of streams had both splash and roll dams, the latter used largely for collecting logs and keeping them afloat. The roll dam was simplicity itself. It was built of cribbed logs, but had no sluice gates. Instead it had well-secured brow logs (atop the dam) and a sloping apron into the stream below. As the water in the dam rose by freshet or water release upstream, the logs rolled over the brow pieces and on their way to tidewater.

The Humptulips River was a good example of the use of multiple dams. The Humptulips Driving Company had two large splash dams (used only to create a man-made freshet), one just inside the Olympic National Forest, the other just outside, about 10 miles above Humptulips City. The one on the west branch was the largest. Cameron & Hoover had a splash dam on the east fork, while the Warren Timber Company and Corkery Brothers had two roll dams on the east fork.

In addition to the main stream dams there were several "side dams," that is, dams on tributaries to the Humptulips. There were five such dams on Big Creek, one on Furlough Creek, another on Deep Creek.

There were several splash dams in the Hoquiam River basin. Alex and Robert Polson built a dam above tidewater on the west branch, another on Bernard Creek, and still another on Davis Creek. They previously had built a splash dam on the Newskah. On the east fork of the Hoquiam there were two dams, one built by Carlson & Callow, the other by the Lytle Logging Company which had a camp at Nisson's Landing. Robert (Bob) Lytle, a store operator in Hoquiam, got into the logging business by accepting timber for the payment of bills.

On the Wishkah were three dams on the west branch, three on the east branch. The east branch dams, built and operated by the Grays Harbor Logging Company, handled logs almost exclusively for the owner of the dams. The firm was headed by Calvin Herbert "Bert" Shutt, who drowned in the pond of the second dam on the East Fork of the Wishkah, November 18, 1915. Shutt was walking along a race stick and stepped upon a dead head resting against the stick. The deadhead rolled and threw Shutt into the water. He was unable to swim. His body was found at the lower end of the deadhead.[25]

The Chambers Company had a big, seven-gate dam on North River some years after John F. Hobi built a seven-gate dam a half mile above tidewater in 1906-07. Hobi's dam, built by Tom Doyle of Aberdeen, had a head of water 26 feet and a pond eight miles long. The dam served until 1915 when extremely high water in the river tipped over the top works. There was always the suspicion the dam tender had been caught with two or three of the false gates down and could not lift the main gates to release the pressure of water. The dam was repaired by John "Jack" Byard and was in service until it outlived its usefulness. It was dynamited in 1921 to clear the stream.

The Hobi family built four dams on Salmon Creek, which empties into North River upstream of Artic, while Lester Brothers had a roll dam on the main stream. In all, at one time or another there were nine dams on North River.

Dan Gillies logged on Little North River, splashing logs to a point where they could be hauled over the divide and shot down into Preacher Slough, and eventually towed into the Chehalis.

The Ellis Logging Company built a splash dam on the Newskah, Jacob Weatherwax one on Porter Creek, Sargent Logging Company a dam on Andrews Creek, while Clemons & Leavitt had a bullteam show and a splash dam on Delezene Creek. Mike Woods and his Woods Logging Company built three splash dams on Delezene Creek and operated a skidroad show into the surrounding hills.

The Wynooche Timber Company had three dams on Black Creek, splashing into the Wynooche. To show the adaptability of loggers to the necessities, Charlie Peterson of Cosmopolis, built a small, single-gate splash dam on Charlie's Creek, named for him, south of Cosmopolis, sluicing his logs into tidewater and pike-poling them into the Chehalis opposite Aberdeen. Where Peterson built his dam a logger with a good rare of snoose could have spit across the stream yet the creek generated enough splash head to carry the logs.

False gate splash dams were monuments to remarkable engineering. They were built by rule of thumb by men who had no training as engineers. The location on a river, the character of the site itself, the availability of fill material and suitable timber, and of course the amount of "head" the owner specified, dictated much of the dam design and structure. The best sites were narrow, with rock bottom, plenty of rubble on adjacent hills and suitable trees.

Dams consisted of four main elements, the "deadhead" (another use of the term) or actual foundation made of long logs, the two wings, the top works and apron. The deadhead was composed of large and long-log sills embedded in the river bottom about 12 feet apart. Length of the sills depended upon the width of the stream, but usually they were tree length to a top diameter of 30 inches, which made them very substantial logs indeed. Into these sills were notched cross logs, then more sills into a cribwork to the height of the dam floor. The top sills were hewn flat to accommodate the heavy plank flooring of the sluiceways.

The wings were cribbed in much the same way with the upstream face of the crib slanting at about 45 degrees so that the fill and water would hold the dam down. The face of the cribwork was covered with either hemlock or fir logs of about 20-inch diameter laid on the perpendicular, at 45 degrees, following the slant of the cribwork. Often called "toepiling" these logs were fastened in place by long drift bolts. In soft ground a ditch was dug with a Bagley scraper to insure a good footing for the toepiling.

The dam apron, built on cribwork, sloped down from the height of the deadhead. Some dams had the apron decked with heavy planks, while others, where logs were to be sluiced over the apron, were decked with small logs similar to the toepiling.

Where the apron was decked with planking, the dam usually had two or three chutes made of small logs leading from the log sluice gates to the river below. This construction tended to let the logs flow in a deep stream of water.

The top works of the dam consisted of gate posts 30 inches square and 30 feet in length. The gate openings through which the logs were sluiced were usually 14 feet wide and 10 to 12 feet in height. The gates were built of heavy timbers six inches thick. The false gates were about four feet higher than the main gates, to allow for the splash boards and provide more lifting power.

The false gates were constructed of lighter material so that they could be raised with a hand-powered winch.

One such dam, not necessarily typical, but close, was what became known as the "Malinowski dam," built and operated by the Wishkah Boom Company in the NW¼ of Section 20, Range 8 West, Grays Harbor County. It was built in 1902 by Robert "Bob" Turner, and rebuilt in 1917 by John A. Byard. It last operated on January 1, 1924, with Joe Malinowski as the tender, a job he held for the last years of the dam's service.

The dam had an overall length of 300 feet with six gates, five of them 8½ feet wide and the sixth, the main sluice gate, 11½ feet wide. The maximum head attainable was 45 feet, while the maximum draw-down was 15 feet. In creating a "splash" the gates were kept open around 1½ hours which would draw the head down around eight feet, the best water in the river below to drive logs.

While the splash dams were a boon to the logger, they made some annoying things happen in the river bottoms. The minute the splash gates lifted, releasing a torrent, the gravel bars below were swallowed in a surge of water, with logs bobbing crazily. Crows lifted from the river bed squawking, and ranchers came down from their barns cursing in several tongues and accents. The blue haze that frequently hung in the hills often was attributed in part to the scorching things ranchers said about the dam operators.

Every splash was a gamble whether a rancher would lose one foot or ten feet of meadow. The surging water swooshed against the bank and logs gouged out great chunks of fine loam and bottomland silt, which would be noticed days later off the Washington coast as a discoloration in the sea. Some horny-handed sailor would peer overside and tell himself his ship was nearing Grays Harbor.

The ranchers were no pale-version pioneers. They were rough and rugged, and could talk a logger's language any day of the week, with embellishments. And they didn't cotton to the idea of having their oat patches and pastures, maybe their henhouses, cut from under them. Individually they made it tough for the boom companies, but when they banded together and hired legal experts, they tied up the rivers tighter'n a bull's eye in fly time.

One individualist on the lower Humptulips, O. P. Burrows, sued the boom company (the Grays Harbor Boom Company started by Al Stockwell) every year just as regularly as he planted spuds or weaned calves. Just as regularly he collected damages. It became sort of a license fee the boom company paid to use the river past Burrow's place. But one year there wasn't any suit. Still the boom company sent a check anyhow, the bookkeeper thinking there had been an oversight somewhere. It was later determined Burrows had fractured his leg, and could not make it to Montesano, the county seat. The check he received, by the way, was for the exact amount he had been suing the company for several years.

O. P. Burrows was just the man to appreciate the driving and rafting company's "thoughtfulness," for he was something of a wag in his lighter moments. He enjoyed telling newcomers that the coming winter was to be a snorter because the hair was growing exceptionally long on the north side of his heifers.

Often fortunes were tied up in the rivers, either with stranded logs, low water, or possible lawsuits, and sometimes log jams such as the one blocking the Humptulips' mouth for years. There was another such jam, not as great or enduring, in the Wishkah in March, 1901, some 18 miles above Aberdeen. The jam contained twelve million feet of logs, blocked the river tight, and caused four logging camps to close.

The small logger was the most likely to be hurt by a tieup of the river for one reason or another. He had to get his logs to market to keep solvent. In some instances he was at the mercy of the boom companies, which had an inclination to move logs for the big operators first, and let the small logger sweat out his next month's bills. But that was the boom companies. Operators of splash dams and splash systems were obligated to carry all the logs in a stream. The boom companies could pick and choose the logs.

Log driving, or "splashing," on Grays Harbor streams lasted around 40 years and carried billions of feet of logs to the always-hungry sawmills. In one splash alone some 17 million feet of logs were sluiced to tidewater, a flood of wood which jammed the boom at the mouth or the river.

There were three major booming companies on the Harbor, the Chehalis Boom Company, George Hubble, manager, with a big booming operation on the Chehalis, the Humptulips Boom and Driving Company, Al Stockwell, manager, operating on the Humptulips and the North Western operation on the Wishkah, which caught and rafted logs for a fee per thousand feet.

Such was the stage set for A. P. Stockwell. When it seemed necessary to splash or "drive" logs out of the vast Humptulips basin, it would take a gambler instinct, venture, financial backing, and guts to pull if off. Al Stockwell seemed to be the man. He already had his initiation into the lumber business, and he would risk. So the Humptulips Boom and Driving Co. was formed.

But there were events and episodes before that, including William Donovan, who parlayed a Stockwell mill into one of the outstanding sawmilling realms of the Northwest.

However, events leading to Al Stockwell on Grays Harbor began more than a century before. Somewhere in England prior to 1770, a family of Stockwells bestirred themselves over the inequities of kings and landowners, and the scrabble of tilling, bundled their possessions and took ship to the New World. As farmers the family worked the virgin lands westward until almost a century later offspring were turning the ground of Michigan. Here Levi L. Stockwell and his wife took up a homestead, which they were farming, at Morenci, May 6, 1863, when a son, Almerion Page Stockwell, was born.

Wedded to the soil like his ancestors Al Stockwell did farmboy chores until he was husky enough to handle a peavey, then he deserted the family tradition and went into the woods and Michigan sawmills. There he learned the rudiments of the lumber business, and heard the tales of that fabulous timber country, Grays Harbor. At 27 years of age, and like so many other men of Michigan, he felt the pull of the western loadstone and hied to the West Coast in 1890. After seven years scuffing through fir chips and sawdust, Al Stockwell joined C. E. Burrows in organizing the C. E. Burrows Company, their first venture building a sawmill in South Aberdeen at the mouth of what was to be known as Donovan Slough. Burrows continued as president of the company until his death in 1907, when Stockwell succeeded to the presidency, then taking over the business of

Bryden & Leitch Lumber Company the same year. The initial mill was sold to the Donovan Lumber Company in 1910 to become known as the Donovan Mill No. 1.

Stockwell at the time would not have known he was doing Donovan any special favor by selling him the mill. But he did. In fact, he was to live to see Donovan pamper and fondle the plant as his most prized material possession until it went into idleness in 1932. Although Donovan, then president of the Donovan Lumber Company, was to acquire another sawmill downstream and call it Donovan No. 2, and gain an interest in the Donovan Steamship Company and the Catherine Donovan Steamship Company to operate the coasters *Catherine Donovan, Carlos* and *William Donovan,* his absorption was with Donovan No. 1.

The mill actually was his life aside from his family and his church. Every day, rain or shine, he donned a stiff-front white shirt with fancy studs, a stiffer upright collar, a bow tie that could upon occasion be a polka dot, a dark gray suit, and a light gray felt hat with a black band that sat purposely and squarely atop his head. A gold watch chain with its dangling crucifix invariably hung from the second buttonhole of his vest into a lower pocket on the port side. All this created a figure of absolved dignity, with just a slight touch of vanity, for he always topped his attire with a diamond stickpin. Besides he wore a whimsical smile, deep far-seeing eyes and a graciousness and compassion that marked him a man apart in the tough, rough-and-tumble business of lumber.

The stiff shirt and bow tie may have been slightly deceiving. When he first hit Grays Harbor William Donovan was 55 and beyond his physical fighting prime, but earlier in life he carried two hard, man-sized fists, something often handy among the Germans, Irish and Swedes of Wisconsin and Michigan timberlands. And it was said of him he had the heart and guts to go with the fists.

However, every day, including Sunday, William Donovan (no one conceivably would call him "Bill") was driven to his mill by Patrick O'Connor, who had been mill manager, companion and right arm for more than 30 years from Michigan to California and finally to Grays Harbor. Donovan never learned to drive an automobile, never cared to; he put all his trust in "Old Pat"

O'Conner. At the mill, Donovan, still in his dress-up attire delighted in lending a hand at lumber-cutting, clearing a jam at the resaw or straightening a tangle on the green chain. He loved the smell of lumber and the feel of it. He even liked the logs in the mill pond, but more than once they proved his undoing. He would often grab a pikepole to "help" the boomman, and as often would fall into the pond. He couldn't swim a stroke, so the boomman would fish him out and call someone to take William Donovan home for another outfit of stiff shirt and collar, bow tie and dark gray suit.

On Sundays, although the mill was idle, Donovan was driven to the mill barn to visit his horses and consult with Barnman Dave regarding them. Donovan loved horses. The mill owned a number to pull lumber trucks around the yard, but one pair of whites was Donovan's delight, they and a mare that had come with the Donovan household goods from Michigan via California. The mare had been pulling Donovan around in a rubber-tired buggy for 23 years when it was pensioned off. Donovan took to motorcars and the driving of "Old Pat" O'Connor and sometimes Pat's son, William O'Connor, who like his father, had been involved in Donovan mill operations from the Michigan days. Patrick O'Connor had another son, Frank, also in the Donovan entourage, who worked in the management end of the enterprises with William Donovan and Donovan's sons, William Jr. and Francis (Barney) Donovan. Barney Donovan had twin daughters, Jane and Nan, a constant puzzle to Grandpa Donovan. He could never tell them apart, so he called each one "Pet."

William Donovan's heritage of horny hands and early poverty working in the mills 12 hours a day for 50 cents was traceable to Clare, Ireland, and the appalling potato famine of the 1840s. His father, William Donovan, was born in Clare, as was his mother Catherine C. Lunch. The two were married in Clare in 1847, and after weathering the famine came to the New World in 1850, settling first near Buffalo, New York, then moving to Fond du Lac, Wisconsin, in 1853. Two years later William Joseph Donovan was born there and lived there until he was 11 years old when it is believed he went to Alpena, Michigan, and the big world of lumbering. He lived in Alpena until 1880 when he shifted to Muskegon and in two years began a lumber career of his own.

Burrows and Stockwell's readiness and willingness to sell the later-called Donovan No. 1, gave William Donovan a lasting home in a timber region so many other men from Michigan had learned to appreciate and acclaim. He was right in his element, and with a satisfaction that lasted until his final breath July 14, 1938.

As a Michigander himself, Stockwell was to appreciate Donovan's enthusiasm in the plant just sold, but in 1910 Stockwell as a born organizer and "plunger" was ready for other things. Back in 1897 not only did he engineer a sawmill with Burrows, but swung the company into purchase of the Grays Harbor Boom Company, which had been incorporated in 1893 with William Balch as president, W. L. Stiles, vice-president, and John Anderson, secretary. Stockwell afterwards became president of the boom company, which was sold in 1910 to the Warren Company, and in 1914 to H. P. Brown.

In 1896, a year before he joined with C. E. Burrows, Al Stockwell made another union that was to have a lasting effect upon his life. He married Carrie Jones, born August 13, 1875 in Montague, Michigan, daughter of Frank E. Jones. She had come to the Northwest with her father, who was to become bookkeeper for Al Stockwell and then Chehalis County Assessor. Carrie Jones was to graduate from the Terrace Heights school in Aberdeen and to work for Al Stockwell, an incident to their marriage.

In 1900 the Humptulips Driving Company was organized with Stockwell secretary-treasurer, a firm with wide ramifications in the Humptulips Valley. It operated a series of splash dams on both the west and east branches of the Humptulips, to sluice logs to tidewater as a common carrier, then a booming grounds on the lower Humptulips River to catch, sort and raft logs for delivery up-bay to the sawmills. It was natural that a towing service should be established, which was done in 1910 by the Warren Company with Al Stockwell as business manager. The firm towed out of the Humptulips with the sternwheeler *Skookum*, Captain "Skovi" Mersich, and the screw *Iloa*, skippered by Captain Richard "Dick" Ultican.

In August 1914 the Humptulips Logging Company was incorporated with H. P. Brown of San Francisco as president; W. B. Mack, vice-president; Clyde A. Pitchford, secretary-treasurer, and Al Stockwell, manager of the Aberdeen office and logging operations in township 21, range 9.

Stockwell liked to tell an anecdote regarding Cameron & Hoover when they teamed to log on the Humptulips. The two operated a primitive stage line carrying mostly settlers and loggers. There was a story that Cameron hired loggers on the Harbor, put them on the stage line for a fee, then Hoover on the other end would fire them and charge them a fare to get to town again. The line was known facetiously as "Cameron up, Hoover down."

Among the several ventures in Stockwell's life was that of the A. P. Stockwell Lumber Company operating at Copalis, getting out spruce for World War I aircraft. From a going business it collapsed into a total loss with the armistice, and in 1920-21 Stockwell's business world tumbled with foreclosures by W. J. "Billy" Patterson and the Hayes & Hayes bank.

Stockwell had been through a similar experience in 1909-10, about the time he was mayor of Aberdeen. He had already been a political figure back in 1899 when he was elected to the state legislature. However, the ever heads-up Al Stockwell had built a mansion in Aberdeen at the northeast corner of Broadway and Eighth Street, and was to come back with his Meadowbrook Farm out of Montesano and his Meadowbrook Dairy in Aberdeen. He became not only a dairy farmer and dairyman, but a horse fancier to the extent of a string of thoroughbreds, some of which placed first in their class at the Alaska-Yukon-Pacific Exposition held in Seattle in 1909.

Al Stockwell, rather than being called a "plunger" perhaps was more of an adventurer. He saw opportunities, he bet on them; some paid off, some didn't. But, what a life! His troubles were not all of his doing. National economic and financial difficulties engulfed him, yet he remained a stalwart and highly respected man in the Grays Harbor woods, and on the tides. He died April 25, 1942, in Aberdeen, some 12 years after Carrie Jones Stockwell.

THERE CAME A TIME when the rivers were no longer the solution to the problem of moving logs. In the first place they had too many problems themselves; river levels and freshets always were uncertain; there was too much log stranding; logs were "broomed," and rock-embedded; booming often was inadequate and, as sometimes charged, unfairly partial; there were lawsuits by riverside landowners; there were dam washouts, and continual arguments and conflicts over brands, grades, log towage and prices. In fact, the splash dam system for all its tremendous effort, was hardly adequate in its time, though a colorful era.

Then came the day when logging was too far from the streams. This was the time the logging railroad came into being and pushed cutting into the farthest reaches of the timberland.

As usual with revolutionary developments of this kind, the first were modest and almost unnoticed, for there was a reluctance to abandon the money and labor that went into the splash dams. Yet the first steam logging railroad was rumbling and screeching in the Grays Harbor woods in the '90s, while the logger and the valley rancher were still locking horns over the splash dam system. But the trend was showing. The splash dam was doomed.

The first railroad actually was a short line operated on Mox Chuck in 1890, with horses instead of a steam locomotive for power. W. D. Mack was to build the first steam line in 1891, announcing in March of that year that his crew of 30 men had completed grading and laying 36-pound steel on cedar ties on 1½ miles of right-of-way near Fords Prairie. He also announced a locomotive from Lima, Ohio, was on the site, with eight logging cars abuilding in Aberdeen.

To supply his new rail line with logs Mack used two teams of oxen (12 oxen, or six yoke each) and a crew of 45 men. The camp was near Sharon, the rail line terminating at a rollway, landing and rafting grounds (for round rafts) on the Chehalis at the Peter Wood's farm. In July 1891 Mack had between 45 and 55 men in his crew, with 28 oxen working. Also a span of horses was kept busy hauling freight, a large part of it being food for men and animals. Clem Brown was foreman for the camp.

The locomotive used by W. D. Mack, built by the Lima Locomotive Works, was described as a "side gearing engine," and was locomotive No. 338, sold to W. D. Mack of Hoquiam, Washington, February 20, 1891. It was a standard gauge with 7" by 12" engines, and 26-inch wheels. Mack eventually sold No. 338 to the S. E. Slade Lumber Company, Elma, for their logging railroad on Newman Creek east of Satsop. The Slade Company sold to Schafer Brothers Logging Company at Brady, Washington. Schafers sold to Linde Shingle Company, Carlisle, Washington, who sold No. 338 to Hofius Steel & Equipment Company, Seattle, and they in turn to the Armstrong Company of Portland, Oregon in February 1931.

Grays Harbor's 1,095 miles of logging railroads used several types of locomotives, both rod and geared. The geared locomotives such as the Shay, Climax, Heisler, Baldwin, Hinkley, and Willamette, were especially useful in steep country, spurs and winding roads, while the rod engines worked mostly the main lines. Rod engines familiar to the Grays Harbor woods were the American, McKay & Aldus, Porter, Baldwin, Willamette and Rogers. At first all were steam, while in later years diesel electrics became popular.

The geared Climax was the bane of the engine crew. Its cylinders were mounted at a 45-degree angle (fore and aft), which caused a jolting action at every thrust of the piston. When traveling fast the locomotive jarred the "bejasus" out of the fireman and engineer with its up and down motion. The engine however, was handy for slow hauls and for switching.

Baldwin had built a saddle-tank machine of 90 tons, which it sent to the Grays Harbor woods. It, too, was good for switching, but proved less than adequate on the long haul.

Chapter 9

BILLY WITH THE BIG FISTS

Any big timber logger will tell you, if you find him in a confiding mood and his tin pants ain't binding, that there are two ways to shake the earth. One way is to drop a Douglas fir upon it. The other is to stomp it aquiver with calk boots. He might even add a third way, for when "Fightin' Billy" McCabe from the Polson works hit town and fists began to thump the results were sometimes seismic.

"Fightin' Billy," (his name is legend on Grays Harbor) was a howling man in whoopin' country. He was fair to middlin' tall until he got a hump in his back packing pump jacks, bull yokes and coils of haulback wire.

In his prime he was about five-foot-nine, weighed 160 pounds in dry socks, and stood shoulder high to a barroom door which, he figured, just about doubled his life span. "It's better to test the temper of a brawl before butting in," was Billy's philosophy and standard procedure. But nevertheless Billy's nose had a so'west kink, and he was well welted above the belt line. And before he was siwashed by a haulback, which left him with a gimp in one leg, he was a fast-stepper in woods or water, or a barroom rumpus. His chaw, which he ruminated placidly even in the heat of battle, he carried habitually on his starb'rd side.

Billy wasn't much of a hand at antecedents, but he was a logger from 'way back. He was born in Brooklyn, New York, where, judging from his later life, he must have been a fistic terror. He was barely more than a weanling when he appeared in the woods of Michigan. From there he came west with the great migration of loggers and millmen. When they closed down the woods and sawmills in Saginaw, Billy lingered with the rest just long enough to load the bullchains. Then he hightailed it to the tall and uncut, west of the Cascades.

He clumped down the waterfront in Seattle and was mighty taken with the big log rafts, but even there the talk was of Grays Harbor. There was loggin' country! Godamighty man, you never saw such timber. It was a whoppin' . . . ten feet on the butt and 100 feet to the first limb. And so thick, the talk said, a man had to walk sideways between the trees and you couldn't see daylight. There was timber from here to hell 'n gone, maybe farther.

She was handsome country. The Almighty must have made it special, because he put so many rivers in it, all logging streams. Due east and west ran the Chehalis. From the north, all of them nurtured by Olympic snows and incredible rains, flowed five parallel tributaries: the Humptulips (called the "Hump"), the Hoquiam, Wishkah, Wynooche and the Satsop. They poured into tidewater through solid forests of the finest fir that ever grew. It cruised three- to four-million board feet to the forty, some stands 20 million to the quarter section and, Fightin' Billy recalled, 20 fights to the million.

Thus was the range readied for the rough and readies — the measureless Scandinavians, the Scots, the Irish, the Poles, the Germans and the Down Easters who had forsaken the timberlands beyond the Plains. All the hosts who stomped the hills and thudded the wooden streets of Plank Island (their name for Aberdeen). All those who could whack an undercut, pull a falling saw, notch a springboard, buck a windfall, set a choker, lay out a skidroad or punch a donkey. Individually each would prefer either black, gray or red two-piece wool underwear, buttoned east of the center line from neck to navel. He would wear stagged and frayed tin pants held belly high with broad galluses. His feet would be shod in Bergman calk boots with frilled false tongues, and oiled with bear grease or whale oil.

When Fightin' Billy McCabe hit the Grays Harbor country in the '90s, the lumber towns of Aberdeen and Hoquiam were spitting on their hands, preparing to outlog anything that had been logged before, to out-saw Saginaw, out-drink Deadwood, Dodge and Denver, out-whore the Barbary Coast, and make Grays Harbor a byword among the rough and tough of the globe.

In the years to come Fightin' Billy was to fit this place as naturally as his underpants. And because it seemed to fit his talents, Fightin' Billy became a bullwhacker. He was good at it. When he rolled his chaw, spat into the underbrush and whooped his bulls into their yokes, Billy could move Hell if it had one end loose. Reputedly he was of such powerful vocal apparatus every bull in the township would knuckle down spraddle-legged and pull when Billy let out a roar. But it made him mightily parched of gullet.

So twice a year, Christmas and the Fourth of July, when they shut down the woods for a spell, Fightin' Billy joined the poundings for town. His was the fraternity of rampallians who tramped down the skidroads, poured down the valleys and hit the planks with their double-ought calks scuffing. They were the giant-killers, skinning out a ripe and raging empire slick and clean. They brought a thousand arid craws and thirsts of all magnitudes for the quenching. And to the women of Hume Street six months of womanless loneliness, and magnificent postures for the ruttings.

What they found were lumber towns of false fronts and scattered dwellings on the banks of the Wishkah, Chehalis and Hoquiam rivers, as though skittish of the deep and dark timber beyond. They found sternwheelers like the *Clan McDonald, T. C. Reed, Harbor Belle, Harbor Queen, Cosmopolis, Montesano* and *Wishkah Chief* churning the rivers, fired with slabwood and gay with a hodgepodge of passengers from the outside world. At their rails were eager Easterners with bank drafts in their pockets, sleek-looking saloon keepers with big watch chains, loggers, millworkers, ranchers, homesteaders, straight gamblers and tinhorns, Siwashes, pimps, sea otter hunters, market shooters, surveyors, timber cruisers, claim locators, tax collectors, housewives, speculators, women of the night and, rarely, a preacher of the gospel.

Before the sternwheelers swung into berth there were indisputable signs of prosperity. Ships at the wharves or anchored in the stream were a sure sign the mills were gushing lumber, while the lumber business itself could be measured almost to a gnat's eye by the stack of empty oaken kegs in the alleys, the number of well-oiled double-swinging doors and the plentitude of women whose morals could have been taken up a dozen round turns and still be considered loose. They had deserted the Barbary Coast and other streets of iniquity for the lusty, well-heeled woodsmen but, keeping to the letter of an unwritten law, they never crossed north of Heron Street.

This was no hindrance to the town's busy dry goods and clothing merchants. They filled large suitcases with dresses a little more racy than those worn on the boreal side of Heron Street, a chemise or two and some flashy appurtenances to which a raring logger would not pay the slightest attention, and toured the "houses." Sales were brisk, and more than one genteel living room was furnished with funds from the skidroad's thighs.

The days dinned with saws, the saloons and dance halls bawled at night when the fiddles quarreled and the strumpets shrieked. Crowds of loggers and millworkers, laced with a generous sprinkling of seamen and fishermen, roared through the boozeries and bawdy houses, the seamen with unconscionable thirsts and ready fists, from the high deserts of the Pacific. The loggers — they were never called "lumberjacks" in this big timber country — came equally ready, hard and tough as spruce knots or timber-bound hemlock, long overdue and throbbing. They, too, came either to frolic or fight, whichever was the more appealing at the time.

And with them came "Fightin' Billy" McCabe who, like the rest, first fought to compose differences of opinion or to settle arguments. But the roustings were so much fun loggers looked forward to town and mixing with other loggers, mill hands, seamen and professional pugilists just for the hell of it. They came to bolt their booze, bewaggle the bawds and settle again who was the best man with the bare knuckles. It was good clean fun, like a tournament, with nothing so serious but what bandages, stitches, splints, casts and cedar coffins wouldn't mend.

The eliminations often began in general melees, as when the Palm dance hall opened, or in rivalry between logging camps, for nearly every camp had its champion. And these were not necessarily scheduled events. It could have been by chance meeting, an overheard boast, a challenge over several shots of straight whiskey, possibly two fingers with a sideboard, or maybe just some camp bully spoiling for a fight.

It was among these events and with this atmosphere that the Palm dance hall began its boisterous career. It stood on the south side and in the 300 block on Hume Street, afterwards changed to State Street in a belated effort to give it respectability, perched on cedar sills and blocks above the swamp. The brawlers, the roisterers, the skylarking hell-busters were ready. The first guests had hardly crossed the threshhold when one lowered the tail end of a 2 x 4 upon another's skull, parting his hair down to his ears. By the time the housewarming had reached the playful stage, two dozen had been picked up by the coat collar and seat of pants to be tossed heave-ho across the 10-foot plank sidewalk into the mud. Even before the whooping stage the bouncers already were spent and weary men. By midnight they were mere caricatures, and the stompers and whoopers turned upon each other. By foggy dawn the Palm was a shambles, its future assured beyond all doubt. A windrow of celebrants reposed along the walls in a multitude of postures, all besodden and in various conditions of batter.

It would be the rankest kind of omission not to mention the Palm had 40 girls, five bartenders and four bouncers; not bad for a backwoods village where Sam Benn's cows could be heard bawling from one end to the other. And it must be mentioned, too, the Palm was a refined place. No rough stuff. To enter, a logger first had to remove his calk shoes, for which he was supplied slippers. Those with feet too big for slippers danced and cavorted in their wool socks, which may or may not have had their six-month washing. Spiked boots played the devil with wooden floors and midriffs. In less elegant places the boorish, uncouth fellows jumped upon each other's kissers, making no distinction between floors and physiognomies.

In any event, the stage was set for "Fightin' Billy" McCabe. This was his time. The lesser were gone to lick their wounds, while the survivors were fit and eager. And along came Charlie "Peavey" Green, who was a professional wrestler. There were very few preliminaries, and the two got right down to the business of pummeling each other for an hour up and down a Hume Street alley, bare knuckles and no holds barred. When both were so fagged they could hardly lift their arms, they shook hands and, bleeding and staggering, stumbled into the back door of a saloon for a drink. Fightin' Billy could make it out the front door under his own power. "Peavey" Green faltered. Fightin' Billy straightened his shoulders and clumped down the street, still the fightingest man in these parts. "Peavey" Green always maintained he would have made it if he hadn't jammed his foot into a spittoon.

In this self-same alley Fightin' Billy came near his comeuppance one long-ago Fourth of July in an eruption that nearly matched Krakatoa. It was the time, but not necessarily the only time, Fightin' Billy got knocked off his feet and bounced on his backsides. The blow that felled him was delivered by "Roughpile" Larson, a hulking man from Minnesota, who started a haymaker away back around Kenosha and caught Fightin' Billy flush on the jaw.

Billy picked up a lot of slivers skidding on his hip pocket, but he boiled up from the planks the maddest man west of Chippewa Falls. What he did to "Roughpile" should be written only in medical journals. He belted "Roughpile" into F Street, north to Heron, west to Paradise Alley and into the Walker "Resort for Gentlemen." Then he got thirsty. And to show he didn't carry grudges, he propped the remnants of "Roughpile" against the bar, slammed down a gold piece, and the pair of them proceeded to get roary-eyed, arm-in-arm drunk.

Contributing to events such as these were eight saloons in 1895 when the town had a population of 2,000 souls in various stages of salvation. But the figure is inexplicable, for in 1891 there had been nine saloons when the population was 1,700. However, Aberdeen was not to falter in that respect again. In 1904 there were 24 bars, despite the disastrous fire of 1903 which wiped out the business district. In 1909 firewater in sousing quantities could be had in 37 oases. The number rose to an all-time high of 39 saloons in 1914.

Take the year 1907; that was the year Grays Harbor began to

open the throttle, and the year Fightin' Billy was drilled through the torso by a bullet fired by a Montesano nightwatchman. Billy had been in a brawl and knocked the town marshal senseless.

Fightin' Billy McCabe not only was a fighter of some distinction, and a character, but durable and something of a public menace as well. In his fighting prime, attempts were made by some of the "sports" in Aberdeen to put Billy in the prize ring, but the attempt came to naught when Billy nearly killed his first sparring partner.

And not only did Billy survive innumerable brawls and fistic entanglements, and the hazards of the canyons, but also the bullet as well.

It was a late May day in 1907, and this is the way the Montesano Vidette put it: "STOPPED BY BULLET" — "Billy McCabe shot by nightwatchman Hilderbrandt. Well known Harbor character brought down by bullet while attempting to escape.

"Billy McCabe, well known lower Harbor character, now lies in the county jail with a bullet clean through his body as a result of creating a disturbance on the city streets, resisting arrest, knocking Marshal Pickering insensible and attempting to escape from Nightwatchman Henry Hilderbrandt.

"McCabe came up from Aberdeen Monday and after getting pretty well boozed up began to create a disturbance in front of the Oklahoma Bar. Marshal Pickering ordered him to desist and when he became abusive called on several bystanders to assist him in arresting the big fellow. As all refused to help, the marshal made the attempt alone, but McCabe struck him a savage blow on the left jaw and knocked him senseless, and after the assault hid in the alley back of the B & B saloon.

"Marshal Pickering finally picked himself up and started off for a warrant and assistance to apprehend McCabe, who had come out of his hiding place and openly boasted nobody in Montesano could run him in.

"City Clerk McCillup hunted up the nightwatchman, Henry Hilderbrandt, and told him of the disturbance which had been created and the big guardian of the peace at once started for McCabe, who took to his heels, running down Main Street and out Wynooche towards the railroad with Hilderbrandt in pursuit.

"Finding his quarry was escaping, Hilderbrandt called upon him to halt and repeated the command but McCabe did not heed it and then the watchman drew his gun, took quick aim and fired. The bullet struck McCabe just above the short ribs on the left side and ploughed clean through his body, coming out in front just below the lobe of the left lung. The wounded man dropped instantly and was taken before Judge Pettijohn's court where he again made a desperate resistance to being handcuffed, overcoming several men who tried to hold him while the bracelets were being put on, until Hilderbrandt was obliged to club him into insensibility before he could be secured.

"McCabe was lodged in the county jail but refused to let physicians dress his wound. Tuesday he was glad enough to have it attended to and the doctors think he can be pulled through, although there is a strong probability of either internal hemorrhage or peritonitis setting in, and in that case his recovery would be doubtful.

"The consensus of opinion here is that officer Hilderbrandt was perfectly justifiable in shooting McCabe and that he was strictly within the limits of his duty, although there have been mutterings of censure heard over the drastic course which he pursued to secure his man. Those who know McCabe on the Harbor where the police of Aberdeen and Hoquiam have had constant trouble with him say he deserved all he got."

Fightin' Billy McCabe survived the bullet wound and a jail term, to live and log and buck timber the rest of his life. Howard Best, who used to work with Fightin' Billy in the Simpson works and traveled back and forth with him between Montesano and Grisdale, recalled Billy as a "rather quiet man, a good worker, tended his own knittin', and in his later years got religion." Best had Billy as a workman bucking wood in 1933 and found him a very agreeable man, although he knew he was a "rip-snorter" in his younger years. Billy lived on the west side of Montesano and died there in 1957.

The Montesano Vidette editor said in print McCabe was a "big fellow," but at least one man who knew Billy McCabe in the flesh said he was of medium height, weighed possibly 160-170 pounds, and was the best fighting machine in the woods or town he had ever seen.

As Fightin' Billy McCabe reached his prime and the pokes of the barons began to swell, the big road engines started to roar in the hills, and Aberdeen's grocery stores were open until 11 o'clock at night. And no one spoke lightly of "making the rounds" in Aberdeen. A full tour of the founts and palaces of joy would call for a superman. "Making the rounds" was merely a figure of speech. However, a man of considerable capacity and means had his choice of bars: the Cub, Grand, Klondike, Lion, Harbor, Board of Trade, Crescent, My House, Log Cabin, Lobby, Our House, Fairmont, Capital, Washington, Star, Fashion, Alaska, North Pole, Humboldt, Heffron, Pioneer, Mecca, Moonshine, Whale, Brook, Central, Royal, Mint, Loop, Combination, Walker and California.

There were of course livelier spots — dance halls and honky-tonks — where the spangles flashed and liquor and flesh went together in sort of a tie-in sale.

Saloons like other businesses flourished and faltered, though many did live out the years until "Prohibition" ended all. There were many other names on Aberdeen's long list of bars. The Bodega burned in the 1903 fire and was re-opened in a tent on the former location by W. J. "Billie" Crosbie, who boasted a curled mustache, a huge watch and charm, and who had a barrel set up in a new saloon building with the sign "Birds of a feather flock together — Bodega Saloon." Then there was the Continental, quiet and much frequented, the Gem dance hall, the Horseshoe, The Aberdeen, The Blue Front, John Kahles, Mose Haufman's, Pullman, Union, Twins (Vidler Brothers), Leaf and Jacobson's, Eagle dance hall run by Eddie Goldsmith, son of Mose Goldsmith, whose Anhaeuser, with its bar and stage for variety shows and tables on the floor, stood at the southwest corner of H and Hume streets.

Another entertainment feature of the day was the Edison theater, 67 Heron Street, which was to be changed to the "Grand" theater, a name later to be applied to an "opera" house built by Ed Benn, son of Aberdeen's founder, and his Grays Harbor Theater Company at the northeast corner of Market and F streets. Two other theaters, the Acme and Olympus, were popular entertainment spots for Aberdeen in their day. R. M.

Cooper of Seattle operated the Olympus. Al Firth, "the singing blacksmith," eventually became Olympus' manager.

And then, of course, there were the Bowes Brothers, prominent figures in young Aberdeen after the turn of the century. The Bowes & Thompson saloon was burned out in the "great fire." In the aftermath Sam Bowes began operating the Capital saloon, Jim Bowes the Fashion saloon. The third brother, Dan Bowes, went into real estate, a booming business. At one time, too, the Our House saloon was listed as operated by "Bowes Brothers."

Jim Bowes quit the saloon business and, with Shirley Randolph, a brother of Dr. Howard C. Randolph, formed an undertaking firm, successor to Undertaker Beardsley, a tall, dark, dignified man who collected bodies on a two-wheel cart with 20-inch rubber tire wheels. Skylarking loggers plagued Beardsley with false calls because Beardsley was accused of sizing up prospects, especially sallow loggers just out of the hospital, which made the loggers "madder 'n 'ell."

Dan Bowes had another claim to early Grays Harbor fame, and that was his inflictions upon the English language. For instance his wife had "social perspirations," or the woman fell "prostitute on the sidewalk," or monotony became "mon-o-tonious." His classic was the time in an Elks Club meeting when he objected to some chandeliers for the lodge hall, clinching his argument with, "besides nobody knows how to play them anyhow."

Sam Bowes eventually quit the saloon business and went into a real estate business with Phil Locke, while later all three Bowes brothers, Sam, Jim and Dan, joined in a real estate office of their own, with a branch office in Seattle where they handled timberlands for the Polson Company.

There were eight saloon licenses issued in Aberdeen in 1895, 12 in 1899, 24 in 1903-04, 30 in 1908 and 37 in 1909. Saloons issued licenses in 1910-11 were: The Cub, The Grand, The Klondike (Mackey & Kauppi), The Lion (J. B. Schier), The Harbor (Chas. Hayes), The Board of Trade (A. E. Anderson), The Crescent (F. C. Scklentz), My House, Our House, Lobby (Fred Hewett), Log Cabin (Selmer Jacobsen), Fairmont, Capital (John O'Hare), Washington, Star (Dolan & McGuire), Fashion

(Mayberry Brothers), California Wine House, Alaska, North Pole, Humboldt (Fred Hewett), Heffron, Pioneer, Mecca (J. S. Jones & P. M. Donaugh), Moonshine, Whale, Brook, Central, Royal, Mint (M. V. Snyder), Loop and Kaufman's Bar. The Owl was added in 1913. In 1914 there were 39 saloon licenses issues and 34 in 1915.

After the last entry December 16, 1915, whoever kept the license accounts wrote: "Last of the wets!"

During the rip-roaring days in that district of Aberdeen usually referred to as "down there," there was one fellow who could and did "make the rounds." He was Victor "Vic" Lindberg, then just old enough to be a paper boy, but to live to become Aberdeen's comptroller and expert on early Grays Harbor lore.

When 14 years of age Lindberg had an "end-of-the-bar" and "throw-it-upstairs" paper route in the roisterous region in Aberdeen. Once a day he frequented that region where doors swung both ways and virtue was not. But Lindberg had no complaints; when loggers had a few belts of firewater they were generous, and tips came frequently from the "second floors."

Early Aberdeen was strict about minors in saloons or houses of ill repute; consequently a young newsboy was limited in his wanderings in forbidden places. Most saloon proprietors had a small office just inside the front door. Lindberg was supposed to leave the Aberdeen Bulletin, forerunner of the Aberdeen World, there, or if there was no office, then on the end of the bar. And then he was to "scoot."

Most of the "houses" were second-floor affairs, usually gained by a narrow and steep stairway from the street. Lindberg had perfected his throwing arm by standing just inside the street entrance and the red light, and tossing the paper into the second-story hallway.

Life on the "skidroad" was often raucous, stormy and stomping, and Lindberg remembered pedestrian traffic was so heavy some nights it was hard to make headway on the wooden sidewalks. Lindberg recalled he was "booted" out of a saloon only once and that was when he stopped to watch a man play the "wheel," a 1908 version of the modern slot machine. Lindberg had barely paused when a big barkeeper with a luxurious mustache appeared and hustled the paperboy out by the seat of his pants.

Like most newsboys Lindberg was "all ears and eyeballs." He was familiar with the town drunks, the saloon swampers, furtive husbands who were where they should not have been, and other denizens incident to the life "below the line" of Heron Street.

After Lindberg shouldered his paper bag, his first stop was at the Kolts Furniture Store in the Masonic Building at Heron and I streets. The Bulletin press was in a room in the rear of the building. Then Lindberg swung eastward down Heron Street to the Golden West Hotel, the Kaufman furniture store, Crammatte's flower and candy store, Marshes' millinery store, Wolff's drygoods store on the corner with the big wolf sign overhead, and the bona fide Hotel Gordon on the second floor.

Then the young news merchant stopped at the Baker Hardware store, Merchants Cafe, Kaufman drygoods store on the southeast corner of Heron and H, then Gabrielson & Homer grocers, I. S. Shey's men's furnishings, and then the first saloon on his route, the Lion, a fancy place with stained glass, ornate backbar and a huge chandelier hanging from the ceiling. Then the D. J. Heffron saloon from which Lindberg was booted, on to the Mecca Cafe, Grays Harbor Hardware, Log Cabin saloon, Fan cigar store, E. Pfund, jeweler, Porter company (men's clothing), Dr. M. I. Pearson (over Porter's), Pennant cigar store, Curtis block (upstairs), and Aberdeen State Bank at the corner of Heron and H.

Then came the Dabney block and Cyr's clothing store, Acme Cafe operated by Captain Thompson, Model Tea & Coffee store, Herricks jeweler, Dan Bowes real estate, John Hanson tailor, Paines book store, L. L. Maley, maker of the famous "Think-of-Me" cigar. Next was the Faulkner real estate office, White House clothing, at G and Heron, the Hub clothing, with Hotel Arlington on the second floor (legitimate), Evans drugstore, Grays Harbor Liquor company, Olympia Oyster & Chop House, Aberdeen Loan office, Brook saloon, Haufman's saloon, on south side of Heron between G and F, then the Boston Oyster House, Fashion saloon (with Fashion "rooms" above), Palace Restaurant, O. K. Baths, Our House saloon, Bailey's cigar store, Bealey's Turkish Bath, Vienna Restaurant, Mont saloon, Butte

Barber Shop, Butte Cafe, Mack's cigar store, the William Doddridge Barber Shop.

Then Lindberg swung across the street to the Pioneer bar at the southeast corner of F and Heron. Next door was the Grand saloon with the office of the Sailor's Union upstairs, haunt of the notorious Billy Gohl, sailors' agent, who had a home at Sixth and Broadway. Next was Dell Doddridge's barber shop and the Colorado "rooms" where Lindberg was supposed to ring a bell when he delivered the paper. At 308 South F was a shooting gallery, then the Lunch Center (310 South F), the Twins saloon, the Humboldt saloon with its amazing collection of curios gathered by "Big Fred" Hewett. Over the saloon was the Humboldt "rooms." Sam's Oyster & Clam lunch counter was on the river side of F Street, and in turn the Union saloon and the Harbor saloon. Houtari & Company was on the corner of Hume, and the Grays Harbor Logging Company nearby, then the Callison Transfer and Cook's ice plant. On the lower end of F Street was the C. E. Burrows Company and its wharf. The company not long before had launched the steamer *Jesse Burrows*, christened by Miss May Jones as whistles blew, crowds cheered and flags whipped in the breeze. The steamer was built by Captain T. C. Reed. C. E. Burrows also boasted the position of secretary and the manager of the Grays Harbor Gas Company.

On lively River Street off F Street stood a two-story brick building called, for obvious reasons, the Merry Widow, then the Diamond Front, operated for the same purpose by one of Aberdeen's better-known characters, Lil White. Not far away was the Combination, a dance hall and crib house, and at 408 South G Street was a colony of Japanese girls. In turn were the saloons Homestead, Three Deuces and the Brook. On the corner was the famed Palm, with "rooms" upstairs, operated by Billy McDonald.

When death finally overtook Billy McDonald, the habitues of the "lower section" put on for his funeral the biggest celebration young Aberdeen had yet seen. They had a parade with two marching bands, while a ragged column of the sober and besotted, the "girls," bar keeps and some of the more ribald young blades, staggered, skipped and cavorted after Billie's hearse to the banks of the Wishkah. Then they put Billy McDonald's coffin into a rowboat, which led a flotilla of "mourners" to Fern Hill, where he was duly interred with pioneer solemnity.

Three saloons stood wall-to-wall on G Street between Hume and Heron, the Corner, Whale and My House, then came the Pullman Cafe and Bonita saloon. The Office saloon was on the west side of G, next to the shooting gallery. Then came three more saloons, the Cub, White Eagle and Klondike. Next to the Klondike was the Peerless, a "house," then the Atlantic, a workingman's hotel. Not too far away was the Aberdeen Steam Laundry, while the Kendall Hotel was at Hume and I streets.

By the time Vic Lindberg got that far he was tired; he could boast facetiously he had visited more saloons than any other man in Aberdeen, but he did his drinking at the old iron fountain that stood on the sidewalk in front of the Wolff store.

The real bonanza days of Lindberg's paper-carrying career were during the trial of Billy Gohl for murder. The Aberdeen Bulletin, other than word of mouth, was Aberdeen's only source of information concerning the trial, and it sold even better than the proverbial hotcakes. Loggers and seamen offered 50 cents (even a dollar) a copy, while the "saloon trade" almost mobbed him.[26]

The extent of some of these goings-on is chronicled in Aberdeen's "Prison Records—1907" under the heading of "House of Ill Fame." On June 28 of that year more than 100 women from the south side of Heron street appeared at the police station to pay $10 fines for being inmates of the houses. In August another hundred put down similar fines, while the keepers and procurers were assessed $25. Thus the city licensed them without avowing them.

The "Prison Record" for June 28 also shows a "muster" of 17 madams or keepers of houses of ill fame: Ruby Scott, Jessie Allen, Mabel Johnson (black), May and Jennie Treda (Japanese), Mabel Montell, June Eavens, Freda Davis, Lillian Marshall, May Loper, Iras Shew, May Woods, Maggie Murphy, Yama Naka and Jessie Taka (Japanese). The Japanese operated houses on River Street, which at the time was prominent in the "district" and contained at least one "international" house, meaning it had women of many races.

One of the better known madams, perhaps the best known,

did a land-office business, but she had her troubles, too. She had the skidroad rollicking with the story of a big, handsome customer who gave her a check for services rendered by the house, with champagne no less. When she went to the bank and Jim Fuller, the man behind the wicket, told her the writer had no funds, she hit the ceiling. She fumed: "And the son-of-a-bitch stayed for breakfast."

Chapter 10

THEY GOT ORGANIZED

It is little wonder the logger, along with his contumacious cousin, the town-working shingleweaver, was heard to screech protest and listen to union organizers and agitators. As early as May, 1898, shingle mill workers on the Harbor went on strike for more pay. And in July of that year employees of Wilson Brothers plant in Aberdeen struck for $1.75 a day. They had been getting $1.50.

For the next 14 years labor relations on the Harbor were quiescent if not agreeable; then came the Industrial Workers of the World, the "Wobblies" as they were commonly called. The organization, founded in 1905, purportedly as an industrial labor union, was, much to its denunciation and failure a quasi-parasitic political catch, using labor as an instrument in its self-proclaimed "class war." The I. W. W. flooded logging camps and mills with inflammatory literature, some of it directed toward organizing labor, particularly in the woods. Much more was directed toward revolution and anarchy and the "war between the working class and the employing class." "The existing parliamentary government will crumble into uselessness," predicted the Industrial Commission of the I. W. W.

Had the I. W. W. stuck to labor organization instead of politics, it no doubt could have become an insuperable power in the industry. However, the Wobblies chose to teach sedition and sabotage when the United States was locked in the First World War, when the nation was in a frenzy of patriotism and war support. The I. W. W. chose that time bitterly to oppose the war as a promotion of the "money mongers" and "exploiters of the laboring class." This more than anything else strengthened the hand of the timber industrialist in opposing the I. W. W. in the woods and mills and to induce the people of the Northwest to side with the lumber interests.

Yet the I. W. W. organizers and agitators made some remarkable gains for the loggers and sawmill labor. Perhaps the greatest change was the eight-hour day which came about by an I. W. W. tieup of the timber industry. Camp conditions were improved, and more moderate labor organizations took hold in the industry.

It was almost inevitable the first skirmish should be on Grays Harbor. The I. W. W. had "free speech" troubles in Spokane in 1909-10, but that was not considered significant. Aberdeen was "the very heart of the lumber trust's domain" so it was here the I. W. W. decided to test its muscle.

Robert L. Tyler in his "Rebels of the Woods: The I. W. W. in the Pacific Northwest" says:

"The I. W. W. fought a less spectacular free-speech fight in Aberdeen, Washington, two years later. (After Spokane). The conflict began in the same pattern as the Spokane conflict with the local business community banding together against the I. W. W. invasion. In Aberdeen, however, the city authorities and the business leaders — sometimes the same persons — prevented the Wobbly victory by responding to the invasion with more efficient tactics of their own. They deported the Wobblies rather than jailing them, thus sparing themselves the expense and trouble of boarding dozens of disagreeable prisoners."

As in Spokane, the Aberdeen disorders grew out of an I. W. W. demand for "free speech," which meant a demand to use the public streets for exhortation of a political philosophy and class war. The city council, learning of the Spokane "invasion" and fearing the same, passed an ordinance prohibiting speechmaking on downtown streets. The I. W. W. immediately passed the word to its other branches in the Northwest to prepare for a descent upon Grays Harbor in force to "persuade" the city to rescind its street-speaking law. Police Chief Templeman purportedly "learned" a large number of Wobblies had been summoned from California.

Meanwhile police arrested five I. W. W. members, J. Johnson, Ed. Marshall, Aloyz Tierog, J. M. Train and W. R. Thorn, for disturbing the peace by attempting to make speeches on downtown streets. The arrests incited a riot by I. W. W. members and sympathizers but was put down by police deputies.

After the riot in the jail the Wobblies attempted to hold a mass meeting in the Empire Theater — on the lower H street — but police-deputized citizens suppressed the meeting by roping off the street between Heron and Hume streets and arresting all who attempted to enter. "W. J. Patterson, president of Hayes & Hayes bank, and Dudley G. Allen, secretary of the Chamber of Commerce, cooperated in making the first arrests," said the Aberdeen Daily World of Novermber 24, 1911.

After the attempted Empire Theater assembly was suppressed, the deputized citizens stormed into the I. W. W. headquarters over the W. M. Mack cigar store at 406 East Heron Street. The place was empty.

Following these events and with an "invasion" imminent, the Aberdeen Chamber of Commerce in a special meeting in the Washington Hotel pledged support to city officials and called for a mass meeting of citizens in the Elks Building. The mass meeting produced 500 volunteers immediately deputized as special police.

Adopted at the mass meeting was a program for "preservation of law and order":

"All roads leading into the city will be patrolled tonight and as long as necessary hereafter.

"Saloons will be ordered closed, under instructions from Mayor Parks, at 6 o'clock tonight.

"Whenever a group of men assembles in large numbers it will be considered a mob and it will be dispersed.

"All suspicious characters will be placed under arrest.

"Five hundred special policemen volunteers from among the business men and others of the city will be sworn in at once to aid the police and city administration.

"A committee of 25 has been named to act with the police and mayor and to have general charge of the arrangements made for resisting the invasion of the workers and maintaining peace.

"All special policemen will report at 6:30 o'clock at police headquarters."

It was determined by the police and the "500" that the Wobblies would not be jailed nor would they be furnished food, but would be held until a "car load" or a "trainload" had been assembled for shipment out of Aberdeen.

In a meeting held in the council chambers in the Aberdeen City Hall, several means of deportation were discussed and "all were rejected for the simple expedient of escorting the men to the city limits under guard of the citizen police and then told to 'beat it.' This was finally done about midnight."

As a result of the determination 25 Wobblies were escorted, each between two citizen police, to the east city limits of Aberdeen, given two loaves of bread, and told to "keep going." None returned.

The news columns of November 25, 1911, summed the situation in Aberdeen: "Industrial Workers of the World created no riot in Aberdeen last night in their endeavors to force the repeal of the city ordinance prohibiting street speaking except within certain limits. They will create no riot tonight, nor tomorrow night, nor the next; in fact, business men and good citizens generally are determined that there shall be no more riots, that the city shall not be overrun by the riffraff of the Coast and that the laws shall be obeyed. For that purpose the 500 special policemen, recruited from the ranks of business and professional men, workers and from all walks of life and armed with unromantic, but business-like hickory wagon spokes and ax handles, of which a supply was laid in during the day, who last night patrolled the streets and alleys of the city and guarded the roads in and out of town, will be on duty again tonight and tomorrow night and so long as their services shall be needed. They signed up for the campaign at a meeting held at the city hall at 11 o'clock last night, at which it was decided to escort those arrested in the night's raid to the eastern boundary of the city, and to make another raid tonight against the wearers of the red tag, and to continue the process as long as need may exist."

Meanwhile 28 Industrial Workers of the World members were taken from trains in Montesano and turned back. They had arrived from British Columbia and points in Western Washington to demonstrate for "free speech" in Aberdeen. All freight trains into Grays Harbor were equally checked for any men riding brakebeams. All thus found were promptly arrested.

While peace officers and vigilantes were proclaiming the attempted general strike on Grays Harbor defeated, there were still a number of lumber mills idle, with the I. W. W. "laying low" to regroup. The Anderson & Middleton and Grays Harbor Commercial Company plants were still operating, with Aberdeen Lumber & Shingle Company plant threatened by 300 pickets. The S. E. Slade, Hulbert, Wilson, Donovan, General Package, American and Western plants were idle.

Emphasis in the Industrial Workers of the World determination to provoke a general strike on Grays Harbor shifted during the winter from Aberdeen to Hoquiam. On March 14, 1912 some 200 I. W. W. and sympathizers swarmed over the North Western lumber yard in Hoquiam, persuading enough workers to strike to close the plant. Once the North Western plant was idled the pickets marched to the Hoquiam Lumber & Shingle Company plant, swarmed over a 12-foot picket fence, and halted all mill operations.

Trouble at the North Western plant reportedly started when W. R. Thorn, a Wobbly leader, interfered with orders given a boy by Mill Foreman M. C. Quinn. In the dispute Thorn allegedly struck Quinn, who subsequently got a warrant for Thorn's arrest. Thorn left the mill at the time to return with reinforcements to block the plant. The demonstrations in Hoquiam drew Dr. Herman Titus, described by some as an I. W. W. sympathizer and founder of the Seattle Open Forum, and by others as a "fanatic reformer thrown out of the Socialist Party." In Hoquiam he promoted a mass meeting for strikers, a typical Wobbly revival with inflammatory speeches and parodies of popular hymns, which caused many to join the I. W. W. organization, but to no avail. The Hoquiam "disturbance" was almost over.

By March 20, after the November shutdown and restart of seven Harbor mills, there were only four plants idle, the

Hoquiam Lumber & Shingle Company and the North Western Company mills in Hoquiam, and the American mill and S. E. Slade plant in Aberdeen.

By this time it was apparent the I. W. W. were using the abortive strike in Hoquiam to establish themselves again in Aberdeen, from where most of the ringleaders had been "deported." They began to drift into Aberdeen in pairs or very small groups in an attempt to escape notice. The town's vigilantes however, were quick to discover and quick to act. But first the Wobblies and sympathizers staged one final riot, this in front of the Anderson & Middleton mill, where a number of pickets attempted to invade the fireroom and blow the mill whistle. Free-swinging night sticks and hickory wagon spokes subdued the riot, while longshoremen loading a vessel at the A & M plant beat off a squad of pickets with cargo hooks.

That night G. A. Biscay and W. R. Thorn, the principal I. W. W. organizers and agitators on Grays Harbor, packed their bags in preparation to leaving the Harbor. A group of masked citizens captured them at the hotel and led them, struggling and yelling, with resounding whacks from the cudgels, to a waiting automobile. More than a hundred spectators watched the reluctant parade, but made no effort to interfere. At the city limits Biscay and Thorn were severely beaten and sent on their way. Peace officers made no attempt to arrest or prosecute the kidnappers even though many working men in the community demanded investigation and action.

The case of a larger-volume deportation in Hoquiam but a short time before had been thwarted by the Chehalis County sheriff, Ed Payette, who learned 150 Industrial Workers of the World and "strikers" had been herded into box cars for transportation out of the county. Sheriff Payette put a stop to the proceedings, but not without vigorous protests from Hoquiam's vigilantes.

As in all confrontations of this kind, there were two sides. The I. W. W., through Ralph Chaplin, who wrote of "The Centralia Conspiracy" in 1924, proposed that the Grays Harbor "affair" was "a strike that started in the mills over demands for a $2.50 daily wage." Chaplin continued, "Some of the sawmill workers were members of the Industrial Workers of the World. They were supported by the union loggers of Western Washington. The struggle was bitterly contested and lasted for several weeks. The lumber trust bared its fangs and struck viciously at the workers in a manner that has since characterized its tactics in all labor disputes.... The jails of Aberdeen and adjoining towns were filled with strikers. Picket lines were broken up and the pickets arrested. When the wives of the strikers with babies in their arms, took the places of their imprisoned husbands, the fire hose was turned on them with great force, in many instances knocking them to the ground. Loggers and sawmill men alike were unmercifully beaten. Many were slugged by mobs with pick handles, taken to the outskirts of the city in automobiles and told their return would be the occasion for a lynching.... This event may be considered the beginning of the labor movement on Grays Harbor that the lumber trust sought finally to crush with mob violence on a certain memorable day in Centralia seven years later."

Events leading to the Centralia Armistice Day Tragedy of November 11, 1919, began almost wholly in Chehalis (Grays Harbor) County, a summer-long strike by the International Shingleweavers Union, joined by the Timberworkers Union and eventually taken over and aborted by the Industrial Workers of the World.

By July 16, 1917 all shingle mills on the Harbor had been closed by the Shingleweavers, while the Wobblies "affiliating" themselves with the Shingleweavers had closed virtually every logging camp in the county. Nine sawmills, including the bucket-making General Package plant in South Aberdeen, were idle; Donovans, Aberdeen Lumber & Shingle, Wilsons, American, A. J. West, Grays Harbor Lumber, North Western and the Carlisle mill at Carlisle.

On July 17, thirteen mills were closed and only two logging companies were operating. Rowland Brothers, with a small camp of 25 men on North River, signed an agreement with the Timberworkers Union. The I. W. W. tried unsuccessfully to keep the crew from returning to work.

At the Wilson Brothers camp at Independence, Manager Dan McGillicuddy engaged in a fist fight with a picket who called him a "scab." McGillicuddy is reported to have won a "decision."

Many I. W. W. camps or "jungles" were set up around the county especially near major logging operations, notably near the Saginaw works at Saginaw, a flag stop and siding on the Chicago, Milwaukee Railroad & Navigation line near the mouth of Delezene Creek, and at the Lester camps east of Montesano.

July 18, 1917 was eventful in that it was the day Secretary of War Newton D. Baker told Governor Ernest Lister of Washington he could use federal troops to subdue strikers interfering with lumber production for the army. There was also the matter of three ships being built on the Harbor for federal account and nine others for private interests, demanding 20 million feet of prime fir.

Governor Lister was not long in exercising his privilege to use U. S. troops. He made the call July 19, 1917 for a detachment to "prevent trouble." Also eighteen Coast Artillerymen were sent to remove arms and ammunition confiscated from the schooner *Annie Larsen* and transport them to American Lake.

The machine gun company, armed with machine guns and rifles, arrived July 20 under command of 1st Lieut. F. U. McCaskrie, to take up headquarters in the Aberdeen armory. The troops were not immediately deployed.

Five men were arrested in a "jungle" near the Lester operations east of Montesano for illegal picketing. The men, B. B. Dupree, R. W. Bicknell, F. R. Harte, R. C. Quint and H. Helms, were picked out by Attorney W. H. Abel, who had obtained an injunction against picketing the Lester works. He had previously seen the men on a picket line after the injunction was issued.

As deputy sheriffs attempted to put the five men into a large truck a crowd of other men in the camp jumped into the truck with the arrested men, saying they were equally guilty.

The next day July 25, 1917, 100 mill owners, loggers and business men met in Montesano to demand the arrest of all pickets obstructing opening of the plants and camps.

On July 28, Grays Harbor Ship Carpenters Union voted not to handle lumber from non-union mills. The Shipyard Laborers Union soon followed with a similar vote, while the Aberdeen Central Labor Council tailed on the Hoquiam Trades and Labor Council, endorsing the International Timberworkers Union and Shingleweavers Union strike.

By August 16, conditions at the entrances to the mills had definitely worsened. On that day the first weapon other than clubs appeared. It was a knife drawn by an Anderson & Middleton teamster, but taken away by Police Captain Joe Searles. That day, too, picketing increased everywhere, even at an employment agency in the City Retail Lumber building across the street from the Aberdeen city hall. Jeers, hoots and clapping became louder and more prolonged. Sabotage was discovered at several mills. The Hoquiam Sash & Door plant at Montesano reported new railroad spikes driven into logs. The spikes were discovered before they hit the bandsaw. Some mills were not that alert and suffered heavy damage.

August 16 was also the day Walter L. Brackenreed of the Aberdeen Labor Council, F. M. McCarthy, business agent for the Ship Carpenters, G. F. Wellman representing the Shipyard Workers and W. H. Stockhouse of the Timberworkers Union went on a tour of all shipyards in the Northwest in an attempt to get others to join the sympathetic strike on Grays Harbor.

The following day Aberdeen police and city officials warned that "trouble was coming" if derisive I. W. W. picketing continued like that at the Wilson and Anderson & Middleton plants. Pickets were reported also going to workmen's homes to alarm wives, and following workers on the street, jeering at them.

On August 20, 1917 the I. W. W. called a general strike for the Northwest, but with little effect on Grays Harbor which was already largely idled by strike.

But then things began to unravel for the Wobblies. Four shipyards of Aberdeen and Hoquiam began operations after five weeks of sympathetic strike. Then two squads of U.S. troops with loaded rifles moved to the Wilson mill, keeping pickets back and moving. The Aberdeen I. W. W. immediately sent an urgent message to Seattle for several hundred Wobblies to back up the local I. W. W. but the help never came.

By August 29, picketing had all but halted on Grays Harbor, and one mill after another resumed operations. By September 10, there was general resumption of operations in Harbor logging camps. A few days later, with its general strike a failure, many of its leaders in jail or prison, and with the once full-blown lumber strike in stalemate, the Industrial Workers of the World called off the strike in the timber industry. The strike was not ended, merely "called off" because strikers, especially family men, "had reached their limit of sacrifice."

The causes of discontent still remained. The 10-hour day was still in effect, wages were low and camp conditions were as deplorable as ever. The call-off of strikes was not to mean operations in the woods and mills would now progress without disruption. Far from it. The strike was now to be taken to the job in a change of tactics. In subsequent issues of the I. W. W. publication, The Industrial Worker, the men were instructed to snipe at the employers by slowdown and sabotage. Old hands in the woods suddenly became inexperienced "farmers" giving foremen fits by following instructions to ludicrous extremes, or merely standing idle awaiting the next instruction for each minor decision, like hooking a choker to the butt rigging, or closing the firebox door.

A particularly exasperating tactic employed by the I. W. W. was to act as though the eight-hour day had already been granted. Workers would walk off after eight hours on the job, or would do "eight hours work" while 10 hours on the job through the expediency of slowdown, waste of material, misuse of tools and machinery and general "louse up" of routine. The Wobblies claimed several advantages to this strike-on-the-job routine. Authorities no longer could arrest pickets, for pickets were working, so to speak. There no longer was need to deal with "scabs" for even the workers were working, and the I. W. W. profited by the money its members earned. And the I. W. W. could attack the "master class" with impunity and watch it rage.

However, the new tactics of crippling lumber production did not cover up the fact the Industrial Workers of the World had lost the leadership in the industry, leaving a leaderless campaign of guerrilla maneuvers. The determination of the Wobblies to continue the fight for the eight-hour day with a leaderless campaign led to virtual chaos in lumber production. At this stage, and to keep the mills and camps producing, the U.S. government set up various avenues of mediation, but all failed largely because there was no representative labor union to speak for the workers, and because of the stubborn open shop stand of the employers. Unable to find a formula to end strife and stimulate lumber production, the government soon found itself creating a labor organization of its own.

Late in 1917, Colonel Brice P. Disque strode upon the scene. He came to the Northwest primarily to investigate why the Division of Military Aeronautics of the War Department was not getting the spruce it needed for airplanes. Disque had been a professional officer in the army who resigned to take a job as a prison warden in Michigan, then rejoined the army expecting to be sent to France. Secretary of War Baker had different ideas; he assigned Colonel Disque to the spruce-production program and sent him to the Northwest.

At the height of the camp and mill strike in 1917, spruce shipments had attained only 2.6 million of the required 10 million board feet, with a large part of the spruce already shipped found to be unusable. Disque noted many mill operators did not even know the government specifications. He also noted the confused labor situation and general discontent in the lumber industry. Then he began to develop plans of his own. First he would organize a special division of troops to work the logging camps along with the regular loggers. Then he would go through the industry getting workers to pledge loyalty to the United States and faithfully to perform their duties in producing lumber to be used against the "common enemies" in the war.

The outcome was the Loyal Legion of Loggers and Lumbermen, the "Four L," the first local of which was established in Wheeler, Oregon, November 30, 1917. Then the War Department allocated 100 officers to Disque to tour mills and camps in Oregon and Washington administering loyalty pledges to workers and employers alike. They pledged:

"I, the undersigned, in consideration of my being a member of the Loyal Legion of Loggers and Lumbermen, do hereby solemnly pledge my efforts during the war to the United States of America, and will support and defend this country against enemies, both foreign and domestic.

"I further swear, by these presents, to faithfully perform my duty toward this company by directing my best efforts, in every way possible, to the production of logs and lumber for the construction of Army airplanes and ships to be used against our common enemies. That I will stamp out sedition or acts of hostility against the United States Government which may come within my knowledge, and I will do every act and thing which will in general aid in carrying this war to a successful conclusion."

While the hundred officer-organizer-pledgers were coursing through the industry, camps and mills, Disque's request for a Spruce Production Division was supplied. These soldiers, eventually to be 25,000, worked where needed in logging camps and mills, were given civilian pay but lived under military discipline.

Colonel Disque at first viewed the Four L merely as an adjunct to the Spruce Division, a device to increase production in the lumber industry. The locals had little to do but reach production quotas and display patriotism. Later they formed grievance committees to handle problems with plant management. Then the locals began electing delegates to district councils, and eventually to a headquarters council where Disque himself presided. In short order the Four L was acting like a union and doing the work of a union. It was enrolling members by the thousand and completely drowning out the I. W. W.

By February, 1918, Colonel Disque felt his Four L organization strong enough to undertake discussion of the eight-hour day, a move advocated not only by labor unions and the I. W. W. but by the governors of Washington and Oregon and by the War Department itself. In fact Disque returned to Washington, D. C. early in 1918 to urge the War Department to designate the Spruce Division as the government's main contractor for lumber, thereby being able to make the eight-hour day a prime requisite for supplying the lumber. This device, however, was found unnecessary. When Disque returned to the Northwest he went into a lengthy conference with a group of 25 lumbermen who, weary of the prolonged confab, told Disque to settle the eight-hour day matter as he wished. He immediately announced the eight-hour day would begin March 1, 1918, throughout the lumber industry.

Created as a wartime indispensable during the troubled days of 1918, the Loyal Legion gained a pledged membership of 100,000 workers, but after 1919 declined rapidly. A decade later it could count only a few thousand members, an organization virtually in name only. Then came the New Deal of President Franklin D. Roosevelt to deal the Four L the coup de grace in the

National Industrial Recovery Act (NRA) of 1933 and the Wagner Act of 1935. Although the Four L changed its name to the Employees Industrial Union to meet the competition of the American Federation on Labor and the newly-organized Congress of Industrial Organizations, which, through its subsidiaries, within a short time took over organization of the labor movement in the timber industry. The Employees Industrial Union, like the Wobblies, faded from the scene.

Chapter 11

WHEN NATURE TURNED MEAN

The conflagration characterized as the "famous fire of 1902" was not limited to the sweep from the Decker settlement to Grays Harbor's North Bay region. It was catastrophic, involving virtually every region in Washington and Oregon from the Cascades to the sea. Fires were burning almost "everywhere." The sky was so overcast with smoke there was actually no daylight. On Grays Harbor the day was almost pitch dark at noon. Households lit lamps, pedestrians carried lanterns. Chickens went to roost at midday.

Fire crept to the outskirts of Elma and Montesano. Sweeping from Summit to Satsop, it cut a swath 13 miles long and from one to two miles wide, leaving a strip of charred and burning ruins. A dam on the west branch of the Hoquiam burned and the New London community was destroyed. Travel on the Wishkah road was impossible. The White Star mill and a million feet of lumber were turned into smoke. Telephone and telegraph lines to Puget Sound were cut by burning and falling timber. East of Elma, Ray's mill was burned and Jack O'Donnell's shingle mill went up in flames.

In Aberdeen and Hoquiam there was near panic as the dark descended. People gathered in the streets, questioning. The air was stifling.

There was no sun. The wind was easterly, blowing smoke from inland fires into the Grays Harbor basin. As night came, so did the fog, which pressed the smoke upon the ground. Fortunately, the next day the wind shifted to westerly, clearing the air with a sea breeze. The danger was over, but the damage remained.[27]

The conflagration creating Grays Harbor's "Dark Day" of September 12, 1902, and giving Polson Brothers a boost to logging greatness, was hardly more than campfires compared to the great fire that swept from the Columbia River to Ozette some time before Columbus sailed the Atlantic. Evidence of that tremendous sweep of flames is best seen in the Copalis Crossing area of the Grays Harbor Country. Here giant cedars fire-killed and long dead, stand like ghostly sentinels in the immense sweep of new forest grown since the fire. That these cedars were all killed at the same time is evident by the growth rings of surrounding green trees.

All similar cedars from south of Willapa Harbor to near Lake Ozette, with several good examples standing just south of the highway entering Ocosta from the east, bear evidence of their death. Most of them are fire-charred. In the Quinault area a 500-year-old cedar was found growing out of a downed cedar whose growth rings set its age at 1,500 years, the two totaling 2,000 years, the same age as some California redwoods.

The fire, if it was but one fire, followed the coast, staying in the low country that produced the cedars. There is no evidence of the fire east of the Humptulips River, perhaps because there were no large, rot-resisting cedars to preserve the evidence. How the fire jumped both Willapa Harbor and Grays Harbor, if it did, is a mystery, although the fire could have burned inland and easily spanned the Willapa and Chehalis rivers. However, there may have been a whole series of fires at the same time, started either by lightning in some unusually dry season, or set by Indians, who were often careless with their campfires, or set fires to create open spaces, or to drive game.

Nevertheless, there is evidence of fire occurring within a span of 10 years for something like 120 miles bordering the Washington coast. If the fire was in one sweep, besides the two harbors it crossed the Humptulips, the Copalis, Moclips, Quinault, Raft, Queets, Clearwater, Hoh, Quillayute rivers, and swung around Lake Ozette and died out before it reached the Sooes.

One result of the fire was that the higher ground came back mostly to fir, which needs open country and sunlight to seed and flourish. The lower country grew heavily to hemlock, with moderate populations of cedar and spruce.

There is evidence of other large forest fires, particularly one that burned the entire North River watershed sometime early in the nineteenth century. The time can be estimated by the age of standing or recently logged timber. Loggers in a five-acre tract found a 100-year-old fir, a 115-year-old fir, a 125-year-old fir a 120-year-old spruce, a 200-year-old cedar and a 500-year-old cedar.

Besides fires, windstorms were another element changing the forests. South of Willapa Harbor, for instance, are timber stands of 500- to 700-year-old cedars sharing the same territory with 125-year-old hemlock. Evidence is that the hemlock was either repeatedly blown down or perished because of age, while the more tenacious cedar stood its ground.

But for sheer destruction, and vast change, nothing yet has equalled the great hurricane of January 21, 1921, resulting in what became known as the "Great Blowdown," when whole sections of prime timber fell like wheat before a hailstorm.

Coming without warning, hitting an area never having known a storm of such intensity, the terrifying winds found both man and nature unprepared. Velocity on Grays Harbor was estimated at 100 miles per hour, enough to topple mill stacks and send roofs flying, down power and telephone lines, uproot ornamental trees, tear log rafts adrift and surge water and logs over the river banks. Deepwater ships and river craft parted mooring lines and crashed into bridges and wharves. The wind, freakish at times, played havoc with everything insecure.

The countless miles of timber from Grays Harbor to Forks and around Lake Crescent, the whole west side of the Olympic peninsula felt the full weight of the hurricane. Whole sections of timber were mowed down; in some regions, near Lone Mountain in the Quinault Indian reservation, for instance, downed trees were piled like jackstraws 20 to 30 feet high. Great spruces, some eight feet through, top-heavy and shallow-rooted, were particularly vulnerable. Tremendous stands of hemlock were literally torn from the ground and tossed into impenetrable tangles.

Destruction was perhaps greatest in the upper end of the Olympic peninsula, where it was estimated one-third of the timber on the west slope of Clallam County was blown down. Between Forks and Crescent Lake the highway was in places smothered in downed timber, mostly prime fir. In all, the estimate of shattered timber was placed in the billions of board feet, with the full extent of damage not known until years later. To add to the destruction, timber too remote to salvage soon became infested and eventually was rot lost.

Shortly after noon the storm hit Grays Harbor, and by 2 o'clock it was roaring up the Peninsula and hammering with unbelievable power at the incredible fir stands in Jefferson and Clallam counties.

The winds were capricious in addition to being of unimaginable velocity. Fingers of destruction were found everywhere, while timber nearby was untouched. Elsewhere whole regions went down. The falling timber killed hundreds of elk, one herd of 200 wiped out to the last animal.

For all its destructiveness, the hurricane was sparing of human lives. Only one man, A. A. Brown, chief engineer for the Anderson & Middleton mill in Aberdeen, was killed on Grays Harbor. There were no deaths elsewhere, although there were a number of injuries, several at La Push where 16 Indian houses were demolished, and many head of cattle killed.

Chapter 12

PLYWOOD, PULP AND PAPER

About the time Grays Harbor was beating itself into a frenzy of lumber cutting and getting the first warnings that tomorrow may not be as salubrious as today, another industry — in fact three — began peeking over the horizon. The first was fir plywood, the others pulp and paper.

Plywood whisperings had been heard on Grays Harbor as early as 1890 when a veneer peeling lathe arrived. There is no record of who used the lathe, or where, but there is a suggestion it was similar to a St. Josepth, Missouri, Iron Works machine installed in the Paulson & Drumm Lumber Company plant in Tacoma in the summer of 1890.

Grays Harbor's next mention in connection with plywood, and it, too, rather wispy, was on December 2, 1902. Paul Autzen, by then a prominent Grays Harbor logger, bought out F. S. Doernbecher and M. L. Holbrook, each with a quarter interest in the Portland Manufacturing Company of which Gustav A. Carlson owned a half interest. Autzen did not move from Grays Harbor to Portland. The firm had been incorporated May 7, 1901, with Carlson assuming the job of manager. Thomas J. Autzen, son of Peter Autzen, joined the firm in May, 1903, as handyman and office man. With Carlson was N. J. Bailey, a lathe operator of some skill who had come from Michigan in May, 1903. The two, Carlson and Bailey, teamed to produce some display plywood panels for the Lewis & Clark Exposition in Portland in 1905, using a hand press and animal glue, an odorous concoction which often made the workmen retch. However, the panels were highly successful and immediately focused nationwide attention to plywood-making in the Northwest.

Carlson died suddenly in September, 1906, while on a duck hunting trip, and his widow asked Peter Autzen to quit Grays Harbor and assume control of the company. This he did, and in 1907 he purchased the Carlson stock, the first known Grays Harborite to be concerned with plywood, although his plywood interest was in Portland and not Grays Harbor.

Grays Harbor's induction into actual plywood making unquestionably was the work of Henry McCleary, a veteran in wood manufacturing long before he built his first plywood plant in 1912.

The saga of Henry McCleary began somewhere back in Guernsey County, Ohio, where he, his father and brothers were doing some sawmilling in the 80's. Like so many other young men of his time, Henry McCleary got itchy feet and a yenning for the West. It is romantically recorded he landed briefly in Montana, where after the fashion of the time and the region he dressed himself in a brace of six-guns and became very proficient in their use; though it is not recorded he ever had a confrontation with another frontier two-gun man. However, it is said he could tack a five of spades against a wall and shoot out the spots as fast as he could pull the trigger. As a young man might say in his fanciful way, McCleary said he never felt fully dressed without his guns. Whether that is believable or not, it added a touch of daring-do to his landing in Tacoma in 1890 and settling for a rather prosaic job as foreman of a small mill at Woodland, about five miles out of Puyallup.

In the spring of 1897, McCleary joined Edward Foy, the firm being known as Foy & McCleary, to log and mill near Garden City. They worked a small patch of timber which was cut out in a matter of months, so the partners moved to South Bend where they built a small mill on the bank of the Willapa river. The difficulty of moving logs against the tides and winds with a small, inefficient tugboat proved the company's undoing. The mill was abandoned.

The next year, 1898, found Foy & McCleary starting a small cedar lumber mill on the Estes mill site in what would someday be McCleary. Logging was done with a six-horse team driven by Joe Thompson, who, after the tradition of his trade, was large and shriveling of vocabulary, and particularly attentive to Old Rock and Rye, the leaders of the team who often felt the weight of Thompson's goad and glossary. Ernest C. Teagle in his schoolboy summer job pounded down the road swabbing each skid with a smear of grease.

In 1899, McCleary bought out his partner Foy, increased the size and output of his sawmill, built the company town of McCleary, and by 1910 was ready to go into the door business with plywood for door panels as an adjunct. A forty-acre site was cleared that year, and in 1911 a nine hundred foot long building on twenty-two hundred piling was raised to house the new manufacturing enterprise.

As part of the preparation, the Chehalis Fir Door Company of Chehalis, acquired by McCleary and George J. Osgood in 1907, but going down hill in 1911, was moved to McCleary, the door-making equipment being installed in the McCleary plant. The Chehalis Fir Door Company was continued under that name for a time, but eventually was absorbed into and lost its identity to the McCleary company. The big door plant was to become outstanding in the industry not only because of the size of its output, but because of the widely-recognized quality of the product. The factory broke all records in 1923 when it made and shipped three hundred thousand doors in sixty days, six carloads a day.

The McCleary sawmill on the other hand closed in 1931 after twenty-six years of operation and cutting a swath of timber from the mill site all the way to Summit Lake. By 1942 the mill, planing mill and shops had been dismantled and sold for junk.

Henry McCleary, late in the afternoon of December 31, 1941, in the Montesano law office of Attorney W. H. Abel, signed a contract of sale with representatives of the Simpson Logging Company, William G. Reed and Chris Kreienbaum. The sale involved the McCleary plants, utilities and company dwellings. The Simpson company sold the water and power utilities to the town of McCleary for $6,000 after the town incorporated in 1943.

The dwellings were sold to the occupants at virtually give-away prices, for Simpson did not want to be in the landlord business. The McCleary mill operated by Simpson continues to be a national leader in panel door production.

Henry McCleary, a lost man for a year and a half with no big operation to manage, died May 8, 1943.

Plywood-making in McCleary was primarily for door panels with no thought for large panels as the industry was to know them. That remained, on Grays Harbor at least, for a gathering of four men from far places. There was a story, which all parties repeated with gusto, of how E. W. Daniels became associated with Harry Knox, a meeting that led in a roundabout way to the formation of the Harbor Plywood Corporation, the first large panel makers on Grays Harbor, and eventually the leader of all the industry.

The story has Harry Knox, an eastern distributor working out of Chicago, purchasing the John A. Gauger & Company there in 1909. The Gauger company was a large distributor of wooden doors and millwork, an operation that fit in with Knox's enterprise. In fact the combine worked so well throughout the Midwest that by 1921, Knox was hard put to find enough doors to sell. That was the year, too, Knox found on his annual trip to the Pacific Northwest seeking doors, his usual suppliers would not set fixed prices for the 1922 selling season. Knox didn't like the situation for he could not quote firm prices to his customers. As an upshot he sought out and bought the Schaefer Company door plant in Hoquiam.

Meanwhile, E. W. "Dan" Daniels, born in Hartford, Connecticut, and a meat salesman for Armour & Company, decided after his return from World War I to set up a sales organization with a fellow employee, Charles Wood. It was called the Daniels-Wood Sales Company, but did not sell for long. The firm was disbanded, with Daniels entering the job market. Early in 1920, Daniels in keeping with his experience as a salesman, wrote Harry Knox, then president of John A. Gauger Company, for a job. The application was written on a Daniels-Wood Sales Company letterhead. Knox mistook the letterhead to mean Daniels was a salesman for wood products. He was a little flabbergasted to learn in the subsequent interview, Daniels had been selling meat, but nevertheless ended up hiring the persuasive applicant. It was a bold stroke for Knox and a little more than fortunate for Daniels. By 1921, Daniels already was manager of Gauger's plywood division, so when Knox bought the Hoquiam plant he sent Daniels to handle financial angles of the transaction. Not long after that Knox made Daniels manager of the operation, by then known as Knox & Toombs — Toombs was the owner of the Roy L. Toombs Sash & Door Company in Fort Worth, Texas, a sales outlet for Gauger.

The Knox & Toombs plant was going great guns under Daniel's management until fire December 1, 1924, destroyed the Sedro Box & Veneer plant in Sedro Woolley, Washington. The fire cut off Knox & Toomb's main supply of door panels, and left a pair of plywood makers at loose ends. They were A. R. "Bob" Wuest and A. R. Welch, who had come up the hard way for plywood experience. Wuest, a bookkeeper, got his first job in the Northwest in the office of a lumber company, later for the McFadden Logging Company near Tacoma, and, becoming interested in veneer-making, worked for the Sprecht & Company. In 1922 he joined Sedro as office manager, but soon became general manager, turning out fir plywood panels. When the plant burned in 1924, Wuest was out $20,000, and looking for a job.

A. R. Welch started with an Astoria door factory in 1911, shifted to the Canadian Western Lumber Company, and then to Elliott Bay Mill as lathe operator when the mill started up. Then William Royse enticed him to the Sedro mill in 1923, where he first teamed with A. R. Wuest. Welch, like Wuest, was out of a job because of the fire. Grays Harbor beckoned, and the pair answered.

The ashes of Sedro were barely cool before all other door panel suppliers in the Northwest raised their prices from $40 to $80 a thousand square feet. This outraged Knox & Toombs, made a travesty of their profits, and prompted E. W. Daniels to propose a plywood plant of their own. Consultation with Wuest and Welch was a determining factor. Knox agreed to put up $95,000 to help finance the new company, while Daniels with $143,000 in bonds started beating the Grays Harbor brush for investors. He sold the whole caboodle to Aberdeen and

Hoquiam men of means. With money in the poke and a mill site just inside the Aberdeen city limits at the Port Dock, the Harbor Plywood Company was organized: Harry S. Knox, president; A. R. Wuest, vice-president and general manager; E. W. Daniels, secretary-treasurer; A. R. Welch, superintendent. On May 25, 1925 the whistle blew for the first time, starting wheels that were to set the pace for the industry. Seventy-eight men and women were on the job, a force that grew to 180 by autumn of that year.

Three years later the always-present fire hazard of the industry wiped out the plant except the green end. Upon the ashes the firm immediately started to rebuild, and by December, only eight weeks after the fire, fir panels again were being produced. This time the machinery was better, the capabilities better, including that of peeling 16-foot logs.

Insofar as the Harbor Plywood Company (it became Harbor Plywood Corporation in 1929) was essentially the Grays Harbor plywood industry, all its gains and vicissitudes, had a bearing on the Grays Harbor economy. It was a stabilizer during the often seasonal afflictions suffered by the lumber industry. Consequently whatever happened to or at Harbor Plywood reverberated throughout the industry, particularly after Harbor chemists perfected a waterproof hot-pressed resin adhesive which revolutionized plywood making.

Development of the new adhesive was a story in itself, with years of trial and error, disappointments, and finally success. It was obvious to Wuest, Daniels and Welch if the plywood business was to expand, it had to make something more than "interior" plywood, a product shunned by a great segment of the building industry, notably those engaged in railway boxcar production, boatbuilders, form-makers for heavy construction, farm buildings, and complete exterior construction for homes. With the demand apparent, Harbor assigned Michel Pasquier, a young chemical engineer from the University of Washington, to the job of finding a waterproof adhesive. In his work studying various formulas, he learned about Dr. James Victor Nevin, then living in California, a man steeped in industrial chemistry and familiar with synthetics and particularly with the experiments in phenolic resins conducted by the German chemist, Dr. Leo Bakeland. It happened that while Pasquier was suggesting Dr.

Nevin to Harbor Plywood, a job-seeking letter from Dr. Nevin appeared on Wuest's desk. Dr. Nevin was summoned and joined the Harbor Plywood research lab in the fall of 1933. With him came William Martin, just graduated from the University of California. The three, Nevin, Pasquier and Martin, worked virtually night and day for a year. Late in 1934, Dr. Nevin was able to announce his waterproof glue. Welch meanwhile had built an improvised hot press to run the first panels as soon as a glue had been found.

After months, and more than a hundred performance tests, Harbor jubilantly announced a perfected exterior waterproof fir panel, a development that shook the industry and changed the whole emphasis and course of plywood making.

Wuest, who had been elected president of Harbor in 1933, guided the firm through the depression years, the development of Super Harboard with the waterproof glue, and with increasing profits to 1936 when, in a dispute with the board, he resigned. In resigning, Wuest took Art Welch with him, the two pairing to establish a plywood plant of their own under the name of the West Coast Plywood Company, with Wuest as president, and Welch as vice president.

John J. Long, a Longview lumberman, then assumed the presidency of Harbor Plywood, but his experience with plywood was insufficient, and with mounting labor, market and log supply problems, coupled with operational losses in 1938-39, he resigned.

The company presidency then fell to E. W. Daniels, who in the next decade gave Harbor Plywood phenomenal growth, especially in marketing and in perfecting specialty products, an outgrowth of Harbor's exterior plywood development. After World War II the plywood business soared, and so did the need for peeler logs. For that matter the necessity for peelers had been felt years before, for when Daniels became president of Harbor he instituted ocean rafting of logs from the Columbia River, later the barging of logs. His next venture into log supply was the purchase of the Pacific National Company holdings near Mt. Rainier. The purchase involved 165 million feet of prime timber and a logging railway and highway. In short order this operation under the direction of Frank Hobi, Harbor vice president, was delivering two and a half million feet of timber, eighty percent peelers, to Harbor every month. However, this timber was but a stop-gap; more timber was needed.

By 1944-45 virtually every plywood outfit in the business was on the prowl for sustaining timber, including Harbor Plywood. Harbor got the commanding position for one of the choice tracts, 28,000 acres owned by the Northern Pacific Railway Company, along the Lewis River in Skamania county. This tract was under contract to Al Peterman of Tacoma. Peterman died and in 1946 Harbor was able to buy the contract from Peterman's heirs. It was March 1947, before the deal was closed. The contract however, had some terrifying provisions, particularly so for a firm seeking only a log supply. The deal required the purchaser to build a sawmill, a plywood mill, a door plant, planing mill and a shingle mill on the site within three years, and required that products from these plants be shipped over the Northern Pacific road. An "emergency agreement" gave Harbor the right to log 90 million feet of timber and ship the peelers to the Aberdeen plant.

In the process a bank loan of two million dollars was arranged to prepare sites and do other preliminary work for construction under the contract since it was supposed no return from the site could be expected for possibly a year or longer.

While all these negotiations were going on, Harbor contracted to purchase, near Redding, California, a billion feet of Ponderosa and sugar pine timber to be converted into plywood in a proposed Harbor Plywood mill in Anderson, Shasta county.

In 1946, Harbor Plywood was presented an opportunity to buy 18 thousand acres carrying 350 million feet of timber, largely Douglas fir, a decrepit sawmill and other acreage near Riddle, Oregon. It signed the deal.

And then troubles developed. Costs started to rise at an alarming rate. In an April 9, 1947 report contract costs at Riddle had become $550,000. Construction in progress — a capital asset — was listed at $390,000, with estimates for completing the construction at $1,375,000. Total Riddle costs then for timber and construction were around $2,300,000. By the end of 1947

Riddle buildings, improvements, machinery and whatever, were listed in the annual report at $2,275,000, plus construction in progress at $595,000.

The rise in the timber purchase contract really stupified Harbor, what with the item of $1,180,000 as "balance payment subject to upward adjustment biennially based on prevailing stumpage." Somewhere down the line Harbor officials had not realized the devastating effect of the escalator.

Harbor Plywood was in a bind. New stock was authorized and sold for $4,500,000. Proceeds were used to retire bank loans of some $3,200,000, with the balance earmarked for Riddle completion and construction foreseen for the Lewis River tract. And then an agreement was made for another loan up to $2,500,000.

Instead of suffering scarcity, Harbor was now topheavy with timber, or at least the financing, so it welcomed an offer from Larry Ottinger, president of U. S. Plywood, to purchase the Redding timber and plywood mill. U. S. Plywood owned ten percent of the Redding layout before it purchased the other ninety percent.

Financial matters caused a Harbor Plywood proxy battle early in 1949, which resulted in E. W. Daniels submitting his resignation as president and general manager effective February 28, 1949. More importantly the shakeup led to the election of Martin N. Deggeller as president and general manager. Deggeller had been a vice-president and director of Rayonier Inc., in charge of the timber division. As director of Rayonier's forestry, Deggeller figured prominently in the purchase of the Polson Logging Company, one of the biggest deals of its kind in Grays Harbor history, and he was particularly involved in the purchase of the Polson timber holdings. Deggeller also personally negotiated deals which increased Rayonier's timber holdings of a few hundred thousand feet in Grays Harbor County to six billion feet in Pacific, Grays Harbor, Jefferson and Clallam counties. Purchases were made from the Polson Logging Company, Bloedel Donovan Lumber Mills, Milwaukee Land Company, Conewango Timber Company, Illinois Timber Company and Clallam Lumber Company, with additional smaller parcels from other outfits in Grays Harbor and Pacific counties.

Deggeller was born and reared in the timber, with years of

experience in timber management and administration. The fact he became disillusioned with Rayonier because he refused to move to Rayonier's New York office was a rare opportunity for Harbor Plywood. Searching the field, Harbor owners found Deggeller was the man to pull them out of the hole. Deggeller knew, when Daniels approached him in Olympia, Harbor Plywood was handing him a hot potato but, seeing the opportunities, he accepted. The move proved trying, but lucrative to both Harbor and Deggeller.

After assessing the company and his position, Deggeller began some agonizing moves. He had learned immediately the company was heavily in hock to the Bank of America, there were internal problems, some relating to personnel in management and the mill, a board that was not all smiles, with the majority convinced management was incapable of salvaging the company. One director dubbed the company the "Harbor Plywood Country Club," with some substance.

It was obvious drastic action was necessary. First came a clamp-down on expenditures, cuts in official and supervisory salaries, elimination of gifts and special favors to certain employees, and finally the release of non-essential employees.

Almost immediately it was found necessary to reorganize the board of directors, a move that ended with a rather purposeful election of outsiders: Roy F. Morse, vice-president of Long-Bell Lumber Company; Ernest G. Swigert, president of Hyster Company, R. D. Merrill, president and partner of Merrill-Ring Lumber Company; Tom Murray, owner of West Fork Timber Company; Harry S. Grande, president of Grande & Company, and E. J. Evans, partner in the First California Company.

Prior to this reorganization the Bank of America, worried by the instability of Harbor Plywood, had installed its own representative in the Harbor office with full authority over monetary matters.

Harbor Plywood went into negotiations with Northern Pacific for better contract terms. This was accomplished by Martin Deggeller as of July 1, 1950. The burdensome phases of the original contract were eliminated, with Harbor given unrestricted cutting rights and a stumpage price of $5.00 per thousand. Harbor, which wanted only the peelers from the tract, and hemlock for trading purposes, made an agreement with Long-Bell Lumber Company to purchase at the market price all logs not wanted by Harbor.

Deggeller next concentrated on personnel, and streamlining plant operations. These problems were resolved so successfully that Fred Ferrogiro, president of the Bank of America, called Deggeller to San Francisco to inform him the bank was removing its watchman from the Harbor Plywood office, and was ready to make Harbor additional loans. With these Harbor started to build a solid plywood empire.

But there were rumblings of change. While Harbor was negotiating for the Northern Pacific timber, management detected a steady sub rosa movement by an outside agency to acquire Harbor Plywood stock. By this time, Harbor with its millions in timber holdings and a good operating and marketing position, was a financial plum. By 1953 it was apparent the seeker of the plum was Norton Simon, board chairman of Hunt Foods, and a director of the Northern Pacific Railway. Late in 1955 Simon announced he had control of eighty percent of Harbor's stock and named himself chairman of the board. The board was reorganized with Martin Deggeller being retained as president. Board members Morse, Murray and Swigert resigned, to be replaced by people from Simon's Hunt Foods. Jack Rehm, vice-president and long-time production manager, resigned to be replaced by Wayne Hagen, his assistant, who himself resigned three years later to take a similar position with Grays Harbor Veneer, where he served as treasurer and board member. Another long-time staff member was Russ Austin, sales manager. He left the company, while E. W. Daniels dropped his "consulting" position and, after 30 years on Grays Harbor, moved to Tacoma to resume his sales activities with Plywood Research Foundation. He died November 11, 1966.

Of the stock not acquired by Hunt Foods and/or Norton Simon, Long-Bell Lumber Company owned the largest single block. Simon threatened a lawsuit against Long-Bell, then in the process of negotiating a sale of the company to International Paper Company. Long-Bell settled out of court and agreed to sell its Harbor Plywood stock to Simon, giving him control of Harbor. Thereupon Simon began liquidating the plywood company holdings, first by sale of the Lewis River properties to International Paper Company and Pacific Power and Light, February 14, 1958, for $17,000,000, then the Riddle, Oregon, operation in September 1958. On May 6, 1960 Harbor Plywood's Aberdeen plant and eighteen sales warehouses around the nation were sold to Aberdeen Plywood & Veneers, Inc., of Aberdeen, then headed by Mon Orloff. Thereafter Harbor Plywood was operated as an investment company and in 1962 was merged with Hunt Foods & Industries, Inc.

The Aberdeen Plywood Company, or at least its plant in Aberdeen was as badly beset. Trouble began almost as soon as the first piling were driven at the foot of Washington street in Aberdeen. Gus Strand, Aberdeen fish packer, lured by the prospering plywood mills, decided to build one of his own. For help he sought out a Swedish engineer purportedly well-schooled in plywood-making. The piling went down, the mill went up, and then Hayes & Hayes bank in Aberdeen, with a wad of Gus Strand money, went broke. Regardless, Strand, already heavily invested, decided to go ahead on his own. But his Swedish engineer proved a mismatch for the project. He installed some of the machinery wrong, some even backwards, and was inept in other phases of plant construction. As a result the mill did not produce a single panel. Disgusted, Strand opted to go back to salmon packing, leaving the plywood plant stand.

At this juncture and two years after Harbor Plywood had blown its starting whistle, two more luminaries lofted into the plywood skies. One was Vernon A. Nyman, who was to bail Strand's plant out of its predicament, the other Mon Orloff, who was to rejuvenate the enterprise and eventually merge it into oblivion.

Vern Nyman came to Grays Harbor by way of Olympia Veneer Company, a worker-owner outfit in which he was an original shareholder. The Olympia undertaking had grown so successful the worker-owners cast about for another mill, and fastened upon Gus Strand's all-but-abandoned plant. This Strand sold to Olympia Veneer for the bargain price of $150,000. Nyman and four veterans of the Olympia plant were sent to Aberdeen to put the mill in running shape and then operate it.

Within a few months Nyman had the operation on its feet and

producing successfully, which it did until March 2, 1940, when the mill was destroyed by fire. The plant was rebuilt and resumed operations in October of that year, continuing under Nyman's direction for almost two decades, when a scarcity of peeler logs and a slack plywood market forced the mill to close.

Meanwhile a Bellingham attorney, Mon Orloff, had more or less backed into the plywood business. Mt. Baker Plywood at Bellingham was upon financial rocks and rapidly breaking up. Panicky management and creditors turned to Orloff to save what he could of the wreck. He not only saved the financial structure, but the plant as well, so successfully in fact Mt. Baker asked him to stay on to run the operation. Creditors agreed. Orloff became a plywood operator, and within the next three years turned Mt. Baker into a surprising money-maker. In fact the success was so pronounced Orloff reasoned that if he could do such a job for others, why not for himself — seek a mill and repeat the performance. Aberdeen Plywood was a logical choice.

Once the decision was made and the possibilities of acquiring Aberdeen Plywood explored, Orloff came to Aberdeen to set up shop. He gathered R. M. "Roy" Landberg, Martell Brown and Lou Goldberg into a huddle for a financial appraisal of the situation and the moves to be made to promote enough capital. It was decided to finance the plan locally with small blocks of stock, mostly in $500 and $1000 bundles, call a public mass meeting to kick off the campaign and create a public-spirited drive for immediate funds. The mass meeting was so successful the capital program was largely subscribed from the floor. Orloff in turn raised a considerable sum from his own resources, mortgaging everything mortgageable he possessed, including, some said, his wife's engagement ring. In any event the money was raised, the mill purchased and put into operation, and as the Aberdeen Plywood & Veneers, Inc., became so well fixed financially that with Orloff's maneuvering skill it could buy Harbor Plywood's mill and warehouses.

Some time later Orloff's operation was phased into Evans Products Company, with Mon Orloff becoming a top official and general all-around manager of the Evans enterprises, including the former Harbor Plywood plant, which was kept in production on specialty panels, mostly cedar. It must be said of Orloff's managing skills he twice retired from overseeing Evans, and each time was recalled to put the company on its feet again after having fallen into disarray financially and in production and marketing. He revived the company each time.

Olympia Veneer Company, the first worker-owner operation in the Northwest, did not conceive the Aberdeen Plywood enterprise under Vern Nyman as a similar institution. The Aberdeen mill hired many outsiders. However, there were two so-called co-ops on Grays Harbor, Hoquiam Plywood (formerly called Woodlawn Plywood) and Elma Plywood managed by James Ladley. Although the plants were called "co-ops," they operated as corporations with no special tax privileges.

Meanwhile Rudy DeLateur started the Grays Harbor Veneer Company with a plant on the Hoquiam River. The operation was eventually sold to Anderson & Middleton and is operated now primarily as a box factory, and maker of other specialty products.

While the Grays Harbor plywood industry was agonizing and prospering, a more chemistry-related industry was toying with a Grays Harbor possibility. This was pulp. Led here by the abundance of raw material, water and a community to cooperate, E. M. Mills, members of the Zellerbach family and Pacific Coast associates in January 1927, came to Grays Harbor to negotiate. They formed the Grays Harbor Pulp Company to manufacture paper pulp, picked a site in Hoquiam upstream on the Chehalis from the mouth of the Hoquiam River and began turning out pulp in 1928. While this was being done, and the mill acquiring water from the east branch of the Hoquiam via a tunnel through what might be called "Campbell Hill," the Hammermill Paper Company of Erie, Pennsylvania, bought into the Grays Harbor Pulp Company. Subsequently a paper mill was built alongside the pulp mill in Hoquiam to produce fine grades of bond paper. The name of the company was changed to Grays Harbor Pulp & Paper Company, which was to struggle through the depression of the early thirties while chemists were working miracles in their test tubes. In the central laboratory in Shelton, Washington, a high grade dissolving pulp product was devised for Eastern rayon mills.

In 1936 the Grays Harbor Pulp & Paper Company became a

part of Rayonier Incorporated and also became one of the great producers in the pulp industry, with one of the big payrolls in the state. Perhaps even more important, the new pulp permitted use of waste wood that once lit Grays Harbor skies in the great sawmill burners.

Long before these Johnny-come-lately diversity-product entrepreneurs, V. G. Posey established a manufacturing enterprise in Hoquiam that has since become the longest continuing operation on the Harbor. V. G. Posey, called "Vertical Grain" Posey because of his initials and his insistence upon fine-grained wood, came to Grays Harbor from California in 1908, to manufacture perhaps the highest grade specialty product made of Grays Harbor wood, piano sounding boards of spruce. During the thirties depression years the plant turned to making gadgets and novelty wood products to earn a dollar, but when piano markets improved, Posey returned to making the specialty sounding boards, a product still in demand and still being made.

The Weyerhaeuser Company not only is a big owner and operator in the Grays Harbor country, it also is a patron of Grays Harbor history, ecology and stimulus to Grays Harbor's future. The company for a great many years has been a heavy timber holder in the Grays Harbor and Willapa Harbor regions, but did little logging of its own until it teamed with the Clemons Company to work southward out of Melbourne.

In 1957 in answer to its own needs and clamor from Grays Harbor the company acquired the historic millsite in Cosmopolis and installed a sulphite pulp mill, now producing somewhere around 150,000 tons of specialty and dissolving pulp each year, one-half of it to international markets, the other half to domestic producers of high-grade papers of various kinds, including photo papers.

This operation not only is a great labor producer but requires huge amounts of timber, much of it not suitable for any other purpose. Establishment of the mill has over the years rejuvenated the once company town of Cosmopolis to make it perhaps the best adjusted, best regulated, best landscaped and most prideful town in the whole Grays Harbor area.

Downstream Weyerhaeuser established what it calls the Bay City Export Center, actually a log-sorting yard for export logs, a huge operation growing out of Weyerhaeuser's enlarged logging operations in the Twin Harbors region.

Downstream further Weyerhaeuser in 1955 acquired the Schafer Company tidewater sawmill, which in 1979 produced 190 million board feet of finished fir, hemlock and spruce lumber, and in a side plant 129 thousand squares of cedar shakes.

In Raymond, on Willapa Harbor, Weyerhaeuser operated for many years a sawmill being phased out in 1980 to be supplanted, it was planned, by a short-log mill to cut second growth.

In connection with the Aberdeen sawmill operation Weyerhaeuser established what it called a "Chip N' Saw Mill" — an operation converting mill waste and small logs, many of them from thinning operations, into chips, some for use locally, but much to export, mostly to Japan. It must be also noted chips were produced in the Raymond mill, which with the Aberdeen production, were sent to the Cosmopolis pulp mill.

There was nothing particularly inspired about N. J. "Nels" Blagen coming to the United States. Born in Denmark July 18, 1859, he spent his first 20 years there, then began to sniff at the opportunities so well fancied across the Atlantic. He wanted a different scene.

Blagen arrived in the United States in 1871, making his way to a farm in Minnesota. Six months there earned him a saving of ninety-six dollars, which took him to Chicago where he could practice his carpenter trade, learned in Denmark. Within four years he began contracting on his own, then moved to California in 1876 and to Portland, Oregon, in 1877, contracting in Oregon and Washington. In 1896-98 he built part of the water system for Boston, Massachussets, and a steel pipeline eight miles long and four feet in diameter for the city of Bedford, which also required building five miles of railway to carry on the work.

Another big construction undertaking was the building of the Northern Pacific road from Ellensburg to a point about four miles east of Green River Hot Springs, including the mountain grade, the switchback over the Cascade summit, and all tunnels with the exception of the main Cascade tunnel. At the time Blagen owned and operated a sawmill supplying all lumber for the rail line, an undertaking which led him to Hoquiam and organization of the Grays Harbor Lumber Company in 1905. He became president and general manager with his son, C. G. Blagen, secretary and assistant manager. Henry W. Blagen, another son, was sales manager for the firm, while Frank N. Blagen was the mechanical engineer and draftsman.

At one time the Blagens operated the Bucoda Lumber Company, but sold out.

Chapter 13

THE SHIPBUILDING YEARS

Ships, shipbuilding and shipping, collectively, were the third element in Grays Harbor's eminence in the lumber trade. Logging and sawmilling were basic, but the carrying of lumber was equally important, especially when much of the lumber was stowed aboard Grays Harbor-built vessels; first the sleek three- and four-masted schooners, later the great procession of steam schooners created on Grays Harbor ways. The ships themselves were a ready and sizable market for fir, vast quantities of which went into the building, so it seemed natural that a shipyard should become an adjunct to the tidewater sawmill. Several mill owners made this decision, with Asa M. Simpson the first.

The North Western plant had already shipped several cargoes to San Francisco when sometime in 1886 Simpson decided to ship his lumber in his own vessels. He liked the lure of profit in ship operation. He foresaw better control of shipping schedules. And in the Hoquiam mill he had an easy supply of building materials. To this end he lured Thomas A. McDonald, a master craftsman and builder, away from California to construct two vessels in Hoquiam. The first, the 128-foot schooner *Volunteer*, McDonald launched in 1887, followed by the 138-foot schooner *Pioneer*.

Two years later the North Western yard launched the 97-foot tug *Printer*. She was towed to San Francisco for her engines, and returned to Grays Harbor to operate for years as a bar tug.

McDonald changed scenes in 1890 to build the 158-foot, three-masted schooner *J. M. Weatherwax* for the lumberman of that name and fellow stockholders in the Weatherwax mill in Aberdeen. With Captain Weatherwax, in the venture were Captain T. H. Smith, Evans, John G. Lewis and Filley of Aberdeen, and A. Anderson & Co. of San Francisco. The keel was laid in January, 1890, in a yard built near the Weatherwax mill. Upon launching, she was fitted with 96-foot lower masts and 56-foot topm'sts, and 2,200 square yards of canvas. The vessel had been put together with 7,000 locust trunnels, and all fastenings were of copper or galvanized iron. All blocks and tackle were made to order. She was fitted with a donkey engine and patented windlass. Her anchors weighed 2,400 pounds, fastened to ten tons of chain. Her entire cost, save for victualing, was $35,000. She carried a crew of 10 men and returned from her maiden voyage November 27, 1890.

From McDonald's initial effort evolved an imposing industry and tradition in wooden shipbuilding to be climaxed by the tremendous performance of two temporary yards during World War I.

Shipbuilding on a scale that would be considered an industry awaited a decision by the E. K. Wood Lumber Company of San Francisco, and the arrival in Hoquiam of Peter Matthews, who had been building ships in Eureka, California. The E. K. Wood Company operated a sawmill in Hoquiam and decided to have a sailing vessel constructed. The company induced Peter Matthews to move his shipbuilding equipment to Hoquiam and establish a yard on the west bank of the Hoquiam, downstream from the company's sawmill. Pertinent to Matthew's undertaking was a fire, which had destroyed the North Western mill in 1896. A new mill replacing the burned plant was equipped to cut long timbers required in the building of ships. In fact, when the mill started cutting in 1897, the year Matthews built his yard, the first raft to arrive at the mill boom contained a fir log 114 feet long and 80 inches in diameter at the top end, which was said to be the longest log ever cut in a Grays Harbor mill. The log was cut into timbers used in constructing Matthews first vessel, the four-masted schooner *Defiance*, of 604 tons.

The second vessel to slide the Matthews' way was the steamer *Dirigo*, which operated a number of years between Seattle and ports in Alaska.

With two ships down the Hoquiam ways Peter Matthews had opened an epoch of wooden shipbuilding on Grays Harbor, and for that matter on the Pacific Coast. He came from Scottish stock that had settled in New Brunswick, Canada, where he was born in 1848. As an infant he moved with his family to Prince Edward Island, again to a farm. There he attended a country school for a total of three months. When sixteen he decided to apprentice himself in the ship carpenter's trade in which he completed his four years of training. All shipbuilding then was by hand tools, from cutting the trees in the forest to hewing out each frame and timber by hand.

Shortly after Peter Matthews completed his apprenticeship on Prince Edward Island he moved to Perry, Maine, in 1868. The town was located on the Bay of Fundy. It was there Peter Matthews married Sadie Eldridge in 1869. In 1874 he learned of the shipbuilding industry in Eureka, California, and of the mild climate, which to him was more than appealing after the hard winters "Down East."

Acting upon the information, young Peter Matthews took a train to San Francisco, then a steamer to Eureka, where he found employment in the H. D. Bendixsen shipyard in Fairhaven, located on the peninsula across Humboldt Bay from Eureka. His wife and their daughter, Lillian, arrived in 1875. Matthews worked on Humboldt Bay for several years. In 1885 a boom in constructing a new type of wood vessel known as the steamschooner, was under way in San Francisco. Matthews spent two years there familiarizing himself with this new and unique type of vessel. When the rush subsided in 1887 he returned to Eureka to contract for and build wooden barges, two schooners and a sternwheeler.

Then came 1892 and a contract to build a steamschooner for the C. A. Hooper Company of San Francisco. The vessel was to have a round stern, the first of this design on the Pacific coast. Up to that time steamschooners had been built with an elliptic stern, the same type of stern used in schooners.

Matthews had his problems designing the new stern with its

circular sidelines, and section lines and diagonals to fit. Fortunately he had George Hitchings with him and the two of them made the frame moulds and moulded the flitch timbers.

The round stern so familiar years later was a great improvement for the steamschooner, for it increased the cargo capacity, the stability and displacement when fully loaded.

She was launched as the *Excelsior*, classed as a single-ender with a triple-expansion engine, the first of the type constructed for a steamschooner, installed as far aft as practical. She was a coal-burner with a Scotch boiler.

Casually and predictably, Peter Matthews met a sea captain on a fateful day in 1896. The mariner, who was to change Peter Matthews' life, had recently made a voyage to Hoquiam, Washington, where he had picked up a cargo of fir lumber at the E. K. Wood Lumber Company plant for delivery to San Francisco. The captain had learned E. K. Wood wanted a shipyard established in Hoquiam to build a four-mast schooner. Also he learned the E. K. Wood mill would cut the timber to construct the vessel.

Matthews was intrigued by the prospect. He wrote the company several letters and finally made a trip to San Francisco to meet E. K. Wood officials, with the result he came away with a contract to construct a four-mast bald-headed schooner to carry 700M feet of Douglas fir, the ship to be constructed at Hoquiam.[28]

Preparation got under way immediately to move equipment to Grays Harbor. Matthews engaged the steamschooner *Del Norte* to call at Eureka and load machinery and tools, along with five experienced shipwrights who wished to go with Matthews, and Matthews' son-in-law, George H. Hitchings, and wife and their small daughters, Ruth and Dora, his daughter Katie, and Matthews' son, Gordon Frazer Matthews. The *Del Norte* lay bar-bound a full day in Humboldt Bay but on March 11, 1897 and at 3 o'clock in the afternoon she cleared for Grays Harbor, where she arrived at 6 p.m. on March 13. The newcomers went directly to the New York hotel in Hoquiam.

That evening Captain Hughes, who lived in Hoquiam with his family, called on Matthews, an old acquaintance, and the two called around to visit several shipmasters in Hoquiam for lumber cargoes. They also met O. M. Kellogg,[29] manager of the E. K.

Wood Lumber Company, and Fred J. Wood, superintendent of the sawmill.

Soon Matthews met James Karr, a pioneer settler on the greater part of the Hoquiam townsite. They made an agreement to establish the shipyard on the Hoquiam River several blocks west of the E. K. Wood sawmill. Work on clearing the land of stumps and debris soon was started, along with buildings for shops, tools and machinery. An empty building suitable for a mould loft was located and work of drafting the vessel's hull lines and making the frame moulds went forward under direction of Matthews and Hitchings. The sawmill started cutting lumber for the new vessel and within a few days the keel timbers were fabricated and laid on the keel blocks.

The North Western Lumber Company by that time had rebuilt its burned sawmill and had in its boom the fir log 114 feet in length and 80 inches in diameter at the top end. It was hauled up the log slip and cut into long lengths for the new vessel. Matthews at the time said the log, largest ever cut on Grays Harbor, made the best ship timber he had ever seen.

Work on the vessel progressed rapidly and by September, 1897, she was ready for launching. Workmen installed the ground ways, well tallowed with beef tallow, then placed the slide timbers atop the ground ways, these well tallowed also. Cribbed timbers were placed to form a cradle for the ship as she slid down the ways. C. A. Thayer of San Francisco, secretary of the E. K. Wood Company, was aboard the vessel at launching time, as was his daughter Katie, who was to be the sponsor and christen the schooner. A band was on board to enliven the launching festivities.

Workmen removed the bilge shore supports and split out the fir keel blocks. But the vessel refused to move. The steam tugboat *Traveler* ran her 9-inch manila hawser aboard in an effort to get the ship started. Still she refused to budge. Peter Matthews gave up for the day, planning to rearrange the launching for the next day. As workmen disassembled the launching cradle and slide timbers they found that the tallow had been put on hot without allowing enough time for it to harden. The soft tallow surface had congealed and frozen solid. In fact the crew had difficulty prying the slide timbers from the ground ways in order to apply a new coat of tallow. This time it was allowed to cool properly. To make doubly sure Peter Matthews had lard oil smeared over the tallow.

With the new preparations completed, the ship slid as scheduled with daughter Katie Matthews, christening the schooner *Defiance,* the first vessel to be built in the Matthews' Hoquiam yard.

With all his preoccupation with the *Defiance* Matthews in August had signed a contract with J. S. Kimball, San Francisco ship operator, to construct a 175-foot double-end steamschooner. This he did on a second slip alongside the one in which the *Defiance* was being completed. The steamschooner was launched in January 1898 as the *Dirigo,* the motto of the state of Maine. She was towed by the *Traveler* to San Francisco for installation of machinery.

The next prospect was to be a four-mast bald-head schooner to carry 650M feet of Douglas fir for the E. K. Wood Company. Before the contract could be signed Peter Matthews became ill and died March 4, 1898. He was buried in Eureka, California, the services a year to the day from the time he left Eureka for Hoquiam.

In 1897 George Herbert Hitchings, born at St. Andrews, New Brunswick, in 1866, joined Peter Matthews in the Hoquiam shipyard. He had learned the trade of sparmaker with his father, Andrew Hitchings, and had worked on vessels Matthews had constructed at Eureka in 1889 and 1893. He had also married Lillian B. Matthews, eldest daughter of Mr. and Mrs. Peter Matthews. Upon Matthews' death Hitchings purchased the equipment in the Hoquiam yard and signed a contract to build a four-mast bald-head schooner for E. K. Wood in the Matthews yard. At this time John Lindstrom, who was years later to figure prominently in shipbuilding in Aberdeen, arrived from Eureka where he had worked for Bendixsen. He helped Hitchings in construction of the four-mast schooner, which was completed and launched in September 1898 as the *Dauntless.* She loaded her first cargo at the E. K. Wood mill and sailed for California under command of Captain T. Smith, who formerly had sailed the two-mast schooner *La Gironde* for E. K. Wood.

The E. K. Wood Lumber Company, so conspicuous in generating Grays Harbor's first large shipbuilding enterprise, was a San Francisco-based firm which entered the Grays Harbor lumber field by purchasing a small mill built and operated by a number of Hoquiam businessmen, including the city's founder, James A. Karr. The purchase was made in 1892, the mill thereafter being gradually enlarged into one of the major lumber mills on the Harbor. It developed a cutting capacity of 160,000 board feet per eight-hour shift, and kept up this pace until final shutdown in 1930.

O. M. Kellogg, original representative of the E. K. Wood Company on Grays Harbor, was a stockholder and the mill's general manager. He came first to Aberdeen and established the S. E. Slade & Kellogg Company affiliated with S. E. Slade & Company of San Francisco. Kellogg's Harbor company bought and shipped lumber to the San Francisco firm. The J. M. Weatherwax Lumber Company and the A. J. West Lumber Company, two of the first three plants in Aberdeen, both supplied lumber to Kellogg's company.

When E. K. Wood purchased the Hoquiam mill Kellogg moved to Hoquiam in 1894 to be near the plant and manage it. He became a stockholder in Wood's Washington operations, including a plant in Bellingham, and a prime factor in E. K. Wood enterprises.[29]

Early in the spring of 1889 George Hitchings signed a contract with the E. K. Wood company to construct a four-top-mast schooner with an 800M foot capacity of Douglas fir. He also signed a contract with Albert Meyer of San Francisco for a duplicate vessel. The first was launched in July as the *Fred J. Wood*, named for Fred J. Wood, superintendent for the E. K. Wood Company in Hoquiam.

The duplicate vessel was launched in September as the *Columbia*.

In August 1899, Captain Robert Dollar, prominent ship owner in San Francisco, came to see Hitchings in regard to constructing a steamschooner. They agreed on terms, the vessel was built and launched early in 1900 as the *Robert Dollar*.

In September, 1899, Hitchings signed a contract for a steamschooner for Pollard and Dodge of San Francisco. She was christened *Rainier* and towed to San Francisco for machinery. In the spring of 1900 Hitchings signed contracts for three four-top-mast schooners, the first for E. K. Wood to be named *Fearless,* then two for Hind, Rolph Company of San Francisco, the first christened *Kailua* the second *Mahukona.* He built another steamschooner for the E. K. Wood Company in 1901, launching her as the *Olympic.*

In 1901 John Joyce came to Hoquiam from Humboldt Bay to become associated with George Hitchings in a new firm of Hitchings and Joyce. Joyce had been superintendent with H. D. Bendixsen in Eureka after having spent some time in his native Nova Scotia in shipbuilding.

In 1901 Hitchings and Joyce contracted with J. J. McKinnon in San Francisco to build a four-top-mast schooner, which was done and launched as the *A. F. Coats,* named for a successful logger in Aberdeen.

In 1902 Hitchings and Joyce contracted for two vessels, duplicates of the *A. F. Coats,* one for the E. K. Wood Company named *Alert,* the other for J. J. McKinnon, launched as the *Melrose.* That same year they built their last sailing vessel, the schooner *Resolute* for E. K. Wood.

In 1903 the firm built the steamschooner *Shasta* for E. K. Wood, and 1904 the steamschooner *Helen P. Drew* for the L. E. White Lumber Company of San Francisco. Both vessels were towed to San Francisco for machinery installation.

In 1904 the firm built a railroad car ferry for the Northern Pacific to operate on the Columbia River between Kalama, Washington, and Goble, Oregon. Several towboats were built that same year. One, the *Redondo* an 85-foot craft, was towed to San Francisco for machinery and completion.

Hitchings and Joyce completed their last vessel together in 1905, launching the *Tiverton* for J. O. Davenport of San Francisco. In the spring of 1906 the successful partnership was dissolved, the two deciding to retire from shipbuilding. Hitchings, who owned the shipbuilding property, negotiated with the E. K. Wood Company for its disposal. He also sold the equipment, machinery and tools. Joyce, who owned Hoquiam property and had a home on a hill overlooking the city, continued to live in Hoquiam until he died at the age of 80 years.

Hitchings continued to live in Hoquiam until 1910 when the

family moved to Berkeley, California, where Miss Ruth Hitchings attended the University of California, and Miss Dora Hitchings a college in San Jose. Hitchings himself spent several years as a shipbuilding inspector, ship designer, and consultant in shipbuilding. Then the Pacific American Fisheries Company of Bellingham, wanted several cannery ships built for its fishing enterprises in Alaska. Hitchings at first declined their offers, but was finally persuaded to Bellingham and opened a yard for construction of the vessels. In January, 1917, about when the first craft was to be launched, Hitchings became ill. Arrangements were made for him to see the first vessel, the *Redwood,* launched; then he moved to Seattle and the hospital. He died in May, 1917, and was buried in the family plot in Washelli.

Despite the departure of Peter Matthews, George H. Hitchings and John Joyce, shipbuilding on Grays Harbor did not languish. Matthews had left behind a highly-skilled offshoot of his own shipbuilding wizardry, his son, Gordon Frazer Matthews.

Gordon Matthews was born in Eureka, California, July 1877, and named for the Scottish friend of his father. He worked with his father in Eureka until March 1897, when Peter Matthews contracted to construct a schooner for the E. K. Wood Company in Hoquiam. Gordon Matthews went north with him. Upon the death of his father, Gordon Matthews went to San Francisco to settle his father's affairs, and then returned to Hoquiam to work for Hitchings. In the course of the Hoquiam shipbuilding activity, Miss Florence Barker was the sponsor of the steamschooner *Dirigo* in January 1898. She had been "keeping company" with young Gordon Matthews, and in October, 1899, they were married. Their first child was born March 23, 1902, a son named Gordon Henry.

Not long after the car ferry was launched by Hitchings and Joyce, the Hoquiam Water Company wanted a flat-deck barge 60-feet long constructed. Gordon Matthews was recommended and submitted a bid which was accepted. The barge was built on E. K. Wood property near their mill. In 1905 a Grays Harbor firm wanted a 65-foot towboat constructed. Gordon Matthews submitted a bid, was accepted, and built the tug *Agnes* on the same location as the barge. In constructing the *Agnes* Matthews had John Stirrat, a highly-competent ship carpenter, as a partner.

Consequently in June, 1905, when the E. K. Wood Company decided upon another steamschooner, Matthews and Stirrat submitted a bid. However, the two could not handle a contract that large, so they consulted W. H. McWhinney of Aberdeen, who had built several vessels near the West & Slade Lumber Company sawmill. His plant had been burned with heavy loss several years before. However, he had saved the Fay and Egan ship bandsaw and some other equipment. He agreed to join Matthews and Stirrat in submitting a bid. The new firm of Matthews, McWhinney & Stirrat was awarded the contract in August. The ship after some delays, including the death of Stirrat, was launched February 1, 1906 as the *Tamalpais.*

Shortly thereafter E. T. Kruse, a ship owner, requested Gordon Matthews to bid on construction of a single-end steam schooner. He was awarded the contract, returned to Aberdeen in April, and found W. H. McWhinney had sold his interest in the firm to James Hood. Hood agreed to join Matthews in a new shipbuilding firm, as did M. Strommer, an experienced shipwright and loftsman The Matthews Shipbuilding Company was incorporated, Matthews assigning his Kruse contract to the new firm. The vessel was launched November 1, as the *Helene.*

The San Francisco earthquake of April 18, 1906, created an immediate demand for lumber to rebuild the city and a resultant demand for ships to move the lumber. The Pacific Lumber Company of San Francisco contracted in August for a single-end steamschooner, while the Hart-Wood Company of San Francisco contracted for a similar vessel in December. The E. K. Wood Company on February 1, 1907, ordered a single-end and a double-end steamschooner.

The Pacific Lumber Company vessel was launched in March, 1907, as the *Temple E. Dorr.* The second vessel for the lumber company was launched June 1, 1907, as the *William H. Murphy,* while the Hart-Wood vessel was launched September 1, as the *Saginaw.* The first of the two E. K. Wood ships was named *San Jacinto* and launched November 1, 1907, the second, the *Shasta,* was launched March 1, 1908.

In 1910 Matthews built the 65-foot tug *Forester* for Grays Harbor, and that same year bought out Hood's third interest in the Matthews Company. In 1911 Matthews started construction on a steamschooner for S. S. Freeman and launched her as the *Daisy Gadsby* in October, with Freeman's daughter Mildred, 11, as sponsor. Early in January 1912 Matthews signed a contract with the E. K. Wood Company to build a steamschooner, a duplicate of the *Daisy Gadsby* except that she was to have accommodations for 15 passengers. She was launched October 1, as the *Siskiyou*. Meanwhile Matthews constructed a tug, the *Petrel*, for the Polson Company, and in July launched the Hart-Wood steamschooner *Avalon*. He also signed a contract with Charles H. Higgins for a steamschooner similar to but five feet longer than the *Daisy Gadsby*. This vessel was launched January 15, 1913, as the *O. M. Clark*. Three days earlier Matthews had made a trip to San Francisco to sign a contract with Freeman for another double-end steamschooner. At the same time work was progressing on the Olson and Mahony vessel, which was launched at high water Friday, June 13, 1913. She was named *Rosalie Mahony* and sponsored by her namesake, daughter of Mr. and Mrs. Andy Mahony.

The Freeman steamschooner was launched in early September and christened *Daisy Putnam* another addition to S. S. Freeman's fleet of "Daisies."

During the early part of 1914 coast shipping was in depression. Many steamschooners were tied up, while virtually every sailing vessel on the coast was idle. There were more than twenty sailing vessels idle on Grays Harbor alone. However, not long after World War I broke out shipping took an upturn and by January 1915, the effects of the war demand were being felt on the Pacific Coast. By May 1, all the vessels on Grays Harbor were loaded and gone.

The following year Matthews launched another vessel for Freeman, this one named *Daisy Matthews*, launched May 25, 1916. A motorship named *Sierra* was launched for the E. K. Wood Company August 15, and another steamschooner, the *Hartwood*, for the Hart-Wood Company, was launched October 15. On March 10, 1917, Matthews launched the *Santa Elena*, first of two motorships for W. R. Grace Company. The second, the *Santa Isabel*, was launched in May 1917. The *Claremont* for the Hart-Wood Company, largest steamschooner constructed on the Hoquiam, slid down the way October 15, 1917. In May 1918 the

San Diego was completed for the Hart-Wood Company. She was the last steamschooner constructed on Grays Harbor and the largest of that type built in the state of Washington.

Two auxiliary four-mast bald-headed schooners were built for Mons Isakason of Norway, the first, the *Mount Shasta*, launched September 1, 1918, the second December 1, 1918, and named *Mount Hood*.

In order to hold his crew, many of whom planned to go to Aberdeen and work in the two yards building Ferris-type craft for the U. S. government, Matthews laid down the keel for a five-mast topsail schooner, a purely speculative undertaking. In October 1919, while work was under way on the schooner, Captain Ralph E. Peasley, master of the E. K. Wood four-mast schooner *Fred J. Wood*, arrived in Hoquiam to load a cargo of lumber. He went to see Matthews and inspect the shipbuilding. Matthews said he would like to have Peasley as master of the new vessel. Captain Peasley said he would like to be the skipper provided it would be agreeable to his owner. Matthews then made a trip to San Francisco to talk with C. A. Thayer of the E. K. Wood Company about Peasley and also to persuade E. K. Wood Company to purchase a controlling interest and manage the new schooner. To all this the company agreed, whereupon Captain Peasley sold his share in the *Fred J. Wood* to the captain who would succeed him. In turn the E. K. Wood Company appointed Captain Peasley as the firm's representative and inspector in the building of the ship.

Work progressed rapidly and by December 20, 1919, at 11 a.m. with a gale blowing and an extreme high tide flooding the Hoquiam River, the five-mast topsail schooner *Vigilant* was launched. Miss Marion Wood, daughter of Fred J. Wood, then manager of the E. K. Wood lumber mill in Bellingham was the sponsor. The towboat *Hoquiam*, Captain Harry Hubble, picked up the *Vigilant* and towed her to the E. K. Wood wharf on the Hoquiam River where the schooner was to be outfitted. Captain Peasley oversaw finishing of the vessel, stowage of 75 tons of gravel ballast and loading of a cargo of lumber for Australia. She sailed in February, 1919, into a long and colorful career with Matt Peasley as skipper.

Gordon Frazer Matthews moved from Hoquiam in 1920 to

undertake a ship repair business in Portland. During his Portland stay he built in 1923 the last steamschooner built on the coast, the *Esther Johnson*. From August 1928 until his retirement in 1950, he was in marine construction and repair in Seattle. He died in March, 1969, at the age of 91.

The year Peter Matthews died, 1898, John Lindstrom, destined to become a luminary in Grays Harbor shipbuilding, arrived in Hoquiam. Swedish-born Lindstrom as a young man had carried his seabag ashore in San Francisco, and was soon drawn to the shipbuilding activities of H. D. Bendixen on Humboldt Bay. He began work as a common laborer. He was energetic and an enthusiast with ships, and as a consequence advanced rapidly in his trade. Within a year he was offered an opportunity to work with a ship carpenter's tools and developed into one of the best ship carpenters and mechanics in the yard.

Lured to Hoquiam by Matthews, Lindstrom went to work for George H. Hitchings as yard foreman constructing the four-mast bald-headed schooner *Dauntless*. In the early part of 1899, Lindstrom leased the small shipyard operated by the West & Slade Lumber Company at the mouth of the Wishkah. This yard had built the four-mast schooner *A. J. West* in 1898 with John Howsen of San Francisco as master builder. A trip to San Francisco and interviews with ship owners rewarded Lindstrom with contracts to build two steamschooners, both launched in 1899, the 499-ton *Aberdeen* and the 674-ton *San Pedro*. Both vessels were towed to San Francisco for the installation of compound steam engines.

In 1899 Lindstrom contracted to purchase a large tract of land on the waterfront in the western part of Aberdeen. On the tract he built ways and shops for the building of ships. His first contract was with the Wilson Brothers Lumber Company for construction of a four-mast bald-headed schooner, the keel for which was laid in the new yard in 1899. She was launched as the *Henry Wilson*.

John Lindstrom then incorporated the Lindstrom Shipbuilding Company with Charles Green as associate, and in the next six years constructed eight steamschooners and seven four-mast schooners. The steamschooners were: the 469-ton *W. H. Kruger* launched in 1900; 330-ton *Brooklyn* in 1901, 453-ton *G. C. Lin-*

dauer in 1901, 382-ton *James H. Higgins* in 1903, 601-ton *Bee* (renamed *Westerner*) in 1904; 579-ton *Coaster* in 1905; 670-ton *Mayfair* in 1905, 339-ton *Sea Foam* in 1905. The sailing vessels were: *A. B. Johnson*, 529 tons in 1900; *Oliver J. Olsen*, 667 tons in 1900; *R. C. Slade*, 673 tons in 1900; *E. B. Jackson*, 682 tons in 1901; *W. J. Patterson*, 645 tons in 1901; *Wempe Brothers*, 675 tons in 1902, and *Andy Mahoney*, 566 tons in 1902.

When the San Francisco earthquake and fire of 1906 created a demand for lumber and ships to transport it, Lindstrom was ready. In the next three years he built eleven single-end steamschooners, launching the first, the *Berkeley*, 571 tons in 1906. Also in 1906 in rapid succession Lindstrom launched the *Carmel*, 633 tons; *Hornet*, 660 tons; *Jim Butler*, 642 tons; *Quinault*, 582 tons; *Thomas L. Wand*, 657 tons. In 1907 Lindstrom's launchings were: *Bee*, 662 tons; *Capistrano*, 648 tons; *Claremont*, 747 tons; *Grays Harbor*, 659 tons, and *J. Marhoffer*, 638 tons.

Even while building ships at a feverish pace, John Lindstrom had time to devote to the city he had chosen. He was mayor of Aberdeen for the years 1905 and 1906. During these years, too, the Lindstrom Company purchased marine railway equipment in Eureka, California, shipped it by steamer to Aberdeen, and installed the only marine railway capable of hauling out ships of the size being built on the Harbor.

John Lindstrom died suddenly in June, 1908, ending all shipbuilding by the Lindstrom Company. His firm did, however, continue to operate the marine railway and repair vessels until 1917, when operations were discontinued and the property leased to the Grays Harbor Motorship Corporation for the construction of wartime wooden vessels.

All of Lindstrom's steamschooners were of single-end design with round stern, a highly successful vessel permitting a greater lumber capacity and more speed. Lindstrom once said he perfected his design by watching a duck in the water, "full-bowed and riding on its tail."

At each launching Lindstrom and his men in the yard formed a "pool" based upon their estimate of how deep the ship would ride upon launching. Each man made his mark upon the hull and signed his name alongside. Lindstrom always made his mark last and never lost a pool, so well did he know his ships.

"Big Fred" Hewett, who was to become one of Aberdeen's most colorful citizens, came to Grays Harbor in 1897 as a shipwright. He worked for John Lindstrom, first at the Wilson Brothers ways, then in Lindstrom's own yard. He liked to tell of building the little steamschooner *Brooklyn*, the first to be built on Grays Harbor bow first, that is with the bow facing the river. All ships up to this time had been built stern first. Grays Harbor shipwrights were not accustomed to this new situation and had difficulties because they were forever getting things backwards. For instance they would truck out a stern frame, carrying it all the way to the bow before realizing their mistake. Or they would get the port and starboard construction crossed up. It was the only ship Lindstrom ever built bow first.

After shipbuilding slackened "Big Fred" opened a saloon on F street, calling it the Humboldt Bar. In time it was to become festooned with curios and a fixture in the double swinging door section of Aberdeen. The saloon was the gathering place of the less volatile natures, though the customers sacrificed nothing in the way of hard heads and harder fists, but "Big Fred" somehow had a calming effect upon those who bellied up to his bar, probably because "Big Fred" was known to have mollified some mighty big men.

"Big Fred" wore tailor-made suits with the coat pockets nothing more than large canvas bags hanging on the inside. Every Saturday Hewett went to the bank and staggered back to his Humboldt with his coat pockets bulging with silver dollars and gold pieces. These he used to cash logger, millmen and sailor paychecks. In this respect "Big Fred" was a unique institution. Most workers would leave the bulk of their pay with Hewett, admonishing him not to give them more, or only a specified amount when next they asked. No man ever complained. And no man ever lost a cent to "Big Fred."

In 1900 Cousins & McWhinney of Eureka, leased the West & Slade yard to build the steamschooner *Coronoda* for Pollard & Dodge of San Francisco, and the four-mast sailing schooner *F. M. Slade* for West & Slade. The builders were barely finished with their second vessel when Cousins died. McWhinney continued the operation building several large four-mast schooners in 1901 and 1902. The plant was destroyed by fire and never rebuilt.

In 1888 regular steamship service was started between Grays Harbor and San Francisco, with the steamer *Cosmopolis*, Captain George Dettmers. The *Cosmopolis* was a steamschooner type, the first of her kind to enter the Grays Harbor lumber trade. She was capable of carrying 325,000 board feet of lumber. She had been launched in San Francisco in 1887, and began her coastwise runs in 1888, to be followed in this trade by the *Point Loma*, Captain Conway, which was wrecked on the California coast several years later.

Other vessels of the steamschooner type immediately followed in the coastwise run, the *Newburg, Del Norte* (Captain Allen), *Centralia, Coronoda, Chehalis, Norwood, G. C. Lindauer, Fair Oaks, Svea*. In the early 1900's these few became a vast fleet hurrying between Grays Harbor and California ports.

In 1888 the *Novelty*, first bald-headed schooner ever built, came to Grays Harbor with her famous Captain Bob Lawson. Without topmasts, she was so unusual that most of Hoquiam's population gathered on the North Western wharf to watch her arrival. Later, another vessel of the same type, the *Volunteer*, Captain Swan, called at the North Western mill. After that the "bald-heads" became quite common, many of them being built on Grays Harbor.

After the little brig *Orient* stowed the first sizeable cargo of Grays Harbor lumber at the North Western plant in Hoquiam and the *James A. Garfield*, Captain Morse, the second cargo, a long list of ships with round-sounding names snuggled up to Grays Harbor wharves, including the schooner *Lottie Carson*, which delivered to Aberdeen the Weatherwax mill machinery. The cargo included the famous mill whistle from the Colby plant in Edmore, Michigan. When the whistle had blown sufficiently on the Weatherwax plant, and there was lumber on the wharf, the schooner *Alcade*, Captain Smith, arrived to lift the Weatherwax plant's first cutting.

In the 80's came the barkentine *Tam O' Shanter*, Captain Dermott, father of the famous actress Maxine Elliott, the two-mast schooner *Wing and Wing*, and the two-mast with single

Peter Matthews' first creation on Grays Harbor, the four-mast, bald-headed schooner, Defiance, fully laden and outward bound on maiden voyage from Hoquiam River in 1897. The tug is the Traveler.

—JONES COLLECTION

—JONES COLLECTION

Achieving "A Billion or Bust," this "Jap Square" being loaded on Grays Harbor in 1924 called for a joyous civic celebration.

—JONES COLLECTION

North Western Mill, right, putting lumber aboard a double-end schooner. National Mill, at left, burned some years later.

Vigilant, *the storied five-mast tops'l schooner in ballast, sail shortened, ready to cross the Grays Harbor bar.*

—ED VAN SYCKLE

Colorful roamer Captain Ralph E. "Matt" Peasley, immortalized by author Peter B. Kyne. Peasley and Vigilant, *man and ship.*

The Wishkah throbbed this 1907 day with schooners Edward R. West, *right;* Charles E. Falk, *left, and* Santa Monica *downstream. At left, American mill.*

—ED VAN SYCKLE

Tom Soule

—KATHLEEN McDONALD HEIKEL

Jim McDonald

—CATHRYN BYARD McKAY

Scene within the McWhinney shipyard showing the massive timbers workmen curved around the bow.

—CATHRYN BYARD McKAY

Two sailing craft built on Grays Harbor by W. H. McWhinney and shown this day with all the men who helped put them together.

Two brass bands helped blow the sternwheeler Montesano *down the ways at her 1890 launching to serve on the Chehalis.*

Early steam schooner Coronado *carried an auxiliary sail on foremast "just in case." Berthed here at mouth of Wishkah, 1907.*

Chief George Dean, seated second from left among Aberdeen's finest, 1913, was the man who snared murderer Billy Gohl.

Tom Swenson (innocent) stands; Billy Gohl sits.

Gohl and his henchmen took many Grays Harbor victims for their last ride in the "Patrol."

—EUGENE PATTERSON COLLECTION

A typical seven-gated splash dam on the Wishkah, this barrier held back a lake until released to wash logs downstream.

Jack Byard, master shipwright and dam builder, later hewed a flagpole for the City of Aberdeen.

—JONES COLLECTION

Men stood back ... way, way back ... when the Malinowski dam on the Wishkah gushed out as its floodgates opened.

Joe Malinowski, Wishkah valley pioneer and longtime City of Aberdeen master mechanic.

—MONTESANO VIDETTE

Bull team at work in a Delezene Creek log dump. Stream held logs behind splash dam for the final spurt to the Chehalis River.

Boom men working logs with long pike poles were responsible for holding "booms" together on the tidal Wishkah.

—MARIE GUSTAFSON WAHL

William "Billy" McLaughlin, scaler for the Grays Harbor Commercial Company, sized up this spruce stick which beached at Cosmopolis.

—HOQUIAM LIBRARY

Air drying yards were typical on the Grays Harbor sawmill scene. Horses pulled lumber on dollies and men watched their step.

—DEWEY WILSON COLLECTION

All built in Grays Harbor yards, these vessels awaiting cargoes include three tops'l schooners, a bald-head and a steam schooner.

—CATHRYN BYARD McKAY

The Watson A. West, a tops'l schooner and one of many graceful windjammers built on Grays Harbor. West's father built Aberdeen's first sawmill.

Oil painting by Ed Van Syckle, "Little Man, Lot of Power," a donkey puncher applying knowledge to his yarder.

Forest fires often ran away, gutting camps and logging operations. This Donovan and Corkery Willamette yarder died in a fire.

—WEYERHAEUSER COMPANY

Now operated by Weyerhaeuser, this former Schafer Bros. plant is the last tidewater sawmill on Grays Harbor.

—WEYERHAEUSER COMPANY

Weyerhaeuser's Cosmopolis pulp mill now flourishes on lands once occupied by the Grays Harbor Commercial Company.

—PORT OF GRAYS HARBOR

A sign of the times in 1980 is this enormous stock of export logs awaiting shipment to Japan from the Port of Grays Harbor.

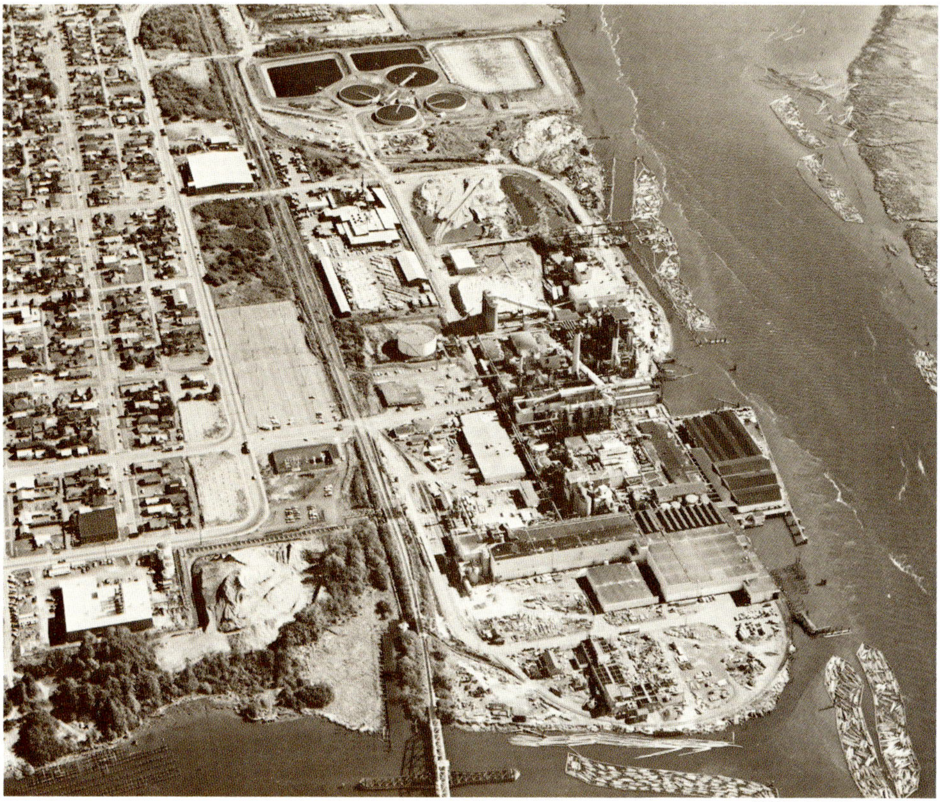

—JONES PHOTO

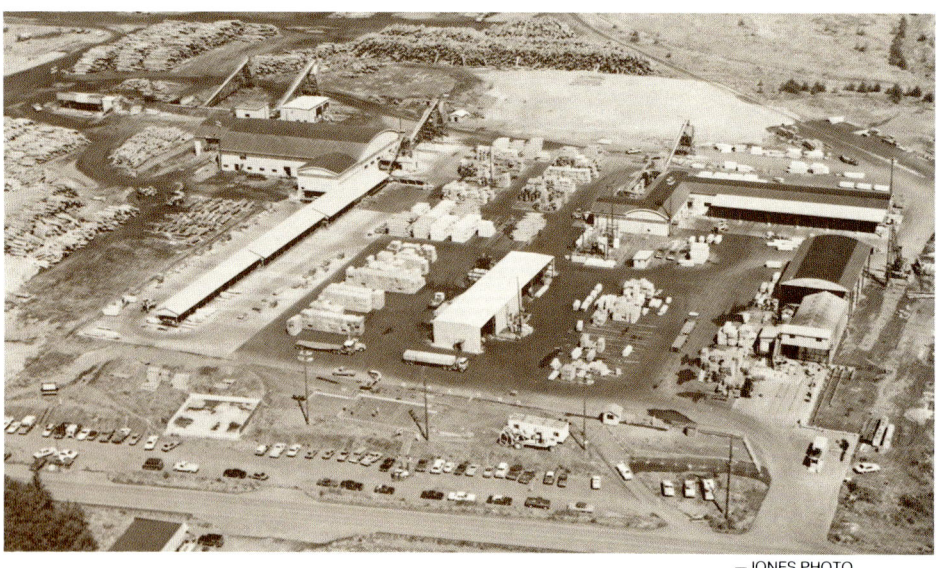

Another block supporting today's Grays Harbor economy is the expanding ITT-Rayonier and Grays Harbor Paper Company complex at Hoquiam.

—JONES PHOTO

An entirely new type of sawmill for small logs has been installed by ITT-Rayonier in Hoquiam to meet future lumber needs.

THE SHIPBUILDING YEARS 229

topmast schooner *Charles Hanson,* Captain Sprague, which made calls so regularly she maintained almost steamer schedules.

The schooner *Trustee* was of particular note, for she was in command of Captain Bill Trainor, one of the three Trainor brothers, all shipmasters on the West Coast, and all State-of-Mainers of the old school. The *Trustee,* lumber laden, was outbound for San Francisco, April 24, 1887, when she went ashore at the mouth of Grays Harbor. The spit upon which she was wrecked was then called "Trustee Spit," now lost in the new configuration of the harbor mouth caused by the south jetty.

Captain Bill Trainor survived the wreck of the *Trustee,* but his brother Captain Charles Trainor, master of the three-mast schooner *Maid of Orleans,* was not so fortunate, for in the relative calm of San Francisco Bay he was knocked overboard by the spanker boom and drowned. The *Maid of Orleans* later called frequently on Grays Harbor under command of Captain Charles Hughes. The third brother of the hard-fisted, hard-stomping and hard-sailing Trainor trio was Captain Sam Trainor, also well known on Grays Harbor, but not in the way of his brothers.

Ships with fascinating names, and shipmasters with arousing ones, gave Grays Harbor rich practical and anecdotal perceptions of the sea. If anything the shipmasters were far more colorful than their commands. They started coming as coastwise and deepwater windjammer skippers, and then in the great era of the steamschooner they rounded out a half century of high-seas and waterfront skill, hardcase commanding, shoreside frolicking and the making of seagoing legends.

In many respects they were awesome, and mostly Scandinavian. They were the innumerable Johnsons, so many in fact they had to be given nicknames to distinguish them, for many had the same given name. Perhaps he was "Single Reef" Johnson, or "Rough Pile" Johnson, "Glassy Eye," "Baby," "Cordwood," "Slabwood," "Scantling Bill," "Swell Head," "Hungry," "Watchtackle," "Coffee," "Doughnut," and "Scarface" Johnson. And others.

Then there was one of the most famous of all, Captain Hans K. "Drawbucket" Johnson, a fixture on Grays Harbor for more than

40 years. In all he spent 60 years deepwater, and as a master of Grays Harbor bar tugs, big tugs, specializing in towing sailing ships into and out of the harbor. Here "Drawbucket" had a succession of such tugs, the *Columbia, Astoria, Printer, Traveler, Daring, Gleanor,* and finally the *John Cudahy*. It was never recorded exactly how "Drawbucket" Johnson acquired his nickname, but it is believed in his younger seafaring days he was a sailmaker and proficient in fashioning canvas buckets for hoisting seawater aboard to wash down the decks. It may have been, too, he was skilled in use of the bucket and thus acquired the nickname.

In any event nicknames were distinguishing, although not always flattering, and most skippers were proud of them. It set them apart and increased their fame, or notoriety, whichever.

There were also Andersons, Hansens, Larsons, Petersons, and others long departed from Scandinavia. They also had nicknames like "Double Reef," "Hoodlum Bob," "Quarter Deck," "Silent," "Breakwater Bill," "Picaroon Charlie," "Picnic Charlie," "Fancy Ben," "Firewood Frank," "Admiral," "Efficiency," "Black Jack," "Holy Joe," "Salvation John," "Berkeley Jim," "Skys' Yard," and then there was Patrick "Stumpin" Olson because he was so short, and Captain Thomas P. "Tin Pan" Dorris of the bald-head schooner *Ethel Zane,* and not forgetting "Midnight" Olson, because he always arrived at midnight, or "Port Wine" Ellefsen, and "Texas Bill" in the *Avalon.*

"Salvation John" can be singled out not only for his own peculiarities, but also for his command, the *Cricket,* an institution on the West Coast. The *Cricket* in her time was unusual in that she was a steel vessel among wooden ones, and had two rather famous skippers, the first being Captain W. J. Maloney, the other Captain "Salvation John" Weideman.

The *Cricket* was built at the United Engineering Works in San Francisco in 1913, and was single-end type, with all her operating units aft. Captain Maloney's claim to fame came with the tow of the British convict ship *Success,* built in 1790 and used almost exclusively for carrying prisoners from Britain to Australia. The *Success* was towed by the *Cricket* into Grays Harbor and berthed by local tugs in the Wishkah River just below the Heron street bridge, where she displayed the "Iron Maiden" and other torturous accommodations to awe-struck Grays Harborites for a fee.

Captain "Salvation John" was something else. His nickname suggested some religious connotation, but his working habits were "full speed ahead and to hell with the gear." His ship, which could carry two million feet of lumber, had two sets of loading booms each ninety feet long. They could reach far over the wharf, some said almost to the pony rig, to lift slingloads of accumulated lumber. Captain "Salvation John" on the wharf side of his bridge, was a man of action. He howled and gesticulated that his loading gear should be over the wharf and the first slingloads coming aboard even before the *Cricket* was made fast. With such antics and fast loading Captain "Salvation John" made a name for himself and his speedy runs between Grays Harbor and California ports.

And the Grays Harbor waterfront was not above waggery. When the schooner *A. B. Johnson* arrived for a cargo of lumber for the West Coast of South America, her master was named Johnson, his brother was mate, Johnson of course, and the cook was named Johnson. Going along with the whimsy the longshore company placed a foreman aboard by the name of Johnson, and a loading crew of ten, all Johnsons. The stevedore company had so many Johnsons on its payroll it numbered them instead of naming them, thus Johnson No. 1, etc. The mill company shipping the lumber put a tallyman by the name of Johnson on the wharf, while the exporting company placed an inspector, Johnson, on the job. The ship was owned by and named after A. B. Johnson of San Francisco. And of course the schooner was towed out by "Drawbucket" Johnson.

Until sometime in 1884 all ships entering Grays Harbor had to come under sail and proceed to their berths or anchorages without assistance, quite a feat of navigation in the narrow water. That year saw the founding of another essential institution — the bar tug, a realm of special skill and daring. The first was the tug *Hunter*, Captain Al Stream, assigned to handle both Grays Harbor and Willapa Harbor bar towing, which essentially was to meet inbound sailing craft off the bar and tow them to their berths and, of course, to tow them out again.

The *Hunter* was appropriately named as a bar tug for she often had to "hunt" for her tows. They would be lost in fog or mist, or if the winds did not serve they could not maintain their station off the harbor entrance and would wander. The *Hunter* continued service for the two harbors until 1890.

The first tug *Argo*, the first of any kind to operate on Grays Harbor, came from Coos Bay in 1883 to tow for the North Western Lumber Company. She tried her best to aid the sailing ships and was barely better than no tug at all when she was afloat. She sank often. In later years the *Argo* was operated by Willis Bergman, brother-in-law of Captain H. A. Benham, who in the early days operated a freight and passenger wharf on the Chehalis River near the mouth of the Wishkah.

In 1886 the tug *Traveler* came into service as a bar tug and remained for 34 years. In 1887 the *Ranger* joined the bar service to remain until 1889 when she was taken to tow on the Humboldt bar. In 1888 the tug *Printer* (97 feet in length, 22-foot beam, 10-foot depth of hold) was built in Hoquiam and towed to San Francisco where machinery was installed. She returned to Grays Harbor in 1890 to undertake bar service, a task she performed until 1913. During the 90's the tugs, *Astoria* and *Columbia* also operated as Grays Harbor bar tugs. Later came the *J. M. Coleman*, the *Daring*, and *John Cudahy*.

In the heyday of Grays Harbor lumber export during the 20's and 30's the bar pilot became as much of an essential figure as the bar tug had been in the sailing ship days. His job was to direct ships in and out of port and he was particularly necessary when big deepwater freighters frequented Grays Harbor wharves.

All the pilots were rated "captains" whether they had actually been or not. However, most had either been shipmasters or tug captains with a peculiar knowledge of Grays Harbor ship channels and other matters pertaining to bar, harbor and river navigation.

Serving during this period of heavy lumber movement were: Captains G. Olson, George Sanborn, Sam Anderson, Harry Hubble, Charles Hansen, Ivar Vaumen, Eric Danielson, Ernest

Smith, "Drawbucket" Johnson, Lloyd Slover, "Tar" Henderson, Marcus Neilson and Henry Stream.

With the proliferation of tidewater sawmills, tugboating "inside" became a booming business. Log towing held attention of most of the towboats, but there were also scows to be handled, gravel barges, ship assists and a number of other chores to keep a big fleet of tugs busy.

A constant flow of log rafts moved up and down the harbor and the Chehalis with the tides. They came from rafting grounds and rollways on the Humptulips, Hoquiam, Wishkah, Preacher Slough, Elk River, Johns River, and the Chehalis itself. The log rafts were snuggled against the racesticks at the mills, where the tugs would pick up the empty boomsticks and tow them back to the rafting grounds. At one time or another there were a number of towing outfits, some independents, and some towing done by boom companies themselves. Eventually the tugboat business narrowed down to two major companies, the R. J. Ultican Tugboat Company and the Allman-Hubble Tugboat Company, the latter operating out of the Hoquiam River, the former out of the Wishkah.

R. J. "Dick" Ultican began his towboat career as skipper of the sternwheeler *Skookum*, towing logs out of the Humptulips. In 1912 he went as skipper of the *Forester* with Jim Wilson as engineer and main stockholder. Warren Egger, owner of the Wishkah Boom Company owned some shares in the *Forester* and upon his death Ultican acquired his holdings in the tug. The first *Forester* was eventually stripped and then the hull burned on Cow Point. In 1921 Ultican, by then owner of a considerable tugboat fleet, built a new *Forester* alongside his office building near the end of Hume street.

Over the years Ultican owned and operated such tugs as the *Tussler, Hustler, Rustler, Warren, Evans, Flora Brown, Richard Jr., Vulcan, Bear* and *Champion*. At one time he had nine towboats operating on the Harbor.

With the advent of truck logging, and the disappearance of tidewater sawmills, log towing declined to a point that would not support the big tugboat fleets. Ultican, who had spent most of his life on Grays Harbor's tides, disposed of his tugs and went to sawmilling, purchasing the Wilson Brothers plant in Aberdeen. He also acquired the lands of the Grays Harbor Commercial Company in Cosmopolis, and during World War II used a portion of the site for a barge yard, building wooden scows for the U. S. government.

The Allman-Hubble Company dates back to 1905 when Frank Hubble and William "Bill" Crawford started a towing business with one tug, *Florence B.* Soon Alzono Hubble replaced Crawford, and along with John Allman, who added his *Advance* to the "fleet," bought out Tom Soule of the Hoquiam Tug Boat Company. In 1913 the operation was incorporated with John Allman as president and manager, and Frank and Alonzo Hubble as vice presidents. Ralph Shivley became secretary-treasurer. Jim Wilson, who had been with Ultican in the *Forester* also became active in the new tugboat company.

In 1914 Frank Hubble became president and manager. Some 13 years later William Geer bought Allman's interest and James "Jim" Walker purchased the Shivley interest. There were no changes in the company until 1944, when Gene Bennett bought out Geer. Two years later Howard Hubble bought out Jim Walker. In 1949 Neil Logue and Carleton Logue bought out Alonzo Hubble. In 1950 Neil Logue became manager of the firm, a position he held until 1972. In 1951 Carleton and Neil Logue, with Howard Hubble, purchased the Frank Hubble holdings. Carleton Logue drowned in the Hoquiam River in 1968, and Gene Bennett, Howard Hubble and Neil Logue assumed the financial interests of the company.

In 1970 Max Wyman bought the company and three years later sold it to Quigg Brothers-McDonald, at which time Neil Logue retired from active operation of the company. He later became a Grays Harbor port commissioner.

While the Allman-Hubble Company was in operation it used the towboats: *Florence B. Advance, Queen, Harbor Queen, Agnes, Laurel, Ranger, Edgar, Watson, Tyee* (lost at Tillamook, Oregon), *John Cudahy, Ryba, Relief, Union, Deck Boy, Daring, Hubble No. 6, H. H. Hubble* (ex-*Tussler*), *F. P. Hubble, E. S. Hubble, Champion, Rose, Lucine* and *Pilot No. 1.*

Actually the Allman-Hubble tugboat enterprise had its

beginning with Thomas C. "Tom" Soule, a stalwart even among Hoquiam's indomitables. He organized a towing company which he eventually sold to Allman and the Hubbles.

Thomas Soule was born December 2, 1874, in Fort Madison, Iowa, the son of T. Soule. He often said in later life it was the wrong place for him to be born. That event should have taken place in Freeport, Maine, where the Soule family had lived, built ships, and put to sea for generations. They moved to Iowa to escape the Down East cold, but apparently still had ties with saltwater, for Tom Soule was virtually raised aboard the ship *Enos Soule* of which Tom Soule's father was master.

Tom Soule at the age of 11 found himself in Hoquiam attending the Hoquiam school. That he came to this coast in the *Enos Soule* is apparent in that "Buck" Bailey, mate in the *Enos Soule* on the East Coast, quit the ship in Port Discovery and came to Grays Harbor to run the steamer *Argo* (40 feet in length, eight-foot beam) in a three-times-a-week service between Hoquiam and Damon's Point. Bailey once picked up a sea otter on the beach and sold it to Jack Kann, a fur buyer, for $200. Charley McIntyre, Steve Grover and Shorty Astell, all sea otter hunters, claimed the animal as theirs. Bailey had removed the marked bullet from the otter and no one of the hunters could prove ownership.

Out of the Hoquiam school, Tom Soule went to Portland, Oregon, to attend Bishop Scott Military Academy, a roommate of Ed Benn, Sam Benn's son, and classmate of Will and Horace Campbell of Hoquiam, Bert Schofield also of Grays Harbor, and John and Herbert Woods of South Bend, Willapa Harbor.

Upon completion of his schooling Tom Soule got a job with salvagers of the rail cargo in the wrecked British bark *Abercorn*.

From the *Abercorn* he went to the *Port Gordon*, a ship wrecked three miles north of the Queets. The vessel was laden with fire brick and pig iron, much of which was removed to the beach. About this time the little sealing schooner *Lucy Lowe* brought a group of settlers to the Queets. After that a number of sealing schooners would approach the beach at the *Port Gordon* wreck on calm days and send sealing boats ashore to load up with bricks and iron, which would be taken to British Columbia and sold. Indians often transferred the heavy cargo in their canoes to waiting sealing ships.

Quite often sealers would get lost in the fog and, unable to find their mother ships, would head for the beach. Some, too, would head for the Strait of Juan de Fuca and Port Angeles where they would leave their boats on the beach, sell their shotguns for $50 and skedaddle.

Tom Soule worked two summers on the *Port Gordon* wreck then gave it up. While at the Queets he became acquainted with William "Bill" Hank, who had the sloop *Mary E* on the Queets lagoon. He wanted to bring the sloop to Grays Harbor so Tom Soule made the trip with him. Bill Hank was the first to file a land claim at the mouth of the Hoh.

Then Tom Soule became teenage owner, with John Allman as partner, of the *Hercules*, a small launch in which he carried freight and supplies to logging camps up the Hoquiam.

In 1899, two years after discovery of gold in Alaska, and at the age of 25, Tom Soule got the fever which was to draw him to the north for two years. Hubert Schafer had gone to Alaska the year before and the letters he sent home gave Soule, Elmer Brady and Jack Knapp the idea of going there themselves. They did find "color" and developed themselves a good mine, but Brady would go into Dawson and listen to rumors of big strikes and bucketsful of gold elsewhere. Soon he had the partners stampeding all over the place. Soule tired of it in 1901 and returned to Hoquiam to start the Soule Tug and Barge Company, first with the old tug *Edgar*. Expanding, the firm purchased the tugs *Rustler*, the *Agnes* and the *Hoquiam*. During this decade in the towing business, Soule found time to salvage the schooner *C. A. Thayer*, which had gone ashore all-standing a short distance north of the Grays Harbor entrance. This time the whole ship was saved by moving her on rollers across Point Brown and relaunching her inside the harbor.

The next salvage venture for Tom Soule was the brand new *Sir Jensey Gee Family* a French bark on her maiden voyage. She piled up on Cape Elizabeth just north of the Quinault River mouth. She had a large quantity of fine liquors aboard, soon to be an enticement for Taholah residents. The crew fought off the first

Indians to approach, but finally, despite their fears, deserted the endangered bark and took uneasy refuge in the Indian village. Within a few days the French crew walked down the beach to Oyehut, from where they made their "escape" to Puget Sound.

Tom Soule was able to purchase five hundred feet of 10-inch hawser from the wreck for $50.

Soule's final venture in salvaging was with the schooner *Zanita*, wrecked two miles south of Oyehut. He hired a crew of loggers to remove ballast from the vessel, but the job was held up momentarily because the skipper would not let the loggers on his deck in their calked boots.

After ten years of tugboating and salvaging, Soule sold his towboat company to Frank, Harry and Alonzo Hubble, who with Soule's partner in the *Hercules,* John Allman, formed the Allman-Hubble Towing Company.

Soule then joined Joe Stearns and Al Kuhn in a company which logged a large portion of the North Bay area and maintained camps and mills at Sternsville, near Aloha, Carlisle and Copalis. Later Soule joined Kuhn in the Robert Gray Shingle Company.

Just to keep his hand in, Soule who held a deepwater master's license, made several voyages in Grays Harbor ships, one of them in the *Pioneer,* first vessel built on Grays Harbor, with Captain Charles Hughes. Another voyage and a notable one, was in the Grays Harbor-built three-mast schooner *J. M. Weatherwax* to the Fiji Islands, with Captain Hughes again. From Suva Soule was invited to visit outlying islands in a private yacht. On one small island he was strolling along a coral road through a small village when four big Fijians approached carrying a hammock slung between two poles. There was a train of several natives behind, all dressed in their Sunday best. Riding in the hammock was a shoeless white man dressed only in dungarees.

Soule peered into the hammock and stood flabbergasted. There with all the aplomb in the world rode "Siwash " Smith, as big as life.

Now "Siwash" Smith, perhaps as late as two years before, had been living in a small houseboat at the mouth of the Hoquiam River. He was a Scandinavian, a hard worker, a jack of all trades, and a seaman when he got the notion. He was nicknamed "Siwash," known as a friend of the Indians. He would often get them whiskey, which he diluted one half with water and saved the other half for himself. At some time unknown to any of his local friends he disappeared from Grays Harbor.

Neither hide nor hair of him had been seen until Tom Soule stood in the hot sun on a dusty road in a small Fiji village and watched "Siwash" Smith pass by in regal splendor.

Soule said: "Howdy, Siwash." But Siwash never batted an eye. Then out of the side of his face: "Meet me here in an hour. I got some doin's to do first."

Soule eventually learned Siwash had shipped out on a lumber schooner for Suva, boarded a missionary brig, taken a liking to one of the smaller islands, and forgotten to return to his ship. He became something of a king or high chief and had lived high on the Fijian hog almost from the day of his arrival. He told Soule he would return to Hoquiam some day and never do another lick of work as long as he lived. But the scalawag never returned.

Next to logging camps and sawmills, seafaring was a way of life for Grays Harbor. When the bandsaw turned the tidewater sawmill into an efficent lumber-cutting prodigy, the waterfront came into its own. Ships swarmed the wharves or anchored anxiously in the stream awaiting lumber cargoes. At first the fleet was entirely sailing craft, then the nature of the vessel changed to steam, to the eclipse of the sail, and eventually to the motorship, with steam becoming an almost forgotten motive power.

In the '90s the few became a host, with Grays Harbor becoming a "home" for a vast sailing fleet. Perhaps it was the *San Buenaventura* just towed in by the tug *Traveler* and loading for San Francisco. The schooner *Norway* discharging ballast, the *American Girl* loading for San Francisco, or the schooner *Premier* loading at A. J. West. It could be the schooner *La Gironde* (January 1, 1891) having her bottom scraped on the beach at Cosmopolis. Perhaps the *Annie Larson*, which in World War I was to figure in the famous *Annie Larson* gun-running episode, arriving for a cargo of lumber. The steamer *Westport*, Captain Conway, stepping a new foremast. The schooners *Lizzie Vance, Sailor Boy, Roy Sommers, Fred J. Wood*, the four-mast bark *Haltalic* and the *Kona*. The ill-fated *American Boy*, Captain

Hammond, loaded at the Weatherwax mill in October 1890, and went aground the following month in the Farallones to become a total loss.

The schooner *Helen N. Kimball* arrived in January 1891, with a cargo of redwood from California consigned to Whitehouse, Crimmins & Company, operators of a sash and door factory. The schooner discharged 168,000 feet of redwood and 500,000 redwood shingles.

Any frequenter of the Grays Harbor waterfront in the earlier days of the lumber trade would have recognized a vast array of vessels: *Orient, Tanner, Melancthon, North Bend, Seminole* (ship), *David Evans, Annie Gee, Volunteer, Novelty, Tam O'Shanter, Portland, Beulah, Charles Hanson, Dora Bluhm, J. C. Ford, J. M. Griffin, Webfoot, Sailor Boy, Signal, James A. Garfield, Omego, Adendo, Pioneer, J. M. Weatherwax, Excelsior, Enterprise, Louis Glide, Newsboy, Wing and Wing, S. L. Wilder, Premier, Robert Levers, Robert Searles, Neptune, Serma Thayer, Jessie Nickerson, Jennie Thelin, O. M. Kellogg, King Cyrus, Lackine, Laura May, Lizzie Vance, Lyman D. Foster, Mary Foster, Endeavor, Ariel, John G. North, Minnie Kane, Oliver Olson, Catherine Sudden, Point Loma, Garden City, Comet, Echo, Bee, Hornet, Trustee, Argo, Dare, Cosmopolis, J. B. Stetson, Kate and Ann, Rebecca, Retriever, Chehalis, John F. Miller, E. K. Wood, C. A. Thayer, Dauntless, S. E. Slade, Fearless, Fannie Adele, J. M. Coleman, Del Norte, Banning, Columbia, Alert, Claus Spreckles, Maid of Orleans, Azalea, Atila Fjord, Irene, A. F. Coats, Amelia, C. C. Funk, Esther Buhner, C. S. Holmes, Coquille River, Gem, Fortuna, Glen, W. H. Talbot, Golden Shore, Jane A. Falkenberg, Harriet Gee, Helene, Geneva, Halycon, General Miles, Gleanor, Forest King, Emma Clandena, Repeat, Crescent City, Borealis, Alliance, Annie Larson, Carrier Dove, Annie Johnson, Occident, Katie Flickinger* and the *Undaunted.*

The *Jessie Nickerson* went ashore on Cape Shoalwater in 1890 to become a total loss. The schooner *Ariel* was lost on Point Adams at the mouth of the Columbia in 1886. The barkentine *Jane A. Falkenberg* was driven ashore on the Oregon coast in 1872. The barkentine *Webfoot* was lost November 21, 1904, near the mouth of the Columbia. The brig *Orient*, which stowed the first sizeable lumber cargo on Grays Harbor, reputedly was wrecked on Point Leadbetter, Shoalwater Bay, May 7, 1875. However, there is a discrepancy here for the *Orient* loaded at the North Western mill in Hoquiam in the early 80's. It is doubtful there was another brig *Orient* on the coast at that time. The source for the date and place of the *"Orient's"* destruction is "PACIFIC GRAVEYARD" a chart published by Binford and Mort, Portland. It could be the chart carried the wrong date.

Steam had come into the coastwise trade as early as 1890. In November of that year the steamschooner *Casper* was loading at Cosmopolis, while a berthmate, the steamschooner *Scocia*, was discharging a cargo of hay for the Grays Harbor Commercial Company, while the steamer *Point Loma* (the first *Point Loma*) was being overhauled with a new deck and upper works. At the same time the schooners *Charles Hansen* and *La Gironde* were loading at Slades. The schooner *J. M. Weatherwax* had just returned from her maiden voyage.

Sail was to continue domination of the waterfront for years to come. For instance on the waterfront November 16, 1903, were the schooners: *F. S. Redfield, Aloha, Fred Sanders, A. B. Johnson, David Evans, Cecilia Sudden, H. D. Bendixen* and *Sophie Christenson*, and only two steam schooners the *Centralia* and *Coquille River*.

This was about the time the *Sophie Christenson* made a classic maneuver and history on the Wishkah. The big schooner was being towed down the stream from the Emery, Mack & Wood mill, deep laden with lumber, her long jib boom angling saucily. As she rounded the tight bend in the Wishkah near the end of Heron street, the jibboom speared an outhouse perched on piling at the rear of the saloon at Heron and F streets.

It was always said Captain Michael McCarron of the *Sophie Christenson* deliberately gave the wheel a sharp turn and, with perfect aim, impaled the privy with a howl from the inmate, who dropped to the wharf planks from the then bottomless structure. The schooner continued on her course, the "two-holer" dangling from the bowsprit, while the waterfront roared. The luckless man on the wharf, desperately hoisting his pants, was identified by a witness to the event, Hugh Delanty of the Grays Harbor Stevedore Company, as Billy Gohl, the "ghoul of the waterfront."

Chapter 14

THAT NO-GOOD BILLY GOHL

There may have been something retaliatory, and perhaps justice, in the Sophie Christenson incident, for Billy Gohl was the scourge of the waterfront, the torment of lumbermen, and an affliction of shipmasters and shipowners. Because he could do so much mischief with but little more than a wave of his hand — and a few threatening axe handles — Gohl tied up ship loading, delayed sailings, fouled up provisioning, caused lawsuits over late lumber deliveries, roused the saloons, intimidated pimps and gamblers, "cut" the whores and generally did pretty well for his finances and his egomania. And already he was on his way to becoming a terrifying criminal, the murderer of many men.

Billy Gohl's story began in 1902. Groomed on the tough San Francisco waterfront, Gohl arrived on Grays Harbor to represent the Sailors Union of the Pacific. He moved into the second-floor union office in Ed Dolan's Grand Saloon building on the southeast corner of Heron and F streets. The rear of the building extended on piling over the Wishkah River. There was also a narrow wharf upon which rested the privy.

It took but a short time for Billy Gohl to commandeer Ed Dolan's saloon for his unofficial Sailors Union base of operations, gather a squad of toughs and prepare to intimidate the waterfront. Ed Dolan and his bartender brother, Tom Dolan, (another brother, Jim Dolan, operated the Horseshoe saloon) soon tired of Billy Gohl and sold the saloon to Patrick "Paddy" McHugh and brother, Neil McHugh.

As Gohl became a settled citizen of Aberdeen he, with Lars Kingstad, opened a cigar store at 313½ South F street, and for his first street address used the Model rooms, and then the Capitol rooms, and finally acquired a house on Broadway at the southeast corner of Sixth street. He also acquired a wife, characterized as a "tough one."

Gohl had been in Aberdeen two years when police began to take concerned interest in the Sailors Union representative and his henchmen. Floating bodies began to show up on the Wishkah and Chehalis, and too many rumors began to float along the waterfront. Gohl himself was responsible for some of the stories, for he was boastful and careless with his talk. And then Gohl nearly overplayed his hand. The schooner *Fearless* was anchored in the lower harbor waiting to cross out. In her crew were two seamen not approved by Gohl for jobs aboard the ship. Told that the *Fearless* was about to sail, Gohl put his armed gang into a launch and headed down the bay. After midnight, with no lights showing, Gohl sneaked upon the *Fearless,* boarded her and made off with the two non-union seamen.

For his act of piracy Billy Gohl was tried and convicted. In his appeal the state supreme court upheld the conviction. The case was eventually settled with Gohl being fined $1,200, which the union paid.

With Gohl boasting he would never go to prison, the Harbor was swept by a series of crimes. The Brunswick Hotel was burned. Many people knew Gohl didn't like Lee Williams, who operated a saloon in the building. Fires burned the Zelasko block and the Grays Harbor Ship Chandlery, with suspicion pointing toward Gohl. A sailor was found shot to death on F street. Gohl bragged of shooting the man from a window in his office. The schooner *R. C. Slade* was looted at a wharf across the Wishkah from the Grand saloon. Frank Becker's sporting goods store was burglarized with a number of guns and ammunition taken. An attempt was made to blow up the house of W. B. Mack, manager of the West & Slade Lumber Company and a particular critic of Billy Gohl. J. B. Mears, a lumber buyer, known to carry a large sum of money, disappeared. His body was fished from the river.

In 1907 an uncommon number of "floaters" began to be pulled from the rivers. The first that year was Askel Johnson, found February 8, spotted by Captain Mersich in the sternwheeler *Skookum*. On February 17, the body of John Andersen, a native of Finland, was found near the Wilson mill. On March 30, C. J. Douglas and Peter Seden, piling lumber on the Hart-Wood mill wharf, spotted a floater, with his throat cut, who never was identified. Soon the body of Gus Lindros was recovered, and on April 26, that of Robert Preist. Sunday morning, May 5, John Hansen, Aberdeen's merchant tailor, was walking across the Heron street bridge. He saw the body of J. B. Meers, who unlike the other floaters, was not a seaman, fisherman or mill hand. He was a timber cruiser employed by the Continental Timber Company. He was last seen alive in some Aberdeen saloons and was known to have had $700 in cash on his person. The next day the body of Connie Lockett, 21, deckhand in the steamer *Harbor Belle* was pulled from the river by the crew of the little steamer *Thistle*. The body of Gabrielle Austad, a 22-year-old Norwegian logger, was found later in the year.

Meanwhile there was a systematic looting of moored ships. Gohl, it was alleged, would supply seamen from among his henchmen for shorthanded ships. The men would go aboard and then when all hands were ashore or snoring in their bunks, would rob the vessel of instruments, money, stores and about everything else that was loose. They would depart overside in a rowboat and be safely away when the crime was discovered.

None of these crimes could be directly pinned on Billy Gohl. There were no witnesses to testify, and Gohl was never caught in the act. But then Billy Gohl made two mistakes: He bragged before a crime was committed, and he kicked Andy Jacobsen's little dog. Then a third element joined in the undoing of Billy Gohl. George Dean, who had been a police officer under J. M. Birmingham, was appointed police captain when Ed Benn became mayor of Aberdeen.

George Dean had come up from the Oregon coast to Westport where his brother had gone as a lifeguard when the Westport lifesaving station was established. Dean worked a year in Westport as a substitute at the coastguard station and drove a team for Charley Yana. Dean then shifted to Aberdeen to drive a team for the Slade mill, and after a time went into partnership with Roy Sargent to operate a grocery store for Slade. As police captain, George Dean gave first priority to building a solid case against Billy Gohl. He found two immediate sources of information: Paddy McHugh in the Grand saloon, who knew every move of Gohl's gang; and Lauritz Jentzen, known on the waterfront as "The Weasel." Jentzen was in on virtually all of Gohl's escapades, and like all of Gohl's gang he felt immune and safe from the law.

But the day came when Billy Gohl leaned over the bar in Paddy McHugh's saloon and confided that he was going down the bay to kill two men, John Hoffman and Charles Hatberg, and that he was taking a sailor named John Klinkenberg in Gohl's launch, the *Patrol*, to a shack Gohl maintained at the mouth of Indian Creek across the upper harbor from Hoquiam. There Gohl was to find Charles Hatberg. Gohl returned to town two days later and immediately shipped Klingenberg out in the schooner *A. J. West*. Hoffman and Hatberg were missing.

A few days later George L. Lightfoot, who had a shack near Gohl's Indian Creek place, saw Hatberg's face sticking out of the water off Indian Creek. He told his brother William Lightfoot, and the brother and Jim Marshall came into Aberdeen to notify authorities.

By this time George Dean was piecing together some concrete evidence against Gohl. He had talked to Paddy McHugh, and now he interviewed Andy Jacobsen, who was ready to tell all he knew. Gohl not only had kicked Jacobsen's dog, but Jacobsen suspected Gohl had the dog thrown into the Wishkah, for several days later the dog was found floating in the river, the fate of Gohl's supposed human victims.

Jacobsen told how Gohl had killed a sailor, a mutual friend, for his money. He also told of two valuable auto robes stolen from Linc Davenport's car parked near Gohl's home. They were traced to a shack known to belong to Gohl, who was charged with the theft. Charles Hatberg testified he had bought the robes at a second-hand store. Billy Gohl was acquitted, but he was to confide in Paddy McHugh that he was going to kill Hatberg because he "knew too much." Later he was to tell McHugh that Hoffman, Hatberg and Klingenberg "would never be seen around Grays Harbor again." This information Paddy McHugh imparted to Captain George Dean, who, when Hatberg's body was found, believed he had his solid evidence.

The next day February 2, 1910, Aberdeen City Detective K. Y. Church, was instructed by Dean, now police chief, to go to Gohl's office and ask Gohl to "walk over to the station for a few minutes." Gohl, who had often been asked to identify dead seamen, many of them allegedly his own victims, thought nothing of the request, and immediately complied. As he walked into the police station Gohl was confronted by Dean and several police with drawn guns. Dean read the warrant charging Gohl with murder.

In a roundabout way Dean had learned John Klingenberg had been sent away as a seaman in the schooner *A. J. West* to Santa Rosalia, Mexico, a port on the gulf side of Baja California. Dean notified Sheriff Ed Payette, who arranged with the American consul to make sure Klingenberg was aboard the schooner on her return voyage to Grays Harbor. As the *A. J. West* crossed into the harbor a deputy sheriff was aboard the bar tug that towed her to quarantine, where Klingenberg was removed and taken before Judge C. W. Hodgdon in Hoquiam, where he made a full confession.

Klingenberg was to repeat at Gohl's trial that he and Hoffman had been summoned by Gohl to go to the shack on Indian Creek where Hatberg was staying, telling Klingenberg he had "work" for Klingenberg to do.

The shack was one of several Gohl maintained around the harbor, at Elliott Slough, Grass Creek, James Rock, South Bay, Chenois Creek and the one on Indian Creek. These he used as hideouts for members of his gang in trouble, or for those who did Gohl's criminal bidding, and even as a place to find a few votes if needed in union elections.

Klingenberg told a frightful story. On the way to Indian Creek in Gohl's launch *Patrol*, Gohl produced a revolver and shot Hoffman, who fell to the bottom of the launch, begging for his life. Gohl shot Hoffman twice more in the body, then seized the man by the throat, pressed the gun against his head and fired. Klingenberg was forced to help Gohl truss the body, weigh it with an anchor and throw it overside.

The two men spent the night in the shack with Hatberg. When leaving the next morning, Gohl ordered Hatberg to row all three out to the anchored launch. Before they departed Gohl slipped Klingenberg the revolver and said he was to shoot Hatberg or he, Gohl, would kill Klingenberg. The sailor was terror stricken by the threat after having witnessed the coldblooded murder of Hoffman.

The three got into the rowboat with Gohl in the stern, Klingenberg in the bow and Hatberg rowing. When half way to the launch Klingenberg put the gun against Hatberg's head and fired. Klingenberg was to testify that Gohl laughed, tied a small anchor to Hatberg's feet and pushed him overboard. Returning to Aberdeen Gohl immediately spirited Klingenberg away in the *A. J. West*.

While Klingenberg was being apprehended, Sheriff Ed Payette arrested the "Weasel," Lauritz Jensen, in Elma. Jensen had been a member of Gohl's gang for some time and reputedly was the toughest of the lot. When he learned of Gohl's arrest he agreed to contribute to the evidence. He related how Gohl had shot a sailor on F street from the window of his office in the Grand saloon building; of the burning of Lee Williams' saloon and the looting of Frank Becker's store for guns and ammunition.

Billy Gohl, faced with at least three documented killings, went to trial May 10, 1910, before Superior Court Judge Ben Sheeks for the slaying of Charles Hatberg. Hoffman's body was never found. Hatberg on May 6, 1910, had been identified by a shipmate, Emil Olson, by the tatooed skin removed from Hatberg's arm.

For the trial, Attorney William E. Campbell, who in later years was to be an outstanding superior court judge, was the prosecutor, with E. E. Boner as assistant prosecutor. Gohl through his wife hired a young attorney, A. M. Abel, for the defense. When Abel visited Gohl in a county jail cell, although he knew Gohl's reputation, he was not prepared for Gohl's boasting of his crimes and the disclosure that Gohl had kept a journal of the more interesting ones. But what turned Abel away from the case was

Gohl's boast that he would never be convicted because he was prepared to shoot his way out of the jail and escape. He showed Abel a loaded revolver and a knife under the cell table held in place by matches stuck into cracks.

That was too much for the young attorney, who sought out Judge Mason Irwin and confided to him Gohl's plans. Without revealing his source of information, Sheriff Payette searched Gohl's cell and removed the weapons.

Three hundred citizens were summoned for jury duty. It took several days for a jury to be selected, most members finally being taken from the east end of the county where Gohl was not well known. Following Abel's resignation from the case A. E. Cross became the court-appointed attorney for the defense, with J. A. Hutchenson as co-counsel.

Gohl's case went to the jury May 11, 1910, at 2:30 o'clock in the afternoon. The twelve jurors filed again into the courtroom at midnight, with Foreman L. O. Stewart delivering the verdict, guilty. Judge Sheeks sentenced Gohl to life imprisonment in Walla Walla. In prison several years later Billy Gohl began to slip mentally. He witnessed a stabbing during a prison altercation and became so deranged he was sent to a prison for the criminally insane at Sedro-Woolley, where he died a maniac.

John Klingenberg was tried in October 1910, for second-degree murder, found guilty and sentenced to 15 years in prison.

Billy Gohl's death ended the career of Grays Harbor's most notorious criminal. Also ended was domination of the waterfront by the Sailors Union and its Gohl gang. Shortly thereafter sail gave way almost entirely to steam and the steamschooner, with union influence fading.

Chapter 15

MASTER OF THE VIGILANT

Captain Ralph E. Peasley was destined for bigger worlds. He may have begun as a Down East State-of-Mainer and sailed lumber-laden windjammers out of Grays Harbor for more than a half-century, but he ended up in libraries of half the nation, maybe more. And many libraries, particularly on the Pacific Coast, still carry copies of Peter B. Kyne's frolicsome "Cappy Ricks or the Subjugation of Matt Peasley." It is a shallow-draft volume of seafaring gimmicks, and shenanigans in maritime law, but it was extremely popular in its day, as one lean, long-shinned shipmaster was to discover.

When Kyne wrote his book (copyright 1915) he perpetuated one of those rare analogies that permits a man to be at once fact and fiction. Buttoned up in the same blue serge suit was the ink-and-paper Peasley, who vanquished All Hands and Feet in Cape Town and went on to marry Cappy Rick's daughter, Florence, and the lively Peasley who stormed up and down and across the Pacific for almost half a century and became far more colorful than the figure Kyne created, or actually lifted from life.

It was not so strange that Captain Peasley, as his voyages multiplied and his deeds gathered, became something of a living legend, with the flesh and fancy of it ever harder to separate. The figment, often so true in Peasley's own life, and the actual facts of his experiences were so mingled that the two Peasleys finally became merged into one.

This similitude came about naturally enough. In his earlier

years the tall Down Easter was inclined toward rollicking ashore, and at sea to hoisting 'em high and to hell with the backstays. He was a fetching figure of a man, standing three inches better than a fathom in his wool socks, not counting the thrum of unruly hair. He carried his weight with the air of a skys'l yarder, straight and lofty. He was blue and sprightly of eye and sharp of wit, outspoken as shipmasters are apt to be, with a sheath-knife tongue, one edge whetted keen, the other harmless. He was able, not only as a seaman but as a yarner and maker of friends. He could cut a dido with the best of the lot. He was laniferous of ear, which gave him only the tinge of a bucko, but his standing rigging was set up with wire. If there was anything soft about him it was his heart, which was balsa, while his soul was lignum vitae. He was not a severe man; he could bend. And it was his fortune the sea spared him the bitter loneliness that abused so many mariners.

He was born Ralph E. Peasley and was meant to be something more than ordinary. It was in his blood and the tradition of his family, the seagoing Peasleys of Jonesport, Maine. Those before him sailed the Atlantic, but the family's fame was to be carried afar by the single son of its last generation. With the instinct of an albatross, Peasley sought salt water as soon as he could hitch up his own britches. He had his first command by the time he turned 20, and in his 22nd year pounded through the graybeards of the Horn to become a man of the Pacific, never to return to the haunts of his people.

While Peasley was being carried by the winds from Grays Harbor to Callao, to Sydney and Shanghai and the islands in between, Kyne was secretary to Dolbeer & Carson in San Francisco, an office-imprisoned man, a sort of desk roach, weary of files and figures. One of his chores was to peruse reports from the company's shipmasters, finding, as the skippers claimed, as much fault as possible.

One day a new kind of report was dropped upon his desk. It was not the customary stuff, flavorless to the point of tedium. This one was terse, there was punch to it, it was salty and a little sacrilegious, not treating with dignity those things that staid old shipping firms expected to be handled with utmost reverence. It was signed "Ralph E. Peasley, Master."

Kyne jotted this down among the mental notes he was accumulating from the shipping business against the day he would quit as an office drudge and buck the winds and tides of fiction writing. In time other tradition-splitting reports turned up, and then one day the office door slammed open and in stormed Captain Peasley himself. There in the flesh stood Kyne's Yankee skipper. As of that moment Peasley blew into fiction all-standing, a ready-made, full-rigged character fresh from the Roaring Forties, with cigar apeak and an effortless roar that rumbled down the corridors of Dolbeer & Carson. Kyne at his best could not have invented better. And he never looked farther. When the time came for the popular "Cappy Ricks" yarns, Peasley was transplanted to print without so much as a changed vest button. Years later Peasley was to say: "I wrote those reports short so there wasn't so much with which to find fault."

Kyne gave credit where credit was due. On the dedication page of his book "Subjugation of Matt Peasley" he wrote: "To the ideal American sailor ... Captain Ralph E. Peasley of Jonesport, Maine, who skippered the first five-mast schooner ever built, brought her on that first voyage through the worst typhoon that ever blew, and upon arriving off the Yang Tse Kiang river for the first time in his adventurous career, decided he could not trust a Chinese pilot and established a record by sailing her up himself."

That was the schooner *Louis* in which Peasley boomed down Alenuihaha channel between Maui and Hawaii on this 30th birthday anniversary May 30, 1896, and fetched his offing on the China coast in the terrible grip of a China Sea typhoon. The *Louis* gave a full set of sail to the demonic winds before she came up to the mouth of the river under bare poles. All the wise heads among the Chinese pilots had long since hightailed for cover, so Peasley, with no river charts, crossed in and took the big windjammer up to Shanghai himself. It was, as Kyne said, a record.

This infinite Yankee was to command many a ship after that, to commute between continents and touch many a fair isle. But as he made port after port he became less certain whether he was his own man or Kyne's. The deeds of fiction followed him wherever he dropped anchor or threw a line over a bollard. He was called upon to elaborate episodes in Kyne's book. People would chuckle over some whimsy Kyne had put to print, thoroughly convinced that the fiction tales were no more than lively accounts of Peasley's own life.

Modesty was of no avail. Denials were turned aside with knowing grins. Peasley was never to live down the prodigious feats of skullduggery that sent Cappy Ricks into tantrums. Nor was he ever to convince his growing "public" he was just a shipmaster earning a shipmaster's pay. He was beset by those who sought to share in some way the fabulous sums the fictitious Peasley made in his waterfront deals. Peasley once declared he inherited everything in Kyne's book except Captain Matt Peasley's Midas touch.

As the years rolled under his keel and his lambent lip straggled into the full bristle of a walrus mustache, Captain Peasley's ear lost its familiarity with the "Ralph E." of his name. He was known everywhere around the Pacific as Captain Matt Peasley, and often called just "Captain Matt." And in some measure the living Peasley began to assume the proportions of his fictitious counterpart. A role was thrust upon him and he began to play the part. It took no serious effort, for he was already in character. Nor did he shrink from the publicity. When ship visitors came to gape at a fiction hero he gave them a real version. Always affable, he found delight in rewarding the crowd with what it wanted. He posed in good humor for the inevitable cameraman, he chatted, he autographed. He gave with the famous Peasley grin.

In the later years of sail there was always a scattering of onlookers at every wharf where few-and-far-between windjammers berthed, and especially if it was a Peasley ship. He strode the poop in the best deep-water fashion, peered over side with a critical eye, bellowed orders aloft and couched his commands in a seagoing lingo that would confound anyone but a pickled-in-brine wooden-ship-and-iron-men sailorman. Where else in his day save from Peasley's deck would you hear: "Pay 'er off handsomely, Mister, I said handsomely!" His limitless and well-barnacled oaths were reserved mostly for landlubbers gathered for a show. They were round but harmless. Peasley was a good showman.

No man could sail so long without some humdrum voyages, but there was enough of adventure and misadventure in Peasley's career to keep waterfronts constantly alert to his doings. Chances were always good that he would come in with a story, like the time in a dense fog he bumped along Australia's Great Barrier, kissing the awesome reef repeatedly and escaping by a miracle with no more damage than a few scratches on the ship's hull.

Captain Peasley in the *Vigilant* rode out the great North Pacific hurricane of January 29, 1921, a storm that struck the big five-master 100 miles off the Washington coast and then screamed ashore to mow gigantic swaths through the magnificent rain forests of the Olympic peninsula. Peasley rated the blow the most terrifying of his life, the only time death had him by the hand.

Another example of how circumstance built up the Peasley legend was the time the *Vigilant* cast off her towboat off the Honolulu harbor late in the Hawaiian afternoon. The great sails filled with the trade that blew down Kaiwi channel past the iron flank of Molokai. Peasley set his course to round Oahu to the westward and then to square away for Puget Sound. Close on his heels the four-masted schooner *Commodore* had towed out and spread her canvas to the same wind, on the same course, for the same destination.

It may have been coincidence, or the two skippers may have designed to make the start neck-and-neck. Nevertheless two of the last big sailing ships on the Pacific were departing under conditions that looked like a race. And race it was. The news soon spread to the mainland, and the progress of the two vessels rated daily front page on most every paper on the coast. It was late in the season, the straining windjammers ran into heavy weather and the race became a thrilling struggle that had followers on edge for three weeks. And then one misty, blustery morning the *Vigilant* stormed up to Tatoosh at the entrance to Juan de Fuca Strait. Peasley had barely taken tow when the tops'ls of the *Commodore* showed above the horizon. Within a matter of hours she, too, was towing in. The race was that close; and neither ship had sighted the other from the time darkness closed on them westward of Oahu. Needless to say Peasley and his *Vigilant* got the big "play" in the newspapers.

And then there was the time — showing Peasley luck with headline — the *Vigilant* was beating up from Australia, coal-laden for Honolulu. She was barely keeping her tops'ls filled in the faint breeze when a smoke-belching steamer passed her close aboard. Peasley wrinkled his nose as coal fumes wafted across his deck — he had no use for steam anyway. He clamped his cigar, muttered, and reluctantly recognized a greeting from the steamer's bridge. The old tramp showed him a churning wake.

But Peasley's hour was coming. The steamer was barely hull down before a breeze gathered. The sweet-sailing windjammer livened. As the wind strengthened the *Vigilant* began to snore with her scuppers under — Peasley once sailed her 315 miles in 24 hours. Throughout the night the wind blew fresh and strong, and by the time the morning bank lifted the big schooner lay off Honolulu harbor, her sail furled with just enough canvas to keep her position until the tug arrived.

Waiting in this position, Peasley was leisurely leaning on his taffrail watching the steamer coming up, dragging a long plume of smoke — the same ship that had been so insulting the day before. The *Vigilant* had passed her during the night.

The steamer's skipper leaned from the wing of his bridge, and shook a fist playfully.

"Where'nell did you come from?" he bellowed.

"Brisbane!" Peasley roared back with a grin.

The steamer sneaked into the harbor ahead of the *Vigilant*, but Peasley burst out in the Honolulu newspapers, with pictures. And it was mentioned, as always, that he was "the Captain Peasley of Peter B. Kyne's Cappy Ricks yarns."

If "copy" was slow from Captain Peasley, likely as not there was Mrs. Peasley — not Cappy Ricks' daughter Florry but the daughter of Captain James Dalton. She married Peasley in 1903, not only for the role of wife but as a shipmate. She sailed something like 250,000 miles with Peasley in his Pacific trampings.

When steam and diesel drove sail from the Pacific deepwater trades, Peasley boxed his "hambone," picked up his long, black topcoat, which had whipped in a thousand winds, and went ashore to stay. He would rather be on the beach than take a berth in some steam kettle. Besides, it was good to settle down in a seafaring community, Grays Harbor, where he could chew a thrum matt with men of his kind. Thus retired, he suffered a stroke in 1945, but even in the hospital he sailed with double-reefed tops'ls across the counterpane, regaled the nurses with seagoing persiflage and confounded the attendants with shipboard instructions: "to starboard with this," or "come up to loo'ard, and lively does it now!"

And so it was. The *Vigilant* and her spirited skipper are gone, with the mortal Peasley dead; but as long as print endures Captain "Matt" Peasley will be hoisting canvas over blue water and thumping the daylights out of All Hands and Feet in Cape Town.

The E. K. Wood Lumber Company had a 60 percent interest in the *Vigilant* and were managing owners. In the late 1920s she was sold to the City Mill Company of Honolulu and operated in their lumber trade between the Northwest and Honolulu. In 1940 a shipping firm in Vancouver, B.C. purchased the vessel and operated her under the British flag, renaming her "*City of Albernie.*" She was put into the lumber trade between British Columbia and Australia, and South Africa. On the last voyage from Port Albernie to Africa the *Vigilant* was seriously damaged in a hurricane in the vicinity of Cape Horn. The captain managed to navigate the vessel 900 miles to a port in Southern Chile where marine surveyors decided the vessel needed such extensive repairs that she was a total loss. Insurance underwriters settled with her owners and the crew was returned to Vancouver and paid off.

Several months later the *Vigilant* was purchased from the insurance company for a very low price, was reconditioned and placed in the coastwise trade. A charter was signed for a voyage from Buenos Aires to Cape Town, South Africa. En route the *Vigilant* caught fire and was abandoned. The damaged hull drifted ashore on the coast of Argentina, a total loss. Thus her career ended.

By December 12, 1910, steamers were outnumbering sailing craft on Grays Harbor, seven steamers to six schooners. By August 9, 1926, the change was almost complete, the five-mast tops'l schooner "*Vigilant*" being the only one of her kind loading, while 15 steamers were stowing lumber, four of them Japanese.

Chapter 16

THE HILLS ARE GREEN AGAIN

Grays Harbor had to run with its tongue hanging out to keep pace with San Francisco lumber demands following the 1906 earthquake and fire. With this feverish lumbering came radical changes in logging, including logging railroads inching out of the valleys. They were being built to make up for the inadequacies of the streams and their splash dams. The timberline was retreating beyond the reach of the rivers and the long skidroads. Rails took to the high and wide watersheds, lifting up steep grades and over breathtaking trestles. They S'ed up the canyons and put steel down almost at the point where the timber felled. Rails brought the geared Shays and Climax locomotives, which squealed around tortuous bends, chugged through the high country, clattering across the broad uplands, which were now being whisked clean and left lay a waste of stumps and discarded timber.

Tremendous fires licked up the debris in the wake of the loggers, and ate into valleys of green timber. Terrifying towers of smoke stood in the still summer air, thousands of feet into the sky. Such ominous pillars could be seen for a hundred miles, bronzing the heavens. They were so common they drew hardly a glance. As the air cooled at evening time, the smoke dropped into the valleys, spreading long fingers of haze over the countryside. The sun sank blood red. Showers of fir needles burned to ash fell upon the city streets. Housewives muttered as they took their sooty wash from the lines and wiped fine dust from their parlor tables. The nights glowed with flame cast against the sky. A thousand acres, ten thousand acres, a hundred thousand acres — hardly anyone batted an eye. There was always more timber over the ridge.

Only Heaven alone can describe those years — timber! — the challenge of it, the appalling labor, the deeds and misdeeds in its name. In the 64 years from the first going sawmill Grays Harbor cut something like 31 billion feet of marketable lumber. This did not include the sawdust that fed the boilers, filled the streets, or the slabs and trims that went into the towering and night-glowing burners as waste. Perhaps 31 billion doesn't sound impressive, but translated into toil and sweat, muscle and men, bacon and beans, booze and bawds and the wear and tear on machinery and forests, it becomes awesome.

In 64 years the first huffing-puffing sawmill grew into an array of timber-hungry, timber-devouring giants, pouring smoke, and distressing days and nights with the screech of machinery, the roar of saws, and the inevitable whistles which pierced or rumbled at dawn and dusk, and at noon sent the crews to their lunch pails. The mills were insatiable. The live rolls rumbled ceaselessly, the edgers snarled, the planers droned deafeningly. Giant cants dropped from riven logs as fast as the great bandsaws could slice the length of a log. The bullchain groaned and complained, but drew an endless supply of logs from the millpond and up the slips. Millwrights frantically hammered and patched the machinery weakening under the strain.

Such a tempo in 1926 produced 1,557,223,000 board feet of lumber in Grays Harbor's two dozen tidewater sawmills. In that year 880 seagoing vessels thumped against Grays Harbor wharves and crammed themselves with 1,416,395,000 board feet. The rest went by rail. The ships slogged away with their plimsol marks awash to Shanghai, Taku Bar, Kobe, Batavia, Sydney, Adelaide, Antwerp, Callao, Southampton, Cape Town, California, New England and elsewhere.

That was the peak year. That was the year the babbit melted in the bearings and pulses raced with frenzy. The throttle was wide open and just about shaking the place apart. But still it was only part of the story. Grays Harbor averaged an annual cut of 1,352,788,000 feet for six straight years, 1924 to 1929.

That was the era of the "Jap square," because it was cut exclusively for Japan. In many cases it was an entire log with but four slabs knocked off to square it. In other cases it was the heart of a log after the clear stock had been removed. It was a compact way of shipping lumber, well recognized by the Japanese, who took it across the Pacific in their own coal-burning ships and sawed it in their own mills with only half the waste in sawdust created by Grays Harbor mills. Besides, the Japanese had ready use for the sawdust. It was a lucrative trade, but it rapidly pushed back the timberline, and far outstripped nature's ability to keep pace with new growth.

The World War I years had been just as bad or worse. Then Grays Harbor had been in a fury of wooden shipbuilding, the bridge that was to span the Atlantic. Long, clear cants went into ships — two million feet to the ship — so green the vessels spewed their calking the first trip out. Millions of feet of timber went into hulls that saw only a year or two of service and in some cases no service at all. When the war ended they were anchored and burned on tideflats in almost every port of the nation.

Those were extravagant times. The war years were a whoop-it-up, saw-'em-down period that had everybody patting everybody else on the back over what a fine job Grays Harbor was doing for the boys "Over There." But in the twenties the first nervous whisperings began to be heard. How long would it last? How much timber is left? The billion-foot years were over in 1929, and water-borne exports dropped to 646 million feet in 1930, when lumbermen began making sober appraisals. They began to count the years left to the industry. Some said thirty; the pessimists went as low as twenty years. The cut-outers and get-outers began to "git." In that tottering decade full nine major sawmill outfits pulled the whistle for the last time, razed their plants, sold the machinery for junk and left sites studded with snags of rotting piling. Total-loss fires were the direct cause of two suspensions, but the prospects were so unpromising the plants were not rebuilt. In some cases the mills had cut out their own timber and were thrown upon the open market for logs. They were through. They paid off their crews, balanced their ledgers, let their cut-over lands go back to the county with taxes unpaid, and wagged their heads sadly over the fate of Grays Harbor.

By then loggers were working 30 to 50 miles back in the hills. The canyon walls were steeper, the high ground higher. Rock ribs began to appear on the hogbacks. Just beyond, the hills began to bald, and patches of snow lay in the wrinkles even in summertime. The logger himself had changed from a hell-roaring, kisser-punching, hard-drinking, harlot-hugging ramstam into a sober, hard-working fellow and family man, who left his spiked shoes in the bunkhouse and went home for weekends. That was partly because the Devil had his comeuppance back in 1915 when the state of Washington voted prohibition, and on December 15 of that memorable year the hard-hearted license collector in Aberdeen scrawled under the last saloon license entry this uninspired comment: "Last of the Wets." That stilled forever much of the thunder in the roaring empire.

As the logger changed, so did his machinery and method of logging. He entered the era of the highlead and the skyline, which together were speedily denuding the landscape. Only superlatives could describe it: the power of the great compounds, the height of the colddecks of logs, the townships of gaunt snags and scorched stumps, and barren ridges like swells on the sea. Only here and there were tufts of trees, bypassed as worthless, to break the desolation. It would no more have occurred to a logger to leave a seed tree purposely than to haul hemlock out of the woods. However, the railroad grades the logger left to grow to brush and saplings would become a godsend in later years. They would be fire trails and access roads when Grays Harbor returned to sanity and began growing timber as well as cutting it.

The Humptulips Valley and its fabulous stands of fir was logged out except on the headwaters. The Hoquiam's many branches threaded vast wastelands. The multi-forked Satsop wended unshaded miles through cut-over country. Timber was gone from the Wishkah watershed and the lower Wynooche, while the North River country wore a nap of hemlock and vast sections of fir stumps. Along the upper Chehalis they were growing strawberries on the prairies and hay in the meadows, and old-timers were remembering when timber stood on the riverbank and none knew how much stood beyond.

But there were changes in the making. In fact, the whole philosophy of timber was in a slow process of change. Somewhere down the line the notion sprouted that maybe timber "land" was worth something, possibly to grow more trees. Some far-seeing men began looking beyond the next ridge. They began hanging onto their cut-over lands. On these they envisioned a perpetual timber supply, to be cropped in rotation.

While they visioned and agonized, a miracle was taking place virtually unnoticed and despite the logger and his kind. Cut-over country that had been free of fire sprang into second growth. It grew with all the vigor of a tropic jungle, cloaking the desolation with ridge after ridge of green. By the time the loggers were working 30 to 50 miles back in the hills, some stands of new growth were almost of saw-log size. Whole townships, once gaunt with sentinel snags and blackened stumps, flourished with new growth.

Today an aged and awed old-timer can stand on some high place and point which way he will without finding a break in the spearing tops of new trees. He could not even find where his bull teams grunted, and only with the greatest difficulty trace the long skidroads that streaked up the hillsides in the days of the big steam yarders, road engines and halfbreeds. The splash dams would have long since been blown out to relieve the streams. And the old steam engines would be rusting away behind the roundhouse.

The new philosophy put a new value on timber too. It no longer was cheaper than a high-sign from a hooker. It was worth real money. In fact, it was worth growing, and despite Grays Harbor's turbulent, to-hell-with-the-future history, it was now witnessing a seeming anachronism: loggers planting trees! This was done on newly-logged and slash-burned areas, and on bald spots, too often burned by fire, where nature seemed unable to replant.

The 1940s brought new concepts in timber management. The forester gained prominence as a man whose knowledge of regeneration, seed gathering, disease and insect control, fire prevention and scientific harvesting methods meant that old "cut and git" could be replaced by permanence.[30]

Federal legislation resulted in better fire control and reforestation. Passage of the Sustained Yield Act of 1944 brought into

Grays Harbor County two permanent forest units, one serving Western Grays Harbor County and the other, called the Shelton Cooperative Sustained Yield Unit, serving Eastern Grays Harbor, Mason and Thurston counties. Now, due to these units and the sustained yield practices of all major operators, harvesting is in balance with the new growth in a true display of perpetual motion.

The State of Washington's Department of Natural Resources has established its own sustained yield units on state lands on the Olympic Peninsula. State, federal and private industry nurseries each year supply millions of seedlings for reforestation.

And fire, once the Devil of blackness on thousands of Grays Harbor acres, had been subdued by a public movement called Keep Washington Green, which from 1940 to this day has inspired a remarkable degree of public participation in protecting Washington's immensely valuable renewable tree resources.

Old-timers may never have thought it would come to pass, but there are "farms" now for the growing of trees. They are "tree farms," an idea originated on Grays Harbor and now used throughout the nation wherever trees grow. The first tree farm significantly was established in the Grays Harbor country in 1942 on a tract of 150 thousand acres logged and, like most every other logged area, notorious for waste and heedlessness. It was called the "Clemons Tree Farm," and it set the standards of forest practices for tree farms everywhere. In the following years Grays Harbor certified more lands to tree farms than any other comparable region in the nation.

As the years remaining of old growth became numbered, Grays Harbor came to caution. It had to get more out of its timber, use more of the tree. The great burners, which were once the night-light of every sawmill and glowed endlessly years on end, disappeared. Small logs of fir and the once-scorned hemlock and alder came to be as valuable as fir. Pulp, paper, plywood, furniture, veneer and other specialty plants replaced the timber-devouring sawmill.

Now timbermen are listening to chemists who have created an entirely new concept of forest products. They speak knowingly of cellulose and fibers, the reduction of whole forests in the chemist's retorts. They are producing things the old timers and their hellions never dreamed of. They expect to use limbs, stumps, roots, bark, needles, perhaps even the soughing of the wind. Even now high-butted cedar stumps, some cut almost a century ago, are being "logged" again, salvaged for their wealth in shake and shingle blocks. Thus Grays Harbor no longer is haunted by the spectre of sagging mill roofs, grass growing on abandoned mill slips. It may not always have big tidewater sawmills, but it will always have loggers.

"We did our damndest," said Fightin' Billy McCabe, "but we couldn't cut 'er out. She growed too fast."

With all this change the logger was changing too. The timber beast became civilized. He slept in iron bunks with real mattresses and, of all things, white sheets and pillowcases, clean each week. There were no cracks in the bunkhouse walls, and the stars did not peek through the shake roof. There was hot and cold water, a place to dry wet clothing, a shower bath and a library with real books.

Some camps were on railway cars and moved along as the timberline retreated. Other camps became permanent communities with streets and light poles and telephones, even movie theaters and churches. Families moved in and there was a school for the children.

Perhaps it was just as well. The old days were gone. The saloons were but dark and cobwebby windows brooding over the forgotten areas of the lumber towns. The merchandised women were gone and there were no longer signs of *"Rooms"* at the bottom of the steep stairways. The red light was gone too. So was the raucous and ribald. Perhaps it was just as well. But Plank Island would never be the same again.

Appendix A

SAWMILLS

The magnitude of timber operations on Grays Harbor can be gained from the number of woodworking mills and logging outfits.

To begin, there were five waterpowered sawmills: Armstrong on Cedar Creek, 1852; Waldrip in the Elma area, 1870s; Estes in McCleary area, early 1870s; Luark at Sylvia Creek Falls, 1873; Charles Stevens, Cosmopolis, 1880.

These were followed by the first steam plants: Asa Simpson's North Western, Hoquiam, 1882; Esmond & Anderson, converting Stevens' mill, 1883; Wishkah Mill Company, Montesano, 1883; M. Z. Goodell, Elma, 1883, relocated in Montesano 1884; A. J. West, Aberdeen, 1884; Capt. J. M. Weatherwax, Aberdeen, 1885; Emory & Mack, Aberdeen, 1885.

In the years that followed, a whole array of big sawmills was built at the edge of tidewater on both banks of the Chehalis from Cosmopolis to Hoquiam, and up the Wishkah and Hoquiam rivers. At one time a tallyman could have counted 46 log-using outfits on tidewater: sawmills, shingle mills and specialty mills.

Within the first two decades of the century, Grays Harbor listened to the roar of these major lumber-gushing operations:

Grays Harbor Commercial Company, Cosmopolis, a Pope & Talbot plant. It also operated a tank factory, box factory and two shingle mills, along with the Chehalis County Logging & Timber Company.

Bay City Lumber Company, South Aberdeen, formerly Union Mill; Sam M. Anderson Sr., president and manager.

E. C. Miller Cedar Lumber Co., E. C. Miller, president, B. B. Averill and G. E. Anderson Sr., other officers.

Aberdeen Lumber & Shingle Co., Clyde A. Pitchford, manager. The plant was built in 1899 and was headed by Ben Averill, Robert Coats, Claude Leitch and Clifford M. Weatherwax.

General Package Corporation was not a lumber mill per se, but it did cut about

10 million feet of timber a year for conversion into wooden tubs and buckets. Fayette Bousfield, manager.

Wilson Brothers & Co., built 1887 by Charles and Henry Wilson who had come from Astoria. Plant later operated by sons John H., William C. and Dewey Wilson.

American Mill on the Wishkah, built in 1885 by Emery & Mack, later operated by Ben Johnson and A. F. Coats, finally acquired by the Hulbert interests headed by Ed Hulbert. His sons Bert, Fred, George and Earle continued the operation.

West & Slade, a plant on the site of the first mill in Aberdeen, A. J. West, operated by W. A. West and John G. Lewis.

E. K. Bishop plant at Junction City was primarily a spruce mill.

Western Lumber Company, established by Walter MacFarlane, later Donovan No. 2, and Bryden & Leitch mill, later Donovan No. 1, headed by William Donovan, president; Patrick O'Connor, vice-president; William Donovan Jr., treasurer; and Francis J. Donovan, secretary.

Saginaw Lumber Company, later Saginaw Shingle plant, built by A. J. Morley and Paul Morley.

Anderson & Middleton, originally the Weatherwax plant, operated since 1898 by A. W. Middleton, president, S. M. Anderson, G. E. Anderson and H. N. Anderson.

Hart-Wood Lumber Co., Fred Hart and Will Wood, since 1916 a unit in the Hulbert operations. Later the site was used by West Tacoma News Print Company.

Eureka Lumber & Manufacturing Co., a Polson Logging Company operation. Robert and Alex Polson were the officers, while J. Clifford Shaw was plant manager. The mill was built in 1910.

National Lumber & Manufacturing Company at mouth of Hoquiam River, east bank, A. L. Paine, manager, started by O. C. Fenalson.

Grays Harbor Lumber Company, built in 1903. N. J. Blagen, president; son Clarence Blagen, manager. Sons Henry and Frank also were officers.

North Western Lumber Company, George H. Emerson, first president, then his son Ralph L. Emerson. Wilfred Dole was an officer, with Thorpe Babcock, vice-president and manager. Plant leveled by fire in 1896; immediately rebuilt with double lumber capacity.

E. K. Wood Lumber Company, mile upstream on the Hoquiam, built by James A. Karr and Associates; sold in 1892 to E. K. Wood. O. M. Kellogg was first president under Wood, then Fred J. Wood.

Hoquiam Lumber & Shingle Company, upstream from E. K. Wood mill on the Hoquiam; built in 1902 and known as the "Lytle Mill" after its original operators Robert F. Lytle and Joe Lytle. Later under another ownership; A. B. Cahill of San Francisco was president and C. M. Fridlender, manager.

SAWMILLS

Downstream from the Aberdeen Lumber & Shingle company plant was the original Durfee mill, a small but efficient operation. The plant was acquired by the Schafer company, later by Weyerhaeuser.

Another mill on the Hoquiam, across from the North Western plant, was the Neff mill, which operated but a short time and burned.

THERE WAS a wide scattering of other woodworking operations throughout the region — some large, and some small sawmills, innumerable shingle plants, and others manufacturing specialized products.

Aloha Lumber Company, a large operation at Aloha.

American Mill Co., founded by Coats Brothers and sold to the Hulbert, Sudden and Christenson interests.

Western Lumber Co., built by Eugene France, sold to Donovan Lumber Co.

Carlisle Lumber Company, a large sawmill at Carlisle.

H. N. Anderson Lumber Co., Aberdeen.

Airplane Spruce & Lumber Co., Hoquiam.

Elma Lumber Co., Elma.

Federal Sawmill Co., Aberdeen.

Michigan Lumber Company, Aberdeen.

M. R. Smith Lumber Company, Moclips.

Schafer Brothers, Montesano, Aberdeen. Sold to Simpson Timber Company in 1956. Now operated by Weyerhaeuser Company.

White Star Lumber Co., large operation at Whites, Elma.

M. E. Morrill Shingle Co., Markham.

Red Cedar Shingle Co., Markham.

Maki & Lewis Co., Markham.

LaBreck Shake Co., Hoquiam.

Soule Shingle Co., Hoquiam.

East Hoquiam Shingle Co., Hoquiam.

Robert Gray Shingle Co., Hoquiam.

Sether Shingle Co., Hoquiam.

Jackson Shake Co., Moclips.

H. E. Bailey Shingle Co., Quinault.

Brown Lumber Co., Quinault.

Merrill Lumber Co., Junction City.

Panama Lumber Co., South Montesano.

South Side Lumber Co., South Montesano.

Stetson Lumber Company, Montesano.

Sunset Shingle Co., Montesano.

Hillview Shingle Co., Montesano.

Picco Logging Co., sold to Blagen, who sold to E. C. Miller.

Vance Lumber Co., Vance Creek.

Elma Shingle Co., Elma.

Ray Shingle Co., Elma.

Henry McCleary Timber Co., McCleary, sold to Simpson Timber Company in 1941.

Swan & Johnson Lumber Co., Malone, sold to Vance, sold to Mumby.

Porter Creek Shingle Co., Porter Creek.

Ultican Lumber Co., Aberdeen.

M. R. Smith Shingle Mill, Moclips.

Deming Shingle Mill, Markham, later Mackie & Barnes.

Bailey & Ingebrigtsen, shingle mill, Wishkah River above North Aberdeen bridge.

Barrel Stave Mill, foot of Washington Street, Aberdeen.

Wilcox Shingle Mill, South Aberdeen.

Posey Manufacturing Co., Hoquiam, piano sounding boards.

Robert Gray Shingle Co., Hoquiam.

American Door Company, Hoquiam.

Knox & Tombs, plywood, Hoquiam.

Hoquiam Plywood, Hoquiam.

George Southern Shingle Mill, Hoquiam.

Woodlawn Plywood, Hoquiam.

Harbor Plywood.

Aberdeen Plywood.

West Coast Plywood.

Olympic Hardwood No. 1 (Henry N. Anderson).

Double Block Shingle Co., mile above Summit on N. P. branch out of Elma; first known as Hamilton & Lee, then Young & Boyle.

I. J. Smith Shingle Mill, on old stage road in Summit area.

Craft & Son Shingle Plant, foot of Maxwell Hill, later Craft & Crosby.

M. R. Smith Shingle Plant, at Rayville, between Whites and McCleary.

Deming Shingle Mill on Mox Chehalis at place called Sine (Archie Deming).

Barrie & Dent Mill, a half mile up Mox Chehalis from Deming.

Royal Shingle Company Mill, four miles west of White Star (Dale Craft); moved to Raymond.

Dale Craft Sawmill (small) at Summit, sold to Church & Sons.

SAWMILL SIGNALS

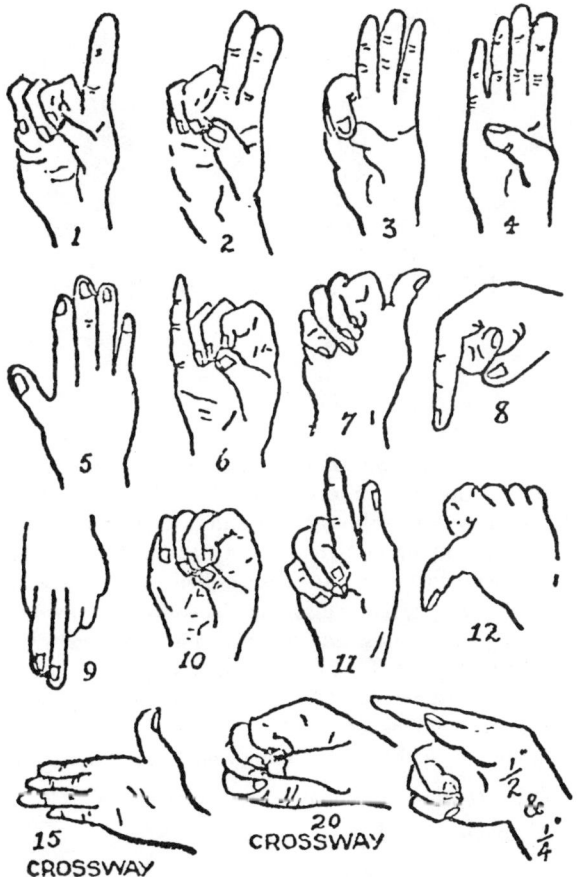

Deafening racket within sawmills made it impossible for the sawyer to yell instructions to the "setter" on the log carriage. Inspired by the communication system used by mute people, sawyers devised hand signals which they could quickly flash at the setter, informing him the thickness of lumber to be cut each time the log carriage passed the screaming bandsaw. This illustration is from a standard handbook of years ago. New employees practiced these signals until their wrists ached but instructions had to be perfected before they could perform the work. 13 to 20 same as 3 to 10 drawn across front of body. Included here for benefit of new employees. These are standard signals used between sawyers and setters and are handy for others in noisy places, also for signaling from distances. The figure with index finger at lower right side is for fractions of inches. Index finger moved back and forth from body toward carriage is for ¼". Index finger moved to and fro parallel to carriage denotes ½". Pointing to floor with up and down motion means ⅛".

Appendix B

LOGGING RAILROADS

For forty years after Alex and Robert Polson started their rail line on the Hoquiam in 1903, logging railroads twisted up the valleys of the Grays Harbor country, clicking across the benches, and in the steeper hills agonizing through cuts and over canyons until there was a maze of steel reaching into the ever-retreating timber. Much of the steel was pulled out in time as the timber was cut away, leaving but the long Polson line (now Rayonier Inc.) as the only remaining stretch of steel, and it serving only as a "mainline" operation in western Grays Harbor County. Simpson Timber Company's railroad extends 42 miles from Camp Grisdale on the Wynooche River in northeastern Grays Harbor County eastward to Shelton.

A summary of rail lines in the Grays Harbor woods at one time read like this:

M. R. Smith Lumber & Shingle Company, Moclips.

Aloha Lumber Company, Aloha.

Thompson & Murray on Joe Creek.

Carlisle Lumber Company, Carlisle.

Lytle on the East Hoquiam, South Bay and Black Hills.

Greenwood Timber Company on East Hoquiam.

A. F. Coats, then Donovan-Corkery.

Schafer Brothers, with previous lines of Lamb Timber Company and Carlson & Callow.

C.C.L.&T. above Sylvia Lake.

Slade on the Satsop.

Hewitt Timber Company on the Satsop.

White Star Lumber Company, Whites.

Henry McCleary Timber Company, McCleary.

Saginaw Timber Company, Delezene Creek, North River-Vesta area.

National Lumber Company in area southeast of Elma.

Mason County Logging Company (Joe Vance).

Clemons Logging Co., out of Melbourne.

Union Timber Company, Oakville.

Wilson Brothers, near Independence.

Homer P. Brown built a line into the rough country south of Elma in the 1920s, but the terrain proved so costly his operation collapsed, bringing down with it the Hayes & Hayes bank of Aberdeen.

Anderson & Middleton, Independence, North River.

Beaulieu & Mackie, Johns River country.

Simpson Timber Company operations on the Wynooche River in eastern Grays Harbor County.

Porter Railroad, Elma.

Hoquiam River Railroad, East Fork Hoquiam.

GRAYS HARBOR'S 1,095 miles of logging railroads used several types of locomotives, both rod and geared. The geared locomotives such as the Shay, Climax, Heisler, Baldwin, Hinkley and Willamette were especially useful in steep country, spurs and winding roads, while the rod engines worked mostly the main lines. Rod engines familiar to the Grays Harbor woods were the American, McKay & Aldus, Porter, Baldwin, Willamette and Rogers. At first all were steam, while in later years diesel electric lokies replaced the smoke-puffers.

MAIN LOGGING STREAMS IN GRAYS HARBOR COUNTY

Appendix C

LOGGING FIRMS

Nearly 300 logging firms have operated in Grays Harbor County since the 1880s. This list is not complete, but it reveals the large number.

Abel Logging Company, operated in Humptulips Valley; Aberdeen Logging Company, East Fork Wishkah; Aberdeen Lumber & Shingle Co., East Branch Humptulips; Airplane Spruce and Lumber Co.; Anderson & Allen Log Co.; Albie Logging Co., Humptulips Valley; Aloha Lumber Co., Aloha; American Mill Co., Montesano; Glen T. Anderson Inc.; H. N. Anderson Logging Co.; Anderson & Middleton Logging Co., Oakville and North River; Arland Logging Co., Montesano, horses, wagons; Arland & Johnson Logging Co., Wynoochee River; Aubal Logging Co., South Bay.

Bale Logging Co.; Bale & Leck Logging Co., Moclips branch NPRR; Beaulieu Logging Co., Elk River; Beaulieu & Maki Logging Co., Johns River; Don Bell Logging Co.; Bernard Logging Co., Bernard Creek, Chehalis River; Big Creek Logging Co., Big Creek; Big Six Logging Co. (Caldwell Brothers), Andrews Creek, South Bay; J. C. Biles Logging Co., Montesano; Blackwell Logging Co., Wishkah River (first splash dam on Wishkah); Cy Blackwell & Jim Gillis Logging Co., New London, Hoquiam River; Blagen Logging Co.; Bocek & White Logging Co.; Tom Bordeaux on Gibson Creek; Brady Lumber Co., Brady; Briscoe Brothers Logging Co., Humptulips Valley; Brittain Brothers Logging Co., Humptulips Valley; Brittain Brothers, Sargent and McDonald, on Humptulips near Stevens Creek; H. P. Burrows and Billy Patterson, near Wilderness in Humptulips Valley; Pete Burrows Logging Co., Lower Humptulips; Burrows & White Logging Co., Humptulips Valley; Burrows Logging Co., Humptulips Valley.

J. E. Calder, North Hoquiam (bull team); Henry Call, Upper Wishkah; Callow & Wray; Caldwell Brothers Logging Co.; Callow & Arthur, Elma; Cameron & Hoover Logging Co., East Fork of Humptulips; Carlisle Logging Co., Carlisle; Carlson Brothers Logging Co., Wishkah River; Carlson & Callow, Chenois Creek, Hoquiam River; C.C.L.&.T. (Grays Harbor Commercial Co.), Wynoochee Valley; Chambers Logging Co., North River; Charman & Traynor

Logging Co., Copalis Crossing; Chehalis Logging Co.; Red Clark Logging Co., Amanda Park; C. H. Clemons Logging Co., Melbourne; Clemons Logging Co.; Clemons & Leavitt Logging Co., Delezene Creek; Climax Logging Co., Elk River; Clyde Brothers, Big Creek, Deep Creek; Coal Creek Logging & Timber Co., near Montesano; F. A. Coats Logging Co.; Coats Brothers Logging Co., Chenois Creek, Wishkah River; Coats-Fordney Logging Co., Wishkah River; Columbia River and Grays Harbor Railway (1883-1891); Corkery Brothers Logging Co., Humptulips Valley; William Corkery — Gus Carlson — Bob Coats — Cliff Weatherwax — Al Coats; — Mike Coats, logged on Humptulips.

Damon & Minard Logging Co., Elma; Dant & Russell Logging, Inc.; Davenport & Payne, East Fork Humptulips; Davis Logging Co., Hoquiam River, Deep Creek; Davis & Payne Logging Co., Deep Creek, East Fork Humptulips; Dineen Brothers Logging Co., Charley Creek; Donovan & Corkery Logging Co.

East Branch Logging Co., Humptulips; Elk River Logging Co., Elk River; Elk Creek and Grays Harbor Railroad; Ellis Logging Co., Wishkah River, Newskah River; Elma Logging Co., Elma; J. J. Esses Logging Co.

Fordney Logging Co., East Hoquiam River; Sol Foss Logging Co., Montesano; Flowers Logging Co., Elk River; R. M. Fox Logging Co., South Bay.

Gateson Logging Company; Dan Gillis Logging Co.; Jim Gillis Logging Co., Hoquiam River, mouth of Humptulips; Fred Green — Parker Creek, Upper Wishkah; Greenwood Logging Co., Wishkah River, Hoquiam River; Green Cedar Shingle Co.; Green Fir Timber Company; Grays Harbor Logging Co., Wishkah River, East Fork; Grays Harbor and Pacific Railroad; Grays Harbor Commercial Company.

Hackett & Corkery Logging Co., Humptulips River; Hackett & Dineen Logging Co., Humptulips River; Haines & Preston Logging Co., Wishkah River; Hewitt Logging Co.; Hobi Brothers Logging Co., North River; John Hobi Logging Co., North River; Hobi Timber Company, Quinault Reservation; Hoefer & Bolja Logging Co., Hoquiam; Hogan Logging Co., Grass Creek; Hoquiam Lumber & Shingle Co.; Hoquiam River Railroad, East Fork Hoquiam River; J. W. Horne Logging Co.; Hopkins & Morley Logging Co., Chehalis River; Hiram Hulet Logging Co., Wishkah River; Humptulips Logging Co., East and West Forks Humptulips; Hoquiam River R.R., East Hoquiam River; M. Huston Logging Co., Montesano.

Independence Logging Co.

C. L. Jackson Logging Co., Aloha; James & Watkins Logging Co.; Samuel James and Wray, Elma; Joe Creek Logging Co., Pacific Beach; B. F. Johnson Logging Co., North River; J & P Logging Co.; Johnson Brothers Logging Co., Wishkah road.

LOGGING FIRMS

Kalb Logging Co.; Keystone Logging Co., Satsop; Kneff Logging Co.; Kuhn Logging Co.

Frank H. Lamb Logging Co.; Larkin Brothers Logging Co., Wishkah River; Larkin & Green Logging Co., Wishkah River; Lester Brothers Logging Co., North River; Lewis & Berg Logging Co., North River; Lindstrom & Haag Logging Co., Elma and Brooklyn; E. H. Lester Logging Co., East Montesano, North River; Llewelyn Logging Co., Quinault Lake; Little Skookum & Chehalis Railroad; Lunch Creek Logging Co., Quinault; Lytle Logging & Mercantile Co., Elma; Louis & Berg Logging Co., Cloquallum Creek.

W. D. Mack Logging Co., West Fork Hoquiam; Mason County Logging Co., Cedar Creek, Gibson Creek; Malone Mercantile Co., Elma; Maubry Brothers Logging Co., Montesano (horse and wagons); Markham Shingle Co., Johns River; Mayr Brothers Logging Co., Artic, Wishkah River; James Murray Logging Co., near Summit; W. D. McCall Logging Co., Moclips branch NPRR; Henry McCleary Timber Co., McCleary; Pat McHugh & Billy Leck, Big Creek; M & B Logging Co., Johns River; McCall Logging Co., near Elma; Melbourne & Northern; Merrill & Ring (with Polsons); Meyer Brothers Logging Co., upper Humptulips; Miller Logging Co.; Milroy, Perkins & Milroy Logging Co., Montesano (bullteams, horses); Monarch Logging Co., Wishkah River; Morgan & Brewer Logging Co., Hoquiam; Moore Logging Co.; Morrison & Son Logging Co., Quinault area; Morrow Logging Company; Mud Bay Logging Co., Porter Creek, Mud Bay; Mumby Timber Co.; Murray & Blackwell Logging Co., Wishkah River; Murray & Johnson Logging Co., Newskah River, Charley Creek; Murray Logging Co., Moclips branch NPRR.

National Lumber & Manufacturing Co., National.

Nelson Logging Co., Chehalis River; Nelson & Shaw Logging Co., Failor Lake, Copalis Beach; Jim Newberry Logging Co., Big Creek; Ninemire Logging Co., Wynooche River; Ninemire and Morgan, Independence; North River Logging Co.; Northwest Logging Co. Inc.; North Western Company, New London, North River, Copalis Beach, Hoquiam River, Fry Creek.

O. K. Logging Co., Wishkah River; Ozette Railroad; Olympia, Sherman & Grays Harbor Railroad & Logging Co.; Ozette Timber Company.

Patterson & Blackwell Logging Co., Wishkah River; Picco Logging Co.; Peninsular Railroad (Simpson), Shelton into Eastern Grays Harbor; Phillips & Watson (1887), Johns River; Picco & Maloney Logging Co.; Ping Pong Railroad, Elma; Pioneer Logging Company; Polson Logging Co., Hoquiam River to Quinault; Pollard Logging Co.; Preston, Allison & Bickler Logging Co., south side Grays Harbor; Port Blakely Logging Co., Summit.

Quinault Shingle Co., Quinault; Quinault Logging Co.

Raisor Brothers Logging Co.; Rayville Shingle Company; River Logging Co., Humptulips River; Roberts Logging Co.; Rowland Brothers, North River; Rayonier Inc. (Ozette Timber Co., Polson Logging Co., Ozette Railroad, Airplane Spruce Co.).

Saginaw Timber Co. (Grays Harbor & Pacific Railroad, E. H. Lester Logging Co., Saginaw Southern Railroad); Arthur Salmon Logging Co., North River; Sargent Logging Co., Andrews Creek; Salmon Creek Logging Co., Artic, Vesta.; Sargent & McDonald, Humptulips River; Shamrock & Western, McCleary; Shaw & Nelson Logging Co., Moclips branch NPRR; Walter Shaw Logging Co., Elma; Simpson Timber Co., Wynooche River (formerly Simpson Logging Company); Schafer Brothers Logging Company, Aberdeen (also operated Chehalis County Logging Co., Grays Harbor Commercial Co., Montesano & Northern, Independence Logging Co., Wilson Brothers Logging Co., National Lumber & Manufacturing Co., Washington & Ohio Logging Co., Wynooche Timber Co.); Slade & Wells Logging Co., Satsop, Newman Creek; Sjoleth & Moe Logging Co., New London, O'Leary Creek; S. E. Slade Logging Co.; M. R. Smith Logging Co., Moclips; J. T. Spradlin Logging Co.; Stearnsville Lumber Co., Stearnsville.; Stimson Mill Co., McCleary; James Stewart Logging Co., two miles up Wishkah from Aberdeen, Stewart Creek, Fern Hill area; Sylvia Shingle Co., Montesano; Frank Stenzel, Deep Creek; Stockwell Logging Co., Deep Creek, Stevens Creek, Big Creek; Al P. Stockwell, who built 27 splash dams on Humptulips and side streams; Arthur Salmon Logging Co., North River, Elma.

Trio Logging Co., O'Leary Creek.

Union Mill Co.; Union Timber Co., near Oakville; Umidon Logging Co., Brooklyn.

Vance Lumber Co., Vance Creek, Malone.; N. Voorhies, 1887, Johns River.

Washington & Southern; Washington and Ohio Logging Co., Oakville; Washington & Ohio Lumber Co.; Walker Brothers Logging Co., Big Creek, school section; Warren Brothers Logging Co., Humptulips River; Weatherwax Logging Co., Porter Creek; West Coast Logging Co., formerly Jones Logging Co.; Western Logging Co., Ocosta; Western Timber Products Co., Copalis; White Logging Co., Humptulips River; White Brothers Logging Co., McCleary; White Logging Co., A. E. White, Summit; Elzy White and Mike Glacier, near Wilderness on Humptulips; White Star Logging Co., Whites; Wiest-Thompson, Pacific Beach; Mike Woods Logging Co., Delezene Creek; Wilson Brothers, Johns River, 1887; Williamson Logging Co.; Wilson Brothers Logging Co.; Womer Logging Company; Workman Creek Logging Co.

Young & Hackett Logging Co., Humptulips River; Young & Hoover Logging Co., West Fork Humptulips; Young & Thompson, Wishkah Valley.

Appendix
D

LUMBER VESSELS

Grays Harbor-built vessels still under registry in 1924.

Name	Type	Year	Launched	Length/Feet
A. J. West	Schooner	1898	Aberdeen	161
Avalon	Steamer	1912	Hoquiam	196
Bee	Steamer	1907	Aberdeen	175
Brookdale	Steamer	1918	Aberdeen	272.5
Caoba	Steamer	1905	Aberdeen	175.2
Carmel	Steamer	1906	Aberdeen	170
Caspar	Steamer	1907	Aberdeen	175.1
Champion	Steamer	1909	Hoquiam	88.5
Claremont	Steamer	1917	Hoquiam	225.5
Columbia	Steamer	1899	Hoquiam	181
Crescent City	Steamer	1906	Aberdeen	180
Daisy Gadsby	Steamer	1911	Hoquiam	189.5
Daisy Matthews	Steamer	1916	Hoquiam	204.8
Daisy Putnam	Steamer	1913	Hoquiam	201
Dauntless	Schooner	1898	Hoquiam	162.2
F. A. Douty	Steamer	1904	Aberdeen	104.3
Forest Dream	Barkentine	1919	Aberdeen	242.4
Forest Friend	Barkentine	1919	Aberdeen	243.3
Forest King	Steamer	1920	Aberdeen	241.5
Forest Pride	Barkentine	1919	Aberdeen	241.5
Fred J. Wood	Steamer	1899	Hoquiam	181
Grays Harbor	Steamer	1907	Aberdeen	172
Grays Harbor	Gas Screw	1917	Aberdeen	266.1
Harbor Belle	Steamer	1902	Aberdeen	98.8
Harbor Queen	Steamer	1910	Aberdeen	86.2

Hartwood	Steamer	1916	Hoquiam	199.3
Helene	Steamer	1906	Hoquiam	172.1
Helen P. Drew	Steamer	1904	Aberdeen	134.6
Henry Wilson	Steamer	1899	Aberdeen	157.8
Hornet	Steamer	1906	Aberdeen	176
Idaho	Steamer	1916	Aberdeen	205.6
Lassen	Gas Screw	1917	Hoquiam	170.2
Marie De Ronde	Gas Screw	1918	Aberdeen	266.7
Mayfair	Steamer	1906	Aberdeen	173.9
Melrose	Steamer	1902	Hoquiam	175.4
Mindanao	Steamer	1902	Aberdeen	164.8
Oregon	Steamer	1916	Aberdeen	201
Phyllis	Steamer	1917	Aberdeen	215.3
Rainier	Steamer	1900	Hoquiam	204.9
Resolute	Steamer	1902	Hoquiam	182.2
Rosalie Mahony	Steamer	1913	Hoquiam	201.1
Saginaw	Steamer	1907	Hoquiam	191.4
San Diego	Steamer	1918	Hoquiam	237.3
Border King	Steamer	1908	Hoquiam	160.3
San Pedro	Steamer	1903	Hoquiam	85.5
Santa Flavia	Gas Screw	1918	Aberdeen	225.6
Santa Isabel	Gas Screw	1917	Hoquiam	216.5
Santino	Gas Screw	1917	Aberdeen	268.8
Sea Foam	Steamer	1905	Aberdeen	125
Shasta	Steamer	1908	Hoquiam	192.3
Sierra	Gas Screw	1916	Hoquiam	210.6
Siskiyou	Steamer	1912	Hoquiam	204.1
Standard No. 2	Steamer	1904	Aberdeen	104.3
Tamalpais	Steamer	1906	Hoquiam	165.2
Tiverton	Steamer	1906	Hoquiam	155
Vashon	Steamer	1891	Aberdeen	149
Vigilant	Schooner	1920	Hoquiam	241.9

Appendix E

POSTSCRIPTS

Mack's Peavey

In the bullteam days when a turn was hard to start, the hooktender or skidder gave the head log a little "hunch" or rock with a peavey or length of vine maple to break the grip of the skids. W. D. Mack, up at Sharon, had his own special instrument, which was bent in the shape of a new moon. Mack let it be known the ash handle got that way by the heave and muscle he had applied in using it. It went without saying, none else used Mack's peavey.

* * *

Both Barrels

John Lindstrom once invited young Dan McGillicuddy to go duck hunting — Dan always maintained he was invited to row the boat, but not necessarily for the near thing that followed. The pair was passing Indian Creek on the south side of the harbor, when a flock of ducks whistled into range. Lindstrom in the stern sheets grabbed his gun, which was muzzle-down on the floor boards. In his excitement he pulled both barrels before the muzzle cleared the gunwhale. The blast almost blew Lindstrom overboard, but more seriously blew a big hole in the boat's side below the waterline.

McGillicuddy looked down to note his leg was still in one piece, but water was gushing into the boat. He picked up a gunnysack, stuffed it into the aperture, and pulled as hard as he could into Indian Creek. For some reason Aberdeen's leading shipbuilder never again invited Dan McGillicuddy to go duck hunting.

* * *

The Hidden Hole

"Big Fred" Hewett frequently told a story concerning the start of the Lindstrom shipyard. There was a huge spruce stump on the site, which Lindstrom had dug out, leaving a considerable crater. There didn't seem to be anything around to fill the hole except wood chips; so the hole was filled with wood chips. The first high and overflowing tide that came along floated out the chips. Then along came a cranky old ship carpenter named John Erickson, who had been sent across the yard to fetch something or another. Erickson, in his usual dudgeon, saw nothing amiss in the terrain and plunged neck-deep into the stump hole. Hewett recounted, once Erickson emerged, spitting chips and shavings, things began to scorch around the Lindstrom shipyard. The soaking-wet Erickson was so mad he reverted to his native tongue for oaths and denunciations of the damn fools who had put chips in the stump hole.

* * *

Tough Country

The Elk River country — the river tended southeasterly from Grays Harbor's South Bay — was a particularly tough country to log. It was hard to reach with waterborne supplies and equipment, the ground was rough and brushy, and it took two tides to get logs out to the mills. This was because South Bay was shallow with wide mud flats and only a narrow channel through which a small tug could pass, and this only at high water. A tug could not get in and out again with a tow on one tide. This upped towing charges considerably and did much to hasten the end of logging enterprises of Roy Sargent and Cyclone Miller. Using a better system the Lytle Company went in with a long railway and operated on a scale that survived the country and the tides.

Over on Johns River, Mackie & Beaulieu, almost in the same township, put in a log dump on Johns River and a railroad that eventually dead-ended against the Hobi works on North River some 10 miles to the southeast.

* * *

The Ruse that Failed

It was almost foregone that there would be shenanigans of various hues and descriptions in the logging and lumbering business, particularly the logging business involving timber ownerships, claims, boundaries, cruises, rights-of-way, damages and a whole list of other pitfalls for a logger.

The history of Grays Harbor logging is permeated with "blocks," "cut-offs," "stops" and other forms of thwarting where one company told or demonstrated to another it could go no further because the thwarting company owned the next section or block of timber.

More than one thriving logging outfit "ran out of timber;" that is, someone else owned the timber just over the ridge, or across the canyon.

A classic example of this situation developed when a company working up Delezene Creek, envisioned an incline rail line across a 40-acre tract, owned by the State of Washington, into timber owned by the Weyerhaeuser Company.

The Clemons Logging Company had its eye on the same Weyerhaeuser timber, and projected a survey across the state tract. Clemons was proceeding southeasterly from Melbourne, the other company southwesterly from Delezene Creek. The two met in a saddle in the state tract. Clemons ran a survey through the state land and on one momentous day appeared in Olympia to seek a right-of-way. He was told that someone from the other works had appeared an hour before and was granted the right-of-way. Clemons demanded to see his opponent's survey. Perusing it he found the survey was a duplicate of his own, to the extent that the other surveyor had in some places actually used Clemons' stakes.

Adding insult to injury, the other outfit bragged how they had the entire area "sewed up;" but they forgot about George Long of the Weyerhaeuser Company. He disliked the management methods of Clemons' opponents, so he told Clemons to go home, calm himself, and continue to operate just as he had been doing. A man respected for integrity, George Long rubbed his long neck, massaged his cheek as was his custom, and conveyed to Clemons that his rivals would never get beyond the Weyerhaeuser line. And they didn't. Clemons was given access to Weyerhaeuser timber, while his opponents, toppled upon their backsides, pulled their rail line and camps out of the Delezene basin.

But the owner of the defeated outfit was not down for long. He moved to another area, built a long rail line and logged out a region of prime timber, even setting some car-loading records in doing it. And he was a man with fruitful ideas. He wrote letters to presidents and board chairmen of the more prominent American railway systems offering to trade them rides on his "railway system" in exchange for trips on theirs. They gave him passes. It was said he did considerable traveling, but it was never revealed whether the other managements took advantage of the logger's offer to ride his rattlers.

* * *

The Chicken Caller

Mrs. Charles H. Fry — nee Amanda Slover — is the source of the information that Emerson located his mill in Hoquiam because of the high price of a Cosmopolis site.

Mrs. Fry also received Emerson at her dinner table. She relates that during his scouting of the Harbor region in the summer of 1880, he stopped at her home for dinner. It was a warm day and Mrs. Fry had left the kitchen door open as she prepared a chicken dinner and set the kitchen table for her guest. The Frys and Emerson had no sooner sat down to dinner when out of the yard, in through the open door, sailed one of the Fry's chickens, landing in the middle of the table. Emerson grinned, while Amanda Fry was beet-red with embarrassment. Emerson grabbed the chicken and tossed it out the door, commenting, "That chicken was sure in a hurry to get into the pot."

* * *

Tough Chipmunk

And then there was Sven Thorson, not long from Karlskoga, who had his first encounter with a chipmunk. When he sat down for dinner in the messhall, he asked his elbow-rubber: "Vot iss dat frisky little feller dat roon round and round the stump? He got bushy tail, too."

"Oh," said the wood-buck between bites, "that's a cougar."

Sven nodded unquestioned acceptance: "Ya, a cougar. Ay never tank ay live to see vun."

* * *

Appendix E

Drop, or Green Chain

The drop, or as it was often called, the green chain, was, and still is, a long sorting table, usually with three flat chains moving along the top to carry lumber. Along either side of the drop are walkways for workmen who pull off lumber onto alongside piles for hauling away. All the boards or timbers are marked with a code, usually for grade, but sometimes for lengths and sizes, or for some special disposition such as shunting into the resaw.

In most sawmills the drop or green chain (because the lumber is still green and not dried) is headed by a bank of trim saws which cuts boards to length and cuts out imperfections. Once on the green chain the lumber travels slowly past the "grader," who inspects each piece and marks it with the appropriate code recognizable by the "pull-off" men stationed on the walks alongside the drop. Some larger timbers are marked for the re-saw, which means literally the piece is to be sawed again to size. This means the piece has to be heaved off the green chain and sent by rollers to the resawyer, who guides it through a bandsaw and onto the green chain again.

A job on the drop was man-killing in the sense it was extremely heavy and hard work. Usually it paid a little more than other common labor jobs in the mill, but in early times the men had to provide their own leather aprons or aprons made from heavy fabric belts, pieces of which often could be purloined from the belt shop.

* * *

He Knew Loggers

Because Druggist Peter M. Nielsen knew his loggers, a couple of would-be swindlers made the Aberdeen hoosegow. And it may have been because Pete Nielsen was a little too trusting, but he realized when he had been had.

The story went this way: Two strangers walked into the Aberdeen Drug Store at Heron and I street, with a check in one hand and a long list of logging camp supplies in the other. A portion of the list was for Peter Nielsen if he would cash the check. Pete did not scan the list just then, but a glance told him it was imposing. He cashed the check and the men departed, leaving Nielsen holding a list of drugs and sundries supposedly for delivery to a logging camp.

The first thing that caught Nielsen's eye was "two hot water bottles." Right off Pete knew that a logger would be caught dead before he would succumb to a hot water bottle.

The bank was closed, so Pete, more than suspicious, called cashier Jim Fuller, who said he would go to the bank and check out Pete's suspicion. Sure enough, Fuller told Pete there was no such account in the bank. Pete then pounded the planks to the police station where he retold his tale of woe. Two police officers, with Pete Nielsen trailing, started checking out the emporiums, both solid and liquid. It took several stops and not a few swinging doors before Peter Nielsen fairly yelled: "That's them!" The police found the remainder of the list of supplies and what was left of Pete's money, a sizeable amount for the two con men had not yet gotten into full swing.

"Two hot water bottles!" Pete always said, "if you want to swindle you can be slick, but not stupid."

* * *

Appendix
F

GEORGE FICKER'S ALBUM

Among those who anonymously built the forest industry of Grays Harbor was a mild little man named George Ficker. He was a handy man at Polson's Camp Eight who whiled away his idle time by taking pictures. The Polson's finally christened him the official photographer of Camp Eight but did not raise his pay. This collection of the postcard pictures taken by George Ficker, the industry's first P.R. man, preserves aspects of camp life which would have vanished but for his dedication and darkroom dabblings.

—*From the Rosalie Spellman Collection.*

Appendix F

Ficker: A Self-Portrait.

Camp hogs which lived on cookhouse scraps. Amused loggers called this group the Spotted Hyenas and admired what they "scaled" in pork chops.

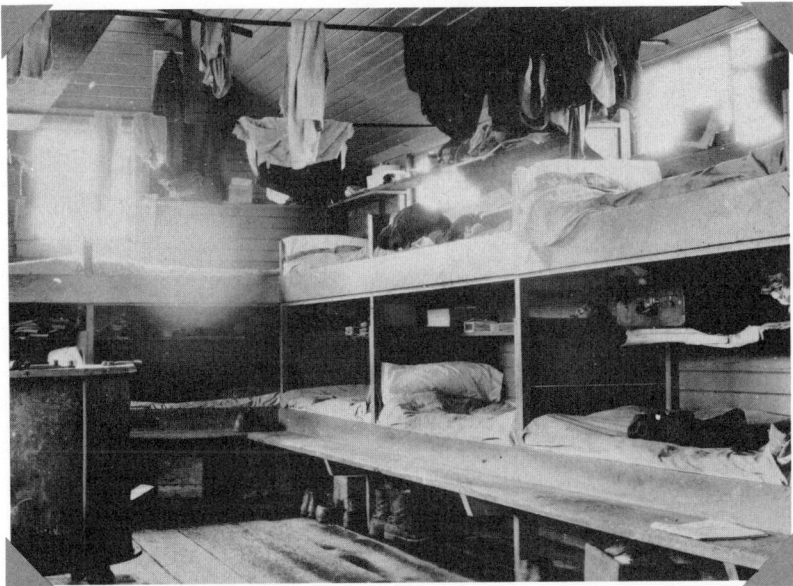

Bunkhouse interior after the men have gone to work and before the bedmaker got around to tidy up.

Ficker's classic "A Rainy Day In Camp."

Preparing meals in the cookhouse. Joe Nieradzik, Sr., center, is father of Aberdeen librarian, Rosalie Spellman.

The flunky and the pot-walloper become entwined. Camp romances were not encouraged, but even Polson could not control the processes of nature.

Notes

1. Three months after sale of the mill to Simpson and Anderson, the same two men with Thomas Bordeaux and M. A. Healey of LaCrosse, Wisconsin, obtained a vast tract of timber in the Black Hills, planning to log to Mud Bay and employ three hundred men in the operation.

    Before Sol Simpson was quit of Montesano, however, he had one nettling experience with a piece of Montesano real estate, and a thorn that really pricked him. The thorn was Dave Harner. On East Pioneer street in Montesano, near the depot, Sol Simpson owned two lots, a house on one, the other empty and somewhat overgrown. Over the years Sol Simpson, preoccupied with other affairs, including his blooming logging business, sort of forgot his Montesano lots and that Dave Harner was living in the house. All of a sudden in December, 1901, Sol Simpson became aware of his oversight and sought to eject Dave Harner and his family from the property.

    "No way," said Dave Harner. "I have been living in the house for ten years and I now claim ownership by adverse possession." Sol Simpson sued, but got a judgment of dismissal with costs in favor of the defendant, and restitution of the property in dispute.

    In January 1902, the same dispute surfaced again. While Dave Harner was out of town Sol Simpson had the house moved to his adjoining lot.

    And then in October 1903 Dave Harner "stole a march" on Sol Simpson "the Shelton millionaire." Harner moved the house back upon the disputed lot. There it remained.

2. George H. Emerson born January 18, 1846 in Chester, New Hampshire, the same town in which his father, Nathaniel F. Emerson, was born 42 years before, and the same in which his mother, Clarissa Goodhue, acquired the Emerson name in 1831. George H. was the fourth child born to the Emersons in Chester. He was moved by them to Massachussets at the beginning of the Civil War. He enlisted in the Union forces, saw active service, and attended Harvard College at the termination of his military services.

    In 1866 young George H. Emerson quit the East by making his way to Kansas City, and then by ox team to San Francisco. There he found employment with Captain Asa M. Simpson and was sent to work in a lumber mill on Coos Bay, Oregon. He grew to like the Coast and decided to stay, but first, in 1868, he returned to Massachussets to wed Lizzie Damon, then taking his bride to the San Joaquin valley in California. He was prepared to farm, but was driven out of the valley by drought, and again turned to Captain Simpson. He was given a job in Simpson's various operations, and by 1881 was in high favor with the sawmill operator and financier. Thus came his Grays Harbor assignment. The famed Simpsons, Sol G. of Shelton and Asa M. of San Francisco, were not related.

3. The Emersons had two children survive to become figures in the Grays Harbor timber industry: Ralph D. Emerson, who was to succeed his father in the North Western Company, and Alice Emerson who married Frank H. Lamb.

   Emerson was president of the Harbor Land Company, president of the Frank H. Lamb Timber Company, president of the Grays Harbor Tugboat Company, vice-president of the Grays Harbor Company, vice-president of the North Western Lumber Company, vice-president of the First National Bank, interested in the Lumbermen's Indemnity Company, the Metropolitan Bank and director of the Metropolitan Building Company in Seattle. He was also proprietor of the Hoquiam Theater, president and principal owner of the North Shore Electric Company, and president of the Wishkah Boom Company.

4. Rennie Island, one of Grays Harbor's more prominent geographic features, was named for William "Bill" Rennie, saw filer in the North Western mill in Hoquiam. About the turn of the century, Rennie got a notion to homestead the so-far unwanted island, built himself a shack on the highest ground available, a patch of willow and bunch grass mostly awash at exceptional high tides. Bill Rennie stayed only a few years, constantly afraid of being carried away by freshets, but his name still clings to the island that successfully divides the Harbor into the North Channel and South Channel.

5. The store which A. J. West saw was taken over within a year by D. R. Edwards and Frank Whitney.

6. The piling for the West mill was driven in the winter of 1883-84 by a crew from Hoquiam: engineer Joe Carnahan, top deckmen Jack Snyder, Bob Durney, Lincoln Snider and foreman Al Kuhn.

7. Two of Peter Emory's brothers, Irwin and Ed Emory, came from Michigan shortly after the store structure was built, Irwin Emory to operate the store, and Ed Emory to work in the mill and on the boom. Ed Emory drowned in the Wishkah and was buried at Fern Hill in a spot barren of trees and near the grave of a man named McCormack, who had also drowned in the Wishkah and was the first person buried in the pioneer cemetery.

8. Ireland born, A. J. West came first to Canada, then to Michigan from where he enlisted as a private in the Union forces. He rose to captain in the service. When the Northern Pacific completed its line to the Northwest, he

bought the first ticket from St. Paul to Portland. In 1865 he married Jennie Robinson.

9. Captain J. M. Weatherwax came by his title as captain of an infantry company under General Phil Sheridan during the Civil War in which he served three years and three months, being twice wounded. He was born in 1826 in Clinton County, New York, on the shore of Lake Champlain. While still a boy he was moved by his father to New Albion in Western New York, and later to Adrian in the new state of Michigan. When 19 years old Weatherwax started the study of medicine and after graduating from a medical college in Cleveland, Ohio, practiced for three years before joining his brother in a lumber business in Michigan. He purchased a half interest in a pine operation in Ottawa County, below Grand Rapids. After nine years of logging and lumber cutting, Weatherwax enlisted with the Union forces, marrying Miss M. E. Keys while in service. He was mustered out shortly before the war ended and returned to his lumber business. By the time he decided to come to the Pacific Coast he had three mills operating in Michigan and several mercantile establishments along with other investments in lands and timber. All these he disposed of a year after starting his mill in Aberdeen.

   Weatherwax was equally successful on Grays Harbor in accumulating properties and making investments. He acquired 25,000 acres of prime timber land on or near Grays Harbor, owned the shipyard adjacent to his mill, built a large foundry in 1888 near the mouth of Wishkah, operated a large general store near the mill with a stock worth $25,000, and owned outright or had a share in several sailing vessels.

10. Edward Hulbert married Laura Jane Wellwood, Sunday April 11, 1880, in Greenville, Michigan, a marriage that in time was to produce seven children, Maude, Elizabeth, Bessie Jane, Albert Edward, Laura Cynthia, Frederick H., George Thomas and William Hulbert.

11. In his time Ed Hulbert established two homes in Aberdeen, the first at Wishkah and H streets; the other, then considered a magnificent mansion, at 807 North M street. For extracurricular activities he became a stockholder in the Columbia Box & Lumber Company in Raymond, Washington, and a partner in the Prosper Lumber Company, Prosper, Oregon.

12. During the "joining" days of the First World War, Dr. O. R. Austin was taken by the army as a military doctor. He was immediately stationed at Fort Lewis to give medical checks to new recruits. He had barely warmed his desk chair when one of the recruits at the far end of the line was Dr. J. B. Kinne, also of Aberdeen, who had joined up, Congressional Medal of Honor from the Spanish-American War and all, including his medical skills.

   Dr. Austin broke a military propriety; he moved Dr. J. B. Kinne to the first in the line. The two were long-time friends and had practiced medicine together in Aberdeen, but upon this occasion there was an immediate understanding, by the wink of an eye, not to recognize each other.

"All right, Dr. Kinne, so it says here on your form, bend over . . . put both hands flat on the floor . . . now kick up your heels . . . now in that position walk across the floor . . . hands flat, mind you."

Dr. Kinne fairly galloped with his hands flat on the floor and his heels kicking like a colt.

The two dozen other recruits in line stood transfixed, flabbergasted.

"O.K.," said Dr. Austin, "you passed."

What all the other recruits did not know, and Dr. Austin did, and Dr. Kinne knew he knew, was that Kinne had been a circus acrobat in his youth while attending medical school. He worked in a circus during the summer tour, and attended medical school throughout the winter.

13. Pap Anderson in his time touched many lives. He had five daughters and three sons by his first marriage, Ida, Martha, Daisy, Carrie, Lulu, and sons Samuel Miles, Henry Neff Jr., George Edgar. After the death of his first wife Pap married Cora Patterson, sister of W. J. "Billy" Patterson, Aberdeen banker.

Samuel Anderson Sr., in turn had three sons, Harold, Sam Jr. and Reginald, while Henry Neff Anderson had one daughter, Priscilla, who married Arnold Polson, son of Alex Polson, and one son, John "Jack" Anderson.

George Edgar Anderson had four sons, Henry Neff 3rd, G. E. "Egg" Anderson Jr. Emmett Dewitt Anderson and Donald Chester Anderson; one daughter Martha Jeanett, who married Charles Moar, a relative of the Wilson sawmill family.

Bert and Martha Anderson Middleton had four children, Edward "Ed" Anderson Middleton, born in Greenville (the name Greenville after an Anderson ancestor named Green) and associated with the Anderson & Middleton Company until his death, two daughters, Sarah and Martha, both marrying in Greenville, and Charles "Chub" Middleton. Edward Middleton had two sons, Edward A. "Ted" Middleton and Richard "Rick" Middleton, who continued with Anderson & Middleton affairs, as did Charles Middleton's son, James "Jim" Middleton.

14. Heine received his nickname from his uncle, Sam Anderson Sr. who collared Henry Neff, 3rd, one day for teasing Sam's son, Harold. "I'm going to call you Heine," said Sam. Heine was what the ill-favored Germans were called at the time, besides Sam had a dog named Heine, and was bent upon "getting Henry Neff's goat." The nickname stuck and was later carried throughout the Anderson realm.

Pap Anderson not only influenced many lives by the name of Anderson, but also fixed his persuasion upon the Elways, also of Altoona. There was a round-about relationship between the Andersons and Elways: Robert "Bob" Elway had a step-brother, Downs Miller, whose mother was an Anderson (daughter of Pap Anderson). After Pap Anderson had coaxed his brood to Grays Harbor and had them settled in Aberdeen, he noted there was no plumbing shop in town, or on the Harbor for that matter. He fastened upon the Elways, Robert and his step-brother, Downs Miller, who were working for another brother, James Elway, in his Altoona plumbing shop. In 1909 Pap's arguments and persuasions induced the Elways to quit Altoona and open a plumbing shop in Aberdeen. Later they brought a brother, Harry, from Altoona and opened a second plumbing shop in Hoquiam. From then on the name "Elway" and plumbing were almost synonymous on Grays Harbor.

15. W. H. "Will" Abel was born in Fernhurst, Sussex, England, December 5, 1870. When still hardly out of diapers he was brought by his parents to Turkey Creek, Kansas. Two years later the family returned to England, but came again to the United States in 1884, settling in Salina, Kansas. W. H. Abel attended a normal school in Salina and was graduated from the commercial course in 1887. While teaching school and despite failing eyesight, he began reading law, a profession in which he was to become outstanding.

    W. H. Abel quit Salina June 2, 1892, shifting to Chehalis County, Washington Territory, upon the heels of Ella Rosmond, of whom he was enamored. The Abel and Henry Rosmond families were neighbors on small farms near Salina, where young Will Abel became so taken with Ella Rose that he followed her to Washington Territory, and married her December 23, 1892. He was thereafter to call her "Rosy," and by her to have five daughters and two sons.

    Will Abel taught school for a short time, and then edited a small paper, the Washington Economist, in Montesano. He was admitted to practice before the Washington territorial supreme court in 1894 and before the United States supreme court in 1897 and thereafter became one of the most outstanding defense and trial lawyers in the state.

    Will Abel, the first of three Abel lawyer-brothers to come to Washington Territory, was followed by A. M. "Mac" Abel, who went first to Snohomish country with Elmer Boner, later to Aberdeen, and by George Abel, who lived in Hoquiam for many years, had four sons and two daughters by a first wife, and moved to Montesano when elected to the Chehalis County superior court. George Abel, like his brother Will Abel, read law, but A. M. Abel was graduated from the law school at the University of Kansas in Lawrence. A. M. Abel likewise married a daughter of Henry Rosmond.

16. The Chehalis Valley Vidette (vidette, or vedette, means watcher, outpost, sentry) in 1883 carried two items of some significance to Alex Polson. The February 1, 1883, issue said George Carlisle had sold his timber to George Emerson for 25 cents a thousand, and Alex Polson, as of December 14, 1882, had sold his logging outfit to Judson Hines for $750. In 1883, too, there was an item concerning Alex Polson's brother, John Polson, who had died in October in Elma from "an attack of quinsey." The following year, in August, Alex Polson was again in print, this time because of an accident as he was working in the woods near Hoquiam. With his axe on his

shoulder, Polson was crossing on a log when he fell and struck the axe into his side, making a deep gash. He was taken to Dr. Mahlon Pearson in Aberdeen.

17. George E. Clemons was married twice, his first wife being Mary J. Dearborn, the surviving children of that union being Charles H. Clemons, and Mrs. Ida M. Ferris of Providence, R. I. His second wife was Sophia G. Jackman, their surviving child being W. G. Clemons of Hanover, New Hampshire, who was on Grays Harbor only three years, starting in 1911.

    Charles H. Clemons was born in North Woodstock, New Hampshire, September 3, 1857. He arrived in Washington Territory the same year as his future wife, Margaret A. Murray.

18. Minot Peak was named for Minot Davis.

19. Apparently J. W. Walsh joined with Joe Calder in this first logging venture for the two signed these "Articles of Agreement" with J. W. Milroy & Co. "Articles of agreement made this 22nd day of January 1884, between J. E. Calder and J. W. Walsh, parties of the first part, and J. W. Milroy & Co., parties of the second part, all now operators in the logging business, _____ that the said parties of the first part are to take exclusive and independent control of the logging camp now located on the land of P. Murray near Elma, W. T., and all its appurtences including the four yoke of oxen now therein, and shall conduct the business of said camp and shall apply the proceeds of all logs sent therefrom to the payment of current expenses and outstanding indebtedness of said camp, profits, if any to go said coportuers.

    "If on the 1st day of April 1884 said expenses and debts are fully paid, then the said parties of the second part shall have the right to take over simply the two yoke of cattle originally put in by them, otherwise said cattle or their equivalent in cash shall remain the property of said coportuers. Further, that if on the said date of April 1st 1884, all debts agains the coportuership as far as they relate to the logging business are paid, the said parties of the second part shall be entitled to a credit of $140.00 on said back indebtedness, and J. E. Calder one of the parties of the part, shall be entitled to a like credit of $45.00, otherwise said parties shall have no such credit.

    J. W. Walsh (*seal*)
    J. E. Calder (*seal*)
    J. W. Milroy (*seal*)
    "Signed, sealed and
    delivered in presence of
    Patrick Murray (*seal*)"

    (Patrick Murray and his wife Anna Keenan Murray were the parents of Margaret Ann Murray, the wife of Charles H. Clemons.)

    J. E. Calder was born August 19, 1860 in Iowa. He arrived on the Sound April 20, 1882. Calder and Walsh printed the first Vidette on February 1, 1883. Calder traded his interest in the Vidette for his partner's interest in a logging deal south of Elma, January, 1884 known as Milroy & Co., which included four yoke of oxen.

The Hoquiam mill managed by George H. Emerson, was the outlet for the logs and the source of supplies and credit. Calder once told a friend that his education had not told him that the scale of the season's delivered logs multiplied by the log price would inevitably equal the indebtedness at the mill store and warehouse.

Calder was given credit for running the first raft of logs down the Chehalis.

In April, 1884, his camp was moved to the Hoquiam River and logged the H. H. Halbert claim. In April, 1885, he moved over to Cosmopolis. In September, 1885, he left for a trip back to his home town in Iowa.

In February, 1886, Emerson notified the loggers that the mill would not be buying logs for some time.

In January, 1887, advertising appeared "J. E. Calder, Real Estate and Intelligence Office." February 27, 1890 he married Nina L. French, a school teacher.

20. George Ninemire was born October 25, 1860 in Weston, Missouri, and was bundled off to the Oregon Country by ox team when only three years old. The family settled on Hood Canal, near Seabeck, in 1864. George Ninemire himself first came to Grays Harbor country in 1877 to drive cattle to Seabeck. He returned in 1885 to become a permanent resident. He was married to Mary Watkins in Montesano in 1887.

Ninemire's partner-to-be, Thomas Grant Morgan, was born in Allegheny, Pennsylvania, April 10, 1860, to Peter Morgan and Rose Grant Morgan, both born in Ireland. Thomas Morgan was married to Margaret Seiling in Allegheny in 1890, the year they settled in Montesano. The Morgans moved from Montesano to Aberdeen in 1890, building a large residence at Wishkah and K streets.

21. In September 1905 Ninemire & Morgan sold 2,300 acres of their south beach and Westport holdings to a Seattle syndicate, and after selling their meat business for reputedly a half-million dollars, divided their Cedarville holdings into 10-acre farms for sale. After the Aberdeen fire in 1903 the partnership engaged in real estate dealings and construction, developing the Commercial block from G to H street on Market street in Aberdeen, including what was first known as the Crescent hotel, later the Lafayette hotel. They also did some developing in Grays Harbor City and Ocosta. Ninemire himself was later associated with Ed Finch in formation of the Aberdeen-Hoquiam street railway system. Ninemire also operated the Montesano Lumber Company, was a mayor and city councilman of Montesano, ending his long career doing a 10-year stretch at farming near Montesano, where he was among the first to grow peas commercially.

22. Robert Lytle was born in Ogdensburg, New York, September 14, 1854, son of Joseph and Elizabeth Foster Lytle. In early boyhood he was moved with the family to Wisconsin where the father started farming near Portage.

Upon finishing the common school, Robert Lytle completed a commercial course at the University of Wisconsin. He then moved to Minnesota, and again to Lincoln, Nebraska, where he engaged in business for himself, supposedly a grocery business.

Robert Lytle was married June 27, 1886, to Ida McDonald and moved with her to Washington Territory three years later.

23. Six children were born to Jerry McGillicuddy and his wife, Agnes, after they arrived on Grays Harbor. They were Jeremiah Ambrose Jr. J. E. McGillicuddy, Cornelius O. McGillicuddy, F. Daniel McGillicuddy, Eveleen, and the last, Blaine H. McGillicuddy, born 1892. An older daughter, Agnes, was born in 1881.

24. There were other heavily timbered regions in the Chehalis country; notable was one township 21-1 in which Stockwell found 120 million feet of timber in one rich section. In township 16-6 every section ran better than 100 thousand feet.

25. A deadhead in timber terms is a log so heavy on one end it sinks to the bottom while the light end floats above the water surface.

26. Vic Lindberg was not the only youngster to deliver papers to the bars and bawds during Aberdeen's palmy days. Two others were John Pinckney, who was to become a prominent Grays Harbor plumbing supplier, and Dan McGillicuddy, to become a logging master, cruiser, Army veteran and much talked-of citizen. McGillicuddy liked to tell how he could sneak a paper into the front of a saloon, then scoot out the back door into the alley to the next stop without having to go all the way around the front.

On one such occasion he was just entering the rear door of a bawdy house, paper sack hanging and the newest edition in hand, when out of a door into the hallway screamed a woman stitchless, with a parrot holding tight, and flapping, to a firm bite on her plump buttocks.

By the time young McGillicuddy had recovered from shock the hall was full of people, all trying to extract the parrot, some by pulling at the bird, others by yanking at the victim. They so managed. And McGillicuddy was to say later he never heard so much laughter and admiration of a unique situation.

27. From the Montesano Vidette, Sept. 12, 1902:

September 12th, 1902 will live in the history of Western Washington as the "Dark Day."

From the Cascades west to the ocean, and probably far out to sea, thick blankets of smoke totally obscured the sun, so that past 10 o'clock this morning darkness reigned supreme.

The darkest night was not darker than the day up to the time mentioned. Toward 11 o'clock the sky began to brighten around the horizon and by 11 o'clock buildings could be distinguished a couple of blocks away. Near the earth the smoke was not any thicker than it had been for several days, and no discomfort was felt by the people, but high in the air there must have been a thick bank of smoke which effectually shut out the rays of the sun.

At 8 o'clock this morning Chief Crane ordered the fire bell rung to gather the firemen and volunteers. A large number of persons were organized into a patrol to guard and armed with lanterns and buckets every part of the town was guarded thoroughly to prevent fire from entering from any direction.

1 p.m. — County Supt. Williams came down from Elma at noon today. He was up the Summit Branch yesterday and brings the latest news from that section. He drove up from Elma yesterday morning and met no fire till near Summit, but on the way back ran into fire this side of Summit. He got through alright until he reached Rayville, which he found in flames. The entire town was burned except the mill, which was saved. The goods from the store and most of the household goods of residents were saved. At White's mill everything was burned, including a million feet of lumber, and the Star mill was destroyed. These two mills are all that were burned in the east end of the county. At Elma, seven to ten small houses on the north side of the R R track were burned and a couple of houses east of the town, one being the Twidwell's. Three railroad bridges and three county bridges on the Summit road were burned and the Loertcher, Hale and Rayville schools were destroyed.

It is reported that it is impossible to save Mack's camp near Satsop. At the time of going to press this afternoon the fires in the east end of the county are under control and no further damage is expected. There are small fires on the prairie west of Satsop but no big fire reached the Satsop River. It is not believed that any lives were lost in the east end of the county.

There were no railroad bridges burned on the mail line. The train went out as usual this morning, passing at Elma the train which should have come in last night. The latter train was probably held on the east side of the line to prevent tying up two trains on the harbor in case bridges were destroyed.

Passengers coming up from Hoquiam this A.M. brought word that nearly all the camps on the Hoquiam had been destroyed, but a special received from Hoquiam at 1 o'clock says that James Cooper had just come down from that section and says that Polson's Camp Three was destroyed and Camp One partly burned, also Ellingson's camp was destroyed; and also the entire settlement of (New) London, except the hotel. The report that the fire was in the neighborhood of Hoquiam seems to be untrue, as at 1 o'clock there was no fire in sight of Hoquiam.

Six men are reported missing from one of Polson's camps, but whether they have been destroyed or have sought safety in some other direction is not known.

At this writing lights are necessary inside the stores and houses but out of doors the sun has conquered the smoke and daylight again holds sway.

Vidette, Sept. 19, 1902

The fire which devastated portions of Chehalis County on Thursday and Friday of last week, was the worst in the history of the county. The total loss will foot up to several hundred thousand dollars, though it is of course impossible to give accurate figures at this time

It is now thought that damage to standing timber will not be as large as first supposed, as the fire was largely in districts that had been cut over.

Chehalis County seems to be the darkest spot on the coast. Reports from other points indicate that darkness was not as intense as in the county, where from early Thursday till 11 o'clock Friday a.m. it was as dark as the blackest night. This was supposed to be caused by a bank of fog keeping the clouds from ascending.

By Friday evening the fires in the different parts of the county were well under control, but hundreds of families had been rendered homeless and much valuable mill, camp and farm property destroyed.

Probably the heaviest losses in the county were Polson Bros., of Hoquiam, whose loss is estimated at $50,000; Allen White, owner of a large mill near Elma, lost in the neighborhood of $40,000, with insurance of $6,000; Frank Stenzil, the Humptulips logger, lost two dams and one camp, besides a large amount of logs, of a total value of $15,000. At Rayville everything was burned except the mill. The loss will be from $8,000 to $10,000. The loss of the Star mill of Elma, of which Wakefield and O'Donnell are the principal owners, will be in the neighborhood of $10,000.

28. A bald-headed schooner is one without topm'sts or tops'ls.

29. Orson M. Kellogg was born in Grand Rapids, Michigan, September 2, 1853. While in Michigan he worked for E. K. Wood for seven years, and in 1877 married Nettie R. Gibbs. They had two children, George and Chester. The elder son, born in July, 1878, was graduated from Leland Stanford University in 1904, married Ida Smith of Seattle, and became assistant manager of E. K. Wood enterprises in Hoquiam, and eventually succeeded his father as manager of the E. K. Wood Company.

30. Turning the tide of timber retreat in Grays Harbor County after decades of relentless logging was not alone the work of Mother Nature. She needed help from trained foresters, economists and the community people who had the most at stake in seeking the preservation of payrolls.

At a time when Grays Harbor was groggily reeling into a slump caused by its having more acres of stumps than standing timber, in 1929, the Western Forestry and Conservation Association came forth with a comprehensive study of what could be done to assure the future of Aberdeen, Hoquiam, Montesano and their neighbors. It was the first time such a timber study had been done in the United States.

Eleven agencies and associations probed the county under leadership of E. T. Allen of Portland, Oregon, one of the brilliant foresters of his time. His participating experts included Col. William B. Greeley, former chief forester of the United States; Richard E. McArdle, later to become chief forester, and Leo A. Isaac of the Pacific Northwest Experiment Station, and a host of other state, federal and private industry experts. The regional community viewpoint was provided by F. W. "Matt" Mathias, then manager of the Hoquiam Chamber of Commerce.

The gist of this report was that by cooperatively managing private and governmental forest resources, and by controlling fire losses that were ruining the county's regrowth, a high yield of production could be maintained permanently. Out of this landmark study came new understandings and a firm foundation for all the communities of Grays Harbor. The area had the soils, the moisture, the tree types; all could be brought together by men using their heads.

Not long after this 1929 report, a new surge of community demand for relief from old and exhausting "cut out and get out" methods emerged in Elma. Aided by Washington state officials, the business leaders of Elma developed the Elma Survey which attracted so much national attention in the 1930's that Author Stuart Chase — the "father of Technocracy" — featured it in an article he wrote for Readers Digest. The Elma Survey became the formula and forerunner for the community protection assured to Eastern Grays Harbor County and Mason County by the formation of the Shelton Cooperative Sustained Yield Unit of 1946.

These two studies made in the depression years which so heavily burdened Western timber areas can now be viewed as responsible for actions which created a new sense of permanence over the hills and into the valleys which once rocked to the roar of the bullwhackers.

Bibliography

City of Aberdeen court records.
Aberdeen Daily World historical files.
Robert M. Cour, "The Plywood Age."
Ralph Chaplin, "The Centralia Case."
Edward Campbell, "History of the Pioneers."
Charles H. Clemons, "History of Clemons."
Chehalis County, Book of Records No. 1.
Hugh M. Delanty, "Along the Waterfront."
David Douglas, The David Douglas Journals.
Firemen's Fund, "Register of Ships."
Ed Hobi, "Logging As I Seen It."
Gordon Frazer Matthews, "Shipbuilding History of the Matthews Family."
Peter Matthews, "Pamphlet on Pacific Coast and Grays Harbor Shipbuilding."
Gordon Frazer Matthews, Biographical Sketch.
Montesano Vidette historical files.
Ed Van Syckle, "Our People: Story of the Fry Family."
Stewart H. Holbrook, "Half Century in the Timber," a history of the Schafer Bros. Logging Company.
Ernest C. Teagle, "Out of the Woods," a history of McCleary.

Helpful informational assistance was given by Cathryn Byard McKay, Howard Best, Dan McGillicuddy, Blaine McGillicuddy, Lester E. Calder, Doyle Barnett, Joe Randich and the Polson House Museum, Robert V. Creech of

Spear and Jackson, Richard Stockwell, June Danielson, Dorothy Z. Collins, Richard E. McArdle, Donald F. Flora, Harriet DeLong, William "Bill" Jones, Marie Gustafson Wahl, Ben K. Weatherwax, Mrs. Victor Lindberg.

Among persons interviewed by the author were Mrs. James Haynes, Samuel Benn, Alex Polson, Joe Malinowski, Mrs. James Gleeson, Cy Blackwell, Tom Soule, Joe Graham, Mrs. Charles Fry, Martin Deggeller, Charles "Chuck" Isaacson, Oscar Rosenkrantz, B. F. "Bim" Morrison, Victor "Vic" Lindberg, Henry N. "Heine" Anderson, Rick Billings, Alex MacLean Polson, Marzell Mayer, Dan McGillicuddy, Blaine McGillicuddy, Arnie Sandlands and Grays Harbor Title Company (land and site locations).

Index

Abel, A. M. "Mac," 198, 246
Abel, Ella Rosmond, 34
Abel, George (Judge), 289
Abel, Marjorie, 34
Abel, W. H., 34, 38, 186
Allen, Captain, 228
Allen, Dudley G., 181
Allen, E. T., 294
Allen, Jessie, 177
Allman, John, 233, 235, 236, 237
Ames, E. B., 46
Andersen, John, 243
Anderson, A. E., 173
Anderson, A. H., 11
Anderson, Donald Chester, 288
Anderson, Emmett Dewitt, 288
Anderson, George Edgar "Ed", 31, 32, 34, 35
Anderson, G. E. Jr. "Egg", 288
Anderson, Harold, 34
Anderson, Henry Neff 1st "Pap", 30, 31, 32, 33, 34, 35, 51
Anderson, Henry Neff Jr., 31, 32, 35
Anderson, Henry Neff 3rd "Heine", 32, 34, 35, 36, 37, 38, 39, 53
Anderson, John, 160, 288
Anderson, Martha (Middleton), 30, 288
Anderson, Martha Jeanette (Mrs. James Moar), 288
Anderson, Priscilla (Mrs. Arnold Polson), 288
Anderson, Reginald, 34
Anderson, Sam (pilot), 232
Anderson, Samuel Miles, 31, 32, 34, 35
Anderson, Samuel Jr., 34
Anderson, Sarah Manola, 51
Anderson, William, 44
Anderson & Nettelblad, 55

Andrews Creek, 116, 117, 118, 153
Arland, Charles W., 83
Arland, Rufus, 85
Armstrong, Benjamin C., 8, 9, 81
Arnold, Miss Ella, 98
Artic, 153
Astell, "Shorty", 235
Austad, Gabrille, 243
Austin, Arthus, 91
Austin, Dr. A. S., 32
Austin, Dr. O. R., 32
Austin, Russ, 206
Autzen, Paul, 196
Autzen, Peter, 82, 196, 197
Autzen, Thomas J., 196
Averill, B. B., 29, 30

Babcock, Lyman, 26
Bailey, "Buck", 235
Bailey, Ed, 56
Baker, J. N., 11
Bakeland, Dr. Leo, 201
Balsh, William, 160
Barker, Miss Forence, 221
Baker Bay, 5
Beardsley Bros (Undertakers), 173
Beardsley, Charles A., 173
Beardsley, Orville, 173
Beaver, Henry, 23
Becker, Frank, 242, 246
Bendixsen, H. D., 215, 218, 220, 225
Bendixsen, Lillian, 215
Benham, Captain H. A., 232
Benn, Ed, 172, 235, 243
Benn, Samuel "Sam", 16, 17, 20, 23, 29, 168, 235
Bennett, Gene, 234
Bergman, Willis, 232

Bernard Creek, 152
Best, Howard, 171
Bicknell, R. W., 186
Bignold, Lewis B., 124
Big Creek, 102, 152
Big Six, 115, 116, 117, 118
Birdwell, Calvin, 115
Birmingham, J. M., 243
Biscay, G. A., 184
Bishop, E. K., 123, 132
Black Creek, 69, 70, 116, 153
Black River, 111, 126
Blackwell, Cyrus "Cy", 25, 57, 82, 85, 86, 91, 92, 93, 131
Blackwell, Ira, 86
Blagen, Clarence, 35, 212
Blagen, Henry, 35, 212
Blagen, N. J. "Nels", 211
Boeing, William, 129, 131
Boling, Sylvester, 62
Boner, E. E., 246
Bordeaux, Thomas, 285
Bower, Earl, 117
Bower, W. Frank, 115, 117
Bowers, H., 109
Bowes, Dan, 173
Bowes, Sam, 173
Boyer, Abe, 25
Boyles, T., 109
Brackenreed, Walter L., 187
Braden, Lee, 93
Brady, 120
Brady, Elmer, 236
Brooklyn, 116
Brown, A. A., 195
Brown, Amos, 103
Brown, Clem, 162
Brown, H. P., 161
Brown, John, 83
Brown, Martell, 208
Bryden & Leitch, 158
Bucks Prairie, 11
Burrows, C. E., 157, 160, 176
Burrows, O. P., 126, 156
Bush, W. H., 123
Byard, John "Jack", 150, 153, 155
Byles, Charles, 9
Byles, C. N., 121
Byles, David, 9, 41
Byles, George W., 41
Byles, Hugh, 91

Calder, Joseph E. "Joe", 106, 107, 108, 109, 110, 290
Caldwell, Byron, 117, 118
Caldwell, Frances (Blaney), 115

Caldwell, George A., 115, 117, 118
Caldwell, Henry "Hank", 115, 117, 118
Caldwell, John L. "Jack", 115, 116
Caldwell, Lucinda "Lucy", 115, 117
Caldwell, Oliver B., 117, 118
Caldwell, William, 115, 116, 118
Callender, M. P., 14
Callow, Bert, 69, 119
Cameron, William, 93
Cameron & Hoover, 95, 152, 161
  W. T. Cameron, Pres.
  W. D. Hoover, Sec.
Campbell, Edward "Ed", 11, 12, 13, 14, 101, 103
Campbell, Mrs. Edward, 11, 12
Campbell, Horace, 235
Campbell, William E., 235, 246
Cape Disappointment, 6
Cape Shoalwater, 6, 239
Carlisle, George, 289
Carlson, Gus, 69
Carlson Brothers, Adolph and Gus, 131
Carlson & Callow, 152
Carnahan, Joe, 286
Carney, John J., 121
Carter, Fred, 44
Carter, T. J., 121
Carter, William Henry "One Arm", 85
Cedar Creek, 9, 32
Cedarville, 119
Central Park, 13, 105
Chalmers, Ed, 83
Charley Creek, 83, 153
Chase, Stuart, 295
Chehalis Indians, 7
Chehalis River, 7, 12, 13, 24, 26, 43, 47, 81, 82, 103, 104, 105, 111, 119, 122, 123, 162, 193, 233
Chenois Creek, 69, 102, 245
Chinooks, 6
Christenson, E. A., 30
Church, K. Y., 245
Clark, Ed, 20
Clark, Grace, 39
Clearwater River, 193
Clemons, Charles H., 83, 86, 103, 104, 105, 106, 121, 122, 126, 153, 289
Clemons, George, 103, 104, 289
Clemons, Isaac, 103
Cloquallum, 42, 111
Clough, W. H., 16
Coats, Albert (VP Coats Logging Co.), 93
Coats, Alfred F. (Pres. A. F. Coats Logging Co.), 39, 93, 220
Coats, Robert, 29
Collins, Chapin, 106, 107

INDEX

Columbia River, 5, 12
Comfort, John, 112
Comcomly, 6
Connor, Thomas, 123
Conway, Captain, 228, 238
Cook, William, 110, 111
Cooney, Neil, 46, 47, 48, 49, 50, 122
Cooper, Jack, 91
Cooper, R. M., 173
Copalis, 161, 193, 237
Copalis Crossing, 69, 193
Corkery Brothers, 152
Corlett, Thomas "Uncle Tommy", 16
Cosmopolis, 12, 13, 21, 42, 45, 47, 49, 50
Cowan, Jim, 82, 84, 126
Cow Point, 14, 19, 233
Cowlitz, 7
Cox, 8
Crane Creek, 101
Crawford, Buster, 92
Crawford, William "Bill", 234
Crosbie, W. J. "Billie", 172
Crowley, Rube, 92

Dalton, Captain James, 253
Damitio, Anthony, 25
Daniels, E. W., "Dan", 199, 200, 201, 202, 204, 206
Danielson, Captain Eric, 232
Davenport, Linc, 242
Davidson, Ed, 37
Davidson, George D., 127
Davis Creek, 152
Davis, Freda, 177
Davis, Minot, 105, 106, 107
Davis, George L., 127
Dean, George, 243, 244, 245
Decker (Settlement), 101, 192
Deggeller, Martin N., 204, 205, 206
Delanty, Hugh M., 240
DeLateur, Rudy, 209
Delezene Creek, 82, 83, 86, 104, 126, 153, 186
Deming, E. C., 116
Dermott, Captain, 228
Dettmers, George, 228
Devonshire, A. D., 129
Dineen, Dan, 129
Dineen, Frank, 129
Disque, Col. Brice P., 189
Doddridge, William "Billy", 26, 176
Doddridge, Dell, 176
Doland & McGuire, 173
Dolan, Ed, 241
Dolan, Jim 242

Dolan, Tom, 241
Dolbeer, 91, 92, 93, 100, 250
Dollar, Harry, 35
Dollar, Captain Robert, 219
Donaugh, P. M., 174
Donovan, Francis "Barney", 159
Donovan, Jane and Nan (twins), 159
Donovan, William, 157, 158, 159, 160
Donovan, William Jr., 159
Donovan Slough, 157
Dorris, Capt. Thomas P. "Tin Pan", 230
Dotson, Frank, 129
Douglas, C. J., 243
Douglas, David, 4, 5, 6, 7, 8
Doyle, Patrick, 129
Doyle, Tom, 153
Dudley, "Walkin' ", 57
Dunbar, H. N., 127
Dupree, B. B., 186
Durney, Robert "Bob", 286
Duval, Milton "Slim", 83
Dzamaria, Michael "Mike", 123

Eastman, John, 11
Eavens, June, 177
Egerer, Joseph, 129
Egger, Warren, 233
Eldridge, Sadie, 215
Elk River, 116, 233
Ellefsen, Capt. "Port Wine", 230
Elliott, E. O., 127
Elliott, Slough, 81, 82, 99, 245
Ellis Logging Co., 153
Ellison, Russ, 52
Elma, 11, 42, 121, 192
Elway, Harry, 288
Elway, James, 289
Elway, Robert "Bob", 288
Emerson, Alice (Mrs. Frank Lamb), 286
Emerson, George H., 11, 13, 14, 18, 84, 85, 92, 108, 109
Emerson, Nathaniel F., 285
Emerson, Ralph D., 286
Emont, Leon, 20
Emory, Irwin, 24
Emory, Peter, 23, 132
Empey, James E., 127, 129
Esmond, John, 44
Ess, Nels, 150
Estes, 42, 81
Evans, E. J., 205
Evans, R. H., 109

Fairfield, J. C., 19, 21, 22, 23
Farnam, A. H., 29, 47
Farquan, John, 129

INDEX

Finch, Edward "Ed", 291
Firth, Al, 173
Fish, Charles, 26
Fleet, D. W. "Daddy", 11, 23, 30
Fleet, Mrs. D. W., 43
Fleet, Reuben, 123
Fletcher, N. W., 42, 44
Ford, Sidney S. Jr., 9
Fordney, J. W. "Joe", 39, 40, 102
Fords Prairie, 82, 162
Forks, 195
Fort George (Astoria), 6
Fort Vancouver, 5, 7
Foster, F. G., 109
Four L — Loyal Legion Loggers & Lumbermen, 189
Fox, Austin I., 21, 25
Fox, Robert "Bob", 35
Foy, Edward, 197, 198
France, Eugene, 27, 30
France, Will, 40
Freeland, John, 68, 69
Freeman, Mildred, 223
Freeman, S. S., 223
Fry, Charles, 44
Fry Creek, 119
Fry, Harvey, 116
Fry, Jason, 10, 42, 43, 44
Fry, John, 10, 11, 43, 44
Fuller, James "Jim", 178

Gabrielson & Homer, 175
Garrison, Charles, 115
Gauger, John A., 199, 200
Garrison, E., 115
Geer, William, 234
Gibbon, William, 109
Gibbs, Nettie R., 294
Gillies, Jim, 85, 86
Gillis, Cliff, 129
Gillis, Dan, 86, 129, 153
Gleed, Thomas F., 114
Gleeson, Dan, 83
Gleeson, James "Uncle Jimmy", 42, 43
Gohl, Billy, 176, 177, 240, 241, 242, 243, 244, 245, 246
Goldberg, Lou, 208
Goldsmith, Eddie, 172
Goldsmith, Mose, 172
Goodell, M. E., 121
Goodhue, Clarissa, 285
Gotsis, Jim, 41
Graham, Joseph "Joe", 16, 17, 18, 19, 20, 21, 22, 23, 26
Grand Mound, 9
Grande, Harry S., 205

Grass Creek, 102, 245
Gray, Capt. Robert, 7
Great Blowdown, 194
Greeley, Col. W. B., 294
Green, Charles, 225
Green, Charles "Peavey", 168, 169
Green, Fred, 86
Grover, Steve, 235
Gustafson, Emil, 141

Hackett, James "Jim", 29, 47
Hagen, Wayne, 206
Halbert, H. H., 291
Hamilton, Alexander, 42
Hamilton & Smith, 82
Hammond, Captain, 239
Hank, William "Bill", 236
Hansen, Charles, 232
Hansen, John, 243
Harner, Dave, 283
Harries, D. S., 129
Harris, C., 129
Hart, Fred, 40
Hatberg, Charles, 244, 245, 246
Haufman, Mose, 172
Hayes, Charles, 173
Hayes & Hayes, 161, 181, 207
Haynes, James B., 25, 83, 99
Haynes, Mrs. James, 25
Heath, Lafe, 129
Heffron, D. J., 174, 175
Helms, H. 186
Hemphill, Jim, 129
Henderson, Alfred "Tar", 233
Herrick, E. M., 46
Hewett, Fred, 173, 174, 176, 227
Higgins, Charles H., 223
Higgins Slough, 85, 104, 105
Hilderbrandt, Henry, 170
Hinsdale, Captain G. S., 46
Hitchings, Andrew, 218
Hitchings, Dora, 216, 221
Hitchings, George H., 216, 217, 218, 219, 220, 221, 225
Hitchings, Katie, 216
Hitchings, Ruth, 216, 271
Hobi, John F., 153
Hodgdon, Judge C. W., 245
Hoffman, John, 244, 245, 246
Hogan, Patrick, 129
Hoh River, 193
Hoquiam River, 14, 17, 25, 86, 101, 102, 108, 116, 152, 233
Hood, James, 109, 222
Hopkins, Willis, 83, 84, 127, 129
Howsen, John, 225

INDEX

Hubble, Alonzo, 235, 237
Hubble, Frank, 235, 237
Hubble, George, 157
Hubble, Capt. Harry, 224, 232, 237
Hubble, Howard, 234
Hudsons Bay, 5
Huffman, John D., 52
Hughes, Capt. Charles, 216, 237
Hulbert, Albert Edward, 30, 47
Hulbert, Bessie Jane, 287
Hulbert, Edward, 29, 30, 40
Hulbert, Frederick H., 287
Hulbert, George Thomas, 287
Hulbert, Laura Cynthia, 287
Hulbert, Maude Elizabeth, 287
Hulbert, William, 287
Hulet, Hiram, 131
Hume Street, 19, 233
Humptulips City, 41, 100, 152
Humptulips River, 42, 86, 126, 127, 128, 152, 156, 160, 193, 233
Hutcheson, J. A., 247
Hutton, Frank, 116
Hyasman, 112, 113

Indian Creek, 245
Independence Creek, 119, 120
Ing, Amos, 83
Ingram, Ernest, 52
Ingram, James, 52
Ingram, Robert, 51
Ingram, Robert Jr., 52
Irwin, Judge Mason, 247
Isaac, Leo A., 294
Isaacson Company, 97
I.W.W. (Wobblies), 48, 49, 136, 179, 180, 181, 182, 183, 184, 185, 187, 188, 191

Jackman, Sophia G., 290
Jackson, A. W. 46
Jackson, Cleve, 126
Jackson, W. T., 21
Jacobsen, Andy, 243, 244
Jacobsen, Selmer, 173
James, John Rogers, 9, 11, 13
James Rock, 245
James, Samuel, 9
James, William, 9, 11
Jentzen, Lauritz "The Weasel", 244, 246
Jerome, Mel, 91
Johnson, Askel, 243
Johnson, Ben, 26, 27
Johnson, Benjamin Franklin, 39, 40
Johnson, Hans K. "Drawbucket", 134, 229, 231, 233

Johnson, J., 181
Johnson, Mabel, 177
Johnson, Mary, 39
Johns River, 23, 43, 44, 116, 233
Jones, Carrie, 160, 161
Jones, Frank E., 160
Jones, J. S., 174
Jones, Miss May, 176
Joyce, John, 220, 221
Jump, Charlie, 3

Kahle, John, 172
Kann, Jack, 235
Karshner, Earl, 53
Karr, James, 13, 217, 219
Keeley, Tom, 92
Keith, George, 91
Kellogg, Chester, 292
Kellogg, George, 292
Kellogg, O. M., 216, 219
Kesterson, Ben, 112, 129
Kesterson, Ed, 112
Kesterson, J. B., 13, 42, 43, 44, 45, 50, 51, 81, 82, 127
Keys, Miss M. E., 287
Keyes, William "Uncle Billy" and Mrs., 26
Kimball, J. S., 218
Kingstad, Lars, 242
Kinyon & Dzamaria, 123
Klingenberg, John, 244, 245, 246, 247
Knapp, Jack, 236
Knox, Harry S., 199, 201
Knox & Toombs, 200
Koehler, E. L., 21
Kolts, L., 175
Kramer, Hubert, 110, 111
Kreienbaum, Chris, 198
Kruse, E. T., 222
Kuhn, Al, 237, 286
Kyne, Peter B., 248, 250, 251, 253

Laberge, Alex, 127
Ladley, James, 209
Lammey, Ernest, 70
Landberg, R. M. "Roy", 208
Larkin Brothers, Jack, Charlie, Ed, 131
Larson, "Roughpile", 169
LaVoice, William, 93
Lawson, Captain Bob, 228
Leahy, J. T., 127
Leavitt, C., 83, 86, 103, 105, 126, 153
Lee, George, 41

Lester Brothers, 153
Lester, Ed, 84
Lewis, George, 15
Lewis, Mrs. John G., 15
Lewis, John G., 23, 26, 214
Lightfoot, George L., 244
Lightfoot, William, 244
Lindberg, Victor "Vic", 174, 177
Lindros, Gus, 243
Lindstrom, John, 225, 226, 227
Lister, Governor Ernest, 186
Little Rock, 111
Locke, Phil, 173
Lockett, Connie, 243
Logue, Carleton, 234
Logue, Neil, 234
Long, John J., 202
Look, C. P. 83
Loper, May, 177
Loveless, Ed, 83
Luark, Michael F., 10, 43, 81, 121
Luark, Patterson F., 9
Lunch, Catherine C., 159
Lutchins, Capt., 44
Lyons, Charley, 21
Lytle, Robert "Bob", 102, 116, 120, 121, 152
Lytle, Joseph, 120

Mace, J. D., 43
Mack, Gilbert F., 23
Mack, William B. "Billy", 36, 130, 161, 242
Mack, W. D. (Mack & Autzen), 82, 105, 132, 162
Mack, W. N. (cigar store), 181
Mackey, Cathy, 53
Mackey & Kauppi, 173
Madden, Tom, 83
Mahony, Andy, 223
Mahony, Rosalie, 223
Maley, L. L., 175
Malinowski, Joe, 155
Maloney, Patrick, 123
Manley, Tom, 22
Marden, Robert and Harry, 18
Markham, 86, 116
Markham, Ed, 129
Markham, John, 10, 119, 129
Marshall, Ed, 181
Marshall, Jim, 244
Marshall, Lillian, 177
Martin, William, 202
Matheson, Alexander McLean, 102, 103
Mathews, Joe, 109

Matthews, Gordon Frazer, 216, 221, 222, 224, 225
Matthews, Gordon Henry, 221
Matthews, Katie, 218
Matthews, Lillian B., 218
Matthews, Peter, 214, 215, 216, 218, 221, 225
Mathias, F. W. "Mat", 294
Mayberry Brothers, 174
Mayr, Dan, 53
Mayr, David, 53
Mayr, Jennie, 53
Mayr, Marzell, 52, 53
Mayr, Marzellinus, 52
Mayr, Mike, 53
Mayr, Tom, 53
Mayr, Werner, 52, 53
McArdle, Richard E., 294
Meadows, Scotty, 113
Mears, J. B., 242
Melbourne, 85, 105
Menzies, Archibard, 5
Merrill, R. D., 205
Merrill & Ring, 102, 205
Mersich, Capt. "Skovi", 160, 243
Meyer, Albert, 219
Meyer, Paul, 106
Middleton, A. W. "Bert", 30
Middleton, Charles, 31
Middleton, Edward Anderson "Ed", 288
Miller, Catherine, 51
Miller, Downs, 288
Miller, E. C., 51, 122, 132
Miller, Harold, 51
Miller, Joe, Mrs., Children Arnold, Anton, Kate, Joseph, 110, 111
Mills, E. M., 209
Milroy, J. W., 82, 85, 108, 131, 290
Minckler, John, 112
Miner, William, 25
Minot — Minot Peak, 290
Moak, Oliver C., 115
Moclips River, 193
Monroe, Dan, 91
Monroe, Simon, 93
Montell, Mabel, 177
Montesano, 9, 11, 13, 30, 44, 82, 98, 183
Montesano Vidette, 11, 16, 106, 108, 170, 171
Moore, Archie, 129
Moore, "Cranky Jack", 84
Morgan, Peter, 291
Morgan, Rose Grant, 291
Morgan, Thomas Grant, 118, 119, 120, 122, 291

INDEX

Moriarity, P. J., 127
Morley, A. J., 83, 84, 86
Morris, T. B., 14
Morrison, B. F. "Bim", 40, 41
Morrison, Victor, 40, 41
Morse, Capt., 228
Morse, Bert, 25
Morse, Roy F., 205, 206
Moulton, T., 109
Mox Chuck, 44, 162
Muller, Anna Bullenbeck, 110
Muller, Chris, 110
Muller, Christine, 110
Muller, Herman, 112
Muller, Julia, 110
Murphy, Dave, 92
Murphy, James, 84
Murphy, Maggie, 177
Murray, Archie, 86
Murray, Margaret A., 104
Murray, Patrick and Anna Keenan, 85, 104, 290
Murray, Tom, 205, 206

McCabe, William "Fightin' Billy", 164, 165, 166, 167, 168, 169, 170, 171, 172
McCarron, Capt. Michael, 240
McCarthy, F. M., 187
McCaskrie, Lieut. F. U., 186
McClay, Jack, 91
McCleary, Henry, 62, 132, 197, 198, 199
McClymont, Sam, 47
McClymont, Charles, 85, 131
McDermoth, Rev. Charles, 27
McDonald, Thomas A., 213, 214
McDonald, William "Billy", 176
McElfresh, J. C., 127
McElfresh, P. J., 127
McGillicuddy, Blaine, 129, 292
McGillicuddy, Bridget, 126
McGillicuddy, Cornelius O., 129, 292
McGillicuddy, F. Daniel, 82, 129, 185, 292
McGillicuddy, Eveleen, 292
McGillicuddy, Flora, 23
McGillicuddy, John, 126
McGillicuddy, Jeremiah Ambrose, 23, 83, 121, 126, 127, 129
McGillicuddy, Jeremiah Ambrose Jr., 139, 292
McGillicuddy, J. E., 292
McGillicuddy, Jerry (Jeremiah H.), 82, 126
McHugh, Neil, 242

McHugh, Patrick "Paddy", 242, 244, 245
McIntyre, Charley, 235
McKinley, Huey, 92
McKinnon, J. J., 220
McManemy, Ed, 16, 21
McWhinney, W. H., 222, 227

Naka, Yama, 177
Nechard, Mary, 9
Neilson, Marcus, 233
Neilton (burn), 101
Nelson, Carl, 59
Nelson, Mary, 53
Nelson, Nels, 59
Nelson, Steve, 53
Nethery, F. L., 127, 129
Nevin, Dr. James Victor, 201, 202
New London, 86, 126
Newell, Ex. Gov., 124
Newman, W. B. D., 9
Newskah (Neushkah) River, 83, 100, 152, 153
Nims, William, 21
Nims, Ruel, 13, 41
Ninemire, George W., 119, 120, 122
Nissons Landing, 152
Norman, Will, 112
North Cove, 16, 119
North River, 84, 106, 116, 153, 194
North Western Lumber Co., 11, 14, 82, 84, 85, 86, 92, 93, 99, 103, 108, 109, 126, 128, 157, 183, 213, 217, 228, 232, 239
Nyman, Vernon A., 207, 209

Oakville, 32
O'Brien, Frank A., 127
O'Connor, Frank, 159
O'Connor, Patrick, 158, 159
O'Connor, William, 159
Ocosta, 10, 116, 118, 193
O'Donnell, Jack, 192
O'Hare, John, 173
Olson, Emil, 246
Olson, Capt. G., 232
Olson, Patrick "Stumpin' ", 230
Olzendam, Roderic, 106, 107
O'Neil, Tip, 129
Onn, G. A., 122
Onn, H. B., 122
Orloff, Mon, 207, 208
Osborn, Tom, 112
Osgood, George J., 198
Ottinger, Larry, 204
Oyehut, 236, 237
Ozette, 101, 193, 194

Parker Creek, 86
Parks, Mayor, 181
Pasquier, Michel, 201, 202
Patterson, W. J. "Billie", 161, 181
Payette, Adolphus, 20
Payette, Ed, 20, 184, 245, 246, 247
Pearson, Billy, 26
Pearson, Judge John C., 20
Pearson, Dr. Mahlon I., 175
Peasley, Capt. Ralph E., 224, 248, 250, 251, 252, 253
Pedler, Billy, 19
Peebles, W. G. "Watt", 125, 126
Perkins, Samuel, 14
Perkins, James A. "Jim", 82, 83, 84, 85, 86, 91, 131
Perry, W. H., 45, 46
Peterman, Al, 203
Peterson, Charlie, 153
Peterson Point, 16
Pettijohn, Judge, 171
Pfund, E., 175
Phelps, Casper "Cap," 25
Phillips, Charley, 129
Picco, Ed, 122
Pickering, Marshal, 170
Pinckney, Ross, 25
Pitchford, Clyde A., 161
Point, Chehalis, 9
Polson, Alex, 23, 45, 50, 98, 99, 100, 101, 102, 103, 107, 116, 152, 123
Polson, Arnold, 45
Polson Company, 96, 99, 100, 101, 102, 103, 110, 173, 193, 204
Polson, Robert, 99, 102, 103, 152
Port Blakely Mill Company, 11
Posey, V. G., 210
Preacher Slough, 23, 153, 233
Preist, Robert, 243
Price, W. H., 106
Promised Land, 95

Quaick, Billy, 112
Queets, 53, 193
Quigg Brothers — McDonald, 234
Quillayute River, 193, 236
Quinault, 53, 101, 118, 193, 194
Quinn, M. C., 183
Quint, R. C., 186

Raft River, 193
Randolph, Dr. Howard C., 173
Randolph, Shirley, 173
Rankin, John, 129
Ray, William "Bill", 83, 105, 192

Raymond, 37, 40
Rayonier, 204, 210
Redman Creek, 10
Reed, Mark E., 36
Reed, Capt. T. C., 176
Reed, William S., 84, 85
Reed, W. G., 114, 198
Rehm, Jack, 206
Reid, William "Uncle Bill", 82
Rennie Island, 17
Rennie, William "Bill", 286
Richling, H., 109
Riddell, John, 9
Ritman, William, 109
Rogers, Jim, 87
Rosendal, Capt. George, 134
Rosenkrantz, William, 40, 41
Rosmond, Henry, 289
Rowland, Brothers, 185
Ruffe, Henry "Hank", 26

Saginaw Station, 84, 186
Sanborn, Capt. George, 232
Sargent, Roy, 131, 153, 244
Satsop, Chief, 9
Satsop River, 42, 83, 101, 111, 112, 116, 192
Scammon, Isaiah, 82
Scanlon, Jack, 129
Chief Schachanaway, 7
Schafer Brothers, 83, 110, 113, 120, 121, 122, 123, 163, 211
Schafer, Albert, 111, 112, 114
Schafer, Anna, 114
Schafer, Anton Dennis, 110, 111
Schafer, Hubert, 111, 112, 113, 236
Schafer, John D., 110, 111, 112, 114
Schafer, Margaret, 110
Schafer, Peter, 110, 112, 114
Schier, J. B., 173
Schofield, Bert, 235
Schumacher, Margaret, 110
Scklentz, F. C., 173
Scott, Ruby, 177
Searles, Police Capt. Joe, 187
Seden, Peter, 243
Seiling, Margaret, 291
Selby & Waite, 122
Sells, J. A., 119
Sharon, 82, 85, 162
Shaw, John, 93
Shearner, James L., 127
Sheasby, Charles, 115
Sheeks, Judge Ben, 246
Shelton, 111

INDEX

Shelton, David, 111
Shew, Iras, 177
Shey, I. S., 175
Shivley, Ralph, 234
Shoalwater Bay, 9, 13, 98, 239
Shutt, Calvin Herbert "Bert", 152
Silby, A. W., 83
Simon, Norton, 206
Simpson, Asa M., 12, 13, 14, 18, 84, 126, 213
Simpson, A. W., 14
Simpson, Sol G., 11, 101, 114, 198, 285
Skeen, Lycia, 91
Slover, Lloyd, 233
Smith, "Blockhouse," 119
Smith, Capt. Ernest, 233
Smith, Ida, 294
Smith, Capt. T. H., 214, 218, 228
Smith, "Siwash", 237, 238
Slade, S. E., 101
S. E. Slade Lumber Company, 24, 36, 101, 163, 183, 184, 219
Snyder, Jack, 286
Snyder, M. V., 174
Soule, John, 47
Soule, Thomas C. "Tom", 235, 236, 237 238
South Bend, 13, 40, 51
Sparling, John D., 120
Spellissy, Martin, 26, 27
Sprague, Capt., 229
Squire, Watson Gov., 124
Stafford Creek, 86
Stearns, Joe, 237
Stetson, George W., 46, 48, 122
Stevens, Charles, 13, 42, 44, 45
Stewart, Hugh, 105
Stewart, L. O., 247
Stiles, W. L., 160
Stirrat, John, 221, 222
Stockhouse, W. H., 187
Stockwell, Almerion Page "Al", 128, 156, 157, 160, 161
Stockwell, Levi L., 157
Stout, Barney, 53
Stout, J. J., 40
Stout, J. M., 20
Strahill, 8
Strand, Gus, 207
Stream, Capt. Al, 231
Stream, Capt. Henry, 233
Stroeder, Charles, 110, 111
Strommer, H., 222
Summit, 192
Swan, Capt., 228
Swan, James G., 8
Swigert, Ernest G., 205, 206

Sylvia Creek Falls, 10, 11, 30, 43, 121, 123
Syverson, H., 122

Taholah, 10, 236
Taka, Jessie, 177
Talbot, W. H., 45, 46
Taylor, E. T., 47
Teagle, Ernest C., 198
Templeman, Police Chief, 181
Tew, Fred, 26
Tew, Tom, 26
Tha-a-muxi, 6, 7
Thayer, C. A., 217, 224
Thompson, Joe, 198
Thorn, W. R., 181, 183, 184
Tierog, Aloyz, 181
Titus, Dr. Herman, 183
Tokeland, 118
Toombs, Roy L., 200
Townsend, George, 62
Train, J. M., 181
Trainor, Capt. Charles, 229
Trainor, Capt. Sam, 229
Trainor, Capt. William "Bill", 229
Treda, May and Jennie, 177
Tucker, W. H., 41
Turner, Robert "Bob", 150, 155
Turner, Ben, 103
Tyler, Robert L., 180

Ultican, R. J. "Dick", 40, 41, 50, 160, 233, 234

Van Metter, Harry, 26
Van Winkle, Rollie, 81, 82
Van Winkle Creek, 82
Varmer, D., 109
Vaumen, Ivar, 232
Vesta, 84, 116
Voorhies, Nathan, 23
Vidler Brothers, 172

Wade, Al, 129
Wade, George, 115
Waite, Nelson, 43
Walker, Cyrus, 46
Walker, James "Jim", 234
Walker, William "Will", 46
Walsh, J. W., 290
Warner, E. B. "Brad", 16, 20, 21
Warren Timber Co., 152
Watkins, Mary, 291
Weatherwax, Addis, 25
Weatherwax, Bion, 25
Weatherwax, C. B., 28

Weatherwax, Carl S., 28
Weatherwax, Cliff M., 30, 47
Weatherwax, George, 20, 24, 25
Weatherwax, J. G., 28, 153
Weatherwax, Capt. J. M., 20, 26, 28, 30, 39, 47, 104, 114, 119, 228, 238
Webster, Frank, 129
Wedekind, Frank, 83
Wedekind, Henry, 115
Weidman, Capt. "Salvation John", 230, 231
Welch, A. R., 200, 201, 202
Wellman, G. F., 187
West, Arnold "Arne", 16
West, A. J., 15, 16, 17, 19, 21, 22, 23, 24, 29, 101, 112, 132, 119, 238
West, E. R., 24
Westport, 116, 118, 119
West, Watson, 24
Weyerhaeuser, 50, 102, 105, 106, 120, 210, 211
Whitbey Harbor, 6
Whitcomb, Capt. James "Jim", 14, 15, 17, 19
White, C. F., 30, 46, 47, 119
White, Lil, 176
White Star, 192
Widow Creek, 126
Wilkie, David, 115
Willey, Sam, 103
William and Ann, 5, 6
Williams, Lee, 242, 246
Wilson, C. N. "Bud", 11, 127

Willapa River-Bay, 6, 13, 40, 53, 193, 194, 235
Wilson Brothers, 119, 132, 185
Wilson, Charles R., 28
Wilson, Fred, 28
Wilson, Henry, 28
Wilson, James, 115, 234
Wilson Creek, 28, 29
Wishkah River, 19, 28, 53, 83, 86, 93, 101, 157, 233, 240
Wolff, George, 175
Wood, A. D., 23, 40
Wood, E. K., 216
Wood, E. K., Lumber Company, 214, 217, 218, 219, 220, 221, 222, 223, 224, 254 264
Wood, Fred J., 217, 219, 224
Wood, Joe, 109
Wood, Miss Marion, 224
Wood, Peter, 162
Woodland, "Poots", 57
Woods, Herbert, 235
Woods, Ike, 23
Woods, John, 235
Woods, May, 177
Woods, Mike, 83, 86, 153
Wuest, A. R. "Bob", 200, 201, 202
Wyman, Max, 234
Wynooche River, 83, 101

Yana, Charley, 244
Young, Ellen, 16
Young, John, 16